AF712061

CRIME AND MENTAL DISORDERS

THE CRIMINAL JUSTICE RESPONSE

Denise Kindschi Gosselin
PROFESSOR OF CRIMINAL JUSTICE
WESTERN NEW ENGLAND UNIVERSITY

WEST ACADEMIC PUBLISHING

The publisher is not engaged in rendering legal or other professional advice, and this publication is not a substitute for the advice of an attorney. If you require legal or other expert advice, you should seek the services of a competent attorney or other professional.

© 2017 LEG, Inc. d/b/a West Academic
444 Cedar Street, Suite 700
St. Paul, MN 55101
1-877-888-1330

West, West Academic Publishing, and West Academic are trademarks of West Publishing Corporation, used under license.

Printed in the United States of America

ISBN: 978-1-63460-409-3

This book is dedicated to
Dr. Hogan, Dr. Nagorney, Dr. Torres
and to the nurses and staff
at the Mayo Clinic in Rochester, MN
with heartfelt appreciation.

Preface

This first edition of *Crime and Mental Disorders: The Criminal Justice Response* has been organized into five sections. It is appropriate at the graduate or undergraduate level. Suggested courses are within majors of criminal justice, sociology, and social work. While the material is largely concerning psychiatric disorders, it is written to bridge the gap of information between the two disciplines of criminal justice as they respond and collaborate with mental health professionals. There are ancillary materials available for the instructor, including an Instructor's Manual, text banks, and PowerPoints. I hope that this is helpful as you plan the semester. The text contains 14 chapters; one might be covered each week. There are chapter questions at the end of each one which can be assigned for homework or used for class discussion. Many of the chapters also have a section entitled: In My Experience . . . there is an experience and question for class discussion. The photo of the Trooper is the author. Also, there is a "crucial question" which can be used to facilitate class discussion at each section of the book. Class participation and discussion is highly encouraged in this course. For some students it will be their first academic course on mental disorders. In-service professionals should know that all of the programs described in the text represent "best-practices" in the field.

Part I UNDERSTANDING MENTAL ILLNESS contains chapters 1–4. These chapters concern the history (past and present), classifications, and introduction to the criminal justice issues on the responses to people with mental illness.

Part II THE CHANGING LANDSCAPE contains chapters 5–7. This section examines the criminal justice involved encounters that occur outside of the traditional system, involving intervention, collaboration, and civil commitment.

Part III CRIMINAL JUSTICE RESPONSES contains chapters 8–10. Law enforcement, criminal court and corrections are represented here.

Part IV ALTERNATIVES TO INCARCERATION includes chapters 11–13. These reflect recent changes to reentry and community corrections. The juvenile justice component includes the brief system responses to juveniles with mental disorders.

Part V GLOBAL ISSUES stands alone as chapter 14 to remind us that we are not alone! The issues and system responses are not unique to the United States. This puts us perspective with the world around us.

Education is the best path to overcome the stigma and recognize the myths surrounding mental disorders. I developed and have been offering a course for six years on *Mental Illness and Disability in the Criminal Justice System*. The widely popular undergraduate course is taken as an elective by various majors on campus, primarily those in criminal justice, social work, sociology, and psychology. Campus police officers have elected an online version and it has been recommended for our campus police officers. This text represents the most up to date information on the topics covered within the course.

Denise Kindschi Gosselin

November 15, 2016

Acknowledgments

I appreciate all of the people who have contributed to this textbook. To the many students who elected the course, thank you for your insightful questions and comments. Some of you have gone on to choose careers in mental health counseling and provide much needed services! I am indebted to Tyler McQuillian who provided invaluable assistance and direction through his careful reading and editing. I would like to recognize and thank Mal Schneider whose contributions in reading and editing this text provided consistency and contributed significantly. I could not have done this without your help! Thank you to Steven Kardys, from Western New England University, who provided his insight along with many of the end-of-chapter questions. To my friend and husband, Robert Gosselin, thank you for your limitless ideas and non-wavering support.

About the Author

Denise Kindschi Gosselin, Ph.D. is a Professor in the Criminal Justice & Sociology Department at Western New England University. She is the author of *Heavy Hands: An Introduction to the Crimes of Family Violence*, now in its 5th edition (Prentice Hall, 2014) and *Smart Talk: Contemporary Interviewing and Interrogation* (Prentice Hall, 2007). Her areas of interest include mental illness, family violence, interviewing and interrogation, and international issues in criminal justice. She has presented numerous papers and authored book chapters on these topics.

Denise is a retired Trooper from the Massachusetts State Police. During her police career she served as a detective, academy classroom and drill instructor, community service officer, and as a patrol officer. Additionally, she has made presentations at professional meetings with the Department of Social Services, Department of Mental Health, and for the Office of the District Attorney. As a Trooper she testified on numerous major crime cases, both in criminal court and in civil hearings.

As an active member in the Academy of Criminal Justice Sciences, Denise has been elected to serve for 6 years on its Executive Board. She is a past President of the Northeastern Association of Criminal Justice and member of the European Society of Criminology. Dr. Gosselin has been an invited speaker at numerous colleges and universities; her major presentations include West Point Military Academy, the Massachusetts State Police Academy, and the UN Congress on Crime in Brazil. She has appeared on the nationally televised "America's Most Wanted" where one of her cases was profiled and the perpetrator apprehended.

Table of Contents

PART III. CRIMINAL JUSTICE RESPONSES

PART V. GLOBAL ISSUES

CRIME AND MENTAL DISORDERS

THE CRIMINAL JUSTICE RESPONSE

PART I

Understanding Mental Illnesses

Photo courtesy of the U.S. National Library of Medicine

The following Chapters are covered in PART I

1. INTRODUCTION TO THE HISTORY OF MENTAL ILLNESS
2. U.S. HISTORY OF MENTAL ILLNESS
3. MENTAL DISORDERS
4. CALLS FOR SERVICE

A crucial question is:

What is the nature of mental illness and how should society respond?

Chapters 1 and 2 deal with the history of mental illness and the influences which shape perception and assumptions regarding mental disorders. Chapter 3 explains classification systems and defines mental disorders. In Chapter 4 the encounters with law enforcement are calls for service, which becomes a significant issue in policing practice.

CHAPTER 1

Introduction to the History of Mental Illness

INTRODUCTION

Mental illness is not new nor newly discovered. Since the beginning of recorded time, abnormal behaviors have been part of the human experience. The search for explanations of the causes of mental illness dates back to ancient times. Conflicting beliefs about demonic possession, punishment by the gods for a sinful state of the soul, and defects of the brain reoccur. Throughout history, attempts have been made at curing people that exhibit abnormal behaviors. Long before doctors had a full understanding of the human anatomy, attempted cures involved making holes in the person's skull for demons to escape. The religious or spiritual practice of evicting demons from a person believed to have been possessed, known as exorcism, also dates to ancient times.

Alternatively, the answer to problematic behavior has been through physical restraint, confinement, banishment, and even death. As this chapter unfolds you will learn about public and private places of commitment. Incarceration in prisons and jails have historically been a dumping ground for undesirables. Examples of periods in history which witnessed mass incarceration of individuals with mental disorders have been disrupted by reformers seeking more humane options. Where we go in the future will likely depend on what we do with the lessons learned from the past. We are at another crossroads in history. Which way will we go?

Key Terms

ASYLUM

BEDLAM

DEMONOLOGY

EXORCISM

PHRENOLOGY

TREPHINING

Chapter Objectives

After completing this chapter, you should be able to:

- Explain the influence of culture and religion on the treatment of those thought to have mental illness
- Compare and contrast European civil commitment with European criminal confinement
- Describe the cyclical nature of responses to individuals having mental disorders
- Compare early religious influences to modern religious influences

CULTURE AND RELIGION

An interesting aspect of mental illness is the historical endeavor to understand it. Insanity is a mystery that continues to challenge researchers to this day. Culture and religion have shaped the level of tolerance, or lack thereof, since the beginning of time. The term "culture" in this book refers to shared patterns of belief among groups of individuals. Religions are diverse, with varying practices and beliefs, and are typically organized. Belief in Gods and demons influence the cultural practices to which we adhere, so the realm is worth exploring.

Ancient Culture

Some individuals experiencing severe mental disorders struggle with a diminished ability to control one's emotions or thoughts, sometimes accompanied by excruciating headaches or pain. This is a difficult concept for others to understand, which may contribute to the marginalization of those who suffer. It does, in part, explain why early therapies to rid individuals of their mental health problems center on surgeries that involve the brain. **TREPHINING** is one example of a surgical procedure that involves cutting a hole in the skull to provide a release for the evil spirits possessing the person. Trephining is believed to be one of the oldest surgical procedures performed by man to alleviate the suffering of individuals with mental disorders. It was performed for epilepsy, infantile convulsions, and headache (Faria, 2013).

In Peru, ancient trephined skulls dating back 2300 years have been unearthed. From excavations of these prehistoric skulls, evidence of bone healing suggests that as many as 70 percent of the subjects initially survived the surgery (Rifkinson-Mann, 1988). Medical instruments discovered in Greece and Rome confirm that surgeons continued the practices of perforating the cranium between 25 BC–AD 216 (Faria, 2013). It is well known that ancient people who committed a crime were considered mentally ill. They were treated like outcasts, tortured, or killed. We can assume that criminals were among those treated for the release of evil spirits.

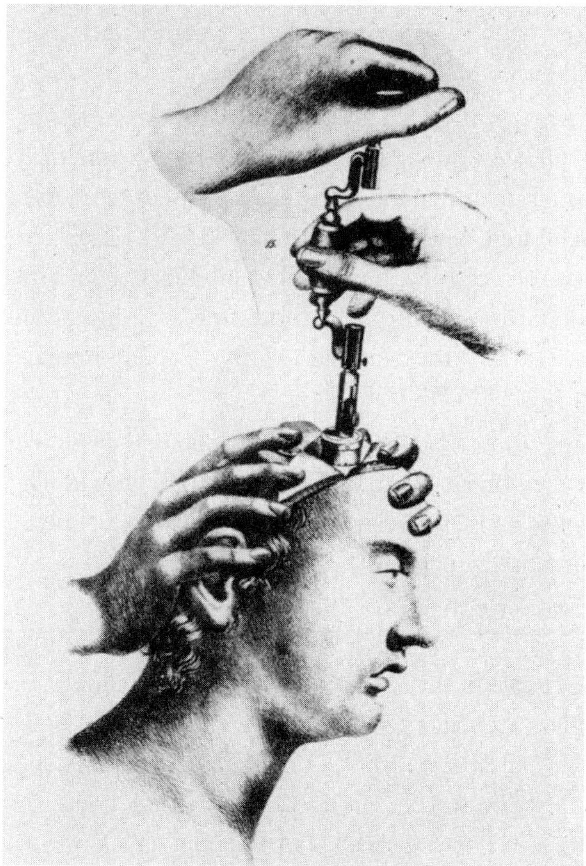

1. CH01-01: *Trephination.* The lithograph demonstrates the use of trephining instruments on a man's head. Photo courtesy of the National Library of Medicine.

Early civilizations often contributed behaviors that they could not understand to animalistic spirits, such as the widespread belief that people could somehow shape-shift into becoming werewolves. It was believed that insanity might cause *wolf-madness*, a term for when a person prowls about graves and bays at the moon (Porter, 2002). No one knows exactly when legends of werewolves began, but they have existed throughout history. As late as the fourteenth century individuals suspected of being werewolves were still being hunted and executed throughout Europe. Another example is found in the use of the phrase "the black dog" for individuals with depression (Porter, 2002). Failing to obey the teachings of the gods and priests might cause individuals to exhibit animalistic or aberrant behaviors as punishment.

IMAGINE THAT . . .

Lycanthrophy or wolf-madness may be one of the earliest diagnosis of melancholy, according to Pietikäinen (2015). The Greek physician, Oribasius of Pergamon (325–403 AD) described the lycanthrophy patient as having a paleness, languid expression, dry hollow eyes and dry tongue.

> Jean Grenier, a self-proclaimed werewolf, was brought to trial in France in 1603. As one of the most illustrious cases of lycanthropy, Grenier confessed to having eaten a baby stolen from its cradle, parts of young children, and to having clawed and bitten several young girls. The court recognized his limited intelligence and mental illness and sentenced him to life in a monastery for moral and religious instruction. He died there at age twenty, scarcely human . . . (Otten 1986, p. 9)

Between 1520 and 1630 AD, there were some 30,000 cases recorded in France alone when werewolves were thought to be meddling in witchcraft. Werewolves are now rare, suggests Pietikäinen (2015), as only 13 reported cases have been documented since 1850.

Question for discussion: Is it possible to explain this phenomenon?

Attempts to explain the symptoms of mental illness have captured the attention of scholars and scientists as far back as the time of Homer, during the eighth century BC (Dalfardi, Yarmohammadi, and Ghanizadeh, 2014). The oldest term thought to describe the characteristics of mental illness is melancholia, now called depression. Per Porter (2002), Hippocrates (460–337 BC) recorded case histories of a woman rambling in her speech and mouthing obscenities; another who would not speak but would pluck, scratch, pick hairs, weep and then laugh.

Hippocrates added the term mania as the opposite of melancholia. In ancient medicine, the concepts of mania and melancholia were broad terms that covered many types of disorders. These included some forms of schizophrenia, schizoaffective disorder, depression, and some forms of psychoses (Dalfardi et al., 2014). The clinical accounts of melancholia would change over time, but anguish and dejection were its essential elements.

There is some historical evidence that individuals thought to be insane might be admired or revered. If the disorder induced behavior that signified mystical powers, such as epilepsy among the early Greeks, then the disordered individuals were honored. Plato (427–347 BC) and Aristotle (384–322 BC), for example, believed that all creative individuals such as artists and poets were prone to a form of mental illness they called melancholy. Although Plato emphasized the difference between clinical and creative mania, the paradox of "creative genius and madness" is one that still prevails.

A few early wise men also challenged the majority view of demonic possession. Hippocrates (c460–357 BC), the father of medicine, believed that mental illness was an organic sickness and not caused by demons. The basis of Hippocratic medicine is the belief that medicine should be practiced as scientific inquiry to recognize the symptoms of diseases through knowledge of anatomy (Kleisiaris, Sfakianakis, and Papathanasiou, 2014). Treatment of mental illness should be attempted in a secure and safe retreat from the crowded urban centers of the day. Hippocrates suggested that these individuals should neither be whipped in public nor held in dungeons. Rather, they should be placed in an asylum. The **ASYLUM**, an enduring term, is an institution that offers shelter and support to individuals with mental disorders.

Mental disorders were studied extensively by Persian scholars during the ninth and twelfth centuries AD, referred to as the *Golden Age of Islamic Medicine.* A Persian physician, Al-Akhawayni Bukhari, classified melancholia into three groups during the tenth century. Based on the writings of Al-Akhawayni, comparisons have been made between his groups of melancholia patients to current DSM-5 disorders (Dalfardi et al., 2014). Group 1 includes patients who are described today as having the major depressive disorders with psychotic features; Group 2 individuals are those who have contemporary concepts of bipolar disorder with psychotic features, schizophrenia, or delusional disorder; Group 3 are those who we now describe as having bipolar mood disorder, major depressive disorder, or eating disorders. Al-Akhawayni prescribed plant materials such as celery stalk, fennel stalk, and cucumber as herbal medication for the management of mental disorders (Dalfardi et al., 2014).

There is little medical literature from ancient China regarding madness because it was considered similar to other illnesses and not the subject of debate. Fabien Simonis (2015) states that around the first century BC Chinese medical texts included the word *kuang*, which describes something like "mania." *Kuang* is discussed in early medical texts alongside illnesses that were neither mental nor behavioral, and treated by similar means. For example, Zhang Lu (1617–99) offers a recipe for curing madness that might also be used to treat headaches (Simonis, 2015). Simonis argues that mental illness among the people of China did not bring about specialized institutions or publications as it did in the Western world. Around the seventeenth century murders committed by people with mental illness were likened to accidental homicides due to a lack of intent (Scull, 2015). By the mid-eighteenth century things had changed, according to Scull. There appeared a presumption of dangerousness as authorities and the law subjected people with mental illness to various forms of confinement.

Early Influences of Religion

Early Christians believed that madness itself was a punishment from God for some wrongdoing. Roy Porter (2002) found a reference that King Nebuchadnezzar, who reigned between 605–562 BC, had been reduced to bestial insanity for having tormented his people. Other passages in the Christian Bible reflect similar beliefs. A well-known passage from Deuteronomy (28:28) states that *The Lord will smite thee with madness, blindness and confusion of mind. . . .* In Zechariah (12:4) it is written that, *on that day I will strike every horse to panic and every rider to madness.* If an individual was possessed by a demon, exorcism was the term to rid the person of the evil spirit.

Soranus of Ephesus, a Greek physician living in Rome during the second century AD, epitomizes the *Methodist* (or medical thinking) school of physicians (Kleisiaris et al., 2014). He believed that living beings were made up of atoms with a tonal quality. If the motion of the atoms was disturbed, the resulting discord could cause mental illness. Interviewing the patient and treating the whole person was at the core of this philosophical approach. This was a non-traditional philosophy. Its believers approached individuals with compassion and care, in sharp contrast to the beatings and starvations practiced during the period. The belief that optimal health involves healing the physical, emotional, mental, and spiritual whole of the patient is very much like the holistic approach to healing practiced today.

2. CH01-02: *Exorcism of a Witch,* 1598. This image is of a demon being exorcised from a woman in front of what appears to be an altar and the bishop. Photo courtesy of the National Library of Medicine.

Per the New Testament of the Christian Bible, Jesus performed many exorcisms and commanded others to do the same. Expulsion of demonic spirits though **EXORCISM** occurs when a demon is commanded by a priest, in the name of God, to stop his activity within a person (Baglio, 2010). This official rite of the Catholic Church began with early religious practices as a remedy for demonic possession. Scripture shows that four of Christ's miracles concern the casting out of demons. Exorcism to expel evil demons may still be one the most widely held religious beliefs in the world (Mercer, 2013).

The Middle Ages

During the Middle Ages, witchcraft and demonology were the predominant explanations for abnormal behavior. Humane approaches to the treatment of individuals with mental disorders were all but abandoned during medieval and post-medieval times. Death was the logical end for those accused of witchcraft. Primitive approaches to mental disorders shared the view that extreme or violent behaviors were the expression of divine magical action, caused by external forces.

A surprising development occurred during the witchcraft and demonology hysteria of the Middle Ages as well. The movement would prove to form the basis of modern psychology.

3. CH01-03: *Johannes Wierus.* Johann Weyer (1515–1588) is depicted in this engraving holding a scroll in his left hand and a skull in his right hand. In the background is a plaque that reads "Vince Te Ipsum" . . . Conquer Thyself. Photo courtesy of the National Library of Medicine.

Johann Weyer (1515–88) is recognized as the first physician to specialize in the treatment of mental illness, or "melancholy" as it was then termed (Cavanaugh, 2015). For his insight into mental illness, Weyer is credited as the "founder of modern psychiatry." He opposed the practice of punishing or killing suspected witches with limited success, contending that these "melancholics" were not demonic but mentally ill. He argued that most confessions to practicing witchcraft were made when the suspect was being tortured. Since the statements were taken under the duress of coercion, Weyer argued, that they were unreliable. Believing that mental illness was treatable, he convinced some like-minded judges who dismissed charges against suspected witches (Cavanaugh, 2015). Unfortunately, the persecution of individuals believed to be under demonic influence as witches continued and even intensified.

Individuals exhibiting evidence of mental illness were accused of having committed sinful offenses and crimes while under the influence of the devil. Those individuals were referred to as witches. The witch hunt that claimed millions of lives over the next 250 years officially began during the 1400s (Cavanaugh, 2015). Witches were suspected of procuring supernatural powers and securing advantages to themselves through an arrangement with the devil. Persons found to be witches were burned alive. This became a common method of ridding the community of undesirables. Catholics and protestants were burned as witches, sorcerers, and heretics (Judd, 1905).

Evil spirits, demons, devils, Satan and the supernatural have been both feared and revered. Believers say that sickness, weakness, or lack of willpower allow the vulnerable to succumb to the influences of the devil. Jinn or genies are an example of supernatural creatures; made of smokeless fire they inhabit an unseen world of the Arabian woods. They are mentioned frequently in Islamic texts. In Muslim societies people have traditionally seen jinn as the cause of mental disorder and epilepsy (Lim, Hoek, and Blom, 2015). Sin, divine will, and faith are among the most commonly held religious ideas in the world. Nearly all cultures and religions have at one time or another embraced **DEMONOLOGY**, which is the science or doctrine of demons (Porter, 2002).

FOUCAULT'S CLASSIFICATION OF SOCIETAL RESPONSES

Philosopher Michael Foucault categorized society's responses to mental illness into three distinct periods of time (Foucault, 2009). The first, the Age of Renaissance, represented a time when madness was considered a state of unreason, the reverse of wisdom. Those who discuss the period typically refer to the years between the fourteenth to the seventeenth centuries. As views shifted from a religious to a more humanistic outlook, the care for individuals with mental disorders began to change. The Classical Age, which spanned the seventeenth and eighteenth centuries, was the second period according to Foucault's classification of societal responses to mental illness. This is the period of time when confinement was used as a way to control the individuals who were mentally ill. The third period envisioned by Foucault is the Modern Age. By the end of the eighteenth-century madness had become an object of scientific scrutiny as a disease to be controlled.

Age of Renaissance

Fear of demonic possession raged extensively in both Catholic and Protestant countries. For more than 125 years, an annual lecture on the enormity of the witchcraft problem was presented at the Queen's college at Cambridge, England. King James was an ardent supporter of witch hunts. In 1602 he wrote a famous treatise on demons and witches that led to an act of Parliament that made witchcraft a felony and encouraged the punishment of suspected witches. It is estimated that in the next eighty years between 50,000 and 100,000 people were put to death as witches across Europe (Scull, 2015).

Classical Age

In the *History of Madness* (2009), Foucault claims that one out of every hundred people living in Paris in 1646 was committed as "mad" into houses that were previously occupied by lepers. Poorer individuals were jailed or placed in charitable public houses, called Almshouses. "Ships of fools" crisscrossed the Rhine and navigated Flemish canals with a cargo of damned souls on pilgrimages supported by hospitals and churches. Exorcism rituals that dated back to ancient times became organized religious traditions of torture resurrected by the Roman Catholic Church and the Church of England (Mercer, 2013).

Modern Age

The medical profession began to note the minor psychiatric problems of educated and polite society. "Nerves" became a popular object of study as physiological defects of the nervous system, in contrast to the traditional demoniacal beliefs that had been widely held. George Cheyne (1673–1743) was one of the originators of the neurological school of psychiatry, making neurosis fashionable (Cheyne, 2013). Health was easier to preserve rather than to cure, Cheyne maintained. Over-indulgence by eating and drinking was to be avoided in order to avoid mental disorders.

Science became consumed in its pursuit of determining the origin of mental disorders. One example that developed in the late 1700s concerned the shape of the skull, which was believed to mirror the development of the brain. Derived from the Greek word for "mind," PHRENOLOGY was based on the belief that the brain is composed of separate organs, each of which corresponds to a skill controlled by the human mind. George Combe (1788–1858) was among the leading phrenologists of the nineteenth century. Having attended lectures and brain autopsies, Combe became convinced of the "science" of phrenology (Jenkins, 2015).

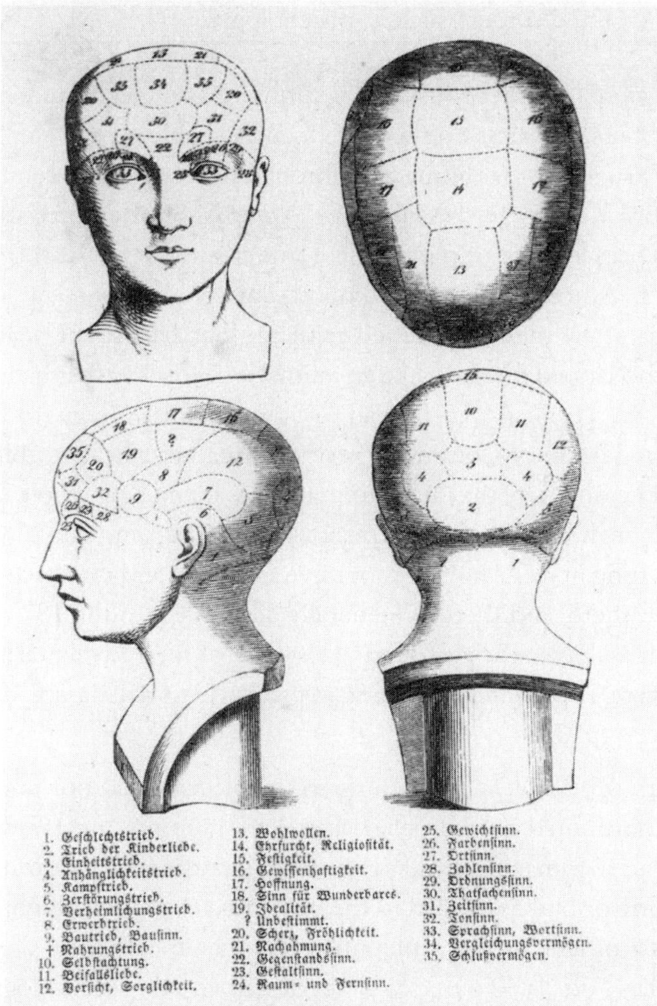

4. CH01-04: *Phrenology, 1841.* Franz Joseph Gall and Johann Caspar Spurzheim founded the "science" of phrenology. Here is the front and side view of a bust with phrenological sections identified. Photo courtesy of the National Library of Medicine.

IMAGINE THAT . . .

In the area of criminology, phrenology became the first comprehensive explanation of criminal behavior (Rafter, 2010). Based on their understanding of the brain, phrenologists would explain all forms of criminal behavior from domestic violence to homicide. They developed guidelines for distinguishing between sane and insane criminals, as well as the concept that people vary in their propensity to crime. By the 1830s, phrenology had lost favor and has been discredited.

Question for discussion: What can we learn from historical efforts to understand mental disorders such as phrenology?

Families were often responsible for caring for and accommodating mentally ill family members, either at home, or if financially able, in private "madhouses." Shorter (1997) suggests that home care through the nineteenth century is nothing less than a horror story. In the *History of Psychiatry*, Shorter cites these historical accounts as representative of the typical home treatment of the mentally ill at the time. In 1798, Anton Muller, chief of psychiatry at a hospital in Wurzburg, described one of his newly admitted patients that had spent years laying in a pigpen and who lapped his food like an animal and another that had been chained to a wall for five years so that he had lost the use of his legs (p. 2). In 1817, a member of the House of Commons described madness in the cabin of the Irish peasant. . . . The only way they have to manage is by making a hole in the floor of the cabin, not high enough for the person to stand up in, with a crib over it to prevent his getting up. The hole is about five feet deep and they give this wretched being his food there, and there he generally dies (p. 1). In the 1870s just prior to introducing an asylum, officials found that 30 out of the 164 mental patients under home care were kept under restraint, typically in dark, damp, unheated, and stinking lockups (p. 3).

Behaviors, which were frightening to people who did not understand their origin, had contributed to the belief that demon spirits must dwell within the individuals. Facial grimacing, head or shoulder jerking, and vocalizations that may include grunting or barking added to the belief that evil spirits might fly out of the possessed into others. It was not until 1885 that the French Neurologist Dr. Georges Gilles de la Tourette first described the neurological disorder characterized by involuntary movements and vocalizations. We now know this as a tic disorder called Tourette syndrome.

In his 1916 edition of *Nervous Disorders of Men*, Bernard Hollander argued that nervous conditions were socially induced. He demonstrated, statistically, that severe mental illness had increased substantially between 1860 and 1913; he presumed it to be a consequence of the increase in brain activity required by men due to the progress of civilization. Hollander argued that the proportion of insane people to the normal population was one in 536 during 1860, a number that had risen to one in 266 by 1913 (Hollander, 2015a). He further argued that mental illness was a functional disorder instead of an organic disease. Functional disorders are conditions believed to be due to psychological dysfunction.

Hollander was also an ardent phrenologist. After careful examination, he concluded that women, on average, possessed a smaller brain than the average male. In his 1916 book, *Nervous Disorders of Women*, Hollander argued that the size of the brain did not render women mentally inferior. However, he concluded that women were more prone to nervous disorders than men. He stated that one reason for the mental disorders women experienced was that they typically "had foolish desires to be regarded as somebody of value in society" (Hollander, 2015b). Women needed to forget their disappointments through the emerging treatments of psychotherapy, Hollander explained.

CIVIL COMMITMENT IN EUROPE

Stories abound on the involuntary institutionalization of individuals who were not dangerous. Prior to the organized construction of places to hold persons with mental disorders, most of the cities of Europe throughout the Middle Ages and the Renaissance, reserved lodging in hotel rooms for the insane (Foucault, 2009). Hospitals were among the first institutions that housed and provided treatment to mentally ill patients. Conceived as asylums for persons with mental disorders, patients were kept in locked wards for their own protection. This kept them out of sight and out of mind of the public.

In 1247, the first institution dedicated to the care and treatment of the individuals with mental disorders was established at Bethlem Hospital in London, England. Starting as a monastery and college, it eventually became a prison for the mentally infirmed. It became known as **BEDLAM**—a term that today is synonymous with chaos and confusion. Bethlem included itself among the "shows of London" which meant that patients were on display, spectacles in a human zoo of demented creatures (Porter, 2002). Patients were identified by their unique clothing and were referred to as Bedlamites. Sometimes allowed to beg on the streets, Bedlamites were often joined by charlatans and fakes trying to make money.

Due to its notoriety, Bedlam has been depicted in numerous cartoons where the argument was made that the insane were those who visited the institution, and that those who lead unhealthy lives would become the inhabitants. Jokes about mad monarchs gave impetus to cartoonists to highlight the corrupting influence of power. Note the final scene of Hogarth's *A Rake's Progress* series, 1735. There is an image of a man holding his head in the historical pose of the maniac. The fallen hero was ruined by drink, gambling, and women of ill-repute, and he is surrounded by other insane patients. An attendant attaches chains to his legs while his faithful lover cries. The well-dressed lady in the background is a visitor come to enjoy the antics of the Bedlam inmates.

5. CH01-05: *A Rake's Progress Scene in Bedlam.* The engraving by William Hogarth (1697–1764) is of the interior of the Bethlehem Hospital in London known as "bedlam." Photo courtesy of the National Library of Medicine.

Private asylums became the most common form of respite for families that could afford the option beginning in the late 1600s. Privatization for profit was viewed as the side effect of a growing surplus of wealth and the undesirability of keeping mentally ill family members in the house. Anyone could open a private madhouse and receive persons that were mentally ill for payment in the for-profit scheme. Passed in England in 1774, the "Madhouse Act" was the first attempt to license private asylums (Bynum, 1981). The act did not regulate the qualifications of the proprietors or require any form of treatment to the residents. Its significance is that it required that a medical certificate be obtained before a person could be committed.

The "Madhouse Act" was significant since there was widespread fear of wrongful commitment in England during the early eighteenth century (McCandless, 1981). Causes for the anxiety may have been justified. The doctors of the time knew little about the pathology of insanity and often confused sexuality and nonconformist behavior as mental disorders. Any doctor could sign certificates of insanity regardless of their specialty. A charge of insanity meant the loss of individual liberty; significantly, it also resulted in the loss of a man's property. Even if the person was later acquitted, the charge would negatively affect his reputation in the community, according to McCandless (1981). Stories of husbands having their wives falsely committed and unscrupulous relatives seeking to take possession of family fortunes fueled the criticisms of the private asylums. In one case, an individual was found insane since he objected to woolen trousers, preferring corduroy because they were better for walking (McCandless, 1981). Despite the fear and abuses, by 1850 more than half of the mentally disordered population of England lived in private institutions (Porter, 2002). Medical supervision was not a legal requirement for early private institutions. Asylums varied widely in quality and the lack of regulation bred corruption and cruelty.

Rise of the Public Asylum

The establishment of public asylums in Europe during the 1700s advanced the professionalism of psychiatry, which led to the employment of doctors who specialized in managing "madness" (Busfield, 2015). Mental illness became a field of study. Research gained from the study of inmates in asylums found links between madness and genius, tuberculosis, and drug use. The doctors of the time sought ways to control and understand mental disorders and conditions. Under the influence of psychiatry, a new model on madness emerged. Roy Porter (2002) reports that madness came to be understood as a psychological condition that influenced the psyche, as evidenced by the patient's behavior.

Asylums provided an abundance of information to diagnosticians in France during the 1800s due to the commitment to clinical observation using the case-history approach (Porter, 2002). A leading authority was Jean-Etienne Dominique Esquirol whose *Mental Maladies* (1838) described the diagnosis of kleptomania, nymphomania, and pyromania in addition to affective disorders involving paranoia. As an advocate of humane treatment of the mentally ill, Esquirol was instrumental in asylum reform in France. Epileptics became distinguished from the insane and were treated in special hospitals that emerged in France, Britain, and Germany.

By 1817, an expansive public asylum system was established in Ireland. An example of the most enduring program of institutional social intervention, it grew to become one of the largest in the world. By 1950, Ireland held the distinction of having the world's highest rate of asylum commitment (Brennan, 2013). Enduring for over 200 years, control over those with mental illness involved long-term removal from society as well as methods of adjustment such as moral intervention, shock treatment, and medication.

John Conolly was appointed resident physician to the Middlesex County Asylum at Hanwell, England in 1839 where he initiated a "non-restraint" system of control for mental patients. The system gained notoriety because of his 1856 book, *The Treatment of the Insane without Mechanical Restraints.* Conolly's system coincided with a movement for "moral treatment" where patients were given food and were not locked in small crates or manacled for long periods of time (Bartlett, 2010).

Not all countries in Europe confined the mentally disordered population with the same vigor. Russia and Portugal stand out as countries where the insane hardly appeared in records at all prior to 1850 (Porter, 2002). Individuals in Russia who were confined due to mental disorders were generally held in monasteries and cared for by clergy. In Portugal, only two asylums existed by the end of the nineteenth century with fewer than 600 inmates between them. It stands to reason that in countries without formalized institutionalization policies, most individuals in need of treatment for mental disorders received care in private institutions or homes.

Criminal Confinement in Europe

It has been argued that while many European cities and towns during the Renaissance gave refuge to individuals with mental disorders, many more simply threw them into institutions. Madness was used as a reason for confining more than 6,000 undesirables and petty criminals in Paris by the 1660s (Foucault, 2009). Commitment and restraint were justified for mental illness through the creation of laws that essentially made it illegal to be mentally ill or homeless. Typified by Louis XIV's France, Foucault described a "great confinement" where troublesome people were confined as a police measure in German prisons, English workhouses, and the hospitals of France.

Prison ledgers from the 1690s reveal inmates labeled as "women who were sick, in a second childhood, girlish old women, epileptics, mad, malformed, damaged simpletons, imbeciles, and those weak in the mind," to name only a few

(Foucault, 2009). Similar patterns for confinement of individuals with mental disorders in prisons continued throughout the 1700s. Violence was interpreted as illogical and sinful and the justification for imprisoning the insane became blurred. Foucault (2009) tells of an inmate who complained about being locked up while being neither "eccentric nor insane." The investigation report included a reply from the guard who justified the confinement:

> *He never kneels at the most sacred moments of the mass . . . and he keeps a portion of his Thursday support for Friday, this last trait revealing that while he may not be mad, he is well on the road to impiety.*

Despite advanced knowledge of scientific principles and medical interventions between the sixteenth and eighteenth centuries, some historians suggest that the custody of the insane was more frequently left in the hands of the jailer (Bynum, 1981). Bynum reports that England's 1744 *Vagrancy Act,* Section 20 provided that any person could detain and claim someone to be a lunatic. With the consent of two justices of the peace, that individual would be kept safely locked up in some secure place. The decision to release the individual was at the discretion of the jailer or the local magistrates.

Spierenburg (2007) disputes the impression that a large population of deviant were imprisoned during the seventeenth and eighteenth centuries, as described by Foucault. However, an early form of confinement, he suggests, is the medieval hospital. From the fifteenth century onward charitable institutions had sequestered areas where "inmates" of the hospital consisted primarily of the insane. Dangerous individuals were kept in custody for long periods of time, typically this population was restrained in some manner. Obviously, they were not free to leave. The hospitals also functioned as asylums for the aged, homeless, the sick, the infirmed, or women in labor. These institutions were different from jails and prisons because there was no responsibility attached to their actions and they were not required to work.

It should be noted that the concept of imprisonment for punishment is a recent one. While places of detention have existed for centuries, these were a means of holding persons for later punishment. Places of detention that held criminal offenders were referred to as *gaols* in England. Gaols are similar to our modern-day concept of the jail—they mainly held debtors and persons for short term stays. Institutions constructed for punishment were first established in the late sixteenth century (Spiernburg, 2007). They have been called *bridewells* or houses of correction in England and *tuchthuizen* in the Netherlands. The *gaols* continued in existence even when houses of corrections were built.

6. CH01-06: Exorcism has recently been sanctioned as official Catholic practice by Pope Francis. The move came as the result of renewed interest in the practice. Photo copyright Neneo/ Shutterstock.com.

Modern Religious Influences

There has been a recent resurgence in the importance of spiritual beliefs as primary mental health treatments. The fastest growing Christian movement in the world is Pentecostalism (Miller, 2006). Pentecostal believers emphasize the role of the supernatural in both causation and treatment of mental and physical disorders. Divine healing, the supernatural, and miracles are attributed to beliefs within the Pentecostal community. Some believers may accept treatment only if it is consistent with Pentecostal deliverance beliefs. Others may reject medical and psychological treatments altogether, even in cases of severe mental disorders. It is estimated that a growing population of more than 80,000,000 Pentecostals live in the United States (Mercer, 2013). Upwards of 64 percent of the diverse American Latino population identifies as Pentecostal (Espinosa, 2014).

Interventions through exorcism are widely practiced today (Mercer, 2013). The ninth annual conference on exorcism, *Exorcism and Prayer for Liberation*, was held in May 2014 in Italy. An Italian newspaper, *Gazzetta del Sud*, reports there were 200 participants from 33 countries attending the event (Allegrezza, 12 May 2014). The Vatican-sponsored conference touched on the resurgence of mystical rites in the Catholic Church and on the renewed interest in exorcisms. According to news reports, Pope Francis has sanctioned exorcism as official Catholic practice, to be used to save people from demons (Withnall, 3 July 2014). More priests will be trained in the practice in order to keep up with increasing demands for exorcism around the world.

IMAGINE THAT . . .

According to Baglio (2010), approximately 8,000 satanic sects with more than 600,000 members exist within Italy alone. These estimates may have fueled the need for exorcisms to cure the large numbers of people who say they are possessed by evil spirits. The current belief is that many mental disorders might be mistaken for demonic possession, but that they are not the same as possession. Each year more than 500,000 people in Italy see an exorcist (Baglio, 2010).

Question for discussion: How has the use of exorcism changed from ancient times?

SUMMARY

Individuals with mental disorders were historically either ignored or institutionalized. Their disorders were not readily understood or treated. Society has often feared and harbored prejudices against people with mental illness based on culture and religious beliefs. Throughout history we have attributed the illnesses to possession by demons or as a punishment for some wrongdoing. Horrific surgeries meant to release demons or cure the brain of abnormalities have been tried to no avail. Brief periods of humane treatment throughout history have occurred.

The distinction between the criminal confinement and civil commitment of individuals believed to have mental illness is blurry throughout history. When vagrancy or idleness is paramount to committing crime, criminal commitment to a jail or prison might have occurred. Confinement in asylums generally occurred when symptoms of mental illness were thought to be treatable conditions or to provide care to individuals who were considered dangerous or unable to care for themselves. Many of the references in history to the imprisonment of the mentally ill may be confusing since the use of restraints suggests punishment rather than confinement. There is disputed evidence that large numbers of individuals were committed to early jails and prisons. Undisputed is that involuntary commitment of persons with severe mental illness has occurred often throughout history; this is generally what we now refer to as civil commitment.

CHAPTER QUESTIONS FOR REVIEW

1. Explain the influence of culture and religion on the treatment of those thought to have mental illness.
2. Describe the cyclical nature of responses to individuals having mental disorders.
3. Compare early to modern religious influences on responses to severe mental illness.
4. What can history tell us about the treatment of individuals who have mental disorders?
5. What does the term asylum mean? Did that change over time?

REFERENCES

Allegrezza, K. (12 May 2014). Vatican exorcism conference warns the devil to get out of you, Life/Religion and Spirituality/Western Religions. *Examiner.* Retrieved from http://www.examiner.com

Baglio, M. (2010). *The Rite: The Making of a Modern Exorcist.* New York, NY: Image Books/Doubleday.

Bartlett, A. (2010). Medical models of mental disorder. In A. Bartlett and G. McGauley (eds.), *Forensic Mental Health: Concepts, Systems, and Practice* (pp. 1–19). Oxford, NY: Oxford University Press.

Brennan, D. (2013). *Irish Insanity 1800–2000.* New York, NY: Routledge.

Busfield, J. (2015). *Managing Madness (Psychology Revivals).* New York, NY: Routledge.

Bynum, W. (1981). Rationales for therapy in British psychiatry, 1780–1835. In A. Scull (Ed.), *Madhouses, mad-doctors, and madmen: The social history of psychiatry in the Victorian Era.* Philadelphia, PN: University of Pennsylvania Press.

Cavanaugh, R. (2015). From Demons to Doctors. *History Today Ltd., 65*(4), 44–45.

Cheyne, G. (2013). *The English Malady (1733) (Psychology Revivals)* (R. Porter, ed.). New York, NY: Routledge.

Dalfardi, B., Yarmohammadi, H., and Ghanizadeh, A. (2014). Melancholia in medieval Persian literature: The view of Hidayat of Al-Akhawayni. *World Journal of Psychiatry, 4*(2), 37–41.

Faria, M. (2013). Violence, mental illness, and the brain—A brief history of psychosurgery: Part 1—From trephination to lobotomy. *Surgical Neurology International, 4*(49).

Foucault, M. (2009). *History of Madness.* London, Eng: Routledge.

Hollander, B. (2015a). *Nervous Disorders of Men (Psychology Revivals).* New York, NY: Routledge.

Hollander, B. (2015b). *Nervous Disorders of Women (Psychology Revivals).* New York, NY: Routledge.

Jenkins, B. (2015). Phrenology, heredity and progress in George Combe's Constitution of Man. *The British Journal for the History of Science, FirstView*, 1–19.

Judd, S. (1905). *History of Hadley: Early History of Hatfield, South Hadley, Amherst and Granby.* Springfield, MA: H.R. Huntting and Co.

Kleisiaris, C. F., Sfakianakis, C., and Papathanasiou, I. V. (2014). Health care practices in ancient Greece: The Hippocratic ideal. *Journal of Medical Ethics and History of Medicine, 7*, 6.

Lim, A., Hoek, H. W., and Blom, J. D. (2015). The attribution of psychotic symptoms to jinn in Islamic patients. *Transcultural Psychiatry, 52*(1), 18–32.

McCandless, P. (1981). Liberty and lunacy: The Victorians and wrongful confinement. In A. Scull (ed.), *Madhouses, mad-doctors, and madmen: The social history of psychiatry in the Victorian Era.* Philadelphia, PA: University of Pennsylvania Press.

Mercer, J. (2013). Deliverance, demonic possession, and mental illness: some considerations for mental health professionals. *Mental Health, Religion and Culture, 16*(6), 595–611.

Miller, D. (2006) *The new face of global Christianity: The emergence of 'Progressive Pentecostalism'/Interviewer: E. O'Connell.* Religion and Public Life, Pew Research Center, Los Angeles, CA.

Otten, C. (1987). *A Lycanthropy Reader: Werewolves in Western culture.* Syracuse, NY: Syracuse University Press.

Pietikäinen, P. (2015). *Madness: A history.* Florence, KY: Routledge.

Porter, R. (2002). *Madness: A brief history.* New York, NY: Oxford University Press.

Rafter, N. (2010). The Murderous Dutch Fiddler. In S. Tibbetts and C. Hemmens (eds.), *Criminological Theory: A Text/Reader.* Thousand Oaks, CA: Sage.

Rifkinson-Mann, S. (1988). Cranial Surgery in Ancient Peru. *Neurosurgery, 23*(4), 411–416.

Scull, A. (2015). *Madness in civilization.* Princeton, NJ: Princeton University Press.

Shorter, E. (1997). *A history of psychiatry: From the era of the asylum to the age of Prozac.* New York, NY: John Wiley and Sons, Inc.

Simonis, F. (2016). Medicaments and persuasion: Medical Therapies for madness in the nineteenth-century China. In H. Chiang (ed.), *Psychiatry and Chinese history*. New York, NY: Routledge.

Spierenburg, P. (2007). *The prison experience: Disciplinary institutions and their inmates in early modern Europe.* Amsterdam, Netherlands: Amsterdam University Press.

Withnall, A. (3 July 2014). Pope Francis makes exorcisms official Catholic practice as demon-fighting priests recognized under canon law, news. *The Independent.* Retrieved from http:www.independent.co.uk/news/world/europe

CHAPTER 2

U.S. History of Mental Illness

INTRODUCTION

This chapter deals with the experiences on mental illness in the United States from a historical perspective. Initially, the care of individuals with mental illness during the colonial period was the responsibility of family members. As the country became more populated, the legal system became more involved. Punishment and shame for the moral failings of individuals with mental disorders subjected them to possible confinement in almshouses and jails. Numerous reform periods have witnessed concern over the imprisonment of individuals with mental disorders along with the use of alternative treatments.

Included in this chapter are the three modern periods of reform which first began during the 1800s. The asylum period is remembered for attempts to introduce a moral treatment approach towards individuals with mental disorders. Institutionalization, the second major period of reform, was built on the foundation of a growing confidence in the scientific advances of psychiatry and psychology. During this second reform period, numerous therapies were introduced, some of which have since been rejected as mental health treatments. A third major reform period is known as the community mental health movement. The contemporary mental health movement orchestrated a massive deinstitutionalization of psychiatric hospitals. Advocates take firm but polarized positions on whether this most recent reform was successful or not. Since families and loved ones of those who have mental disorders are no less desperate for help, what will happen next?

Key Terms

AMERICANS WITH DISABILITIES ACTS

ANOSOGNOSIA

DEINSTITUTIONALIZATION

EUGENICS

INSTITUTIONALIZATION

PSYCHIATRISTS

PSYCHOLOGISTS

TRANSINSTITUTIONALIZATION

Chapter Objectives

After completing this chapter, you should be able to:

- Describe the three modern periods of mental health reform in the U.S.
- Explain the concepts of institutionalization and deinstitutionalization
- Discuss the problems of homelessness in the U.S.
- Define the *Americans with Disabilities Act*

CARE OF THE MENTALLY ILL IN THE COLONIES

Similar to the European example, individuals with mental illness in colonial America were generally cared for by their family members. According to Grob (2009), there was no need for special facilities to care for people with mental disorders in the early American colonies since there were not enough people for the situation to be a problem. The population density was low and communities were primarily rural and agricultural. As the population grew in the colonies, so did the social problems that required community attention.

Early American attitudes attributed mental disorders to moral or spiritual failings. Historian and author Grob states that the first legal code in Massachusetts, adopted in 1641, made several references to "distracted" persons and idiots. By 1694, the rise in the numbers of "distracted persons" had been noted by the Court, prompting passage of the "Act for the Relief of Ideots and

Distracted Persons" (Grob, 2009). Essentially, it allowed for the overseers of the poor to take legal responsibility for the care of these individuals, including the liquidation of their assets to defray costs. Individuals exhibiting unusual behaviors were subjected to punishment and shame, sometimes ending up in almshouses or jails.

1. CH02-01: *Witchcraft.* Many people are still fascinated with the idea of witchcraft. During the Colonial period the mere accusation of being involved with witchcraft could result in death. Today, most of those who call themselves witches belong to the Wicca religion. Some believe Wicca to be the fastest growing non-traditional religion in America. Photo copyright Tibanna79/Bigstock.com

Witchcraft

While the existence of witchcraft was a universal belief in Europe, it was also spreading to the New World. Early settlers were firmly convinced of the reality of witchcraft. The practice of witchcraft was a capital crime in the New England colonies in the late 1600s and continued into the 1700s. Prior to the Salem witch trials an estimated ten people had been found guilty of witchcraft and hanged in Massachusetts and Connecticut, though many more were found not guilty and released (Judd, 1905). The witch trials of Salem in 1692 resulted in the deaths of 20 more.

Joseph and Bathsheba Pope, Quakers who lived in Massachusetts, joined the numbers to claim torment by witches. In 1692 they accused three of their neighbors of practicing witchcraft, John Procter, Martha Cory, and Rebecca Nurse

(Baker, 2015). All three were convicted in court and executed during the notorious Salem witch trials. However, the belief in witchcraft was short-lived in the colonies. From the infamous Pope family was born one of the most prominent leaders of the American Enlightenment. Baker (2015) states that Bathsheba's youngest sister, Abiah, was the mother of Benjamin Franklin. By 1693, grand juries refused to indict for witchcraft in the colonies, looking back at the Salem witch-hunts with horror and remorse (Judd, 1905).

During the seventeenth and eighteenth centuries the trend in the colonies was to provide guardianship and support of the poor insane. However, hospitals were opened to secure, rather than cure, the individuals with mental illness (Tomes, 1981). In 1752, the newly opened Pennsylvania Hospital provided rooms in the basement complete with shackles attached to the walls to house a small number of patients with mental disorders. It was quickly expanded to an entire hospital wing. According to Tomes (1991), medical treatment provided to patients, while considered humane at the time, consisted of bleedings, purges, and medications that caused vomiting.

Among the most influential individuals credited with promoting the construction of asylums to care for individuals with mental disorders was Dr. Benjamin Rush (1745–1813). Referred to as the "father of American psychology," Rush served in numerous prominent positions as well as on the staff of the Pennsylvania Hospital from 1783 until his death (D'Elia, 1974). Rush taught that the patients suffered from a disease of the mind and not a demonic possession. Among his many accomplishments, he is credited with writing the first psychiatric textbook printed in America.

By the 1800s care for the individuals with mental illness was largely left to jails and poor houses in the absence of available family (Grob, 2009). More pressing social problems included threats of smallpox, yellow fever, diphtheria, and malaria, which resulted in high mortality rates. Conditions were deplorable as the houses of correction and jails became the dumping ground for individuals with mental disorders. Similar to the European experience, workhouses and almshouses began to take in some of the poor and jails were used as a means of punishing the vagrant and criminal population (Scull, 2015).

2. CH02-02: *Pennsylvania Hospital for the Insane.* This bucolic scene depicts the first institution in Pennsylvania devoted exclusively to persons with mental disorders. It was located in Philadelphia. Photo courtesy of the National Library of Medicine.

ASYLUM PERIOD OF REFORM—MORAL TREATMENT

The first modern period of reform began during the early 1800s. Scull (2015) suggests that there were a handful of small charitable asylums built in the U.S. that were heavily influenced by the *moral treatment* practiced by the Quakers of England. Moral treatment advocates did not believe in the use of any medicine or drug; they denounced bloodletting, vomiting, blisters, or the use of restraints. Instead they advocated warm baths, compassionate treatment for the patients (Tomes, 1981). Opening in the early 1800s, examples of the asylums using the moral treatment approach include the Friends Asylum in Pennsylvania, the McLean Hospital in Waverly, MA, and the Massachusetts General Hospital in Boston. The moral treatment approach was not widely practiced, however.

The first institution in Pennsylvania devoted exclusively to persons with mental disorders opened as the Pennsylvania Hospital for the Insane in 1841. The hospital was not intended as a permanent residence—the stated goal was to improve the patients' health and then return them home. *The Code of Rules and Regulations for the employees of the hospital* included the philosophy that insanity is a disease over which individuals have no control (Pennsylvania Hospital for the

Insane, 1850). Employees were instructed that the patients would never be exposed to rude remarks, rough actions, and were always to be treated with courtesy, respectful kindness and sympathy. Ridicule and violence by attendants was strictly forbidden as a condition of employment.

IMAGINE THAT . . .

Mary Todd Lincoln had lost three of her four sons to death. In the theater, she was holding the hand of her husband, President Abraham Lincoln, when he was assassinated (Emerson, 2012). Numerous historical accounts describe her as a reckless spender and a self-indulgent woman. She was scorned by the American public for her lavish spending on repairs to the White House. Mary invited spiritualists to the White House. Spiritualists believed in the continuity of life into the afterlife; that the dead could communicate with the living through a medium. It was a controversial religion in the 1800s. Some suggest that Mary's beliefs contributed to her fate.

On May 19, 1875, Mary Todd Lincoln was brought before the Illinois court at the direction of her only surviving son, Robert, on the charge of being insane. A juror later said that it was clear that Mrs. Lincoln suffered from fear of fire and manic purchasing. She was found guilty and committed to Bellevue Place Sanitarium. There is still much disagreement as to whether Mary Lincoln was, in fact, insane. With the help of friends, Mary left the asylum to visit her sister. She never returned to Bellevue from that visit. Assisted by her attorney, James, and his wife, Myra, Mary was given a second trial a year later. Adjudicated to be sane, her property and money was returned to her.

Question for discussion: What does the story of Mary Tod Lincoln have in common with other historical accounts of insanity?

By the mid-1800s urbanization and the influx of large numbers of poor immigrants to the American colonies made the care for people with mental illness more difficult. Dorothea Dix, a leading prison reformer, strongly advocated for the moral treatment of jail and prison inmates through asylum care rather than criminal commitment. She described inmates that were naked, filthy, and held in solitary confinement. Some inmates were so disturbed that they self-abused. Dorothea Dix wrote a scathing report to the Massachusetts legislature in the early 1840s, saying in part (Dix, 1843):

> *I proceed, Gentlemen, briefly to call your attention to the state of Insane Persons confined within this Commonwealth, in cages, closets, cellars, stalls, pens: Chained, naked, beaten with rods, and lashed into obedience.*

Dix recognized that the jails and prisons were not designed to provide the treatment that mentally disordered individuals so desperately needed. She pointed to the asylums run by moral treatment methods as the most desirable (Scull, 2015). During a 40-year campaign to remove persons with mental disorders from prisons and jails to more humane lodgings, Dix influenced the building of 32 new mental institutions across the United States. Increased demands for institutional care prompted expanding the asylum populations to include advanced cases of mental illness with the least chance of recovery (Morrissey and Goldman, 1986).

Custody and community protection eventually became the major focus of asylums, rather than treatment. Deplorable prison conditions and the lack of care prompted the growth of the asylum movement. Asylums were considered the most humane way to care for persons with mental illness and they were welcomed by families and communities struggling to care for relatives with severe mental illness and disability (Knapp, Beecham, McDaid, Matosevic, and Smith, 2011). By the time of the 1880 census, 99 percent of individuals with mental illness lived in asylums or at home, while only a few hundred remained in jail or prison (Knapp et al., 2011).

The first professional medical specialty organization in the United States, called the Association of Medical Superintendents' of American Institutions for the Insane, was established in 1844 (NIH, 2015). Its organizers shared information with each other for improving the treatment and the rights of the mentally ill, and to clarify the civil and criminal relationships of the persons with mental illness. In 1921, its name was changed to the American Psychiatric Association (APA). Eventually the APA would dominate the field of psychiatry and psychology, specifically driving the care for individuals with mental disorders.

THE EUGENICS MOVEMENT

As advances in the scientific study of evolution and the role of biology emerged, demonology and witchcraft were no longer considered to be viable causes of mental illness. New labels and definitions were created to describe mental disorders. Psychiatric classifications included "idiocy" as the most severe form of mental disorder. It was popularly believed at the turn of the century that personal traits were passed down from generation to generation; a very crude conception of genetics was being developed.

Adding to the scientific revelations was Sir Francis Galton (1822–1911). Galton hypothesized that heredity explained more than merely the transmission of physical characteristics of individuals, but mental, emotional, and creative qualities as well. Galton conducted research of London families, and he became convinced that two people of bad blood would produce progressively defective offspring. He called for strict marriage licensing as a social control to the problems of bad blood. Galton coined **EUGENICS** as the term to refer to his "science of selective breeding."

In 1912, American psychologist Henry H. Goddard published *The Kallikak Family: A Study in the Heredity of Feeble-Mindedness.* His case study explored the genetics of mental illness, concluding that mental traits were hereditary. Goddard argued that society should limit reproduction by people who possessed traits of mental illness. With the link between heredity and feeble-mindedness established, there came a fear of worsening generations of undesirables. In response, the U.S. legalized eugenics as a means of fighting the spread of mental disorders. Poverty, low intelligence, epilepsy, or African or American Indian ethnicity were all reasons individuals were deemed feeble-minded (Black, 2012). Mandatory sterilization laws were passed in 27 states to prevent targeted inferiors from reproducing, according to Black (2012).

In the *Buck vs. Bell* decision of May 2, 1927 (274 U.S. 200), the United States Supreme Court upheld a Virginia statute that provided for the eugenic sterilization for people considered genetically unfit. The Court's decision, delivered by Oliver Wendell Holmes, Jr., included the infamous phrase "Three generations of imbeciles are enough." Like animals, boys and girls at young ages were sterilized and released. Most were unaware of what had been done to them. Approximately 70,000 individuals were forcibly sterilized across America during the eugenics movement (Black, 2012). While most states stopped enforcing sterilization statutes in the 1970s, the practice continued under federal provisions. Black reports that over 3,500 Native American women and men were sterilized between 1972 and 1976 after threat of losing welfare benefits or custody of their children. Since 2002, the governors of Virginia, California, Oregon, North Carolina and South Caroline have formally apologized to victims both living and dead for decades of eugenic sterilizations.

INSTITUTIONALIZATION PERIOD OF REFORM—RISE OF PSYCHIATRY AND PSYCHOLOGY

Around the turn of the twentieth century, a growing pessimism towards the therapeutic value of asylum care gave way to the rejection of the asylum model. Optimism regarding scientific advances in psychiatry and psychology led to the creation of a small number of 'psychopathic hospitals' and mental health clinics which were meant to address the previous lack of treatment through mental hygiene (Morrissey and Goldman, 1986). However, individuals that needed long-term care eventually were sent to state institutions.

Reformers turned to the relevance of psychiatry as the means to correct moral hygiene. Institutions increasingly assumed the care of individuals deemed to be feebleminded, alcoholics, abnormal children, and criminals (Morrissey and Goldman, 1986). Between 1903 and 1950, per Morrissey and Goldman (1986), the number of patients in mental hospitals increased by 240 percent, a rate of growth nearly twice as large as the rate of increase in the U.S. population. This period of **INSTITUTIONALIZATION** refers to the inpatient care model, in which patients live in psychopathic hospitals and state institutions with treatment by professional staff with increased access to mental health services. Professional staff included psychiatrists, psychologists, and social workers. **PSYCHIATRISTS** are medical doctors with a specialty in the assessment and treatment of mental health disorders. **PSYCHOLOGISTS** are not medical doctors; they have advanced degrees in philosophy or psychology with a specialty in counseling. Only psychiatrists can prescribe medications, but both categories are trained to practice psychotherapy. Different types of institutions throughout the U.S. include private hospitals as well as government hospitals.

States assumed greater financial responsibility for the care and treatment of individuals with mental illness during the institutional period (Morrissey & Goldman, 1986). Unfortunately, funding was affected by the earlier reform period. For example, Dorothea Dix had also led a movement to establish a national policy for the care of people with severe mental illness and the use of federal land for the building of asylums. The 12,225,000 Acre Bill, as it was called, mandated federal funding for the building of state psychiatric hospitals that were to assume the care of the mentally ill who were in jails, poorhouses, or on the street (Parks, Radke, and Haupt, 2014). Although the legislation passed Congress in 1854, President Franklin Pierce vetoed the bill, stating that the responsibility for care of persons with mental illness should be placed on the states, not the federal government.

According to Parks, et. al (2014), this action has had lasting fiscal and philosophical effects to this day. When the federal government established the Medicaid program in 1965, Congress insisted that the costs for state and local psychiatric hospitals should not be funded. Based in part of the precedent created by President Pierce, Congress created the Institution for Mental Disease (IMD) Exclusion rule. The IMD Exclusion Rule prohibits Medicaid reimbursements to any facility in which more than 50 percent of the beds are occupied by patients with a primary diagnosis of mental disease. U.S. Code: Title 42—*The Public Health and Welfare Law* defines an institution for mental disease as a hospital, nursing facility, or other institution of more than sixteen beds, that is primarily engaged in providing diagnosis, treatment, or care of persons with mental diseases, including those which provide medical attention, nursing care, and related services. Marginalized in federal reimbursement and regulatory structures, state psychiatric hospitals continue to depend predominantly on state funding.

Many suggest that the state hospitals were underfunded and understaffed, and that these conditions eventually led to poor living conditions within the institutions (Novella, 2010). Despite the lack of federal assistance, every state had built one or more psychiatric hospitals by 1890 (NIH, 2015). In the United States, state hospital populations peaked in 1955 at 560,000 people (Talbott, 1979). State psychiatric institutions, in addition to private hospitals, had become long term chronic care facilities where psychosurgery and other radical treatments for mental illness flourished as mainstream medicine (Valenstein, 1986).

Shock Therapy

Therapies to cure individuals of mental disorders entered a new phase during the 1930s when three types of treatments meant to "shock" the body out of mental disorder were introduced for patients with schizophrenia: the insulin-induced coma, medically induced convulsions, and electroshock convulsions. Convulsion therapies were thought to be effective treatments for depression as well. An estimated 75,000 patients across America received shock treatments between 1935 and 1941 (Valenstein, 1986).

In 1941, the Mental Hygiene Division of the *United States Public Health Service* conducted a survey on the use and efficacy of shock therapy in hospitals across America (Kolb and Vogel, 1942). Federal, state, and city hospitals in addition to private hospitals and psychiatric wards in general hospitals were included in the study. Of the 305 institutions that responded, 85 percent were using some kind of shock therapy or had in the past. Insulin shock was introduced in 1935, metrazol in 1936, and electric shock in 1942. The study showed that there was a tendency for institutions to discontinue use of any one type of shock therapy when a new form became available. Prolonged coma, pneumonia, fractures, dislocations and death were among the reported complications of shock therapy. Solicited comments in the study on shock therapy ranged from "highly valuable" to "I do not believe that we can scramble brains and expect to have anything left but scrambled brains" (Kolb and Vogel, 1942). Little evidence on the efficacy of these treatments could be produced, however, and the incidence of these procedures lessened after the advent of anti-schizophrenic drugs.

IN MY EXPERIENCE . . .

Since the state police had jurisdiction of the asylum, called the "state school," I was called to investigate an alleged sexual assault. As I entered a locked ward, the blood-curdling screams echoed against the bars that locked behind me. It was my job to protect the rights of the people to be free from predatory abuses. However, as a Trooper with the Massachusetts State Police, I envisioned crime fighting to be the only job of a police officer, and this was not what I expected. . . .

Question for discussion: What role SHOULD the police have in the protection of individuals with severe mental disability?

Psychosurgery

Psychosurgery is a general term used to describe surgical procedures that are used to destroy specific areas of the brain to improve conditions of mental illness. One well-known type of psychosurgery is the prefrontal lobotomy. In this procedure, a surgeon will drill two or more holes in a patient's skull, according to Valenstein (1986). Without being able to see what he was cutting, the doctor will then insert into the brain any of various instruments used to destroy parts of the brain. Typical instruments included an apple corer or ice pick. Between 1949 and 1952 approximately 5,000 lobotomies were performed each year in the U.S.; tens of thousands of these brain mutilation operations were performed as cures for individuals with mental disorders around the world (Valenstein, 1986). The procedure is seen as a last resort for patients who lack any alternative treatment. An estimated 60,000 frontal lobotomy procedures were performed in America and Europe between 1936 and 1956 (Faria, 2013). The procedure fell into disrepute by the 1960s, leaving in its wake many people with serious brain damage as well as critics who claimed it was nothing more than trephining. Psychosurgery played a significant part in the ongoing dispute between psychiatrists and neurologists over the responsibilities of treating individuals with mental disorders. Additionally, these desperate measures to cure individuals highlight the despair of both patients and their families. Surgical destruction of specific regions of the brain is now a discredited biological treatment.

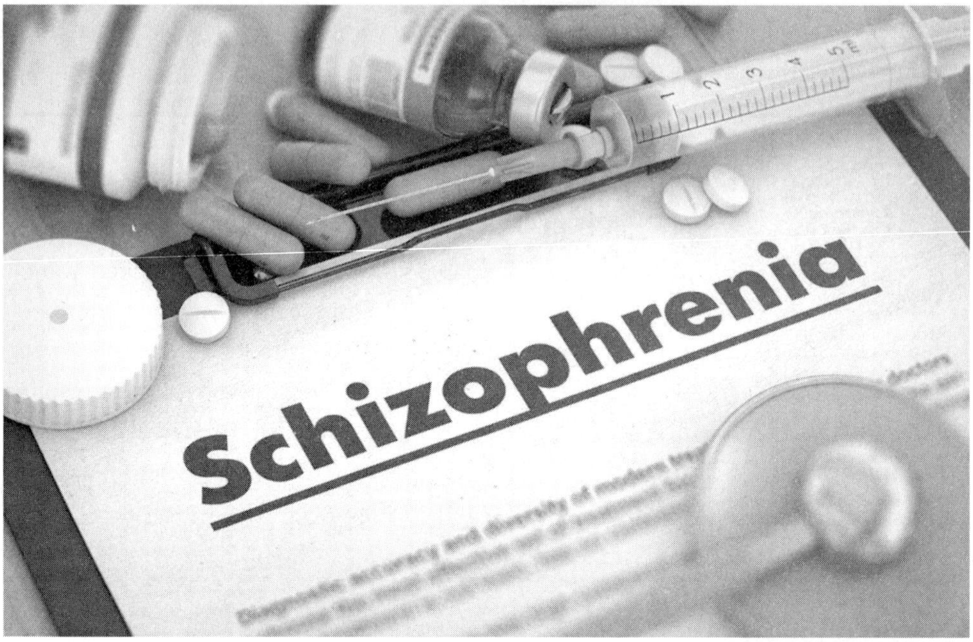

3. CH02-03: *Medication Therapy.* When medications became available for the treatment of mental disorders during the 1950s they were quickly embraced as a viable option to replace earlier barbaric methods. Shock therapy or electroconvulsive therapy (ECT) that is used today to treat depression now uses electric currents given in a controlled setting under general anesthesia. A modern psychosurgery, called a craniotomy, may be used to remove tumors of the brain in areas under the skull by removing a portion of the skull and then reattaching it after the procedure. Brain mapping and 3-D computer images assist surgeons during this delicate operation. Photo copyright tashatuvango/Bigstock.com

Drug Therapy

Reliance on psychiatric hospitals as the primary management for individuals with mental disorders continued at an accelerated pace during the first half of the twentieth century. By 1955, almost 600,000 beds in the U.S. were occupied by seriously ill psychiatric patients (E. Torrey, Fuller, Geller, Jacobs, and Ragosta, 2012). Individuals with schizophrenia, bipolar (previously called manic depressive illness), dementia, and other chronic brain diseases along with persons who suffered developmental disabilities filled the beds. Psychosurgeries failed the test of time as more than three-quarters of the schizophrenic patients treated with lobotomy were reported to be in a state of dependency in homes or hospitals by the 1970s (Faria, 2013).

The medical profession eagerly embraced the advent of drugs that could replace the often gruesome and debilitating psychosurgery and shock therapies that had become mainstream. Ushering in the drug therapy revolution, the drugs chlorpromazine and haloperidol were introduced in the U.S. between 1953 and

1967 (Faria, 2013). Almost immediately, a trend towards deinstitutionalization began as drugs were seen as the most effective means to stabilize patients with psychiatric illness.

Patient Abuses

Psychiatric institutions came under attack following high profile abuses and human rights violations. The scientific and research community viewed vulnerable institutionalized populations as among those who were appropriate to be used as test subjects. Numerous human experiments involving individuals confined in psychiatric hospitals and prisons have been discovered. In the 1950s, for example, an institution for mentally handicapped children in New York experienced unsanitary conditions so severe that outbreaks of hepatitis were occurring. The doctor sent to investigate the outbreaks, Dr. Saul Krugman, proposed that children would be deliberately infected with hepatitis as an experiment to assist in developing a vaccine (Education Development Center Inc., 2009). It was hinted in at least one report that obtaining permission of the parents was the only way to guarantee admittance into the overcrowded institution (Pecorino, 2002). The controversial experimentation on children in the institution continued for fourteen years. Referred to as the Willowbrook Study, it was among several human experiments that occurred between 1932 and 1979 that led to the creation of the Institutional Review Board (IRB), which was formed to protect human subjects involved in future research. Mainstream therapeutic responses used during the period of institutionalism period eventually gave way to policies to protect vulnerable populations from human experimentation.

DISABILITY RIGHTS MOVEMENT

Over time, long-term chronic care institutions also housed individuals with severe physical and motor impairments. There was little distinction made in the institutionalization of people with psychological disabilities versus those with physical disabilities. During the 1950s and early 1960s, people with severe physical disabilities began leaving institutions, attending colleges, and entering the American workforce. Individual mobility and communication techniques improved and progress was made toward the main goals of deinstitutionalization and independent living. The trend during the 1960s towards deinstitutionalization allowed individuals with severe physical disabilities to begin entering mainstream society.

A chronology of the Disability Rights Movement by Fleischer and James (2001) suggests that the disabilities rights movement had slowly begun in the

1800s when the first school for deaf students opened in Hartford, Connecticut. Other significant historical points in the chronology include the publication of the autobiography of Helen Keller in 1903 and the passage of several laws to aid disabled American Veterans during the 1920s. In 1932, Franklin Delano Roosevelt, crippled due to childhood polio, was elected president of the United States. The disability rights movement prompted activism and was responsible for numerous legislative changes including funding for accommodations that enabled individuals with physical disabilities to live independently (Fleischer and Zames, 2001). Activism also brought changes in social understanding for individuals with physical disabilities.

The two populations of the mentally and physically disabled are dissimilar in their needs and abilities to live independently, yet they do share the history of institutionalization, discrimination, and ultimately deinstitutionalization. During the early 1970s, around the same time as the rights movement of people with physical disabilities took hold, the rights movement of people with psychiatric disabilities expanded. Legislative protections that resulted from the disability rights movement are still being applied to assist and protect all individuals with physical and psychological disabilities.

COMMUNITY MENTAL HEALTH REFORM—DEINSTITUTIONALIZATION

The next reform period is referred to as the community mental health (CMH) movement. Civil libertarians and other activists called for reforms in response to charges of patient abuses and dehumanizing conditions in the state mental institutions. Reforms were stimulated by psychiatrists returning to the U.S. following World War II that brought back techniques for brief hospitalization and treatment of mental health disorders (Morrissey and Goldman, 1986). Activists from the movement worked to tighten the procedures under which individuals with mental disorders could be involuntarily committed, resulting in changes to the laws on civil commitment.

There are multiple causes that lead to the large-scale deinstitutionalization that began as the CMH movement. **DEINSTITUTIONALIZATION** is the policy of moving physically and mentally disabled persons out of state hospitals and then closing the institution fully or in part. Researchers cite two significant developments in the early 1960s that quickened the deinstitutionalization of individuals with mental illness across America (Sisti, Segal, and Emanuel, 2015). In 1963, individuals with psychological disabilities became eligible for federal financial assistance through Aid to the Disabled (ATD), later known as Supplemental Security Income (SSI). It became more affordable for communities to maintain patients outside of hospital settings.

IMAGINE THAT . . .

Early pioneers of disability rights made significant progress in establishing college programs for persons with disabilities, including disabled veterans. Yet prior to the 1950s it was widely believed that individuals living in long-term chronic care institutions would remain institutionalized their entire lives. In 1958, an early experiment took place at New York City's Goldwater Memorial Hospital. A twenty-one-year-old woman named Anne Emerman was selected as a test case for independent living. Anne was a quadriplegic wheelchair user who ultimately graduated with a master's in social work, became a psychiatric social worker, served as the director of the Mayor's Office for People with Disabilities in New York City, and became a wife and mother (Fleischer and Zames, 2001). Changes in the ways of thinking about social inequality have occurred since that time.

Question for discussion: What are your views about independent living for people with physical disabilities?

The second significant development was the passage of the *Mental Retardation Facilities and Community Mental Health Centers Construction Act of 1963*. The *Act of 1963* required local governments to provide community-based settings so that patients could continue their treatment, medication, and therapy outside of state mental health facilities (Talbott, 1979). Unfortunately, the large number of community-based facilities required to meet the needs of this population was never built (Fleischer and Zames, 2001). The importance of psychoactive medication and a stable financial support system was conceived, but not implemented, according to some studies (Sisti, Segal, and Emanuel, 2015; Smith, 2015). States were reluctant to allocate funds for community-based services and existing mental health centers were resistant to providing services to the chronically mentally ill transient population (Lamb, 1984). Despite the lack of resources in the community, by 1979 the institutionalized population had declined to 170,000—a drop of more than 60 percent (Talbott, 1979).

The belief that most individuals could live outside of institutions, with drug treatment and assistance from community facilities, was commonly accepted among advocates of reform. It was not even considered that some patients might need to live in a long-term, locked, and supervised community facility when the institutions were closed. Civil commitment laws had become so restrictive that institutionalization was no longer a viable alternative. Some experts now question whether the policy of ignoring those patients that are never free of psychosis and dangerous in every setting is a humane response (Sisti et al., 2015; Smith, 2015). By 1971, deinstitutionalization was decried as a mess by local communities that were inundated by hundreds of discharged patients (Talbott, 1979). When psychiatric professionals or lay people refer to the disaster created by deinstitutionalization, according to Talbott (1979), they are referring to several events. . . .

> *"Most striking [however] was the dramatic increase of large numbers of obviously mentally ill people on city streets, people who were dirty, who wore torn or inappropriate clothing, who hallucinated and talked to themselves or shouted to others, and who in general acted in a strange or bizarre way."*

WHERE DID THE PATIENTS GO?

Many ask, where did the institutionalized patients with severe mental illnesses end up? Disputed facts and conflicting research is still emerging. Some believe that the policies of deinstitutionalization led to the unintended consequence referred to as transinstitutionalism. **TRANSINSTITUTIONALIZATION** is the phenomenon where individuals with severe mental health issues are alternately moved between different institutions such as homeless shelters, hospitals, and the criminal justice system (Sisti et al., 2015). Blau (1992) stated that many of the released patients from mental institutions were transferred to nursing homes. He asserted that as a result of closing institutions, half of the 1.3 million nursing home residents had a mental disorder by 1977. A large percentage of patients immediately became homeless, according to others. Markowitz (2006) revealed that 27 percent to 38 percent of deinstitutionalized patients became homeless within six months after discharge when the psychiatric hospitals in the U.S. closed.

IMAGINE THAT . . .

Lionel Penrose published a study in 1939 maintaining that an inverse relationship existed between the number of mental hospital beds and the number of prisoners (Penrose, 1939). He argued that by increasing the number of psychiatric hospital beds, a society could reduce serious crimes and imprisonment rates. When psychiatric hospital beds are reduced, he suggested, prison and jail populations would increase. Now referred to as 'Penrose's Theory' there is continued research and debate on the theory.

Question for discussion: Find contemporary articles and debate in class the value or lack of value you see in this theory.

IN MY EXPERIENCE . . .

Deinstitutionalization in Massachusetts meant that some former patients were temporarily relocated to hotel rooms. Shortly after the Northampton State Institution was closed, Alice was deemed by the Department of Mental Health as able to live independently with periodic supervision by a case worker. Considered mildly mentally ill, she could balance her checkbook, but unable to deal with people, I was told. It happened that the hotel she was staying at had difficulty in keeping hot water supplied to rooms farthest from the furnace, resulting in the owner increasing the 120-degree water temperature (which was code) to 160 degrees.

One morning Alice received first degree burns over most of her body as the result of scalding herself in the shower. On investigation, I found that she had walked three-quarter miles from the hotel into town to visit the pharmacy in order to get something for her burns. It was Sunday morning and the pharmacy was closed, so she walked back and knocked on the door of a neighbor saying "the water was so hot." The ambulance was called and Alice lingered in horrific pain at deaths door for almost a month before she died.

Question for discussion: How much weight should the ability to make self-care decisions be taken into account in decisions on the protection of individuals with mental disability?

Still others point to the population explosion within prisons and jails following deinstitutionalization. Research confirmed that in 1968 there were 399,000 patients in state mental hospitals and 168,000 inmates in state prisons (Goldman, Adams, and Taube, 1983). By the time that the mental hospital population had dropped by 64 percent in 1978, the prison population had grown by 65 percent (Steadman, Monahan, Duffee, and Hartstone, 1984). A suggestion has even been made that while psychiatric beds in mental hospitals have been reduced, the number of psychiatric beds in general hospital settings have continued to be filled (Shen and Snowden, 2014). Both the advocates and critics have responded to these issues with explanations for the outcomes that followed community mental health reform and its policy of deinstitutionalization. There is a growing realization that some severely disabled individuals need structured and stable controlled living conditions (Sisti et al., 2015). At the same time, considerable controversy exists regarding the absolute right of people to live freely versus the rights of society to protect itself.

4. CH02-04: *Victimization.* Extremely high rates of victimization have been documented among the adult population of homeless individuals who have mental disorders. The relationship (if any) between violent behavior and violent victimization of the homeless with mental disorders is a current subject of interest to researchers. Copyright Lisa F. Young/Shutterstock.com

Homelessness

Many individuals are thought to have become homeless after deinstitutionalization occurred because they are unable to care for themselves. Some experts argue that mental illness itself is not the cause of homelessness; instead, it is the way that deinstitutionalization was implanted in the U.S. that has caused chronic homelessness (Lamb, 1984). As late as 2004, the National Alliance on Mental Illness (NAMI) reported that mental illness and the lack of needed services was the second most frequently sited reason for homelessness. NAMI reports that as many as 55,000 homeless people benefited from substance abuse and mental health services each week during 2004 (NAMI, 2004).

More recently, as many as one-third of the homeless in America are individuals thought to be experiencing mental illness (E. Torrey, Fuller, et al., 2012). Experts tell us that these individuals live under appalling conditions on the streets and that they are frequently victimized. Victimization rates among homeless adults with severe mental illness range between 73 percent and 87 percent (Roy, Crocker, Nicholls, Latimer, and Ayllon, 2014). Unfortunately, there is some evidence that mental health professionals may not be inclined to treat street people, in part due to the lack of trust and transient nature of the population (Sisti et al., 2015). Creating stable and secure living arrangements for the population of severely disabled individuals is considered a more humane and cost-effective way to help those who are unable to care for themselves.

From a review of research estimating the prevalence of criminal behavior among homeless adults with severe mental illness, authors found that lifetime arrest rates range between 62 percent and 90 percent (Roy et al., 2014). These rates are much higher than for the general U.S. population, in which lifetime arrest rates are estimated to be about 15.0 percent and for community dwelling adults with mental illness which ranged between 25.0 percent and 33.0 percent (Roy et al., 2014). Many are too sick to understand their own mental illness due to anosognosia. **ANOSOGNOSIA** is a medical condition experienced by someone with acute mental illness who does not think clearly enough to know that he or she is sick. It is estimated that 50 percent of people with *schizophrenia* and 40 percent of people with *bipolar disorder* are affected by Anosgnosia, placing them at greater risk of homelessness, victimization, or arrest (NAMI, 2015).

Psychiatric Facilities

The policy of deinstitutionalization in the U.S. resulted in the closing of most psychiatric hospitals and the loss of 95 percent of hospital beds that were once available for patients with chronic and severe mental disorders (E. Torrey, Entsminger, Geller, Stanley, and Jaffe, 2012). There are not enough facilities left to meet the needs of long term chronic care. While most agree that the system of institutionalism had become flawed, the abrupt closing of so many psychiatric hospitals has resulted in large numbers of individuals being without necessary services. It is estimated that 10 percent of the seriously mentally ill cannot be supported in the community (E. Torrey, Fuller, et al., 2012). Concerns about the abandonment of thousands of persons with severe mental illness has brought us to what some frame as the current crisis in mental health care. The number of psychiatric beds available is approximately fourteen per 100,000 people, roughly the same number as were available in the year 1850 (E. Torrey, Fuller, et al., 2012).

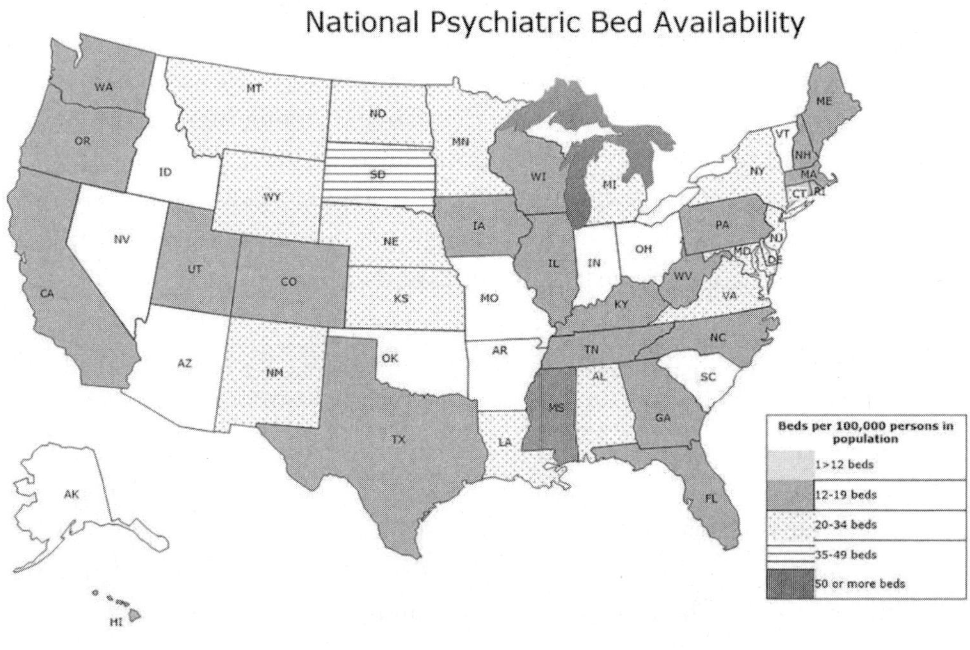

5. CH02-05: As illustrated in this figure, Mississippi is the only state in the United States that maintains the minimum number of psychiatric beds that experts suggest is needed to meet the needs of those suffering with severe mental illness in the country. Source: Torrey, Fuller, Geller, Jacobs, and Ragosta, 2012.

In a report published by the Treatment Advocacy Center, a minimum of fifty psychiatric beds per 100,000 in the population is the absolute minimum necessary to provide adequate psychological services for individuals with mental disorders. Facilities across America have fallen far short of this requirement, only one state in the country has yet to meet that minimum standard (E. Torrey, Entsminger, et al., 2012). Refer to Figure CH02-05 to see how your state fares. Additionally, America's community psychiatric treatment centers did not materialize as expected, and fewer than half of patients in need receive community services according to Torrey, et al. (2012).

Criminalization of Mental Illness

Referred to as the *criminalization of mental illness*, there are more people with mental illness in jails and prisons than there are in psychiatric hospitals. Using 2004–2005 data, researchers documented that it is three times more likely that individuals with serious mental disorders reside in jails and prisons than in psychiatric hospitals (E. F. Torrey, Kennard, Eslinger, Lamb, and Pavle, 2010). Many experts, however, dispute that deinstitutionalization is the cause of the criminalization of mental illness. Steadman, et al. (1984) conducted one of the earliest studies to challenge the assertion that deinstitutionalization was directly responsible for exploding prison populations. The authors concluded that the U.S. prison population between 1968 and 1978 did not appear to be significantly more disordered than during previous years (Steadman et al., 1984). Authors of the Steadman study suggest that the significant increase in prison populations were more likely caused by baby boomers coming of criminogenic age along with the criminal justice trends towards punitive sentencing. The study also noted, that during the period of deinstitutionalization there was an increase in clientele of mental hospitals who had been involved previously with the criminal justice system. The researchers assumed that it was jails, rather than the state prisons, who were functionally interdependent with mental hospital releases.

While there is disagreement over the cause of the criminalization of mental illness, experts agree that individuals with mental disorders are overly represented throughout the criminal justice system today. Jails and prisons have become the de-facto mental health institutions in the U.S. It is generally accepted that American jails and prisons have become the nation's largest mental health care facilities. This means that the criminal justice system has the primary responsibility for the care, protection, and treatment of these individuals whether they suffer minor disorders or are severely disordered.

AMERICANS WITH DISABILITIES ACT

The most significant example of the protection that has been afforded to individuals experiencing psychiatric and physical disabilities was enacted in 1990. The Americans with Disabilities Act (ADA) Title II § 12112 provides that "no qualified individual with disability shall, by reason of such disability, be excluded from participation in or be denied the benefits of the services, programs, or activities of a public entity, or be subjected to discrimination by any such entity."

This means that all state and government services, regardless of whether the person receives federal financial assistance, are mandated to provide services without discrimination. The ADA covers a wide range of disabilities, including both psychiatric and physical conditions. Those conditions do not need to be severe or permanent to be considered a disability. The Americans with Disabilities Act (ADA) requires that people with disabilities and their advocates file complaints and lawsuits, when appropriate, as a means of monitoring compliance (Americans with Disabilities Act, 1990). Due to the ADA mandate, the criminalization of mental illness, the shortage of psychiatric beds and mental health facilities, along with homelessness, criminal justice interactions with the disabled community has taken on great significance.

6. CH02-06: The Americans with Disabilities Act (1990) provides opportunities and protection from discrimination to individuals with physical challenges and psychological disabilities. Photo copyright Michaelpuche/Shutterstock.com

SUMMARY

The reasons why there is an overrepresentation of individuals with mental illness in the criminal justice system today is complicated. Medical practices and horrific abuses within psychiatric hospitals hastened the closing of institutional care facilities. Deinstitutionalization itself represents only a part of the historical explanation. And while deinstitutionalization has provided meaningful opportunities for many individuals, the mental health support system is lagging. An unintended consequence is that the criminal justice system has been given the task of policing within the context of disability. The Americans with Disabilities Act (1990) and its subsequent changes are slowly being integrated into the system, with court decisions continually refining criminal justice responsibilities. Future chapters will discuss the ways in which current reforms have changed criminal justice policies.

CHAPTER QUESTIONS FOR REVIEW

1. Explain the concepts of institutionalization and deinstitutionalization.
2. Describe the three major periods of reform in the United States.
3. What is the eugenics movement?
4. Why is anosognosia relevant to the issue of homelessness in the U.S.?
5. Is there a link between deinstitutionalization, homelessness, and the availability of psychiatric hospital beds?

REFERENCES

Americans with Disabilities Act, 42 U.S.C. 12101 (1990).

Blau, J. (1992). *The visible poor: Homelessness in the United States.* New York, NY: Oxford University Press.

Baker, E. (2015). *A storm of witchcraft: The Salem trials and the American experience.* New York, NY: Oxford University Press.

Black, E. (2012). *War against the weak: Eugenics and America's campaign to create a master race* (2nd ed.). Washington, D.C.: Dialog Press.

D'Elia, D. J. (1974). Benjamin Rush: Philosopher of the American Revolution. *Transactions of the American Philosophical Society, 64*(5), 1–113.

Dix, D. (1843). *Memorial, to the Legislature of Massachusetts.* Boston, MA: Munroe and Francis.

Education Development Center Inc. (2009). *Exploring bioethics.* (NIH 09-7386). Newton, MA: National Institutes of Health Retrieved from https://science.education.nih.gov/supplements/nih9/bioethics/guide/pdf/teachers_guide.pdf

Faria, M. (2013). Violence, mental illness, and the brain—A brief history of psychosurgery: Part 1—From trephination to lobotomy. *Surgical Neurology International, 4*(49).

Fleischer, D., and Zames, F. (2001). *The disability rights movement: From charity to confrontation.* Philadelphia, PA: Temple University Press.

Goldman, H. H., Adams, N. H., and Taube, C. A. (1983). Deinstitutionalization: The data demythologized. *Psychiatric Services, 34*(2), 129–134.

Judd, S. (1905). *History of Hadley: Early History of Hatfield, South Hadley, Amherst and Granby.* Springfield, MA: H.R. Huntting and Co.

Knapp, M., Beecham, J., McDaid, D., Matosevic, T., and Smith, M. (2011). The economic consequences of deinstitutionalization of mental health services: lessons from a systematic review of European experience. *Health and Social Care in the Community, 19*(2), 113–125.

Kolb, L., and Vogel, V. (1942). The use of shock therapy in 305 mental hospitals. *American Journal of Psychiatry, 99*(1), 90–100.

Morrissey, J., and Goldman, H. (1986). Care and treatment of the mentally ill in the United States: Historical developments and reforms. *The ANNALS of the American Academy of Political and Social Science, 484*(1), 12–27.

NAMI. (2015). Anosognosia. Retrieved July 10, 2015, from http://www.nami.org/Find–Support/A–Family–Member-or-Caregiver/Helping-a-Family–Member–Who–Doesn-t-Think–They-re.

NIH. (2015). Diseases of the mind: Highlights of American psychiatry through 1900. Retrieved May 24, 2016.

Novella, E. J. (2010). Mental health care and the politics of inclusion: a social systems account of psychiatric deinstitutionalization. *Theor Med Bioeth, 31*(6), 411–427.

Parks, J., Radke, A., and Haupt, M. (2014). The vital role of state psychiatric hospitals. Alexandria, VA: National Association of State Mental Health Program Directors.

Pecorino, P. (2002). Medical Ethics. Retrieved May 22, 2016, from http://www.qcc.cuny.edu/SocialSciences/ppecorino/MEDICAL_ETHICS_TEXT/Chapter_7_Human_Experimentation/Case_Study_Willowbrook_Experiments.htm

Pennsylvania Hospital for the Insane. (1850). *Code of rules and regulations for the government of those employed in the care of the patients of the Pennsylvania Hospital for the Insane, near Philadelphia*. Philadelphia, PA: T.K. and P.G. Collins Retrieved from http://resource.nlm.nih.gov/101560452

Penrose, L. S. (1939). Mental disease and crime: Outline of a comparative study of European statistics. *British Journal of Medical Psychology, 18*(1), 1–15.

Roy, L., Crocker, A. G., Nicholls, T. L., Latimer, E. A., and Ayllon, A. R. (2014). Criminal behavior and victimization among homeless individuals with severe mental illness: A systematic review. *Psychiatric Services, 65*(6), 739–750.

Scull, A. (2015). *Madness in civilization*. Princeton, NJ: Princeton University Press.

Shen, G. C., and Snowden, L. R. (2014). Institutionalization of deinstitutionalization: a cross-national analysis of mental health system reform. *International Journal of Mental Health Systems, 8*(1), 47.

Sisti, D., Segal, A., and Emanuel, E. (2015). Improving long-term psychiatric care: Bring back the asylum. *JAMA, 313*(3), 243–244.

Smith, C. (2015). Transinstitutionalization. *Correctional Mental Health Report, 17*(No. 1), 3–4.

Steadman, H., Monahan, J., Duffee, B., and Hartstone, E. (1984). The impact of state mental hospital deinstitutionalization on United States Prison Populations, 1968–1978. *Journal of criminal law and criminology, 75*, 474–490.

Talbott, J. (1979). Deinstitutionalization: Avoiding the disasters of the past. *Hospital and Community Psychiatry, 30*(9), 621–624.

Tomes, N. (1981). The discovery of the asylum revisited: Lunacy reform in the new American Republic. In A. Scull (Ed.), *Madhouses, mad-doctors, and madmen*. Philadelphia, PA: University of Pennsylvania Press.

Torrey, E., Entsminger, K., Geller, J., Stanley, J., and Jaffe, D. (2012). The shortage of public hospital beds for mentally ill persons (p. 17). Arlington, VA: Treatment Advocacy Center.

Torrey, E., Fuller, D., Geller, J., Jacobs, C., and Ragosta, K. (2012). No room at the inn: Trends and consequences of closing public psychiatric hospitals. Arlington, VA: Treatment Advocacy Center.

Torrey, E. F., Kennard, A., Eslinger, D., Lamb, R., and Pavle, J. (2010). More mentally ill persons are in jails and prisons than hospitals: A survey of the States. Arlington, VA: Treatment Advocacy Center and the National Sheriffs' Association.

Valenstein, E. (1986). *Great and desperate cures*. New York, NY: Basic Books, Inc.

CHAPTER 3

Mental Disorders

INTRODUCTION

Though they are rarely dangerous, individuals with mental disorders have typically been viewed by society as problematic. Societies throughout history believed that creativity and physical deformity were both evidence of mental illness. Culture, superstition, and religion have provided justification for legal intervention. Psychiatry and science are also involved in classifying and defining mental disorders. As these disciplines develop and change, so does their influence on the law. Criminal justice developed independently from psychiatry, so the two perspectives often differ and sometimes conflict with one another. Some conditions exist that are acknowledged by law and criminal justice practices that are not specifically recognized by psychiatry. It is important to note that definitions of mental disorders have changed over time and are based on societal standards.

This chapter contains an introduction to the terminology, disorders, and selected diagnostic classifications from psychiatry that pertain to crime and criminal justice specifically. References to the psychiatric diagnostic classifications is for the purpose of drawing parallels between the disciplines; however, mental health, psychiatry and psychology are very different professions from criminal justice. Diagnosis and treatment is the prevue of clinicians, those who are educated and work in the mental health field. Criminal justice professionals are tasked with responding to crisis and criminal situations. Having a set of shared definitions allows for a foundation on which interventions can occur in behalf of individuals with special needs.

Key Terms

COGNITIVE DISABILITY

MAJOR DEPRESSIVE EPISODE

MENTAL DISORDER

MENTAL ILLNESS

PSYCHOSOCIAL DISABILITY

SCHIZOPHRENIA

SERIOUS MENTAL ILLNESS

Chapter Objectives

After completing this chapter, you should be able to:

- Compare and contrast the three modern diagnostic systems
- Explain the role of the media in perpetuating myths regarding mental disorders
- Define various categories of mental disorders
- Explain the relationship between crime and mental disorder

MODERN DIAGNOSTIC SYSTEMS

To make a diagnosis, the clinician considers the patient symptoms against a list of the mental disorders from a classification system. The selection reflects the signs and symptoms that are exhibited by the individual being evaluated. There are three versions of diagnostic systems for mental illness that are widely used today. The most well-known of these systems is the *Diagnostic and Statistical Manual of Mental Disorders* (DSM), published by the American Psychiatric Association. The second is the Mental and Behavioral Section of the *International Classification of Diseases* (ICD), developed by the World Health Organization. The third system is the RDoC project of the *National Institute of Mental Health* (NIMH). The scope and focus of each system differs somewhat, resulting in what may appear to be conflicting information. However, these are not mutually exclusive systems since they share some common terminology and some disorder classification categories.

Diagnostic and Statistical Manual of Mental Disorders

The most recent version of the *Diagnostic and Statistical Manual of Mental Disorders* (DSM) is the DSM-5 (APA, 2015). First published in 1952, the Diagnostic and

Statistical Manual focuses on clinical aspects of mental disorders. Psychiatrists and psychologists depend on input from patient self-reports, caregivers, parents, and teachers in making an assessment. This approach to classification was groundbreaking for its time and is still credible today.

The American Psychological Association DSM-5 defines a **MENTAL DISORDER** as:

- A behavioral or psychological syndrome or pattern that occurs in an individual;
- reflecting an underlying psychobiological dysfunction;
- the consequences of which are clinically significant distress (e.g., a painful symptom) or disability (i.e., impairment in one or more important areas of functioning);
- must not be merely an expectable response to common stressors and losses (for example, the loss of a loved one) or a culturally sanctioned response to an event (for example, trance states in religious rituals);
- not primarily a result of social deviance or conflicts within society.

International Classification of Diseases (ICD)

The second method of classification is found in the Mental and Behavioral Section of the *International Classification of Diseases* (ICD), developed by the World Health Organization (ICD-10, 2016). The ICD classification is intended for use by practitioners with different levels of expertise and in different cultural settings around the world (Cuthbert and Insel, 2013). The World Health Organization (WHO) is the directing and coordinating authority for global health matters within the United Nations system, which includes the United States. WHO provides leadership for shaping the health research agenda, setting standards and publishing evidence-based policy recommendations. The international community situates mental disorders under an umbrella of disabilities by using the term *psychosocial disability*. **PSYCHOSOCIAL DISABILITY** refers to the disabilities of individuals with either diagnosed or perceived mental health conditions and/or intellectual impairments, which may be caused by stigma, discrimination or exclusions.

Research and publications from WHO inform and recommend response strategies for global mental health issues. For example, WHO estimates that 80 million people are currently impacted by emergencies arising from natural disasters and armed conflicts around the world, causing depression in as many as

10 percent of those populations (WHO, 2015a). The *mhGAP Humanitarian Intervention Guide* is available for non-specialist health-care providers working in humanitarian emergencies. Contents of this guide include modules on assessing and managing conditions such as acute stress, grief, moderate-severe depressive disorder, post-traumatic stress disorder, epilepsy, and harmful use of alcohol and drugs.

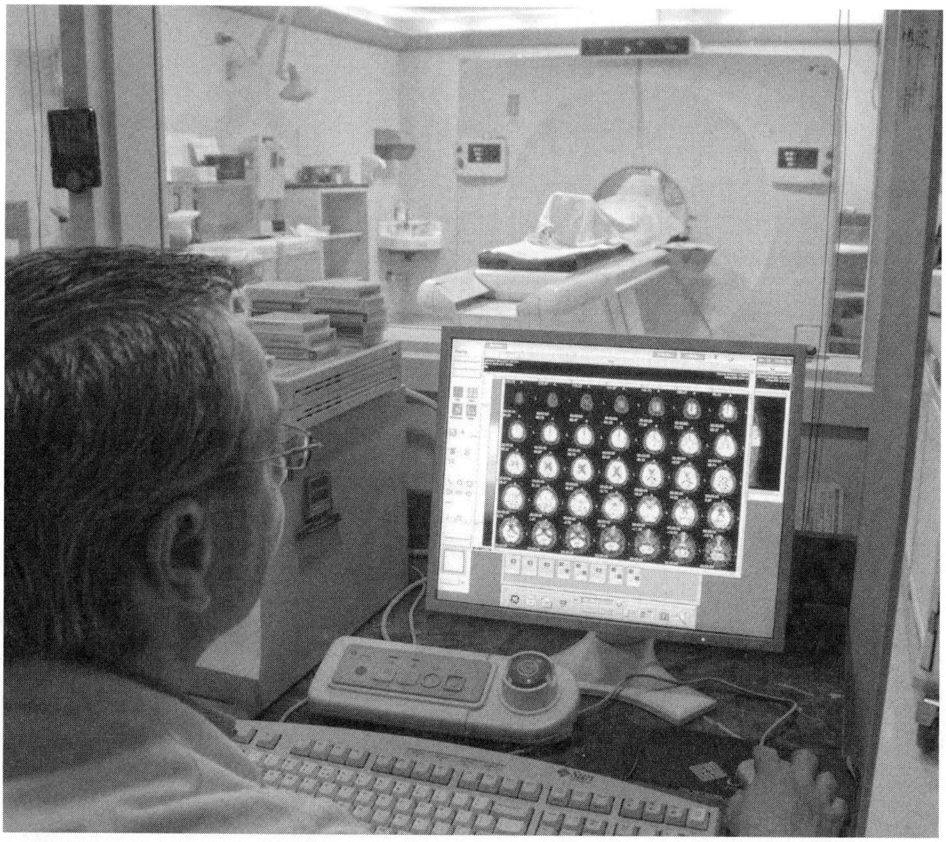

1. CH03-01: *RDoC.* The purpose of the RDoC project is to promote science so that advances in genomics, pathophysiology, and psychology can substantially inform the diagnosis and treatments of mental disorders. Photo courtesy of the National Institutes of Health, Department of Health and Human Services.

Research Domain Criteria (RDoC)

The third system is the Research Domain Criteria (RDoC) project of the *National Institute of Mental Health* (NIMH, n.d.). This is the most recent development in mental illness research. It was developed to bridge the gap between science and psychology to advance our understanding of mental illnesses through basic and clinical research. Consistent with precision medicine in general, *RDoC* does not rely on patient self-characterization of symptoms. Instead, it forms medical diagnoses based on behavioral science and neurosciences (Cuthbert, 2015).

The National Survey on Drug Use and Health (NSDUH) is the newest survey developed for the *RDoC* standard and used by the National Institute of Mental Health (NSDUH, 2014). Its findings are grouped into three categories to provide estimates on the extent of mental illness among adults aged 18 or older within the general population of the United States and their use of mental health services. It does not include for measure the prevalence of mental illness among individuals institutionalized in jails, nursing homes, mental institutions and long-term hospitals, or homeless persons, or military personnel on active duty, or for childhood and developmental disorders. The three categories in NSDUH are *Any Mental Illness* (AMI), *Serious Mental Illness* (SMI), a*nd Major Depressive Episode.*

THE PROBLEM(S) WITH MENTAL ILLNESS IN THE U.S.

In developed countries, mental illness accounts for a larger proportion of disability than any other group of illnesses, including cancer and heart disease (Centers for Disease Control and Prevention, 2011). Among the many challenges associated with mental disorders is the cost to the United States economy. Mental disorders were one of the five costliest conditions in the United States in 2006, with expenditures at $57.5 billion (AHRQ, 2009). One report estimates current costs of over $300 billion annually (McCall-Hosenfeld, Mukherjee, and Lehman, 2014). This figure is comprised of both the direct cost of mental health care and indirect costs such as income compensation for unemployment. Experts suggest that the cost of lost earnings alone due to major mental disorders in the United States is approximately $193 billion each year (Kessler et al., 2008). As people are expected to live longer in the future, these costs alone represent an impending crisis.

Mental Disorders Are Common

Research on mental health shows that mental disorders are very common throughout the United States today. In 2013, almost 43 million adults were affected (NSDUH, 2014). The National Survey on Drug Use and Health (2014) reports that approximately one in four adults and one in five children have a diagnosable mental illness. Diagnoses made of the same disorder do not necessarily manifest the same way with different people. Diagnosed disorders are also on a continuum; symptoms may lessen or worsen over time—or they may remain the same. There are a lot of variables within each of the disorder categories that people may experience. Having a mental disorder does not predict any specific outcome, so much is dependent on individual pathology and life conditions.

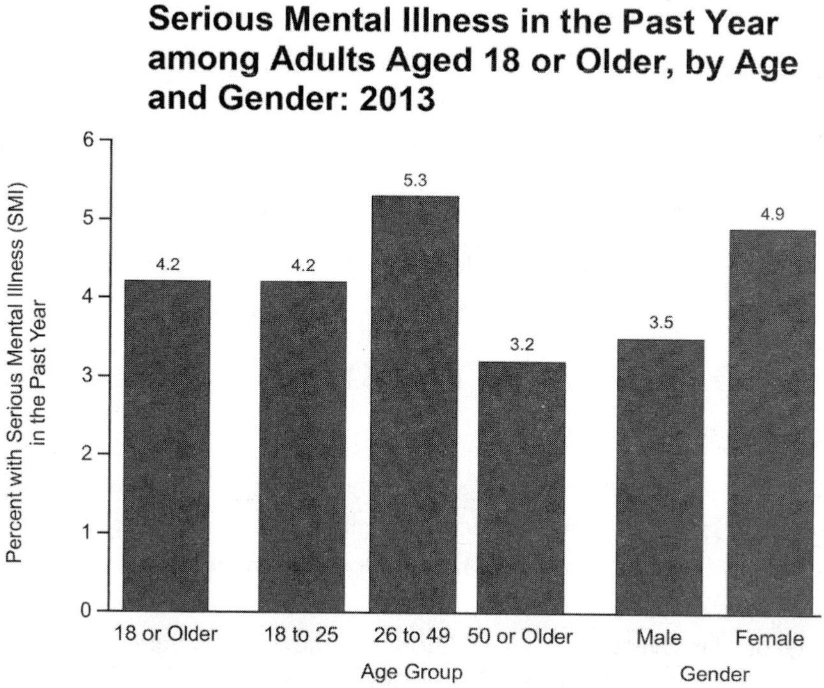

2. CH03-02: *Serious Mental Illness Among Adults.* It is estimated that less than 5 percent of adults, or 10 million people, experienced serious mental illness disorders in 2013. Pictured here is a breakdown by age and gender. Source: Substance Abuse and Mental Health Services Administration (2014).

The term **MENTAL ILLNESS** refers collectively to all diagnosable mental disorders. While mental disorders are common in the United States, their burden of illness is particularly concentrated among those who experience disability due to serious mental illness. The NSDUH (2014) defines a **SERIOUS MENTAL ILLNESS** (SMI) as a diagnosable mental, behavioral, or emotional disorder which results in serious functional impairment. The NSDUH estimated that 10 million adults aged 18 or older, roughly 4 percent of the population of adults in the United States, experienced SMI in 2013. SMI is believed to be more prevalent in women versus men and it is most common among adults aged 26 to 49 (refer to figure CH03-02 for illustration). NSDUH also provides estimates of having a past year major depressive episode (MDE) among adults.

Adults are defined as having a **MAJOR DEPRESSIVE EPISODE** (MDE) if they had a period of two weeks or longer in the previous twelve months when they experienced a depressed mood or loss of interest or pleasure in daily activities, and they had at least some additional symptoms, such as problems with sleep, eating, energy, concentration, and self-worth. In 2014, NSDUH estimated that 15.7 million adults, approximately 6.6 percent of the population aged 18 or older, had at least one MDE in the past year (Center for Behavioral Health Statistics and Quality, 2015). Examples of these serious mental health disorders that criminal justice professionals may encounter include *psychosis* and *major depression* (Frank and McGuire, 2011).

The Role of the Media

The public is bombarded with simplistic and often inaccurate information through the media portrayals of violent criminals which depict horrific acts as normal behavior of those with SMI (Slopen, Watson, Gracia, and Corrigan, 2007). It is believed that sensationalized violent crimes involving people with mental disorders tend to cause negative attitudes about mental illness and increase stigma (Corrigan, Powell, and Michaels, 2013). The relationship between mental illness and criminal conduct is far more complex than the handful of violent crimes suggest. Although mass shootings are extremely rare events, dramatized media coverage has increased the perception of individuals with SMI as dangerous (McGinty, Webster, Jarlenski, and Barry, 2014).

The Role of Research

Its dominance notwithstanding, the DSM diagnostic scheme is far from perfect in meeting the needs of our population of individuals with mental disorders. The outdated methods of relying on self-reported patient symptoms results in a hit-or-miss response in diagnosing patients. Experts tell us that, on average, a marketed psychiatric drug works for approximately half of the patients who take it (Cuthbert and Insel, 2013). Therapies are adjusted only after frustrating delays in reaching effective relief. Unresolved problems with the treatment of schizophrenia include unpleasant side effects that lead many patients to discontinue therapy with only modest effectiveness for less than half of the patients (Frank and McGuire, 2011). The problem, in part, is due to a failure of the American Psychological Association to assimilate recent breakthroughs in genetics and neuroscience (NSDUH, 2014).

We don't have all the answers. Research on the effectiveness of interventions, including medical treatment and mental health services, remains a priority. The relationship between mental disorder and violence indicates that the likelihood of committing violence is greater for people with a mental disorder than for those without, even though most individuals with mental disorders do not commit violent acts (Hiday, 2006). Recent and emerging research supports the idea that violent offending and violent victimization are related outcomes among individuals with mental disorders (Silver, Piquero, Jennings, Piquero, and Leiber, 2011). Co-occurring mental and substance use disorders are highly represented in the criminal justice system and present a higher risk of recidivism for both juvenile and adult offenders, compared with persons who only have one type of disorder (Peters, Lurigio, and Wexler, 2015).

Having mental disorders may contribute to violence, yet they may not be the direct cause of criminal behavior. After all, crime and violence occur among individuals who are not known to have mental disorders. There is a significant amount of research which suggests that severe mental illness alone does not predict violent behavior (Elbogen and Johnson, 2009) or that programs designed to increase mental health services are only minimally helpful in reducing recidivism (Peterson, Skeem, Kennealy, Bray, and Zvonkovic, 2014). These findings bring a renewed interest in shifting intervention strategies away from mental disorders and towards a focus on that are directly linked to criminal behavior which can come and go. Therapeutic interventions in these major areas may be effective in reducing crime.

3. CH03-03: *Recovery.* When a person is diagnosed with mental illness the services to optimize recovery typically include some combination of psychosocial supports such as family involvement, work or school support, psychotherapy, and self-management strategies and medications. Photo courtesy of the National Institutes of Health, Department of Health and Human Services.

The Role of Cooperation

Forensic science specializations suggest the recent trend of new interdisciplinary fields which bring together psychology, psychiatry, and the law. Generally, however, behavioral scientists, legal scholars, and practitioners don't even speak the same language (Schug and Fradella, 2015). Schug and Fradella provide evidence that these disciplines rarely interact. They state, for example, that the study of mental illness is the province of social and behavioral scientists who often lack education or training about the law, crime, and criminal justice. On the other hand, crime is defined by law and applied by practitioners who have little training in the behavioral sciences. Cooperation is sometimes strained and each uses vocabularies that are native to their respective disciplines.

The disciplines have developed independently and continue to work without significant influence from the other. A movement that is often overlooked in contemporary literature is referred to as the "medicalization of behavior," which is the process of defining deviant behavior as an illness and mandating physicians to treat it (Melick, Steadman, and Cocozza, 1979). Put another way, what used to be "bad behavior" under the province of criminal law, has shifted to "mad behavior" with mandated psychiatric intervention. Throughout the text, students may notice that conflict and controversies do exist between the psychiatric and mental health community with the legal and criminal justice perspectives (MHA, 2015).

CRIME, DISABILITY, AND MENTAL DISORDERS

As noted earlier, the relationship between mental illness and criminal behavior is unclear. To deny that some relationship exists is unrealistic, we just don't know the extent of the relationship at this time. It appears that there may be a modest but significant link between mental disorders and violence in the community (Swanson, McGinty, Fazel, and Mays, 2015). Impulsivity and impaired response inhibition can be said to incite criminal behavior among all individuals who are mentally disordered or not. Some argue that criminal characteristics are similar between individuals that commit crime with or without a history of mental disorders. Experts consistently confirm that most crimes committed by individuals having mental illness are minor nuisance behaviors.

There is overlap between the classifications of mental disability and mental disorders that bear explanation. One example concerns the difference between cognitive disabilities and mental disorders. A **COGNITIVE DISABILITY** is a comprehensive term used to describe a variety of medical conditions affecting different types of mental tasks (Bronson, Maruschak, and Berzofsky, 2015). Examples of cognitive disabilities which are prevalent in the criminal justice system include Down syndrome, autism, dementia, attention deficit disorder, learning disorders, intellectual disabilities, or traumatic brain injury. Examples of mental disorders include depression, anxiety disorders, and schizophrenia. A cognitive disability is not the same as a mental disorder, although they often co-occur and a mental disorder can be considered a disability as well.

ANXIETY DISORDERS

Anxiety is a normal reaction to stress and can be beneficial in some situations. For some people, however, anxiety can become excessive. The person suffering from anxiety may realize it is excessive and still have difficulty controlling it, sometimes negatively affecting their day-to-day living. There are a wide variety of anxiety disorders which make up the most common mental disorders experienced by Americans (NSDUH, 2014). The three categories of anxiety are *Generalized Anxiety Disorder (GAD), Panic Disorder, and Social Anxiety Disorder (SAD).* Some evidence exists that there is a relationship between anxiety disorders and some forms of violence. From an analysis of the National Comorbidity Survey (NCS) it was revealed that people having a diagnoses of anxiety disorders were almost four times more likely to engage in violent behavior compared to people who did not have a psychiatric diagnosis (Corrigan and Watson, 2005).

DEPRESSIVE DISORDERS

Depression has been associated with an increased risk of suicide and self-harm and, to a lesser degree, with an increased risk of violent crime (Fazel et al., 2015). Depressive disorders in the DSM-5 (APA, 2015) include *major depressive disorder*, *persistent depressive disorder*, *premenstrual dysphoric disorder*, and *disruptive mood dysregulation disorder*. Adults are defined as having a *major depressive episode* (MDE) with severe impairment if their depression caused severe problems with their ability to manage at home, manage well at work, have relationships with others, or have a social life. The Center for Behavioral Health Statistics and Quality (2015) reports that over 10 million adults experienced a MDE with severe impairment in 2014. The number of individuals with severe impairment was almost two thirds of the total number of adults who had a past year MDE. Refer to figure CH03-04 for an illustration.

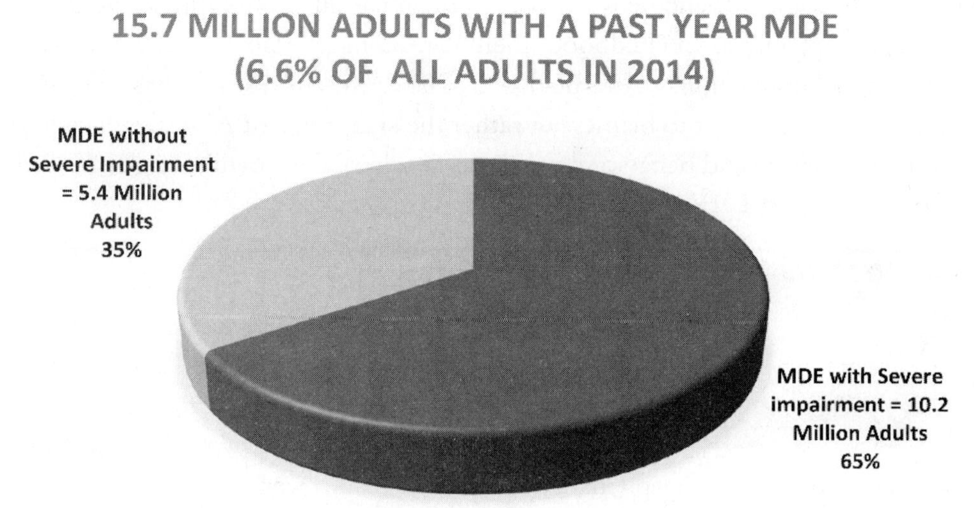

4. CH03-04: *Major Depressive Episode.* The vast majority of individuals experiencing a MDE experience severe impairment. Source: Center for Behavioral Health Statistics and Quality (2015).

DISORDERS OF INFANCY, CHILDHOOD, OR ADOLESCENCE

Neurodevelopmental disorders and disorders identified in childhood are not included in the National Survey on Drug Use and Health (NSDUH, 2014). These include *autism spectrum disorder, attention-deficit/hyperactivity disorder, intellectual disability, communication disorders, specific learning disorder, and motor disorders* (APA, 2015). Individuals with neurodevelopmental disabilities are four to ten times more likely to be represented in the criminal justice system, as both victims and criminals, than those without disability (Davis, 2009). Individuals with cognitive or developmental disabilities are represented as much as three times more in jail than in the general population (Davis, 2009).

Attention-Deficit/Hyperactivity Disorder (ADHD)

Although it can also affect adults, *ADHD* is among the most common mental disorders in children. *ADHD* is a multifaceted disorder that varies widely in terms of the type and severity of its impact. It may be expressed through inattention, excessive movement that is not appropriate to the setting, and impulsivity. These symptoms can cause difficulty in learning, completing tasks, staying focused, and losing possessions. ADHD has been linked to numerous different forms of misconduct in children and as risk factors for adult criminal conduct (Savolainen et al., 2010). Some evidence exists that for individuals diagnosed with ADHD who do not have problems in childhood, there is no longer an increased risk of later adult criminal convictions (Satterfield et al., 2007). Resent research has suggested that ADHD itself is not to blame, but rather the symptoms of ADHD which lead to academic failure and behavioral problems at school that predict a risk of future criminality (Watts, 2016).

IN MY EXPERIENCE . . .

I was close to a family with a ten-year-old boy who doctors had determined was "retarded" and in need of being institutionalized. We know that condition today as having a *learning disability*. The parents declined and chose to keep Charles at home instead. Over the years it became apparent that Charles had difficulty in reading and comprehension. He attended a special school to help him maximize his potential. He found it impossible to understand the test for getting a driver's license, but wanted to drive a car. His grandmother decided to teach him the test . . . I was told that he actually memorized it and was able to get his license!

He went into the Navy—it took him two times to get through basic training. . . . But he made it. A few years of peeling potatoes on a ship was exactly what he needed to boost his confidence. Coming back from his tour of duty he got a tutor and earned his GED. As a veteran, he was eligible for a federal job. He became a "stitcher" and sewed canvas tents for the military. I am told Charles is now retired on a federal pension. He owns two homes—one is a trailer in Florida where he spends his winters. Like most people, he has had two divorces and now is with a live-in girlfriend. Charles is a veteran, he worked his entire life without receiving disability payments or food stamps. He was never arrested. Everyone has challenges in life; it seems he handled his just fine.

Question for discussion: Do you know someone who has a mental disorder?

Disproportionately higher rates of ADHD have been noted among offenders than within the general population (Young, Goodwin, Sedgwick, and Gudjonsson, 2013). Young et al. (2013) have found that individuals with ADHD tend to give a disproportionate number of 'don't know' responses when questioned by the police, which may be misconstrued as being uncooperative. Individuals with ADHD may also be prone to make false confessions during police questioning. Once in a custodial environment, offenders with ADHD may become a management problem as their symptoms are reportedly associated with aggressive behaviors, which may be due to excessive emotional reactions and mood swings.

Asperger's Disorder

Asperger's disorder has been described as involving communication deficits which impair social interactions that might involve inappropriate gestures, personal space, difficulty recognizing humor, irony, or sarcasm (Haskins and Silva, 2006). Quick to become aggressive and violent, individuals with *Asperger's disorder* are also described in the literature as socially and sexually deviant, arsonists, and antisocial without regard for the consequences of others (Barry-Walsh and Mullen, 2004; Haskins and Silva, 2006; Schwartz-Watts, 2005).

Intellectual Disability

A child having difficulty in problem solving and academic learning at an early age is now referred to as has having an *intellectual disability*, a term that replaces mental retardation. Unless the condition is severe, individuals with *intellectual disability* are not often perceived as having a disorder. Approximately 2 percent to 3 percent of the population has an intellectual disability, yet rates as high as 30 percent have been documented among prisoners (Griffith and Fedoroff, 2014). The disability is characterized by a decreased ability to learn and is often accompanied by a lower IQ than those in the general population. It is thought that individuals with *intellectual disability* are more vulnerable to being misled due to a strong need to be accepted and an inability to read social cues. It is possible that cognitive distortions associated with mental illness may erode interpersonal relationships and lead individuals to approach situations in a maladaptive fashion, leading to crime (Frank and McGuire, 2011). The primary offenses committed by persons with intellectual disabilities leading to criminal charges are sexual offenses, arson, and violent conduct (Lindsay, Steele, Smith, Quinn, and Allan, 2006).

BIPOLAR DISORDERS

Bipolar disorder, previously known as manic-depressive illness, is a brain disorder that causes unusual shifts in mood, energy, activity levels, and the ability to carry out day-to-day tasks. Rates of violent behavior since age 15 has been found to be greater for *bipolar disorder* (27.58 percent) than for other mood disorders (Pulay et al., 2008). Symptoms of *bipolar disorder* are severe. They are different from the normal ups and downs that everyone goes through from time to time. *Bipolar disorder* symptoms can result in damaged relationships, poor job or school performance, and even suicide. But *bipolar disorder* can be treated, and people with this illness can lead full and productive lives.

Bipolar disorder is considered the most expensive behavioral health care diagnosis. Mainly due to indirect costs such as the result of lost productivity related to absenteeism, the disorder costs more than twice as much as depression per affected individual (Laxman, Lovibond, and Hassan, 2008). Experts suggest that early intervention with outpatient care could decrease the financial impact of this disorder. For every dollar allocated to outpatient care for persons with *bipolar disorder*, \$1.80 is spent on inpatient care (Peele, Xu, and Kupfer, 2003). The prevalence of *bipolar disorder* is likely higher than you would think. Approximately 2.4 percent of people around the world have had a diagnosis of *bipolar disorder* at some point in their lifetime (Merikangas et al., 2011). The United States has the highest lifetime rate of *bipolar disorder* at 4.4 percent, per the first comprehensive international figures on the topic (Merikangas et al., 2011).

DISRUPTIVE AND CONDUCT DISORDERS

Disorders that are defined as a disruptive or conduct disorder in the DSM-5 include *oppositional defiant disorder* and *conduct disorder* (APA, 2015). Among children with early externalizing behavior problems an increased risk for later antisocial behavior or mood dysfunction may be identifiable in early childhood based on levels of overt aggression and emotion dysregulation (Okado and Bierman, 2015).

5. CH03-05: *Conduct Disorder*. Children and adolescents diagnosed with CD are frequently involved in serious and harmful conduct. Behaviors include weapons use, bullying, and cruelty to people or animals. Photo copyright Ted Denson/Shutterstock

Conduct Disorder

Conduct disorder (CD) is a pattern of behavior in juveniles which involves frequent serious and harmful rule-breaking and unlawful conduct. According to the DSM-5, CD conduct can include using weapons, bullying, breaking into people's homes, and physical cruelty to people or animals (APA, 2015). *Antisocial personality disorder* is the adult equivalent, which may be diagnosed when a person is age eighteen or older. Childhood conduct disorder (CD) is one of the strongest childhood behavioral predictors of later criminality, frequently it is associated with a diagnosis of ADHD (Dalsgaard, Mortensen, Frydenberg, and Thomsen, 2013).

Oppositional Defiant Disorder

Oppositional defiant disorder (ODD) is defined as a persistent pattern of defiant, disobedient and antagonistic behavior toward adults (ICD-10, 2016). This disorder is distinguished from CD due to the absence of the more serious acts of aggression or antisocial behavior. ODD is a common childhood disorder which has consistently been found to predict later depression and anxiety (Burke, Boylan, Rowe, and Waldman, 2014; Copeland, Shanahan, Costello, and Angold, 2009).

FACTITIOUS DISORDER BY PROXY

Buried among the new classifications of mental disorders created in the DSM-5, *Munchausen* is now referred to as *factitious disorder*. It is defined as a person who seeks help for a physical complaint while aware that no physical problem exists, or hides the fact that he or she caused the physical problem on purpose (APA, 2015). *Munchausen Syndrome* (as it is often referred by medical and criminal justice professionals) is a serious form of *factitious disorder* in which the person often visits doctors and hospitals (Vaglio, Schoenhard, Saavedra, Williams, and Raj, 2011). The sufferer may produce his or her own symptoms by taking medication and other substances, contaminating urine tests or creating infections. The person may take injections to produce symptoms. An example is a woman who simulated arrhythmias by taking caffeine overdoses and using an ECG rhythm generator, demonstrating knowledge of medical equipment (Vaglio, Schoenhard, Saavedra, Williams, and Raj, 2011).

IMAGINE THAT . . .

Fictitious Disorder by Proxy is known as *Munchausen by Proxy* among medical and law enforcement professionals. It got its name from the literary Baron von Munchausen, known for his tall tales of travel and adventure. British physician Richard Asher coined the term *Munchausen* in 1951 to refer to individuals who sought the "sick role" by fabricating dramatic physical ailments in themselves. *Munchausen syndrome by proxy* was named in 1977 by pediatrician Roy Meadow when he saw that parents sometimes induced sickness in another person to meet their own needs for attention, nurturance, and perverse control. Considered to be an underestimation of the MBP prevalence, over 550 published case reports from almost thirty countries attest to the reality of MBP (Feldman, 2004).

Munchausen by Proxy is a dangerous kind of child abuse in which caretakers, typically parents, deliberately and repeatedly exaggerate, fabricate, and/or induce a problem or problems in someone who is under their care (Lasher and Sheridan, 2004). The disorder is under recognized and underreported, according to Lasher and Sheridan. One study found MBP in one in 100 children treated for allergies (Warner and Hathaway, 1984). Another surveyed 451 published cases to conclude that 6 percent of known MBP victims died and 7.3 percent suffered permanent injury (Sheridan, 2003). Additionally, 25 percent of victims' known siblings were also dead and over 61 percent of siblings had similar illnesses. The majority of known perpetrators of MBP are mothers to the victim.

Question for discussion: What would you do if you suspected a child might be sickened by MBP?

Munchausen by proxy is a form of the factitious disorder which occurs when a person produces medical symptoms in either a child or older adult. It is also a dangerous form of child abuse that mandated reporters of child abuse in every state must report, or themselves face criminal and civil consequences (Bursch, 2014). Examples of professionals who are identified by law as mandatory reporters include police officers and medical personnel (Gosselin, 2014). The severity of the disorder, like any other mental disorder, ranges from minor to very serious. Medical procedures inflicted on child victims causing death are rare, but have been documented in serious cases. *Munchausen by Proxy* has been estimated in occurring against 2.8 per 100,000 children (Criddle, 2010). Hospital personnel and child abuse investigators are the most likely to encounter this disorder.

NEUROCOGNITIVE DISORDERS

Neurocognitive disorders make up a new category in the DSM-5 (APA, 2015). These disorders used to be called dementia. The category includes nine disorders that are characterized by damage to the brain which can affect memory, thinking or reasoning. Symptoms of a major neurocognitive disorder include evidence of significant cognitive decline from a previous level of performance in one or more cognitive areas such as learning, memory, language, perceptual-motor or social cognition. Examples of these disorders that criminal justice professionals may recognize in persons they encounter are *Alzheimer's disease* and *Excited Delirium.*

Alzheimer's disease is a common neurocognitive disorder among older adults, however, it is not a normal part of the aging process. The disease kills nerve cells in the brain, which ultimately results in memory loss and personality changes. A diagnosis is typically initiated by the individual, a friend or family member, or a clinician who notices that the person has experienced a significant decline in their ability to perform familiar everyday tasks. An estimated 5 million Americans are affected by *Alzheimer's disease* (Hebert, Weuve, Scherr, and Evans, 2013). During the middle stages of *Alzheimer's disease* some individuals experience confusion which may result in frustration and irritability. Patients also experience restlessness, causing some to pace or wander and get lost. It is not uncommon for the police to be called when an older adult with *Alzheimer's disease* is discovered to be wandering.

Delirium is a condition characterized by an abrupt onset that impairs attention, memory and cognition. It may be caused by a drug, illness, intoxication, medication or a medical condition. People are at risk for delirium when normal brain signals are not working. Risk factors include immobility, a history of falls, and the use of drugs and medications which change mood and behavior. Delirium is a medical emergency associated with a risk of sudden death seen frequently in intensive care units at hospitals, per the DSM-5 (APA, 2015).

OBSESSIVE-COMPULSIVE DISORDERS

Obsessive-compulsive disorder (OCD) has been reclassified in the DSM-5 and now resides among a list of four other disorders (APA, 2015). Previously grouped among anxiety disorders, both *major depressive disorder* and *anxiety* are acknowledged as frequently co-occurring but distinct disorders (APA, 2015). According to the APA, the obsessions and compulsions are unique characterizations of OCD, which led to the new grouping. Obsessions are persistent ideas, thoughts, impulses, or images that are intrusive and inappropriate and that cause marked anxiety or distress. Compulsions are repetitive behaviors or mental acts that are used to prevent or diminish anxiety, tension or distress.

PARAPHILIC DISORDERS

Paraphilias are defined in the DSM-5 as well as the International Classification of Diseases (APA, 2015; ICD-10, 2016). Individuals with *paraphilic disorders* have sexual interests or preferences outside of the sexual norm lasting for at least six months with behaviors involving a nonconsenting person or which causes clinically significant distress or impairment in functioning (APA, 2015). The paraphilic spectrum of behavior ranges from almost normal behavior to being hurtful or destructive to oneself or others. While the prevalence of paraphilias is unknown, estimates suggest that 1 percent to 3 percent of men in community settings are affected (Seto, 2014). Individuals with paraphilic disorders are commonly seen in forensic and correctional settings since behaviors are often illegal if acted on, such as accessing child pornography or having sexual contact with a child (Seto, 2014).

A small but significant portions of mentally disordered sexual offenders require special treatment and resources. Booth and Gulati (2014) state that mentally disordered sexual offenders (MDSOs) are those who have committed sexual offenses and have co-occurring major mental disorders. The exact rate of severe mental illness among sexual offenders is unknown since only a handful of studies have shown interest in studying this population. From these efforts experts report that co-occurring disorders among sexual offenders is common for most major areas of mental disorder: as high as 85 percent with substance use disorder; 74 percent had a paraphilia; 58 percent had a mood disorder; 38 percent had an impulse control disorder; 23 percent had an anxiety disorder; 9 percent had an eating disorder; 45 percent had antisocial personality disorder, 4.3 percent to 16 percent had a psychotic disorder, PTSD, dementia, and adult ADHD are also represented in case studies (Booth and Gulati, 2014). When screening for psychiatric disorders, studies of male sexual delinquents found high rates of ADHD (Dalsgaard et al., 2013).

According to a large population study of all individuals born in Denmark from January 1944 through December 1947, researchers found that having psychotic disorders with co-occurring personality disorders (PD), or substance use disorder (SD), was associated with a six-fold increased risk of physically aggressive sex offending and a three- to five-fold increased risk of non-physically aggressive sex offending (Alden, Brennan, Hodgins, and Mednick, 2007). Unlike the U.S., the police in Denmark have no discretionary powers regarding arrest or plea bargaining, according to Alden and colleagues. If offenders are suspected to have a psychotic disorder, they are arrested then transferred to treatment only after a charge has been filed. The decision on whether to prosecute will be made later. The Denmark study has implications for understanding and treating psychotic disorders, for the prevention of sex offending, and for the rehabilitation of sex offenders. The Denmark study also concluded that men with psychotic disorders or organic brain disorders alone were more likely than the never-hospitalized male cohort members to have been arrested for a sexual offense. Men with affective psychoses, bipolar, or manic conditions were related to an increased risk of sex offending only when combined with a PD or an SUD.

PERSONALITY DISORDERS

Personality disorders are a group of illnesses that involve long-term patterns of thoughts and behaviors that are unhealthy and inflexible. Disorders can affect how someone thinks and lives, often leading people to ignore their own safety and the safety of others and to be distrustful of others. People with personality disorders have trouble dealing with everyday stresses and problems. The most common personality disorders among jail and prison inmates are antisocial personality and borderline personality disorder (Fellner, 2003).

Antisocial Personality Disorder

Antisocial personality disorder is a type of chronic mental condition in which a person's ways of thinking and relating to others are destructive (APA, 2015). People with antisocial personality disorder typically have no regard for right and wrong and often disregard the rights, wishes and feelings of others. Those with antisocial personality disorder tend to antagonize, manipulate or treat others either harshly or with callous indifference. They are highly represented in the criminal justice system and do not exhibit guilt or remorse. They may lie, behave violently or impulsively, and have problems with drug and alcohol use. Fire-setting, cruelty to animals, and bullying behaviors during childhood may be signs of early development of antisocial personality. Follow-up studies of children and adolescents diagnosed with ADHD have provided evidence of high rates of antisocial behavior and substance use disorder (Dalsgaard et al., 2013).

Borderline Personality Disorder

Borderline personality disorder (BPD) is a serious mental illness evidenced by unstable moods, behavior, and relationships (APA, 2015). More than 1.5 percent of the adult population in the United States is diagnosed with BPD each year

(Lenzenweger, Lane, Loranger, and Kessler, 2007). People with this disorder also have high rates of co-occurring disorders, such as depression, anxiety disorders, substance abuse, and eating disorders, along with self-harm, suicidal behaviors, and completed suicides, which may bring them to the attention of the criminal justice system. While rates of BPD in the community are 1 percent to 2 percent, rates among inmates have been estimated as high as 45 percent (Conn et al., 2010). Self-harming behaviors associated with borderline personality disorder include cutting, burning, hitting, head banging, hair pulling, and other harmful acts. People with borderline personality disorder may self-harm to help regulate their emotions, to punish themselves, or to express their pain. About 40–80 percent of people with borderline personality disorder have suicidal behaviors and approximately 10 percent commit suicide (Oumaya et al., 2008).

POSTTRAUMATIC STRESS DISORDER

Posttraumatic Stress Disorder (PTSD) is included in a new chapter in the DSM-5 on Trauma- and Stressor-Related Disorders (APA, 2015). This represents a change from the DSM-IV, which addressed *PTSD* as an anxiety disorder. The diagnostic criteria for the DSM-5 identify the trigger to *PTSD* as exposure to threatened death, serious injury or sexual violation. The disturbance, regardless of its trigger, causes clinically significant distress or impairment in the individual's social interactions, capacity to work or other important areas of functioning. It is not the physiological result of another medical condition, medication, drugs or alcohol.

Four distinct diagnostic clusters are associated with post-traumatic stress disorder. They are described as re-experiencing, avoidance, negative cognitions, and arousal. Re-experiencing includes spontaneous memories of the traumatic event, flashbacks, recurrent dreams of it, or some other intense or prolonged psychological distress. Avoidance is a common reaction to trauma, but in PTSD it becomes an extreme way to avoid thinking about or feeling emotions about a stressful event, distinguished by aggressive, reckless or self-destructive behaviors including hypervigilance and sleep disturbances.

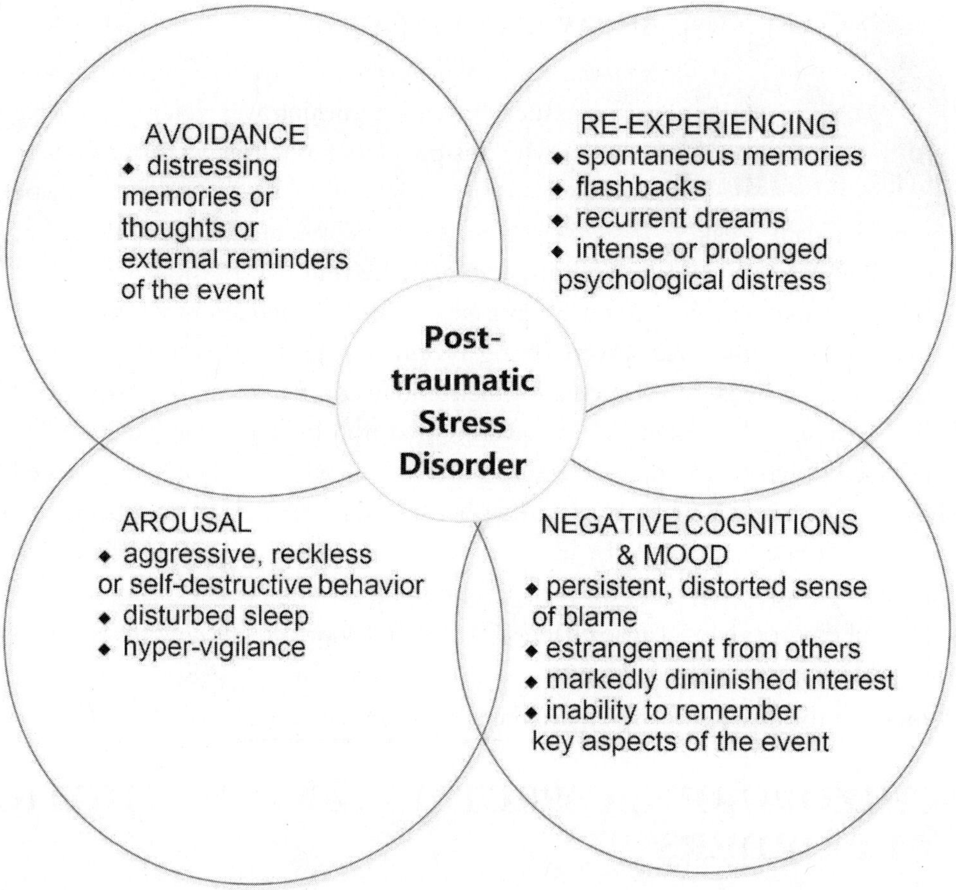

6. CH03-06: *Post-traumatic Stress Disorder:* Pictured are some of the ways individuals with post-traumatic Stress Disorder will react to stress, arranged in four distinct diagnostic clusters.

Negative cognitions may involve a persistent and distorted sense of blame, a diminished interest in activities, or an inability to remember aspects of the stressful event. Arousal is distinguished by aggressive, reckless, or self-destructive behaviors including hypervigilance and sleep disturbances. Historic terms for PTSD in the military include "war neurosis," "combat fatigue," and "shell shock." Commonly associated with combat exposure, *PTSD* is also highly represented in specific occupations, including law enforcement and corrections. Among other stressors, *PTSD* may also be experienced by individuals who have lived through natural disasters and children who have been severely abused. Common mental health symptoms associated with traumatic exposure are *PTSD*, anxiety, sleep problems, depression, withdrawal, and isolation. *PTSD* symptoms may not develop for six to twelve months after a traumatic event.

IN MY EXPERIENCE . . .

Post-traumatic stress disorder is a well-known syndrome often associated with returning war veterans. People wonder why this problem has surfaced in our society. Are we different than in the past, maybe psychologically weaker? It seems that so many people are affected. What has changed? A friend of mine told me that after he returned home from service during the Vietnam War he was surprised to hear so much about the problems of *PTSD*. His father had served during World War II, so an obvious question was asked, "Why is *PTSD* such a problem today compared to previous wars?" His father sighed deeply before answering that nothing had changed at all. He had lived down by the railroad tracks in Chicopee when the soldiers returned home after World War II. He said that hardly a day went by when at least one man didn't commit suicide by jumping onto the railroad tracks in front of an oncoming train. That went on for a long time. For some, reactions to ongoing stressful environments cause change. There are no records linking the suicides to PTSD, only anecdotal evidence.

Question for discussion: What are the symptoms associated with *PTSD*?

SCHIZOPHRENIA SPECTRUM AND PSYCHOTIC DISORDERS

There is some evidence that symptoms of specific forms of mental illness, such as bipolar disorder, schizophrenia, and depression directly account for a small percentage of criminal activity (Peterson, Skeem, Kennealy, Bray, and Zvonkovic, 2014). Of controversy is whether specific types or severity of mental illness have a direct causal link to criminal behavior. The exact causes of psychotic disorders are unknown, but several genetic, medical, psychological, and social risk factors have been identified. *Schizophrenia Spectrum and Psychotic Disorders* are characterized by disordered thought processes. The most well-known disorder is *schizophrenia*. Other examples include *brief psychotic disorder* and *schizoaffective disorder*.

Schizophrenia

SCHIZOPHRENIA is a chronic, severe, and disabling mental disorder characterized by deficits in thought processes, perceptions, and emotional responsiveness. Its symptoms are typically described as "positive" or "negative." Positive symptoms may include delusions, thought disorders, and hallucinations. Affected individuals may hear voices other people don't hear or believe other people are reading their minds, controlling their thoughts, or plotting to harm them. The negative symptoms may resemble depression such as a lack of desire or motivation to accomplish goals, form social relationships, and blunted affect and emotion. These symptoms make holding a job, forming relationships, and other day-to-day functions especially difficult. Organizing thoughts, prioritizing tasks and some memory functions may be a challenge for the sufferers. While there is no cure, the disorder is highly treatable.

Schizophrenia affects men and women equally and at similar rates across all ethnic groups around the world, according to NAMI (2008). Symptoms usually start between ages sixteen and thirty. More than 2.2 million Americans over the age of eighteen are affected, twice as many people live with *schizophrenia* than with HIV/AIDS (NAMI, 2008). While people with the disorder are not usually violent, some symptoms are associated with violence, such as delusions of persecution. Substance abuse may also increase the chance a person will become violent. If a person becomes violent, the violence is usually directed at themselves or family members and tends to take place at home.

Some psychotic symptoms, such as feeling threatened, may lead directly to criminal conduct (Frank and McGuire, 2011). The risk of violence among people with *schizophrenia* is small, but individuals with this condition are fifty times more likely to attempt suicide than individuals without the disorder, per the Treatment Advocacy Center. About 10 percent of those diagnosed with the disease (especially young adult males) die by suicide (Torrey, 2013). It is hard to predict which people will be prone to suicide. Extreme depression or psychoses that can result due to lack of treatment are the usual causes of suicide attempts.

Some people who abuse drugs show symptoms similar to those of *schizophrenia*. Therefore, people with *schizophrenia* may be mistaken for people who are affected by drugs. Most researchers do not believe that substance abuse causes the disease. However, people who have *schizophrenia* are much more likely to have a substance or alcohol abuse problem than the general population (Blanchard, Brown, Horan, and Sherwood, 2000).

Brief Psychotic Disorder

Individuals with *brief psychotic disorder* lose contact with reality and experience a range of extreme symptoms which have sudden, short periods of psychotic behavior. Symptoms are similar to schizophrenia, but fully go away in a short time. These same symptoms can also occur in people with other health problems, including *bipolar disorder*, *dementia*, *substance use disorders*, or *brain tumors*. According to the DSM-5 *brief psychotic disorder* may include at least one of the symptoms below for at least one day but less than one month (APA, 2015):

- Hallucinations—hearing or seeing things that are not real, such as voices
- Delusions—believing things to be true that are not true
- Disorganized speech

The current DSM-5 does not recognize post-partum psychosis as a distinct disorder, however, patients who meet the criteria for a *brief psychotic disorder* may be diagnosed by adding the specifier "with postpartum onset" if symptoms occurred during pregnancy or within four weeks following delivery. Postpartum psychosis is a rare disorder, occurring in less than 3.4 percent of women overall, but can occur in 20 percent to 30 percent of women with known bipolar disorder (Monzon, Scalea, and Pearlstein, 2014). Women with bipolar disorder and a family history of postpartum psychosis may experience postpartum psychosis at rates as high as 74 percent (Monzon et al., 2014). Postpartum psychosis has been the basis of acquittal and reversal of convictions in criminal cases involving women who have killed one or more of her children in the period within four weeks of giving birth.

SUBSTANCE-RELATED DISORDERS

Alcohol and drug use disorders contribute more to the public health burden of violent behavior than all other psychiatric disorders combined (Pulay et al., 2008). Experts exploring patterns of justice involvement substantiate that co-occurring substance use disorders and severe mental illness increases the risk of offending for both men and women (Elbogen and Johnson, 2009). The odds of any justice involvement, any criminal convictions, or any jail days are each significantly higher for men with bipolar disorder and a substance use disorder than for men with schizophrenia or bipolar alone (Robertson, Swanson, Frisman, Lin, and Swartz, 2014). Among women, the combined effect of bipolar disorder and substance use disorder is even stronger (Robertson et al., 2014).

Alcoholism and drug dependence are well-established risk factors for violent offending (Boden, Fergusson, and Horwood, 2012). It is also thought that mental illness can make it more likely that individuals abuse drugs and alcohol, both of which also contribute to crime (Frank and McGuire, 2011). Increased risks of violence, however, are not equal among those with psychiatric disorders, state Pulay and colleagues (2008). Factors associated with increasing the risk of violence in connection with substance use disorders are antisocial traits and behavior.

DISPELLING MYTHS

Myth: *Schizophrenia* is a mental disease characterized by split or multiple personalities that incapacitates an individual for the remainder of his or her life.

Fact: According to the National Alliance on Mental Illness, more than 60 percent of people falsely believe that split or multiple personalities are symptoms of *schizophrenia* (NAMI, 2008). This common misconception about *schizophrenia* stems from the fact that its Greek word origin means "to split" and "mind". Additionally, with ongoing medical treatment, these individuals can live independent and productive lives.

Myth: Personality weakness or character flaws cause mental health problems. People with mental health problems can "snap out of it" if they try hard enough.

Fact: Mental health problems have nothing to do with being lazy or weak and many people need help to get better. Many factors contribute to mental health problems, including biological factors such as genes, injury, or brain chemistry. Life experiences such as trauma due to child abuse, domestic violence, combat exposure, and police service can contribute to disorders.

Myth: People with mental health needs, even those who are managing their mental illness, cannot tolerate the stress of holding down a job.

Fact: Under the right circumstances, individuals with mental health problems can be just as productive as other employees. Employers who hire people with mental health problems report good attendance and punctuality as well as motivation, good work, and job tenure on par with or greater than other employees. Research shows that when people with schizophrenia or other severe mental illness engage in structured and meaningful work, the severity of their symptoms decrease (McGurk and Mueser, 2014).

Myth: High rates of mental disorders and decreasing institutional care options are problems unique to the United States.

Fact: According to the World Health Organization, mental disorders occur at high rates in all countries around the world and there is evidence of a decrease in mental hospital beds. Globally, an estimated 676 million people experience mental disorders (WHO, 2015b).

SUMMARY

Historically, the field of psychology has been recognized as the authority on defining mental disorders and prescribing therapeutic responses. The Diagnostic and Statistical Manual (DSM) is the standard tool for these purposes. Advances in genetics and neuroscience has expanded our knowledge of mental illness, making it possible to diagnose some disorders through scientific analysis. The United States contributes to the advances within the global community to address the needs of individuals with mental disorders through the International Classification of Diseases (ICD). This is a very exciting time in the history of medicine that promises to treat mental disorders based on scientific developments. With an increase in research and a fuller use of technological advances, the Research Domain Criteria (RDoc) contributions are a promising direction for the future.

The current challenges must be met in ways that recognize the fact that individuals are not all the same, with or without mental disorders. We know that most individuals can live full and productive lives with disorders that were thought to be debilitating in the past. We also know that mental disorders are more common than previously thought. Some individuals in desperate need of intervention are falling through the cracks of society. There is no one-size-fits-all solution for the complex mental health issues that we face.

CHAPTER QUESTIONS FOR REVIEW

1. What are the major differences between the Diagnostic and Statistical Manual (DSM) and the Research Domain Criteria (RDoC) classification and diagnostic systems?
2. Explain the role of the media in perpetuating myths regarding mental disorders
3. Define the disorders of infancy, childhood or adolescence
4. Explain the relationship between crime and personality disorders
5. What are the four distinct diagnostic clusters associated with post-traumatic stress disorder?

REFERENCES

AHRQ. (2009). Mental health research findings. Rockland, MD: AHRQ.

Alden, A., Brennan, P., Hodgins, S., and Mednick, S. (2007). Psychotic disorders and sex offending in a Danish birth cohort. *Arch Gen Psychiatry, 64*(11), 1251–1258.

Andrews, D., and Dowden, C. (2006). The recent past and near future of risk and/or need assessment. *Crime and Delinquency, 52*, 7–27.

APA. (2015). *Understanding mental disorders: Your guide to DSM-5*. Washington, D.C.: American Psychiatric Association.

Barry-Walsh, J., and Mullen, P. (2004). Forensic aspects of Asperger's Syndrome. *Journal of Forensic Psychiatry and Psychology, 15*, 96–107.

Blanchard, J., Brown, S., Horan, W., and Sherwood, A. (2000). Substance use disorders in schizophrenia: Reviews, integration and a proposed model. *Clinical Psychological Review, 20*, 207–234.

Boden, J. M., Fergusson, D. M., and Horwood, L. J. (2012). Alcohol misuse and violent behavior: Findings from a 30-year longitudinal study. *Drug and Alcohol Dependence, 122*(1), 135–141.

Booth, B., and Gulati, S. (2014). Mental illness and sexual offending. In J. Bradford and A. Ahmed (eds.), *Psychiatric Clinics of North America* (Vol. 37). Ontario, Canada: Institute of Mental Health Research.

Bronson, J., Maruschak, L., and Berzofsky, M. (2015). Disabilities among prison and jail inmates, 2011–12. Washington, D.C.: U.S. Department of Justice.

Burke, J., Boylan, K., Rowe, R., and Waldman, I. (2014). Identifying the irritability dimension of ODD: Application of a modified bifactor model across five large community samples of children. *Journal of Abnormal Psychology, 123*(4).

Bursch, B. (2014). Munchausen by proxy and factitious disorder imposed on another. *Special Reports*. Retrieved April 5, 2016, from http://www.psychiatrictimes.com/special-reports/munchausen-proxy-and-factitious-disorder-imposed-another

Center for Behavioral Health Statistics and Quality. (2015). Behavioral health trends in the United States: Results from the 2014 National Survey on Drug Use and Health: HHS Publication No. SMA 15-4927, NSDUH Series H-50.

Centers for Disease Control and Prevention. (2011). Mental Illness Surveillance Among Adults in the United States. *MMWR, 60*(Supplement), 1–20.

Conn, C., Warden, R., Stuewig, J., Kim, E. H., Harty, L., Hastings, M., and Tangney, J. P. (2010). Borderline personality disorder among jail inmates: How common and how distinct? *Corrections compendium, 35*(4), 6–13.

Copeland, W., Shanahan, L., Costello, J., and Angold, A. (2009). Childhood and adolescent psychiatric disorders as predictors of young adult disorders. *Arch Gen Psychiatry, 66*(7), 764–772.

Corrigan, P. W., Powell, K. J., and Michaels, P. J. (2013). The effects of news stories on the stigma of mental illness. *The Journal of Nervous and Mental Disease, 201*(3), 179–182.

Corrigan, P. W., and Watson, A. C. (2005). Findings from the National Comorbidity Survey on the frequency of violent behavior in individuals with psychiatric disorders. *Psychiatry Research, 136*(2), 153–162. 10.1016/j.psychres.2005.06.005 0165–1781.

Criddle, L. (2010). Monsters in the closet: Munchausen Syndrome by Proxy. *Critical Care Nurse, 30*(6), 46–55.

Cuthbert, B. N. (2015). Research Domain Criteria: toward future psychiatric nosologies. *Dialogues in Clinical Neuroscience, 17*(1), 89–97.

Cuthbert, B. N., and Insel, T. R. (2013). Toward the future of psychiatric diagnosis: the seven pillars of RDoC. *BMC Medicine, 11*, 126–126.

Dalsgaard, S., Mortensen, P. B., Frydenberg, M., and Thomsen, P. H. (2013). Long term criminal outcome of children with attention deficit hyperactivity disorder. *Criminal Behaviour and Mental Health, 23*(2), 86–98.

Davis, L. (2009). People with intellectual disabilities in the criminal justice system: Victims and suspects. Retrieved June, 2015, from http://www.thearc.org/document.doc?id=3664

Elbogen, E. B., and Johnson, S. C. (2009). The intricate link between violence and mental disorder: results from the National Epidemiologic Survey on Alcohol and Related Conditions. *Arch Gen Psychiatry, 66*(2), 152–161.

Feldman, M. (2004). Forward. In L. Lasher and M. Sheridan (eds.), *Munchausen by Proxy*. Binghamton, NY: The Haworth Press.

Fellner, J. (2003). Ill-equipped: U.S. prisons and offenders with mental illness. New York, NY: Human Rights Watch.

Frank, R., and McGuire, T. (2011). Mental health treatment and criminal justice outcomes. In P. Cook, J. Ludwig, and J. McCrary (eds.), *Controlling crime: Strategies and tradeoffs* (pp. 167–207). Chicago, IL: University of Chicago Press.

Gosselin, D. K. (2014). *Heavy hands: An introduction to the crimes of family violence* (5th ed.). Upper Saddle River, NJ: Prentice Hall.

Griffith, D., and Fedoroff, P. (2014). Persons with intellectual disabilities and problematic sexual behaviors. In J. Bradford (ed.), *A Ahmed* (Vol. 37). Ontario, Canada: Institute of Mental Health Research.

Haskins, B. G., and Silva, J. A. (2006). Asperger's disorder and criminal behavior: Forensic-psychiatric considerations. *Journal of the American Academy of Psychiatry and the Law Online, 34*(3), 374–384.

Hebert, L., Weuve, J., Scherr, P., and Evans, D. (2013). Alzheimer disease in the United States (2010–2050) estimated using the 2010 census. *Neurology, 80*, 1778–1783.

Hiday, V. (2006). Putting community risk in perspective: A look at correlations, cause and controls. *International Journal of Law and Psychiatry, 29*, 316–331.

ICD-10. (2016). International classification of diseases. Retrieved March 10, 2016, from http://www.who.int/classifications/icd/en/

Kessler, R., Heeringa, S., Lakoma, M., Petukhova, M., Rupp, A., Schoenbaum, M., Zaslavsky, A. (2008). The individual-level and societal-level effects of mental disorders on earnings in the United States: results from the National Comorbidity Survey Replication. *American Journal of Psychiatry, 165*, 703–711.

Lasher, L., and Sheridan, M. (2004). *Munchausen by Proxy*. Binghamton, NY: The Haworth Press, Inc.

Laxman, K. E., Lovibond, K. S., and Hassan, M. K. (2008). Impact of bipolar disorder in employed populations. *The American journal of managed care, 14*(11), 757–764.

Lenzenweger, M., Lane, M., Loranger, A., and Kessler, R. (2007). DSM-IV personality disorders in the National Comorbidity Survey Replication. *Biological Psychiatry, 62*(6), 553–564.

Lindsay, W. R., Steele, L., Smith, A. H., Quinn, K., and Allan, R. (2006). A community forensic intellectual disability service: Twelve year follow up of referrals, analysis of referral patterns and assessment of harm reduction. *Legal and Criminological Psychology, 11*(1), 113–130.

McCall-Hosenfeld, J. S., Mukherjee, S., and Lehman, E. B. (2014). The prevalence and correlates of lifetime psychiatric disorders and trauma exposures in urban and rural settings: Results from the National Comorbidity Survey Replication (NCS-R). *PLoS ONE, 9*(11).

McGinty, E. E., Webster, D. W., Jarlenski, M., and Barry, C. L. (2014). News media framing of serious mental illness and gun violence in the United States, 1997–2012. *The American Journal of Public Health*(3), 406.

McGurk, S., and Mueser, K. (2014). Vocational rehabilitation for severe mental illness. In P. F. Buckley and F. Gaughran (eds.), *Treatment-Refractory Schizophrenia* (pp. 165–177): Springer Berlin Heidelberg.

Melick, M. E., Steadman, H. J., and Cocozza, J. J. (1979). The medicalization of criminal behavior among mental patients. *Journal of Health and Social Behavior, 20*(3), 228–237.

Merikangas, K., Jin, R., He, J.P., Kessler, R., Lee, S., Sampson, N., Zarkov, Z. (2011). Prevalence and Correlates of Bipolar Spectrum Disorder in the World Mental Health Survey Initiative. *Arch Gen Psychiatry, 68*(3), 241–251.

MHA. (2015). Position statement 55: Confining sexual predators in the mental health system. Retrieved June 5, 2016, from http://www.mentalhealthamerica.net/positions/sexual-predators

Monzon, C., Scalea, T. L. d., and Pearlstein, T. (2014). Postpartum psychosis: Updates and clinical issues. Retrieved June 5, 2016, from Psychiatric Times http://www.psychiatrictimes.com/special-reports/postpartum-psychosis-updates-and-clinical-issues

NAMI. (2008). Schizophrenia: Public Attitudes, Personal Needs. Arlington, VA: National Alliance on Mental Illness.

NIMH. (n.d.). Research Domain Criteria (RDoC). Retrieved April 25, 2016, from https://www.nimh.nih.gov/research-priorities/rdoc/index.shtml

NSDUH. (2014). Results from the 2013 *National Survey on Drug Use and Health*: Mental health findings *NSDUH Series H-49* (Vol. HHS Publication No. (SMA) 14-4887). Rockville, MD: Substance Abuse and Mental Health Services Administration.

Okado, Y., and Bierman, K. L. (2015). Differential risk for late adolescent conduct problems and mood dysregulation among children with early externalizing behavior problems. *Journal of Abnormal Child Psychology, 43*(4), 735–747.

Oumaya, S., Friedman, A., Pham, T., Abdallah, J. A., Guelfi, D., and Rouillon, F. (2008). Borderline personality, self-harm and suicide: a review of literature. *Encephale, 34*(5), 452–458.

Peele, P., Xu, Y., and Kupfer, D. (2003). Insurance Expenditures on Bipolar Disorder: Clinical and Parity Concerns. *American Journal of Psychiatry, 160*, 1286–1290.

Peters, R., Lurigio, A., and Wexler, H. (2015). Co-occurring substance use and mental disorders in the criminal justice system: A new frontier of clinical practice and research. *Psychiatric Rehabilitation Journal, 38*(1), 1–6.

Peterson, J., Skeem, J., Kennealy, P., Bray, B., and Zvonkovic, A. (2014). How Often and How Consistently do Symptoms Directly Precede Criminal Behavior Among Offenders with Mental Illness? *Law and Human Behavior, 38*(5), 439–449.

Pulay, A. J., Dawson, D. A., Hasin, D. S., Goldstein, R. B., June Ruan, M. W., Pickering, R. P., . . . Grant, B. F. (2008). Violent behavior and DSM-IV Psychiatric Disorders: Results from the National Epidemiologic Survey on alcohol and related conditions. *The Journal of clinical psychiatry, 69*(1), 12–22.

Robertson, A. G., Swanson, J. W., Frisman, L. K., Lin, H., and Swartz, M. S. (2014). Patterns of justice involvement among adults with schizophrenia and bipolar disorder: key risk factors. *Psychiatric Services.*

Satterfield, J. H., Faller, K. J., Crinella, F. M., Schell, A. M., Swanson, J. M., and Homer, L. D. (2007). A 30-year prospective follow-up study of hyperactive boys with conduct problems. *Journal of the American Academy of Child and Adolescent Psychiatry, 46*(5), 601–610.

Savolainen, J., Hurtig, T. M., Ebeling, H. E., Moilanen, I. K., Hughes, L. A., and Taanila, A. M. (2010). Attention deficit hyperactivity disorder (ADHD) and criminal behaviour: the role of adolescent marginalization. *European Journal of Criminology, 7*(6), 442–459.

Schug, R., and Fradella, H. (2015). *Mental illness and crime.* Los Angeles, CA: Sage.

Schwartz-Watts, D. (2005). Asperger's disorder and murder. *Journal of the American Academy of Psychiatry and the Law, 33*(3), 390–393.

Seto, M. (2014). Assessment of the paraphilias. In J. Bradford and A. Ahmed (eds.), *Psychiatric Clinics of North America* (Vol. 37). Ontario, Canada: Elsevier Health Services.

Sheridan, M. S. (2003). The deceit continues: an updated literature review of Munchausen Syndrome by Proxy. *Child Abuse and Neglect, 27*(4), 431–451.

Silver, E., Piquero, A., Jennings, W., Piquero, N., and Leiber, M. (2011). Assessing the violent offending and violent victimization overlap among discharged psychiatric patients. *Law and Human Behavior, 35*(1), 49.

Slopen, N. B., Watson, A. C., Gracia, G., and Corrigan, P. W. (2007). Age analysis of newspaper coverage of mental illness. *Journal of Health Communication, 12*(1), 3.

Swanson, J. W., McGinty, E. E., Fazel, S., and Mays, V. M. (2015). Mental illness and reduction of gun violence and suicide: bringing epidemiologic research to policy. *Annals of epidemiology, 25*(5), 366–376.

Torrey, F. (2013). *Surviving Schizophrenia: A Manual for Families, Patients, and Providers* (6th ed.). New York, NY: Harper Collins.

Vaglio, J. C., Schoenhard, J. A., Saavedra, P. J., Williams, S. R., and Raj, S. R. (2011). Arrhythmogenic Munchausen syndrome culminating in caffeine-induced ventricular tachycardia. *J Electrocardiol, 44*(2), 229–231.

Warner, J. O., and Hathaway, M. J. (1984). Allergic form of Meadow's syndrome (Munchausen by proxy). *Archives of Disease in Childhood, 59*(2), 151–156.

Watts, S. J. (2016). ADHD symptomatology and criminal behavior during adolescence: Exploring the mediating role of school factors. *International Journal of Offender Therapy and Comparative Criminology.*

WHO. (2015a). Clinical Management of Mental, Neurological and Substance Use Conditions in Humanitarian Emergencies: Mental health Gap Action Programme Humanitarian Intervention Guide. Geneva, Switzerland: World Health Organization.

WHO. (2015b). Mental Health Atlas 2014. Geneva, Switzerland: World Health Organization.

Young, S., Goodwin, E. J., Sedgwick, O., and Gudjonsson, G. H. (2013). The effectiveness of police custody assessments in identifying suspects with intellectual disabilities and attention deficit hyperactivity disorder. *BMC Medicine, 11*(1), 1–11.

CHAPTER 4

Calls for Service

INTRODUCTION

Attempting to address the needs of persons with mental illness over the past several decades in the United States has resulted in their overrepresentation within the criminal justice system. According to the *International Association of Chiefs of Police* (IACP, 2010), we have replaced one dysfunctional system with another: from institutionalization in state hospitals to jails and state prisons. An overrepresentation of people with mental illness in the criminal justice system is well documented at every point, beginning with police encounters and ending with reentry from prison or jail (Babchuk and Lurigio, 2012). Understanding mental disorders from the first point of entry into the criminal justice system illustrates the appropriateness of diversion and highlights opportunities for treatment intervention.

Routine police work is anything but routine. Police officers are described as "first-line, around-the-clock, emergency responders, mediators, referral agents, counselors, youth mentors, crime prevention actors and much more" (Reuland, Schwarzfeld, and Draper, 2009). Law enforcement officers encounter all sorts of individuals, including some who exhibit bizarre behaviors, are suspected of committing crimes, and those who are witnesses or victims of crimes. A recent survey concluded that calls related to mental disorders outnumber calls for routine larceny, traffic accidents and domestic disputes combined (Biasotti, 2011). Responding to calls for service involving individuals with mental disorders is a relatively large part of the police officers' job since they are often disproportionately time-consuming and without long term benefit for individuals in need of treatment.

Key Terms

DELIBERATE INDIFFERENCE

EXIGENT CIRCUMSTANCES

MISDEMEANOR CRIMES

NUISANCE BEHAVIORS

SUICIDE-BY-COP

Chapter Objectives

After completing this chapter, you should be able to:

- Describe how persons needing psychiatric care affects police practice
- Discuss the ADA Title II claims applicable to police arrests
- Define misdemeanor crimes and nuisance behaviors
- Explain the debate on the prevalence of violence among individuals with mental disorders

CALLS FOR POLICE SERVICE

Dramatic increases in calls for service involving persons needing psychiatric care have been noted by police departments nationwide. Law enforcement officers find themselves in the position of having to balance issues of public safety with the needs of a vulnerable population. Benton County, Oregon is an example where alarming spikes in law enforcement contacts with individuals who have mental illnesses have recently been studied (Akins, Burkhardt, Lanfear, Stevens, and Amorim, 2014). In 2012, a 60 percent increase in the number of individuals taken into police custody and transported to the emergency room due to mental illness was noted. According to the analysis, some possible causes for the increase include the final closing of the Oregon State Hospital in November of 2011. While there is disagreement over the importance of this cause for such increases, there is little doubt that overrepresentation of this population exists at various levels within the criminal justice system which must be addressed (Akins, Burkhardt, and Lanfear, 2016). The majority of encounters between law enforcement officers and people with mental disorders involve individuals suspected of committing misdemeanor crimes or are exhibiting nuisance behavior (Green, 1997).

1. CH04-01: *Police Contacts.* Individuals with mental disorders come in contact with the police as criminal offenders, disorderly persons, missing persons, complainants, victims, and persons in need of services. Adapted from Cordner, 2006.

MISDEMEANOR CRIMES are relatively minor acts described by federal or state criminal code, and are punishable by incarceration or by fine. **NUISANCE BEHAVIORS** are acts that disturb the health and safety of a community, including things that annoy the public and prevent people from being comfortable in a community. Calls for misdemeanor crimes or minor nuisance behavior occupies an increasing amount of police attention that no other entity can resolve. While rare, these minor problems have the potential for dangerous situations to erupt. According to the FBI Uniform Crime Reporting statistics, during a ten-year period (1997 to 2006) 1,058 officers were assaulted and three officers feloniously killed in the line of duty when handling persons with mental illness.

Calls for service involving individuals with mental disorders might involve disturbing behaviors or when someone else notices that emergency help is needed. In most jurisdictions, the response options for law enforcement officers is limited (Akins, Burkhardt, Lanfear, Stevens, and Amorim, 2014). For minor or inappropriate behaviors, the officer may informally handle the incident, calm the person, or guide him or her to a different location. In cases where the individual is suicidal, homicidal, or unable to care for himself or herself, an officer can place the person in emergency protective custody (EPC) and transport him or her to a mental health facility (dependent on state law). Obtaining treatment services for this population is likely to be a more appropriate resolution than making an arrest.

DEMAND FOR POLICE SERVICES

Modern policing faces significant challenges due to the high demand for services, chronic consumers, and the time that it takes to resolve complex cases involving individuals with mental health issues. Researchers estimate that police encounter an individual with mental disorders on average four to six times per month, and may be as high as 110 times per month (Cordner, 2006; Kerr, Morabito, and Watson, 2010). Upwards of 7 percent of police contacts in jurisdictions with a population of 100,000 or more involve persons with mental disorders, impacting over 90 percent of patrol officers (Cordner, 2006). The evidence suggests that encounters between law enforcement and individuals with mental health issues may be frequent.

Chronic Consumers

The high incidence of repeat calls to a small group of individuals has left agencies wondering what might be done to provide more meaningful assistance to those in mental health crises. For example, the Los Angeles Police Department identified 67 people with mental disorders that resulted in a total of 536 calls for service during the first eight months of 2004 (Reuland, Schwarzfeld, and Draper, 2009). These calls typically involve people that become well-known to the police because of the frequent calls to the same place. Just 17 locations in Lexington, Kentucky were identified in 20 percent of its 507 calls for police service over the span of one year (Cordner, 2006). These calls often involved a person with mental illness. Since some individuals are in such frequent contact with the police, officers get to know them. In Honolulu, responding police officers knew the individual in 64 percent of the incidents involving individuals believed to have mental illness (Reuland et al., 2009).

There is a small but growing body of research which maintains that it is a subset of individuals experiencing psychotic symptoms who frequently and repeatedly come to the attention of the police (Green, 1997; Houston Police Department, 2011; White, Goldkamp, and Campbell, 2006). Commonly referred to as *frequent fliers*, repeat encounters between individuals having crisis due to mental illness and the police appear to be increasing (Santos and Goode, 2014). The term *frequent fliers* refer to a group of justice-involved individuals who often cycle between jail, halfway houses, hospital emergency rooms, to the streets and back again.

The suggestion that a small group of individuals may be responsible for a significant amount of police contact and service use is not new, suggests Akins and colleagues (2016). In their analysis of Benton County, Oregon, contacts between individuals with mental disorders and the police, the authors proposed a simple method to define and quantify *frequent fliers* in that jurisdiction (Akins et al., 2016). Benton County police officers have the right to take a person into custody, a *peace officer custody* or POC, someone that is believed to be a danger to self or others due to mental illness. These persons under POC are taken to the nearest mental health facility. Investigators discovered that nearly half of all repeat POC detentions occurred within 60 days of the initial POC custody, 25 percent had occurred within just fourteen days of the initial POC. The authors maintain that these individuals present frequently due to unmet mental health needs. Once identified, they suggest, law enforcement and mental health can collaboratively determine what approaches are most promising for these individuals.

Resolution Time

Due to the complex nature of police responses to individuals with mental disorders the situations may be difficult to resolve. The amount of time that law enforcement officers spend on a call for service varies, however, officers do spend a significant amount of time trying to resolve situations involving individuals with mental disorders. For example, a study of the Lincoln, Nebraska Police Department found that mental health investigation cases took more time than injury traffic accidents, burglaries, or felony assaults (Cordner, 2006). In a more recent study law enforcement officers were found to be spending twice the amount of time in order to resolve cases involving individuals with mental disorders than any other call for service (Akins et al., 2014). Strain on public safety resources occurs since officers are unavailable to respond to other calls during these cases.

In addition to the growing demands in calls for service, transportation and hospital security for people in acute psychiatric crisis is further straining public safety resources. The most time-consuming disposition is when law enforcement officers transport an individual to an emergency medical facility, frequently needing to wait for medical clearance or hospital admission of the individual. Providing transportation may require officers to leave their jurisdiction and travel long distances to hospitals or mental health units. During 2010, North Carolina sheriff's deputies reported transporting more than 30,000 psychiatric patients for involuntary commitments (Torrey, Fuller, Geller, Jacobs, and Ragosta, 2012). A study in Hawaii concluded that when officers respond to incidents involving individuals who have mental disorders, the time commitment was significantly more when emergency transportation was involved (Green, 1997). This study found that an informal disposition time was 23.3 minutes on average. If an arrest was made, the officer spent an average of sixty-four minutes on the incident. In cases where an individual was transported to a hospital for an emergency evaluation, the officer spent an average of 145 minutes on the incident. The manpower necessary to handle such situations can be substantial.

Most police officers report that the amount of time spent on calls for service has increased over the length of their career (Biasotti, 2011). Law enforcement officers in Virginia have found it very difficult to implement state mandates requiring that people who qualify for emergency assessment remain in the custody of law enforcement until an emergency service clinician can complete an assessment (Reuland, Draper, and Norton, 2010). Mandatory custody is up to six hours in order to provide sufficient time for medical clearance. During this time the individuals cannot be placed in a jail cell. Connecting people with mental illness to emergency services under similar mandates can involve greater police resources than more traditional responses of arresting the individual.

THREAT OF SUICIDE

Mental illness is strongly associated with an increased risk of suicide, which accounts for over half of U.S. firearm-related fatalities. Individuals receiving public health services for schizophrenia, bipolar disorder, or major depressive disorder are four times more likely to die by suicide than the general population a recent study in Florida concluded (Swanson et al., 2016). The violent crime rate for the Florida study group was also twice that of the general population. Swanson and his colleagues found that 62 percent of violent gun crime arrests and 28 percent of gun suicides were not legally permitted to have a gun at the time. They suggest policy reforms to include risk-based gun removal laws and prohibiting guns from people involuntarily detained in short-term psychiatric hospitalizations.

IN MY EXPERIENCE . . .

Police received a call from a passing motorist that there was a body by the side of the road. Responding officers found an unconscious victim who was bleeding but still alive. Evidence at the scene indicated that he had attempted to commit suicide by cutting off his head with a hacksaw. There was a broken blade nearby which he had replaced with a spare blade. The man had lost consciousness due to the loss of blood from the wound to his neck and the alcohol that he had consumed. He was transported to the hospital where he survived. One week later, this man was successful with another suicide attempt. He left a message to his wife saying that he had left enough gas in their car for her to go to his funeral, he was too depressed to go on living.

In some states there may be a law prohibiting an attempt of suicide. Common law which exists in Massachusetts is an example. An individual may be brought before the court by a police officer for an attempted suicide. I know that sounds strange, but it is not for the purpose of punishing the individual. It is within the power of the judge to order an individual into mental health treatment for evaluation, when they are a risk to themselves.

Question for discussion: What could have been done to intervene in this situation?

Threat of suicide or attempted suicide is thought to be one of the most common and most difficult situations for police officers to handle. San Diego police have seen a 54 percent increase in the number of mental health and suicide-related calls in recent years (Torrey, Entsminger, Geller, Stanley, and Jaffe, 2012). The suicidal continuum includes three levels: serious thoughts of suicide, making plans of suicide, and attempting suicide. The Substance Abuse and Mental Health Services Administration reports that over 9 million adults had serious thoughts of committing suicide in 2013, some of which may have been verbalized to someone they knew; approximately 2.5 million people made plans; and 1.5 million people attempted suicide (NSDUH, 2014). A small percentage had not made any prior plans before the attempt. Depending on the circumstances, police officers could be called at any time during the suicidal continuum. Thankfully, most of individuals who seriously think of suicide do not plan or attempt the act.

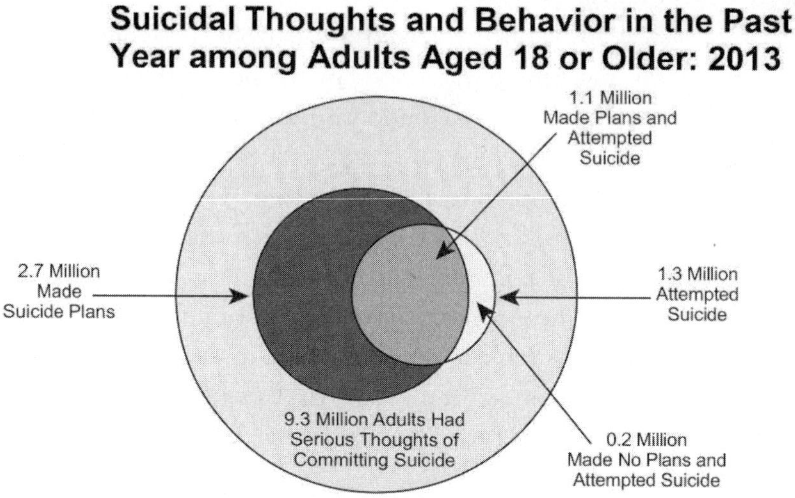

2. CH04-02: *Suicidal Behaviors Among Adults 2013.* The vast majority of adults who attempt suicide have seriously thought of committing suicide. Many others plan a suicide. If someone you know makes statements or takes actions towards suicide it is important to take this seriously. Talk to him or her, if you feel comfortable, and suggest that they seek professional help. If you do not feel comfortable, speak with someone who can intervene. We can all help to lower the rates of suicide at home, school, and in the workplace by taking this simple step of getting involved. Source: Substance Abuse and Mental Health Services Administration. (2014).

Approximately 34,000 Americans commit suicide each year (NSDUH, 2014). It is the tenth leading cause of death among adults and the third-leading cause of death among adolescents (CDC, 2015). Studies have found that about 90 percent of individuals who die by suicide experienced mental illness (NAMI, 2015). These startling figures emphasize why the police must be trained to respond to any situation. Calls involving individuals with mental illness cannot be ignored despite the patience and time required to resolve them. Properly monitoring and counseling an individual after a suicide attempt can be just as important as prevention. If a suicide attempt is unsuccessful, there may be the risk of multiple future attempts unless intervention is successful.

Referrals by the police officer to a mental health agency may help to prevent future attempts at suicide. Not all individuals who contemplate suicide will make plans to do so. However, there is a substantial number of individuals who do make plans to commit suicide and then attempt the act. This is significant since every person, in addition to police officers, has a moral duty to care for those who are in need.

Suicide-by-Cop

In 2001, Secret Service agents wounded Robert Pickett, the man holding a gun and firing shots at the White House. The *National Alliance of Mental Illness* promptly issued a statement that the agents had faced a situation which could occur anywhere in the country, police-assisted suicide. **SUICIDE-BY-COP** (SBC) occurs when an individual deliberately seeks to create a dangerous situation so that police are forced to shoot him (NAMI, 2001). Like Pickett, sometimes the person is only wounded. Other times, the shooting is fatal. The American College of Emergency Physicians reported that suicide-by-cop constitutes an actual form of suicide and define it as "an incident where a suicidal individual intentionally engages in life threatening and criminal behavior with a lethal weapon or what appears to be a lethal weapon toward law enforcement officers or civilians specifically to provoke officers to shoot the suicidal individual in self-defense or to protect civilians" (Pinizzotto, Davis, and Miller, 2005).

There is no standardized record keeping for instances thought to be suicide-by-cop, so estimates on its frequency are quite broad. Depending on the definition used, estimates in the United States range between thirty-five and 120 people annually who use the police as instruments of their own destruction (Dahl, 2011). As many as 25 percent of officer-involved shootings may involve suicide-by-cop (Parent, 2011). Weapons used against the police officer have ranged from firearms, stabbing instruments, blunt instruments, and firearm replicas. From cases that have been examined, researchers suggest that only a very small percentage of suicide-by-cop cases involve women, approximately 3 percent (Mohandie and Meloy, 2011).

This form of suicide reflects two tragedies. One involves the person who suffered from mental illness and lacked clear, rational, balanced judgment at a critical moment and may not have received adequate or continuing treatment beforehand. The other victim is the law enforcement officers who are forced to shoot. Approximately 85 percent of law enforcement officers involved in such cases experience at least transitory symptoms of emotional trauma; as many as a third have moderate to severe reactions according to the National Alliance on Mental Illness (NAMI, 2001). NAMI (2001) estimates suggest that 3 percent to 5 percent of police officers experience long-term problems such as post-traumatic stress disorder in the aftermath of a suicide-by-cop incident. Among the many symptoms reported by police are hypervigilance, fear, anger, sleeplessness, recurrent nightmares and depression.

Some suggest that suicide-by-cop instances can be stopped (Dahl, 2011). Contrary to public opinion, law enforcement officers are not trained to kill people simply because they ask for it. It is true that officers are trained to protect themselves and others against lethal threats which is a component of suicide-by-cop. As in all potentially lethal encounters, police do have the responsibility to de-escalate the situation if possible and to use lethal force only as a last option. Taking the time to properly assess the dangerousness of the situation is an important part in any case where weapons are involved.

Researchers disagree on what constitutes a case of suicide-by-cop. While most agree that individuals with severe mental illness are at high risk for suicide, others suggest that situations involving people with severe mental illness should not be included in profiles of the phenomena (Violanti and Drylie, 2008). Typologies of individuals typically fall into two groups: the cornered felon who decides to die rather than be arrested and the emotionally disturbed person whose aim is to provoke the use of deadly force. Crisis intervention teams, specifically trained to intervene in cases involving an emotionally disturbed person, are a promising means by which to resolve these difficult situations.

CONTROLLING LEGISLATION AND COURT ACTION

In Chapter 2, students were briefly introduced to the Americans with Disabilities Act ("ADA," 1990). While the ADA was not written specifically for application to the criminal justice system, law enforcement was not exempted from its original requirements or subsequent amendments. Police officers and their departments face liability under the ADA in circumstances that are defined by the court. The ADA mandates affects policy and procedures concerning encounters that police have with individuals defined as having a physical or mental disability.

The specific circumstances during which the ADA is applied to police action has been an ongoing process (Duffy, 2003). In the years since its inception, various courts have settled issues surrounding the extent to which the ADA applies to law enforcement. The mandate of the Americans with Disabilities Act of 1990*,* affects much of what law enforcement officers do. The courts have even expanded the definitions of what constitutes police action when applying ADA requirements (*Schorr v. Borough of Lemoyne*, 2003). For example, arrest itself is now broadly interpreted to include pre-arrest investigations and violent confrontations not technically involving an arrest. Police action includes receiving citizen complaints, interviewing witnesses, interrogating, arresting, booking and holding suspects, operating telephone (*911*) emergency centers, providing emergency medical services, and enforcing laws. Law enforcement officers and their police departments face civil liability for failure to observe the mandates of the ADA.

Courts have consistently recognized two types of ADA Title II claims applicable to police arrests (*City and County of San Francisco v. Sheehan,* 2015):

- Failure to make reasonable accommodations—where, although police properly investigate and arrest a person with a disability for a crime unrelated to that disability, they fail to reasonably accommodate the person's disability in the course of investigation or arrest, causing the person to suffer greater injury or indignity in that process than other arrestees
- Wrongful Arrest—where police wrongly arrest someone with a disability because they misperceive the effects of that disability as criminal activity

Sporadically, courts have also recognized department liability due to a failure to train—where the failure to train amounts to deliberate indifference to the rights of persons with whom the police come into contact.

Reasonable Accommodations

In part, the ADA requires that law enforcement makes every possible effort to communicate with all citizens. In some cases, effective communication may include the use of auxiliary devices, an interpreter, or a third party to assist. The department may not require payment from a disabled individual for the use of any auxiliary aid. While public entities are required to provide alternative auxiliary aids, if available, they are not required to alter the nature of the service, program, or activity if it results in an undue financial or administrative burden.

The earliest case to recognize a federal claim of discrimination under the ADA in the context of a police arrest alleged failure to provide reasonable accommodations involving an individual in a wheelchair who sustained injuries after being transported in a police van which was not equipped with wheelchair restraints (*Gorman v. Bartch*, 1998). In *Gorman*, a paraplegic plaintiff alleged that police officers discriminated against him in violation of Title II of the ADA by failing to provide a proper transportation vehicle to accommodate his condition and failing to modify department policies and procedures dealing with the arrest and transportation to accommodate such disabled individuals.

Whether reasonable accommodations must be made by police when confronted with an individual known to have psychiatric disability in crisis is a question that is frequently challenged in court. As of this writing, exigent circumstances may absolve public entities of their duty to provide reasonable accommodations (*Hainze v. Richards*, 2000). **EXIGENT CIRCUMSTANCES** is defined as those circumstances that would cause a reasonable person to believe that entry (or other relevant prompt action) was necessary to prevent physical harm to the officers or other persons, the destruction of relevant evidence, the escape of the suspect, or some other consequence improperly frustrating legitimate law enforcement efforts (*United States v. McConney*, 1984). When an individual behaves in a way which suggests that he is a threat to himself or others, reasonable accommodations are not constitutionally required.

IMAGINE THAT . . .

In *Hainze v. Richards* (id 797), a woman requested that police transport her suicidal nephew to a mental facility. The officer observed the nephew outside a convenience store standing with a knife in his hand next to an occupied truck. The deputy exited his vehicle and ordered the nephew away from the truck. When the nephew was within four to six feet, the deputy fired two shots into his chest. Holding that the deputy's use of excessive force was not actionable under the ADA, the Fifth Circuit explained (*Hainze v. Richards*, 2000):

> Law enforcement personnel conducting in-the-field investigations already face the onerous task of frequently having to instantaneously identify, assess, and react to potentially life-threatening situations. To require the officers to factor in whether their actions are going to comply with the ADA, in the presence of exigent circumstances and prior to securing the safety of themselves, other officers, and any nearby civilians, would pose an unnecessary risk to innocents at Id 801.

Question for discussion: The Supreme Court has determined that police officers faced with exigent circumstances are not required to take ADA into consideration, do you agree or disagree with this?

Wrongful Arrest

Two cases set the precedent for wrongful arrest claims against law enforcement officers and their departments. The earliest case to recognize a federal claim of discrimination under the ADA in a police encounter involved a man who was arrested for drunk driving but was actually sober (Jackson v. Inhabitants of Town of Sanford, 1994). His unsteadiness and slurred speech had resulted from a past stroke. The second case involved a man who was deaf. He could not understand the commands issued by the police and was beaten and arrested for resisting arrest (Lewis v. Truitt, 1997).

To prevail on a wrongful arrest claim under the ADA, plaintiff must prove that:

- he was disabled;
- the officers knew or should have known he was disabled; and
- the officers arrested him because of legal conduct relating to his disability.

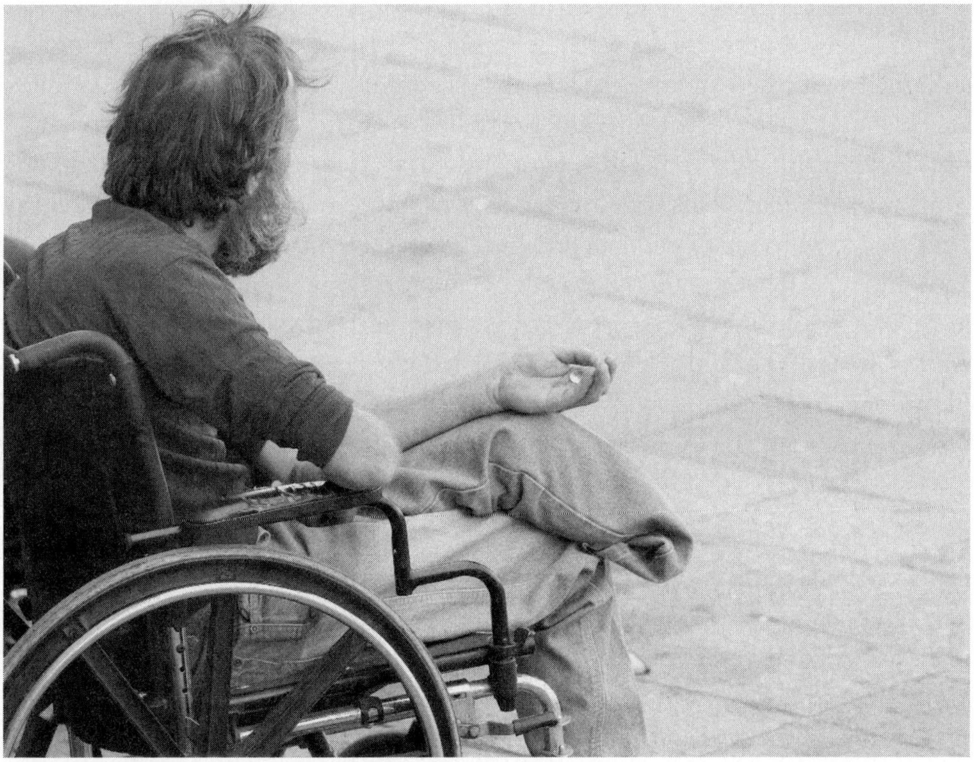

3. CH04-03: A key component to successful liability in wrongful-arrest cases involve a reasonable claim that the police officer had knowledge of the individuals' disability and disregarded it. Co-occurring disorders may include either physical or mental disabilities or a combination of either. Photo copyright John Sohm/Shutterstock.com

Failure to Train

Schorr, a case where police officers shot and killed a man who had bipolar disorder provides an example where the court accepted a claim for "failure to train police" under the ADA requirements (*Schorr v. Borough of Lemoyne,* 2003). The shooting occurred while officers were executing an involuntary commitment warrant. The Court stated that in that circumstance, the police department had failed to institute polices to accommodate disabled individuals such as Schorr, by failing to give the officers the tools and resources to properly de-escalate the situation. While there is no specific training that law enforcement officers must complete to meet the ADA requirements, adequate training to respond to individuals who suffer from physical and psychiatric disabilities is a requirement for law enforcement. Police departments across the country have since developed training programs for their officers to meet this mandate.

LIABILITY ISSUES IN POLICING

Within reason, police are expected to recognize a situation in which a person has a disability and then act in a manner that accommodates that disability. Liability attaches under the American with Disabilities Act for failure to recognize and respond appropriately to persons with physical or psychiatric disability, including some forms of mental illness. Court actions taken against police officers under the ADA require proof of deliberate indifference (*Meagley v. City of Little Rock*, 2011). **DELIBERATE INDIFFERENCE** was defined by the United States Supreme Court in *Farmer* holding that "a prison official may be held liable under the Eighth Amendment of the Constitution for acting with 'deliberate indifference' to inmate health or safety only if he knows that inmates face a substantial risk of danger of serious harm and disregards that risk by failing to take reasonable measure" (*Farmer v. Brennan*, 1994).

However, there is immense social and legal pressure on law enforcement officers to make the correct decisions and to develop the expertise to de-escalate and safely handle cases involving individuals with mental disorders. Specialized response training is advocated for law enforcement officers so that they may better understand the complexities of mental illness and to debunk myths, reduce fear, and learn methods of defusing potentially difficult situations.

Awareness and compassion are among the qualities of law enforcement officers around the country. Still, there are many ways in which a law enforcement department might need to modify its normal practices to accommodate a person with a disability. Flexibility during periods of confinement and at times when there is no risk to the individual under arrest enhances the police-public relationship in the spirit of the reasonable accommodation mandate. You should notice when reading the examples below that one common theme emerges: you must *never* ignore the concern of a medical condition regardless of how you personally feel about the accommodation.

Example: A police department modifies a rule that detainees are not permitted to have food in their cells. To accommodate an individual with diabetes who uses medication and needs access to carbohydrates or sugar to keep blood sugar at an appropriate level, some food is permitted.

Be Aware: Look to see if the detainee wears a medical ID that confirms diabetes as a medical issue for them. Does the person carry a blood sugar monitor or have test strips in the car? Ask the suspect what is needed to make sure that you do not compromise his or her medical condition while in custody. If in doubt, call for a paramedic to confirm the medical needs of the detainee.

Example: When an individual has a physical disability and the police department modifies its regular practice of handcuffing arrestees behind their backs. Individuals who are deaf might be handcuffed in front to allow them to sign or write notes. Physical limitations of an individual might also be cause for some flexibility in handcuffing procedures.

Be Aware: While it may be necessary to handcuff an individual in the front to accommodate a physical need, this method of handcuffing also makes it easier for an individual to remove their handcuffs. This can be avoided by double-locking the handcuffs. Individuals that are handcuffed in the front are considered more dangerous to the officer since they have greater access to items that may be hidden, such as handcuff keys or knives. Explain to the person that you will need to empty their pockets and do a thorough search for weapons prior to their being transported.

Example: A police department modifies its practice of confiscating medications for the period of confinement to permit inmates who have conditions that require self-medication, such as cardiac conditions or epilepsy, to self-administer medications that do not have abuse potential.

Be Aware: If medications are left in a cell with the detainee, there is always abuse potential. Confirm the stated medical condition through a paramedic or other medical person and log the situation with a supervisor.

4. CH04-04: If a police department has the option of administering a breathalyzer at the scene, it can be helpful in making an immediate determination of whether the driver is under the influence of alcohol, particularly in situations when a disability is suspected. In some cases, the driver will have to be placed under arrest and transported to a station for the breathalyzer test. The driver is later released from custody if the breathalyzer test is failed and safety is not an issue. Photo copyright Nikamo/Shutterstock.com

ADA CONDITIONS

Defining disability is a difficult task since it is not necessarily an absolute or static condition. An individual that has a disability cannot be identified by any single common characteristic. Some persons will be readily distinguishable as having impairment due to obvious aids like wheelchairs, canes, or handicap parking stickers; others will not. Psychiatric disability may be less difficult to determine. The individual's response to law enforcement will often be a more precise guide for police interaction.

Law enforcement officers have broad discretion in deciding whether to make an arrest or bring someone to the hospital emergency room when called to intervene in a crisis situation. Once 911 is called and law enforcement officers arrive on the scene, they determine if a crime has occurred and if they have the power to arrest someone that is suspected of committing that crime. If a community has a mental health crisis team, law enforcement can (and often will) call for assistance with mental health emergency situations. The crisis team may assist police in deciding what options are available and appropriate. Likewise, the crisis team may decide to respond with law enforcement. Law enforcement officers encounter individuals having a variety of disorders that cause impairment and they must be prepared to react accordingly.

Suspicious Behaviors

Some unexpected actions may be misconstrued by law enforcement officers as suspicious or illegal activity. Failure to follow directions of the officer, making quick movements (as if hiding something), or reaching behind (as if reaching for a weapon), are all actions that heighten police suspicion during a confrontation. Officers frequently respond to individuals who disregard or even attack them, so it is important that individuals with special needs make the officer aware of their disability so that police officers can respond appropriately. Training, sensitivity, and awareness on the part of the police officers will help to ensure equitable treatment of individuals with disabilities as well as promote effective law enforcement.

> **Example:** An officer observes a vehicle with only one working headlight and pulls the vehicle over. When the driver hands their registration to the officer, the officer notices that the driver's hand is trembling and her speech is slurred. The officer concludes that the individual is under the influence of alcohol, when in fact the symptoms are caused by a neurological disability.

Be Aware: Some people with disabilities may have a staggering gait or slurred speech related to their disabilities or the medications they take. These characteristics, which can be associated with neurological disabilities, mental/emotional disturbance, or hypoglycemia, may be misperceived as intoxication. Even after the driver informs the police officer that he or she has a disability, the officer may need to conduct tests to rule out impairment. It is not uncommon for a person with a physical disability or mental disorder to suffer from co-occurring disorders such as substance abuses. Almost 8 million adults with mental illness in 2013 abused illicit drugs or alcohol. Individuals with SMI are roughly three times more at risk for substance dependence or abuse compared to adults without psychiatric disorders.

Uncooperative Behavior

Individuals with intellectual or cognitive disorders may exhibit moods or behaviors that do not fit the situation. These individuals may erroneously be perceived as uncooperative. An officer's first response should be to wonder why a person acted in a seemingly inappropriate way.

> **Example:** Police respond to a complaint of larceny in a local store. The suspect is not far from the scene and is pointed out by the owner. The officer questions the young man about the items in his pocket that belong to the store. In response, the man looks away and laughs softly. The officer believes that the suspect is intentionally refusing to provide answers and disregarding her authority.

Be Aware: Individuals who have intellectual or cognitive disorders may exhibit moods or behaviors that seem inconsistent with the situation. Failure to follow the commands of a police officer coupled with some inappropriate action may indicate disability or fear rather than overt disregard for police authority.

Threatening Behaviors

Police officers must respond appropriately to real threats to health or safety, even if a person's actions are a result of her or his disability. It is important to distinguish behaviors that pose a real risk from behaviors that do not, and to recognize when an individual, such as someone who is having a seizure or exhibiting signs of psychotic crisis, needs medical attention. It is imperative that behaviors resulting from a disability not be criminalized where no crime has been committed:

> **Example:** A store owner calls to report that an apparently homeless person has been in front of the store for an hour. Customers are complaining that he is scary; he is loudly yelling and gesturing while talking about the end of the world. The individual, who seems to be suffering from mental illness, is not violating loitering or panhandling laws.

Be Aware: Officers arriving on the scene could make an arrest for disorderly conduct, but this should be avoided unless the person is clearly a danger to himself or someone else. Armed with knowledge of local shelters, food pantries, and mental health services, the officers should first attempt to arrange services and care for the man.

> **Example:** Police receive a call in the middle of the night about a teenager with mental illness who is beyond the normal control of her parents. All attempts to get services for the teenager at that hour fail.

Be Aware: If the responding officer arrests her until he can get her into treatment, the girl ends up with a record, even though she committed no offense. This is a situation that can be anticipated, so options should be determined as a matter of department policy based on the available resources in the area.

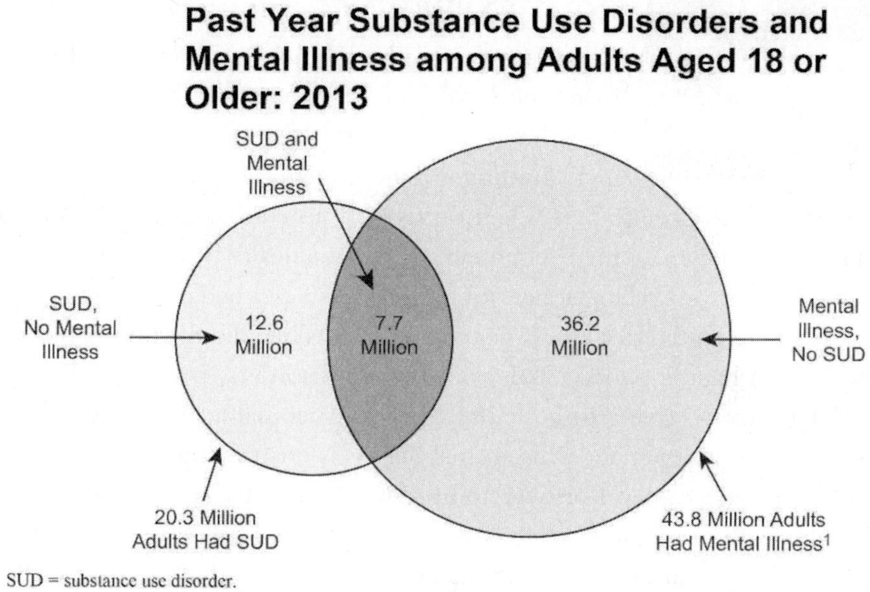

5. CH04-05: *Past Year Substance Use Disorders, 2013.* These numbers suggest that individuals with any mental illness are at higher risk of developing drug and alcohol abuse issues than the general public. Source: Substance Abuse and Mental Health Services Administration. (2014).

PREVALENCE OF VIOLENCE

The question of whether individuals with psychiatric disorders are more violent than the general population is an active ongoing debate. The question is particularly relevant when determining if diversion is an acceptable option for public safety. The issue has been hotly debated since the 1970s. The *MacArthur Community Violence Study* conducted between 1992 and 1995 made an important contribution to the question of dangerousness among individuals with mental disorders (Steadman et al., 1998). The purpose of the study was to determine the rate of violence by former mental patients and compare it to the rate of violence by other members of the community. The study concluded that drugs and alcohol increase violence in people with mental disorders more than they do in the general population, but otherwise, individuals with mental disorders are not more violent than anyone else. This study is widely cited as proof that individuals with mental illness are not violent due to mental disorders. As you can see in figure CH04-05, an estimated 7.7 million adults over the age of eighteen are estimated to have past year substance use disorders and mental illness in 2013. This represents a considerable challenge to law enforcement public safety efforts.

IN MY EXPERIENCE . . .

A call came into the barracks that a young woman from the local halfway house was on the building roof threatening to jump. She was armed with a 15 inch knitting needle which she was using to spear anyone who came close to her. When I arrived, I noted that there were lots of people at the scene including firefighters and mental health workers. They were looking up at the roof yelling at her not to jump. As I climbed the ladder against the house she retreated to a far corner of the roof. When did the police become the experts on handling individuals with mental disorders, I wondered? I just kept talking quietly, trying to get closer to her. Eventually I was able to grab her from behind and pin her arms against her body, instructing someone to get the needle away from her. For over an hour we sat like that on the roof before I let her go. She cried and struggled. She screamed and called me every nasty name in the book, but I held tight and talked . . . gently, softly. Then she started crying about how her mother doesn't love her. . . . It started to rain and someone put raincoats over us. We needed time. These things take time. Eventually she calmed down and we all went down the ladder. I was hopeful for her on that day and often wonder how she is doing.

Question for discussion: Discuss how this case was handled. Can a person be harmed by a knitting needle?

Unfortunately, the debate has not been settled. In an analysis of the MacArthur study shortly after its release, researchers state that the report contradicts the findings of numerous studies over the previous thirty years which had concluded that individuals with mental illness *were* more likely to be involved with serious violence (Satel and Jaffe, 1998). These critics state that the MacArthur study purposely excluded many potentially violent people such as those who were currently in or recently released from a prison, jail, forensic hospital, or a long-term psychiatric hospital. In a published debate ten years after the MacArthur study, its authors responded to these and other concerns regarding its influential findings (Torrey, Stanley, Monahan, and Steadman, 2008). Maintaining the validity of the original study, its authors conceded misuse of some of its findings by the public. For example, the study was not designed to assess evidence of violence among all people with mental disorders, only of those patients with psychiatric illness discharged from acute psychiatric inpatient facilities. Further, the conclusion three years after the MacArthur study by its authors on the effectiveness of psychiatric treatment in reducing violence had been stated with "guarded optimism" and presented only as one way to manage violence risk (Torrey et al., 2008). It may be that persons who are unlikely to commit violence are more likely to adhere to treatment. How does this information inform law enforcement practice? Alpert suggests that the question of greater importance is whether police officers are competent at determining who is mentally disordered and if particular types of training will improve that skill (Alpert, 2015).

Despite the low risk of violence among people with mental illness, research does substantiate that they carry a modest elevated risk of violent behavior when compared to the general public (Swanson, McGinty, Fazel, and Mays, 2015). The occurrence of violence increases the probability that the offender may be arrested at the street level stage. Swanson et al (2015) point out that when persons with mental illness do behave violently, it is often for the same reasons that non-mentally ill people engage in violent behavior. Violence is a complex societal problem that is often caused by other things besides mental illness.

Mass Shootings

Recent shootings at Virginia Tech and the Washington Navy Yard and in Aurora, Colorado; Newtown, Connecticut, Tucson, Arizona; Santa Barbara, California, and Orlando, Florida have focused immense national attention on people with seeming mental illnesses who use guns to victimize strangers. To provide empirical information on gun violence directed at strangers, Steadman and colleagues reexamined the *MacArthur Violence Risk Study Assessment* population (Steadman, Monahan, Pinals, Vesselinov, and Robbins, 2015). Within the first year, almost 30 percent of the population had committed at least one violent act, with an average of 2.3 acts per person and almost 30 percent involving a weapon threat or use. The authors found also that 2 percent of the population committed a violent act involving a gun, with only 1 percent committing a violent act with a gun that involved a stranger (Steadman et al., 2015). Among the violent group were a high incidence of major depression and a diagnosis of alcohol or drug abuse. For the small group of people at risk of committing gun violence, their prior violence, substance use, and early trauma are more likely to contribute to subsequent violence than the mental illness per se (Steadman et al., 2015).

Some experts contend that the proliferation of gun control statutes poses a dilemma for advocates of persons with mental disorders, including psychiatrists and their national organizations (Appelbaum, 2006). Only a tiny fraction of violence, including gun violence, is perpetrated by persons with severe mental disorders. Efforts that center disproportionately on restricting access to firearms reflect a deeply irrational public policy, Appelbaum suggests. Nevertheless, the media displays these acts of public massacre over and over. A recent study from the FBI confirms that mass shootings are on the rise, an increase by 10 percent during 2007 to 2013 (McCarthy, 2014). Another study suggests that the illusion of an increase in mass shootings is due to the short time frame utilized in the FBI report, revealing its bias. Examining the period from 1977 through the first half of 2014, research shows only a slight, statistically insignificant increase in mass shootings (Lott, 2015). By linking mental disorders and violence in the public mind, advocates for more restrictive firearm laws reinforce the stigmatization of persons with mental disorders as inherently dangerous (Appelbaum, 2006). In an open letter to Congress in 2013, the Treatment Advocacy Center emphasizes:

"... individuals with mental illness are no more violent than the general public. But when an individual with a serious mental illness is untreated, the risk of violence rises. An estimated 10 percent of homicides and 50 percent of rampages killings are committed by a small subset of people with untreated mental illnesses..." [to change the math] we need to add treatment to the equation (TAC, 2013).

High profile mass shootings do attract the attention of the public but mental disorder alone is not a predictive variable. However, most active shooters do suffer from mental illness (PERF, 2014). There is no way to predict who will become violent and who will not among any group of people. The Department of Homeland Security (DHS) has taken the lead to enhance active shooter preparedness through a "whole community" approach by providing training, products, and resources to a broad range of stakeholders. Active shooter awareness, incident response, and workplace violence are among the issues for training. Since there is no pattern or method to the selection of victims by an active shooter, these situations are by their very nature are unpredictable and evolve quickly. DHS offers courses, materials, and workshops to help schools and businesses prepare to deal with an active shooter situation and to raise awareness of behaviors that represent pre-incident indicators and characteristics of active shooters.

SUMMARY

Increased calls for service require that police officers be trained to meet the needs of individuals with mental disorders. This is not the same population as individuals who are suspected of committing crimes. Individuals may be involved in nuisance behaviors or minor crime situations where treatment rather than making arrest is a more appropriate response. The needs of individuals with are often complex and require a disproportional amount of time to resolve. Individuals with mental disorders are at an increased risk for suicide and suicide attempts.

The Americans with Disabilities of 1990 has been very influential in setting priorities for police action concerning individuals with physical and psychiatric disabilities. The mandate to law enforcement has slowly been defined though court action in the years since the ADA was passed. ADA Title II claims that have been recognized by the courts include the 'failure to make reasonable accommodations' and the wrongful arrest sections. The failure to train police officers has also been cited when the failure amounts to deliberate indifference to the rights of individuals with whom the police encounter. In some situations, behaviors that might be perceived by police officers as suspicious, uncooperative, or threatening may occur due to the physical or psychological disabilities of the suspect. It is imperative that police officers learn to recognize mental illness and react appropriately.

The question on whether individuals with mental illness are more violent the general public has been answered in part. Unless substance use is involved, experts maintain that the answer is 'no'—individuals with mental disorders are not more dangerous than anyone else. Questions remain about the generalizability of this response to all individuals. Of concern is the reliability of statements that all individuals can be treated successfully. The subject is too complex to fully settle here, more research is needed to clarify and settle the debate. However, the deadly encounters occurring when individuals have encounters with law enforcement officers is highly contentious. Why is this happening and what can be done to improve outcomes between law enforcement and individuals that have mental disorders.

CHAPTER QUESTIONS FOR REVIEW

1. How would you explain the mandates to police officers according to the Americans with Disabilities Act?
2. What does the term "reasonable accommodations" mean to law enforcement action?
3. Provide examples of behaviors that may wrongly be construed by police that a person is involved in illegal behavior. How could officers avoid these situations?

4. What is meant by suicide-by-cop?
5. What is the relationship of substance use to violent behaviors among persons with mental disorders?

REFERENCES

Akins, S., Burkhardt, B., Lanfear, C., Stevens, K., and Amorim, M. (2014). *Law enforcement response to people with mental illness in Benton County: Executive Summary.* Oregon State University. Corvallis, OR.

Akins, S., Burkhardt, B. C., and Lanfear, C. (2016). Law Enforcement response to "Frequent Fliers": An examination of high-frequency contacts between police and justice-involved persons with mental illness. *Criminal Justice Policy Review, 27*(1), 97–114.

Alpert, G. (2015). Police use of force and the suspect with mental illness. *American Society of Criminology, 14*(2), 277–283.

Americans with Disabilities Act (1990).

Appelbaum, P. (2006). Violence and mental disorders: Data and public policy. *American Journal of Psychiatry, 163*(8), 1319–1321.

Babchuk, L. C., and Lurigio, A. J. (2012). Responding to probationers with mental illness. *Fed. Probation, 76*, 41.

Biasotti, M. (2011). *The Impact of Mental Illness on Law Enforcement Resources.* Retrieved from http://www.prweb.com/releases/2011/12/prweb9053827.htm

CDC. (2015). Deaths: Final Data for 2013 *National Vital Statistics Reports* (Vol. 64). Hyattsville, MD: Centers for Disease Control.

City and County of San Francisco, California, et al. v. Sheehan (575 U.S. 2015).

Cordner, G. (2006). *People with mental illness.* Retrieved from http://www.popcenter.org/problems/pdfs/MentalIllness.pdf

Dahl, J. (2011). How to Stop Suicide by Cop. Retrieved from http://www.psmag.com/health-and-behavior/how-to-stop-suicide-by-cop–27758

Duffy, S. P. (2003). ADA applies in context of police arrest. *The legal intelligencer, 228*(38), 3.

Farmer v. Brennan, 511 U.S. 825 (1994).

Gorman v. Bartch, 152 F.3d 907 (1998).

Green, T. (1997). Police as frontline mental health workers: The decision to arrest or refer to mental health agencies. *International Journal of Law and Psychiatry, 20*, 469–486.

Halleck, S. (1987). *The mentally disordered offender.* Washington, D.C.: American Psychiatric Press.

Hainze v. Richards, 207 F.3d 795, 801 (2000).

Houston Police. (2011). Chronic Consumer Stabilization Initiative. Retrieved from http://www.popcenter.org/library/awards/goldstein/2010/10–13(F).pdf

Jackson v. Inhabitants of Town of Sanford, 1994 WL 589617 (1994).

Lott, J. (2015). The FBI's misrepresentation of the change in mass public shootings *Academy of Criminal Justice Sciences Today, October 6, 2014.*

McCarthy, M. (2014). Mass shootings on rise in US, says FBI report. *BMJ, 349.*

Kerr, A., Morabito, M., and Watson, A. (2010). Police Encounters, Mental Illness and Injury: An Exploratory Investigation. *Journal of Police Crisis Negotiation, 1*(10), 116–132.

Meagley v. City of Little Rock, 639 F.3d 384, 389 (2011).

Mohandie, K., and Meloy, J. R. (2011). Suicide by Cop Among Female Subjects in Officer-Involved Shooting Cases. *Journal of Forensic Sciences, 56*(3), 664–668.

NAMI. (2001). White House Shooting Reflects National Issue: "Suicide By Cop". Retrieved 2016, from http://www.nami.org/Press–Media/Press–Releases/2001/White–House–Shooting–Reflects–National–Issue–Sui

NSDUH. (2014). Results from the 2013 *National Survey on Drug Use and Health*: Mental health findings *NSDUH Series H-49* Vol. HHS Publication No. (SMA) 14-4887. Rockville, MD: Substance Abuse and Mental Health Services Administration.

Parent, R. (2011). The Police Use of Deadly Force in British Columbia: Mental Illness and Crisis Intervention. *Journal of Police Crisis Negotiations, 11*(1), 57–71.

PERF. (2014). The Police Response to Active Shooter Incidents *Critical Issues in Policing Series.* Washington, D.C.: Police Executive Research Forum.

Pinizzotto, A., Davis, E., and Miller, C. (2005). Suicide-by-Cop: Defining a Devastating Dilemma. *FBI Enforcement Bulletin* (February), 1–20.

Reuland, M., Draper, L., and Norton, B. (2010). Improving Responses to People with Mental Illness: Tailoring Law Enforcement Initiative to Individual Jurisdictions. New York, NY: Council of State Governments Justice Center.

Reuland, M., Schwarzfeld, M., and Draper, L. (2009). Law enforcement responses to people with mental illnesses: A guide to research-informed policy and practice. New York, NY: Justice Center.

Santos, F., and Goode, E. (2014). Police confront rising number of mentally ill *New York Times, Late Edition (East Coast) ed.*

Satel, S., and Jaffe, D. (1998). Violent fantasies. *National Review, 37*, 36–38.

Schorr v. Borough of Lemoyne, 243 F. Supp. 2d 232 (2003).

Steadman, H. J., Monahan, J., Pinals, D. A., Vesselinov, R., and Robbins, P. C. (2015). Gun violence and victimization of strangers by persons with a mental illness: data from the MacArthur Violence Risk Assessment Study. *Psychiatric Services.*

Steadman, H., Mulvey, E., Monahan, J., Robbins, P., Appelbaum, P., Grisso, T., . . . Silver, E. (1998). Violence by people discharged from acute psychiatric inpatient facilities and by others in the same neighborhoods. *Arch Gen Psychiatry, 55*, 393–401.

Swanson, J., Easter, M., Robertson, A., Swartz, M., Alanis-Hirsch, K., Moseley, D., . . . Petrila, J. (2016). Gun violence, mental illness, and laws that prohibit gun possession: Evidence from two Florida Counties. *Health Affairs, 35*(6), 1067–1075.

TAC. (2013). An open letter to Congress after defeat of gun legislation. Retrieved October 20, 2015, from http://treatmentadvocacycenter.org/about-us/our-blog/69–no?start=297

Torrey, E., Fuller, D., Geller, J., Jacobs, C., and Ragosta, K. (2012). *No room at the inn: Trends and consequences of closing public psychiatric hospitals.* Retrieved from http://tacreports.org/storage/documents/no_room_at_the_inn–2012.pdf

Torrey, E., Stanley, J., Monahan, J., and Steadman, H. (2008). The MacArthur violence risk assessment study revisited: Two views on ten years after its initial publication. *Psychiatric Services, 59*(2), 147–152.

United States v. McConney, 728 F. 2d 1195 (1984).

Violanti, J., and Drylie, J. (2008). *"COPICIDE": Concepts, Cases and Controversies of Suicide by Cop.* Springfield, IL: Charles C. Thomas.

White, M., Goldkamp, J., and Campbell, S. (2006). Co-occurring mental illness and substance abuse in the criminal justice system: Some implications for local jurisdictions. *The Prison Journal, 86*, 301–325.

PART II

The Changing Landscape

Photo copyright monkeybusnessimages/Shutterstock.com

The following chapters are covered in PART II

5. JUSTICE INVOLVED INTERVENTION

6. MULTI-AGENCY COLLABORATIONS

7. CIVIL COMMITMENT

A crucial question is:

What do you think is the most important intervention strategy?

In Chapter 5 we envision the entire criminal justice process as a continuum of intercept points with opportunities for intervention. The goal is to keep people out of the criminal justice system in situations where nuisance behaviors and minor law violations are the product of an illness. Chapter 6 addresses the commitment to collaborative relationships between agencies and sufficient resources to meet the needs of the population. Civil commitment resources for assessment and treatment remain an important asset. The processes are explained in Chapter 7.

CHAPTER 5

Justice Involved Intervention

INTRODUCTION

There is little doubt that people with mental illness are overrepresented within the criminal justice system. People with mental illness who come in contact with the criminal justice system represent a highly diverse group of individuals with varying levels of need for psychiatric intervention. Many come to the attention of law enforcement due to nuisance behaviors and minor law violations simply because of their mental disorders or lack of access to treatment. This is sometimes referred to as the *criminalization of the mentally ill* (Slate, Buffington-Vollum, and Johnson, 2013). It has been established that this group of people with mental disorders are best served if their underlying conditions were addressed affectively (Steadman, Morrissey, and Parker, 2015). Whenever possible, treatment intervention should occur outside of the criminal justice system.

Community-based alternatives to prosecution is considered the optimum goal. A sequential intercept model is the conceptual framework that communities use when considering diversion (Munetz and Griffin, 2006). This chapter addresses diversion practices that commonly occur during the five intercept points. These range from informal police responses to postplea diversion and specialized mental health courts in intercept points one through three. During intercept four and five the reentry and community corrections stage offer opportunities for intervention and community support.

Key Terms

DIVERSION

MENTAL HEALTH COURT

REENTRY

SEQUENTIAL INTERCEPT MODEL

THERAPEUTIC JURISPRUDENCE

RECIDIVISM

Chapter Objectives

After completing this chapter, you should be able to:

- Describe multiple intercept points when diversion may occur
- Define the difference between prebooking and postbooking diversion
- Compare and contrast opposing prosecution diversion perspectives
- Explain the role of specialty courts in diversion programs

SEQUENTIAL INTERCEPT MODEL

The **SEQUENTIAL INTERCEPT MODEL** (SIM) developed by Muntez and Griffin (2006) provides a way to organize and structure community-based alternatives to traditional prosecution. The SIM describes five intercept points during the standard criminal justice process of policing, adjudication, and incarceration. An intercept point is the time of diversion or reentry during which an intervention can be made to prevent individuals from entering or going deeper into the criminal justice system. These five points of intercept would interrupt the process and produce a different route for the individual with mental health needs: 1) law enforcement and emergency services; 2) initial detention and initial court hearings; 3) jails and courts; 4) reentry; and 5) community corrections and community support. The first point of intercept is the most critical, it occurs prior to an arrest. During intercept one, individuals may be diverted informally or before an arrest (see law enforcement involved diversion) (DeMatteo, LaDuke, Locklair, and Heilbrun, 2013). Jail diversion often describes the pretrial programs which identify detainees who can be supervised safely in the community pending trial. Other programs collectively referred to as jail diversion parallel the pretrial diversion by offering alternatives to adjudication (see *Mental Health Courts*). Reentry, suggests Muntez and Griffen (2006), occurs throughout the criminal justice process. Ideally, most people with mental health needs would be intercepted early on during the process to avoid criminalization. The SIM model should act as a filter, with fewer and fewer individuals needing to be diverted as stakeholders develop active collaborations and community mental health alternatives. Although programs vary, a program will typically have only one intercept point. Refer to the illustration figure CH05-01 to see the points of the SIM in relation to the criminal justice system. Note the types of diversion which occur as well as the intercept category.

INTERCEPT POINTS OF DIVERSION

Intercept points occur as early as street level decision making and as late as community corrections and community support. **DIVERSION** is a general term that refers to the movement of cases out of the criminal justice system into community-based options as an alternative to prosecution. Program variations exist based on eligibility criteria that is consistent with the goal of the specific program. While diversion might take place at any time during the criminal justice process, it is typically occurring within the first three intercept points. These common intercept points are at the law enforcement stage, the pretrial or prosecution stage, and at the court phase. There are numerous diversion opportunities during the first three intercept points.

Formal diversion options developed through multi-agency collaborations are widely used today. In the absence of formal diversion policies, informal diversion is a discretionary option used by law enforcement officers. The term jail diversion refers collectively to formal initiatives that connect offenders with serious mental illnesses (and often co-occurring substance abuse issues) to community-based treatment and support services prior to incarceration. Prebooking diversion is considered optimum since it occurs before the person is arrested and therefore avoids pretrial detention. As you will see, jail diversion does not adequately describe the many opportunities for diversion that have emerged in recent criminal justice policy and practice. All programs require substantial resources to identify the individuals who qualify for diversion through referral, screening, and acceptance. The process involves a collaborative and team approach model. Team members include a variety of stakeholders such as criminal justice and mental health professionals, medical and clinical staff, peer counselors, and other members of the community.

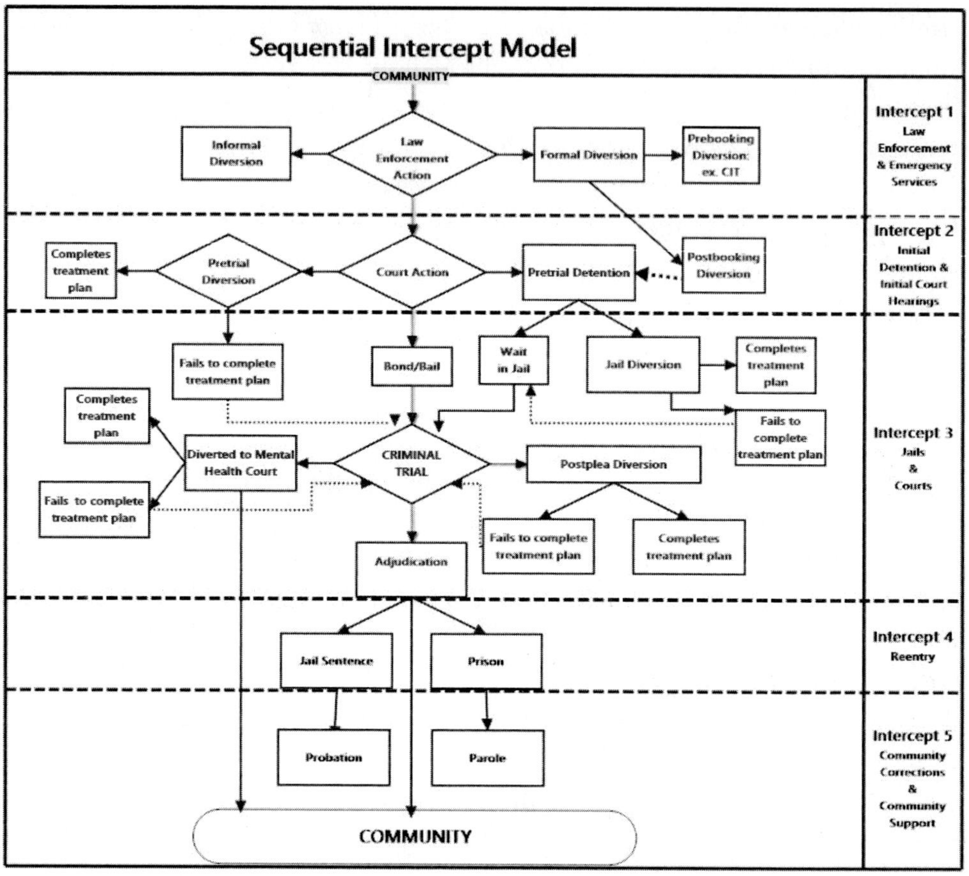

1. CH05-01: *Sequential Intercept Model.* The chart in this figure illustrates the five primary intercept points envisioned by Munetz and Griffin (2006) where individuals with mental illness may be diverted out of the criminal justice system and into supportive reentry and community mental health initiatives. Notice the complex criminal justice system which has been adapted to provide diversion and treatment services. Adapted from Munetz and Griffin (2006).

Scope of Diversion

Per the *International Chiefs of Police* (IACP) National Policy Summit, numerous agencies are actively funding pilot projects to address the recovery of persons with mental illness (IACP, 2010). Among these are the *Substance Abuse and Mental Health Services Center* (SAMHSA)'s Gain Center, the *Bureau of Justice Assistance* (BJA), the *Council of State Governments*, and the *National Alliance on Mental Illness* (NAMI). Each has a variety of test programs and research on best practices. The *Sequential Intercept Model* is incorporated as a foundation for interventions during all stages of the criminal justice process (Mental Health Weekly, 2015).

In 2004, Congress authorized the Mentally Ill Offender Treatment and Crime Reduction Act, administered by the U.S. Department of Justice's Bureau of Justice

Assistance ("MIOTCRA," 2004). The *Act* provides funding for collaborative initiatives among criminal justice agencies and mental health organizations which specifies "low-level, nonviolent mentally ill offenders" as the target population for the services the legislation aims to support. $8.5 million in grant funding was invested in MIOTCRA in 2015 to improve services for individuals with mental illnesses (Justice Center, 2015b). Likewise, an amendment to *Title I* which provided funding for the development of mental health courts, specified that "only those offenders who have been charged with misdemeanors and non-violent offenses—loitering or theft, for example—are eligible to participate in the state and local mental health courts" (*"America's Law Enforcement and Mental Health Project,"* 2000). Programs that limit participation to only nonviolent misdemeanor offenders are common in states across the country. Federal funding for mental health court programs requires a program focus on nonviolent misdemeanants only (Fisher, Albert J. Grudzinskas, Roy-Bujnowski, and Wolff, 2011). However, the criteria for inclusion is not universally accepted.

Experts contend that a growing body of evidence suggests inclusion criteria for diversion program funding should be expanded beyond the nonviolent population (Fisher et al., 2011). Based on the conclusion that more felony arrests than misdemeanor arrests involve persons with severe mental illnesses, Fisher and colleagues argue that the change is necessary to significantly impact incarceration rates among persons with mental illnesses. The *National Association of Pretrial Services Agencies* (NAPSA), which has provided definitions for pretrial diversion intervention, state that eligibility criteria should be broad enough to encompass all potential participants (NAPSA, 2008). Still another suggests that diversion programs have achieved extraordinary successes in treating offenders with mental disorders and in reducing recidivism, even in programs that accept violent offenders (Danjczek, 2008). **RECIDIVISM** is one of the most fundamental concepts in criminal justice, it refers to a person's reoffending, or the repetition of criminal acts by a convicted offender. Danjczek suggests that MIOTCRA's limitation to nonviolent offenses for diversion programs should be eliminated.

Another significant difference in the scope of diversion is evidenced by the program's position on case processing. The NASPA argues that diversion programs require alternatives to regular case adjudication and dismissal of charges if the individual successfully completes the agreed treatment plan. It contends that pretrial supervision programs which seek to minimize the short-term risk of missing scheduled court appearances and rearrests during case processing are not true pretrial diversion, since defendants under these programs remain under regular case adjudication (NAPSA, 2009b). When a case remains under traditional adjudication an individual may still go through a trial and be found guilty. Diversion may or may not involve case dismissal. In some situations, a diverted individual may have to serve a criminal sentence once their treatment is completed. Many jail diversion programs do maintain regular case processing and cases move to traditional judgment and sentences based on the severity of the offense committed.

Goals of Diversion

The main policy goal of diversion is to either reduce recidivism or remove individuals from the criminal justice system altogether without compromising public safety. Per the standards established by the NAPSA, the purpose of jail diversion and intervention programs is to enhance justice and public safety by addressing the root cause of the arrest provoking behaviors of the defendant and reducing the stigma which accompanies a record of conviction (NAPSA, 2008). Having a mental illness which impacts behavior is not a choice; it is a psychological condition. The balance must be made between public safety and the rights of defendants. A proliferation of treatment developments that rely on evidence-based psychological intervention have joined pharmacotherapy as treatment options for a range of disorders (McHugh and Barlow, 2012).

While one can live well in society with appropriate intervention, relapses do occur. It is unrealistic to think that diversion may only be needed once in a lifetime, however. It is estimated that 20 percent of the individuals who are diverted may need rediversion at least once, according to a study that examined two postbooking jail diversion plans in Florida (Boccaccini, Christy, Poythress, and Kershaw, 2005). The study determined that fewer than 6 percent of the diverted individuals had been re-diverted two or more times. The specific goals of diversion practices vary significantly since programs are designed to address the needs of the community.

2. CH05-02: *Law enforcement action*. Both formal and informal diversion occurs at this this first point of intercept. Prebooking diversion is considered the most desirable outcome for people with mental disorders involved in nuisance behaviors and minor law violations. Copyright John Roman Images/Shutterstock.com

LAW ENFORCEMENT INVOLVED DIVERSION

Police are commonly called to a scene to restore order when someone's behavior disturbs others in restaurants, stores, or on the street. Prior to the advent of diversion, law enforcement officers used an informal approach in as many as 75 percent of calls involving individuals with mental illness (Lamb, Weinberger, and DeCuir, 2002). An informal response does not require record keeping or reports. Informal diversion occurs when disturbed individuals are not formally categorized as mentally disordered because of practices that occur within the legal discretionary powers of police officers. There is no accurate data on the extent of informal diversion of individuals with mental illness, yet the practices are believed to be common (Halleck, 1987).

Lurigio maintains that there is no evidence that the police are biased against individuals with severe mental illness or that they deliberately treat them inhumanely (Lurigio, 2011). To the contrary, he asserts, police officers commonly take steps to obtain services, including food and a place to sleep during extreme weather, for persons who are most in need. These cases for informal diversion may involve minor infractions and public nuisance calls to which police officers frequently respond. Typically, this category of response does not involve someone that is in a psychiatric crisis. The individuals in this category are not arrested or formally processed in the criminal justice system.

Prebooking Diversion—Intercept One

Prebooking diversion can be difficult to implement since it requires sufficient availability of mental health services for a population that may be volatile and is often in crisis at the point when diversion is needed prior to an arrest. Prebooking diversion consists of programs and practices that intervene in the criminal justice process, on behalf of individuals with severe mental illnesses, prior to an offender being arrested for a crime. Highly trained law enforcement officers are taught to recognize the symptoms of serious mental illness and form collaborative policing relationships in the community. One example of a program used for prebooking diversion is the *Crisis Intervention Team,* or CIT. This collaborative program will be discussed fully in the next chapter. Prebooking diversion is thought to be the most beneficial type of diversion for individuals with severe mental illness and co-occurring disorders because these programs keep individuals out of jail altogether (Camilletti, 2010). Pre- and post-booking diversion are sometimes called *street-level law enforcement intervention* or *jail diversion* since major goals are to obtain services and mental health treatment for the individual rather than funnel them into the criminal justice system through incarceration.

IN MY EXPERIENCE . . .

While on patrol during the winter months I saw a woman walking on the side of the highway. She was not wearing a coat or shoes, despite the bitter cold. To be clear, pedestrians are not allowed on this highway; the misdemeanor crime she was committing was trespassing after notice because there are clearly posted signs that pedestrians are not allowed on the highway. It would have been perfectly legal to arrest her for the misdemeanor act of trespassing. It was readily apparent when I stopped the cruiser and spoke with her that she was confused and disoriented. The woman was dirty and clearly was not dressed properly for the weather. The woman did not want to go for a psychiatric evaluation and there were insufficient grounds to take her involuntarily. I gave her a ride to a local shelter where she was given food and clothing.

Question for discussion: What type(s) of diversion does this describe?

Postbooking Diversion—Intercept Two

Postbooking diversion also occurs at the law enforcement stage of the criminal justice response. Postbooking diversion of offenders involves assessment and screening of offender's after they have already been arrested for a crime. This is the most common type of diversion program (Camilletti, 2010). Offenders are diverted through negotiations between diversion staff and criminal justice personnel. Treatment plans are developed and offenders' charges may be waived after completion of the diversion program. The availability of mental health assessment services on a twenty-four-hour basis is a desirable component to complement law enforcement intervention and therefore enhance a successful prebooking or postbooking diversion effort.

EVALUATIONS OF LAW ENFORCEMENT DIVERSION

With the realization that individuals with mental illness are overrepresented in our criminal justice system, diversion efforts have received increased attention among policymakers and practitioners. A wide variety of diversion systems are being implemented to explore the available options. One study identified over 100 different diversion programs across the country that divert prior to a criminal conviction (Rodriguez, 2014). Advocates for diversion have long argued that jail detention causes harm to individuals with severe mental illness without serving a legitimate public safety need (Fisher et al., 2011).

All contemporary diversion programs focus on linking offenders to community treatment services rather than incarceration. Experts recommend widespread adoption of diversion for individuals will mental illness, yet few studies look at whether the approach is cost-effective. Cowell et al. (2013) examined the prebooking component of an award-winning jail diversion program which involves the use of highly trained dispatchers, police officers, and clinicians. Cowell and colleagues have concluded that prebooking diversion can be fiscally justified (Cowell, Hinde, Broner, and Aldridge, 2013). Program inclusion criteria require the responding officer to identify that the person is eligible for a misdemeanor offense arrest and also be in a moment of personal crisis with indications of serious mental illness. All diverted individuals are diagnosed after the person is transferred to the Crisis Care Center. Police custody is relinquished at that point. Treatment is offered in the community, but not as a condition of release. The cost of implementing prebooking diversion in San Antonio, Texas was assessed at approximately $370 per person, most of which was incurred by community mental health agencies for short-term monitoring and screening (Cowell, Hinde, Broner, and Aldridge, 2015). Per Cowell and colleagues (2015) a taxpayer savings of $2,800 per person two years after the point of diversion was realized.

Law enforcement diversion has caused an observable decline in the number of individuals who are arrested. Specialized police responses to individuals with mental illness in crisis have been successful in reducing arrest rates by a range of 2 percent to 13 percent (Steadman, Deane, Borum, and Morrissey, 2000). Since a primary goal of the law enforcement approach is to lower recidivism rates among individuals with mental disorders, subsequent studies have evaluated the effectiveness of diversion as well. Skeem, Manchak, and Peterson (2010), for example, conclude that prebooking and postbooking programs made little to no difference in re-arrests over a one-year period. Since programs are being implemented without standardization, they suggest, this calls for a closer look at the programs that are successful to improve outcomes in locations where no change is noted (Skeem, Manchak, and Peterson, 2010). Widespread diversion efforts at the law enforcement phase are new, therefore, evaluations are an important aspect of determining what works and what does not for future implementation.

IMAGINE THAT . . .

Here is an example of a program funded by the Substance Abuse and Mental Health Services Administration (SAMHSA). The Knoxville Early Diversion Program is a collaboration between the Helen Ross McNabb Center (HRMC), Knoxville Law Enforcement, and the Tennessee Department of Mental Health and Substance Abuse Services (TDMHSAS), in coordination with community partners and stakeholders. The Knoxville Early Diversion partners provide screening, assessment, referral, and treatment to individuals at risk of entering the criminal justice system. The diversion team is made up of early diversion liaisons and diversion case managers. The liaisons are available during high-volume times to work side-by-side with law enforcement. They intervene and effectively divert individuals at police encounters. Once an individual encounters the diversion team, the liaison triages, assesses, and identifies possible treatment options. Individuals who need further assistance accessing resources are assigned to an early diversion case manager. Case managers work with individuals to ensure that treatment options are reviewed, referrals are made, appointments are set, and all barriers to the individual engaging in or receiving treatment are identified and addressed.

Question for discussion: What type(s) of diversion does this describe?

3. CH05-03: *Non-Violent Offenders*. Although the policy is controversial, national funding sources for mental health diversion programs require that the primary target participants be non-violent misdemeanor offenders. Copyright Pixel4Images/Shutterstock.com

PROSECUTION INVOLVED DIVERSION

The point at which the prosecution phase formally begins can vary. Typically, when an individual is charged with a crime by law enforcement and not released post-booking, the court assumes jurisdiction and the prosecution period begins. Diversions during the prosecution phase frequently occur pretrial or postplea.

Pretrial Diversion—Intercept Two

Pretrial diversion is a voluntary option that provides alternative criminal case processing for a defendant charged with a crime and it ideally results in a dismissal of the charge (NAPSA, 2008). The pretrial stage is the period after someone has been arrested and prior to being adjudicated in a trial. During this stage an individual may be released into the community on bail or personal recognizance, or held in a jail pending trial. Pretrial detention is limited to the purpose of assuring that an individual will return to court at the time of trial, and that he or she not pose a risk to public safety (i.e. commit a new crime) prior to adjudication. Approximately 17 percent of individuals entering jails during pretrial meet the criteria for a serious mental illness; approximately 60 percent of the jail population is made up of these pretrial detainees (Fader-Towe and Osher, 2015). Since a significant number of severely disordered offenders comprise the American jail population, an ongoing agenda of the justice community is the identification of individuals with behavioral health needs who do not pose a public safety risk so they can be diverted into community-based services.

Pretrial diversion programs operate at the federal, state, and local levels of the criminal justice system. The first pretrial diversion program, called the Citizen's Probation Authority Program (CPA), started in 1965 in Flint, Michigan. Today the *National Association of Pretrial Services Agencies* recognizes 298 pretrial diversion programs in forty-five states, the District of Columbia, and the U.S. Virgin Islands (NAPSA, 2009b). Nonviolent offenders who may be eligible for diversion are identified through a risk assessment process. Pretrial diversion attempts to eliminate factors that may drive an individual's criminal behavior, such as mental illness or substance abuse, through programming that meets the specific needs of the offender.

Diversion at the pretrial stage can occur when a prosecuting attorney and the defense agree that a prosecution will be suspended for a specified period, after which it will be dismissed if the offender has met specific conditions during the suspension period. Pretrial diversion models differ substantially. In some jurisdictions, the defendant must enter a guilty plea upon entering the diversion program, while in others this is not required. A diversion decision may be made within days of arrest, but the decision can also take months.

4. CH05-04: *Prosecution Involved Diversion.* The prosecution diversion may involve release from jail while the offender is awaiting trial or it could signal the end of traditional court processing. The primary decision-making lies with the prosecuting attorney. Copyright Africa Studio/Shutterstock.com

Programs may be available for persons charged with any nonviolent offense, or only for specific offenses. Based on the needs of the offender, restitution, community service, and counseling are common elements of the diversion. Pretrial diversion programs may be located in a variety of agencies: stand-alone agencies, District Attorney's offices, pretrial agencies, probation, courts, private nonprofits, or Sheriff's offices. In a study on pretrial diversion models, the most common eligibility criteria are the defendant's prior criminal history and the current charge (NAPSA, 2009a). Both the victim and the arresting officer have a voice; their approval is required in approximately 33 percent of the programs. Successful completion of the terms for diversion results in the case being dismissed and the record being expunged. If the diversion is terminated for noncompliance, the case is reinstated to the court docket for prosecution.

Postplea Diversion—Intercept Three

Postplea diversion programs require regular court processing and a guilty plea for diversion eligibility, a practice that is inconsistent with NAPSA diversion standards (NAPSA, 2009b). Under postplea diversion, courts hold guilty pleas or convictions in abeyance, pending a defendant's completion of community-based supervision and/or treatment or service programs. Pleas and convictions are vacated following successful program completion. Postplea diversion programs incorporate supervision, service, and treatment similar to that offered under pretrial diversion. If an individual does not complete the negotiated program of treatment, the court is free to continue criminal processing. This approach to diversion is likely to be used when the past criminal history of an individual suggests that he or she is not likely to commit to treatment but appears genuinely motivated to change, therefore the court is willing to give the person another chance to change. This diversion approach is also used when the court determines that the individual needs motivation to complete the treatment plan, therefore the incentive of a pending criminal sentence may be warranted.

EVALUATIONS OF PRETRIAL DIVERSION

A 2010 research summary on pretrial diversion programs noted that little work has examined their effectiveness as a whole (Camilletti, 2010). However, cost savings have been noted. Cowell et al (2015) reported that jail diversion at the pretrial stage saves approximately $205 to $238 per person, depending on whether the measure is implemented as a postbooking bond determination or at the postbooking docket stage. The clear majority of these expenses are incurred by court personnel in both instances. Significant evidence exists of program effectiveness in terms of time benefits as well, since it controls the growing court dockets of criminal justice systems and jurisdictions that implement the programs (The Center for Health and Justice at TASC, 2014). The positive outcomes for participants of pretrial diversion include less time spent incarcerated, avoidance of criminal convictions that make finding gainful employment difficult, reduced rates of substance abuse and improved mental health conditions.

While most pretrial diversion programs do not collect data on recidivism, the Center for Health and Justice (2014) reports that a program in Hennepin County,

Minnesota significantly reduced recidivism rates among participants that successfully completed the program (6 percent) compared to those who did not (40 percent). Recidivism is when an individual has been convicted of or, has a case pending, for any new crime while involved with the program or within six months after completion. Diversion appears to be a successful alternative for eligible defendants maintains NAPSA. In a survey of pretrial diversion programs of eligible defendants who entered diversion, an average of 85 percent successfully completes the program (NAPSA, 2009a). Noncompliance problems are typically met with increased sanctions and problem-solving initiatives. Rediversion is practiced in some jurisdictions (Boccaccini et al., 2005).

COURT INVOLVED DIVERSION

The emphasis on court reform typically centers on the overrepresentation of individuals with mental illness that are in prisons and jails. The reality is that they must have gone through the court system to get there. Almost 20 percent of defendants have a diagnosis of a serious mental illness at arraignment (Broner, Lamon, Mayrl, and Karopkin, 2003). Without adequate treatment or linkage to community services, many people with mental illnesses who are caught in the system risk falling into a cycle of repetitive involvement within the justice system. **THERAPEUTIC JURISPRUDENCE** attempts to view law in a way that values psychological health and avoids anti-therapeutic consequences whenever possible, without subordinating due process principles. Research has suggested that the voluntary nature and procedural justice of the approach may lead to decreased rates of new arrests and increased court compliance (Redlich and Han, 2014). The Mental Health Courts (MHCs) are modeled after drug treatment courts on the principle of therapeutic jurisprudence.

Mental Health Court—Intercept Three

A **MENTAL HEALTH COURT** is a specialty court that attempts to reduce the incarceration and recidivism rates of people with mental illnesses by linking them to the mental health services and support programs that might have prevented their arrest in the first place. MHCs substitute a problem-solving model for traditional criminal court processing. They operate with limited jurisdiction and a specialized court docket for qualified defendants. While this may refer to a building, it is typically a room or rooms where the judge will hear cases that have been deferred from the criminal court docket. Their focus on the population of persons with severe mental illness uses the criminal justice system's authority to provide behavioral health care and psychiatric services in lieu of incarceration.

Like other diversion programs, there is variability among mental health court models. The two general approaches to MHCs are a preplea and a postplea model. Findings suggest that in response to accepting felony cases, the next generation of mental health courts has moved towards favoring a postplea approach along with the use of jail as a sanction (Redlich, Steadman, Monahan, Petrila, and Griffin, 2005). Recall that when defendants remain under regular case adjudication, the program is not considered true diversion per the definitions of NAPSA (NAPSA, 2009b). In contrast, the preplea model requires that no plea is entered and there is agreement that charges will be dropped upon successful program completion.

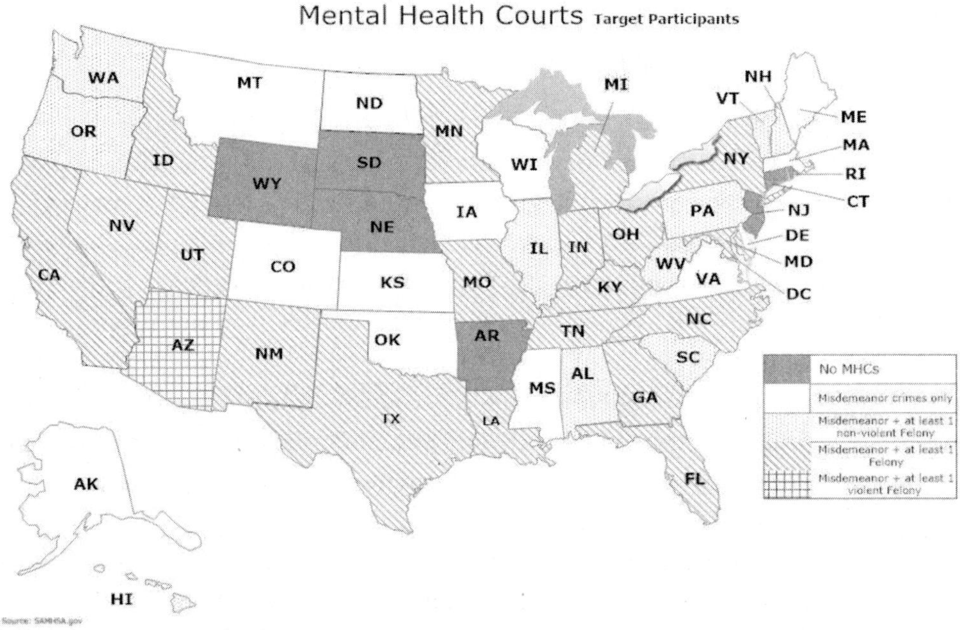

5. CH05-05: *Mental Health Courts.* A Mental Health Court is a specialty court that tries to reduce the incarceration and recidivism rates of people with mental illnesses by linking them to the mental health services and support programs that might have prevented their arrest in the first place. Since 1997 the system has grown to over 300 courts, with programs in almost every state. Adapted from SAMHSA.gov

The first jurisdictions to establish Mental Health Courts (MHCs) were Broward County, Florida; King County, Washington; and Anchorage, Alaska. Since 1997 the system has grown to over 300 courts, with programs in almost every state (Justice Center, 2015a). These courts seek to improve outcomes for offenders with mental illness in the criminal justice system by connecting individuals to treatment and other social services in the community. By using a team approach to address public safety concerns MHCs also reduce jail overcrowding. Common core elements of a Mental Health Court include:

- Voluntary participation by the offender
- A multidisciplinary approach to problem solving
- Intensive case management that includes supervision and accountability
- A judge that oversees treatment and facilitates collaboration

In a study examining MHCs in the state of Illinois, most programs utilized personal appearances before judges and active, flexible staff programing to meet individual needs of participants (Staton and Lurigio, 2015). The courts typically have special pretrial service personnel who are responsible for developing treatment plans, as well as dedicated probation officers who monitor defendants' compliance with the conditions of the court order. The same study described notable differences between these Illinois courts in their disparate uses of rewards versus punishments. The court may sanction verbal praise and admonishments, community service hours, brief jail stays for the most serious rule violators, and an increased or decreased number of required court appearances. The authors note that, given the continued growth of MHCs, further research should examine the sanctioning of rewards to motivate participants.

Participants in Mental Health Courts

Mental Health Courts typically involve offenders that suffer from serious mental illnesses including schizophrenia, schizoaffective disorder, bipolar disorder, severe depression, and anxiety disorders. A subset of serious mental illnesses is severe and persistent, including conditions that involve long-term and profound impairment of functioning. Some courts accept individuals with a broader spectrum of disabling conditions than mental illness alone such as developmental disabilities, traumatic brain injuries and dementias that may also co-occur with serious mental illnesses. Addictive disorders are considered mental illnesses in the American Psychiatric Association's *Diagnostic and Statistical Manual of Mental Disorders* and may be an included criterion in some jurisdictions. Approximately 75 percent of the individuals with mental illness who are involved in the criminal justice system also have co-occurring substance use disorder (Justice Center, 2008).

As you can see in figure CH05-05, there is great variation among the states on the target participants they serve (SAMHSA, 2015). Most states have at least one court that is dedicated to a specialized mental health docket. There are seven states that do not yet have a Mental Health Court. Note that most states process cases that involve felony offenses in at least one court. The clear majority of states have between one and five MHCs; states with more than twenty include California, Florida, Illinois, New York, and Ohio. Alabama is unique in that it is the only state that specifies that a specialized court must be dedicated to involuntary commitment cases.

Health Care Information Sharing

Mental health courts and criminal courts become involved with the mental health treatment system in many ways, including postbooking and therapeutic courts. These programs require an ongoing exchange of information between court personnel and treatment providers at every stage of the process. Courts are neither "covered entities" within HIPAA nor "federally assisted programs" within 42CFR Part 2. Obtaining healthcare information from treatment providers that are covered entities can occur though a court order. Most state laws will require a judicial order before information is released to the court; both HIPAA and 42 CFR Part 2 contain specific provisions governing the issuance of such a court order.

In lieu of obtaining a court order, court officials can also obtain permission for the release and sharing of healthcare information from the participant. Mental health courts frequently require that a potential participant be willing to provide permission to share information between criminal justice and health-care clinicians as a condition of admission to the program. The Council of State Governments states that HIPAA does not require that hearings in a mental health court be closed to the public, even if protected health information may be disclosed (Petrila and Fader-Towe, 2010). This does not mean that courts disregard privacy concerns. Some courts do choose to close hearings where particularly sensitive information is likely to be discussed. Other options include discussions at the bench or in chambers.

EVALUATIONS OF MENTAL HEALTH COURTS

Studies that examine the effect of Mental Health Courts are adding to anecdotal evidence suggesting that the approach is successful in meeting the primary goal of reducing recidivism. Skeem, Manchak, and Peterson (2010) have found MHCs to have a positive effect on recidivism rates. The probability of re-arrest following intervention by MHCs is around 40 percent, versus 55 percent observed in a control group after eighteen months (Skeem et al., 2010). Research concluded that even when misdemeanor offenders with mental illness have similar services, after one year the proportion arrested is significantly lower among MHC defendants than among those who were processed in traditional courts (Aldigé Hiday, Ray, and Wales, 2013). Individuals who successfully complete and graduate the Mental Health Court program exhibit a lower frequency of illegal drug use and recidivism. Among the benefits associated with successful program completion in a Mental Health Court, several studies find decreases in new jail bookings, fewer days spent in jail, increased frequency of treatment services, and a more favorable perception among defendants that they were treated with fairness and respect (Justice Center, 2008).

A study of the outcomes of the Cook County MHC program among felony probationers with chronic mental illness problems found substantial improvements in all measures (TASC, 2012). The average number of arrests per participant decreased by 81 percent; days in custody decreased by 71 percent; and among the program graduates, 70 percent had no new arrests in the year following completion. Additionally, the program has saved taxpayers an estimated $4.2 million in custody costs, a 70 percent cost decrease. Between 2004 and 2011, there have been 369 active participants in the Cook county program.

REENTRY INVOLVED DIVERSION

The goal of diversion is to avoid or radically reduce jail time through referral to community-based services (Steadman et al., 2015). As stated earlier, the goal should be accomplished at early intercept points. Munetz and Griffin (2006) argue however, that the reentry stage represents yet another opportunity for intervention, which may include reductions in jail time though good behavior and affect recidivism. Per DeMatteo et al. (2013):

> **REENTRY** includes all institutional and community-based programming dedicated to assisting individuals with mental illness to re-integrate into the community following release from incarceration, including efforts to prevent further criminal justice involvement (pg. 68).

More than 36 percent of prison inmates and 43 percent of jail inmates in the NIS-3 survey reported having ever been told by a mental health professional that they had a mental disorder (Beck, Berzofsky, Caspar, and Krebs, 2013). Cited disorders include manic depression, bipolar disorder, other depressive disorders, schizophrenia or another psychotic disorder, posttraumatic stress disorder, or an anxiety or personality disorder. Counseling and medication during incarceration are common responses to these mental health issues, according to the NIS-3 survey. The federal government has recognized that the failure to prepare inmates for the transition from corrections into the community would likely contribute to high rates of recidivism (Fisher et al., 2014). Program initiatives to address reentry concerns has received support in the form of *The Second Chance Act of 2008* (SCA). Efforts at this point in the criminal justice process are to prevent rearrest of persons with mental illness though the essential elements necessary for community reintegration, including housing, treatment and support services, and access to medication and entitlements (Fisher et al., 2014).

Reentry Programing—Intercept Four

Programming for persons with mental illness begin with institutional efforts at the time of incarceration, transitional planning, and includes facilitating continuity of care between correctional settings and the community (DeMatteo et al., 2013; Munetz and Griffin, 2006; Steadman et al., 2015). Reentry initiatives are broadly grouped into three areas; programs from assertive community treatment, intensive case management, and correctional reentry programs (Heilbrun et al., 2012). There is significant overlap in service initiatives associated with reentry since community programing occurs at every intercept point (DeMatteo et al., 2013). For example, assertive community treatment (ACT) is a mobile mental health crisis team collaborative response associated with reentry is also a major community intensive treatment and intensive case approach initiative.

Providing adequate services in jail and prison is constitutionally required under the Eighth Amendment's prohibition of cruel and unusual punishment (*Estelle v. Gamble*, 1976). *Estelle* was the first Supreme Court case dealing with correctional health care, a case typically remembered for the court's determination that 'deliberate indifference' is the standard for review of correctional health care. The court concluded that the failure to treat an inmate's serious medical needs is inconsistent with contemporary standards of decency.

Since *Estelle* the courts have revisited discharge planning and found it to be an essential component of mental health care (*Brad H. v. The City of New York*, 2004). *Brad H.* was an inmate who had been admitted to the NYC Department of Corrections (DOC) twenty-six times, received treatment for his mental illnesses, but had never been provided discharge planning prior to release (Mellow and Greifinger, 2008). The court in *Brad H.* found that inmates are "entitled to discharge planning because they are patients of a mental treatment provider" pg. 118 [i.e. the New York State Office of Mental Health under NYC DOC] (Barr, 2003). Mellow and Greifinger (2008) suggest that under the American Medical Association code of ethics physicians have a moral obligation to provide continuity of care for their patients upon discharge from corrections and reentry. At the very least, they argue, the duty at reentry involves the requirement for a needs assessment, a summary of essential medical information, an appointment for follow-up care in the community or a referral to a community resources along with a prescription or bridge supply of medication for the period between release and the next appointment in the community (Mellow and Greifinger, 2008).

EVALUATIONS OF REENTRY PROGRAMING

The development of financial resources and the ability to adopt technology which allows for information sharing between agencies who provide a continuum of health care for inmates are the two biggest problems facing correctional agencies in their development of reentry programs (Mellow and Greifinger, 2008). In a recent evaluation of challenges to reentry program development, Steadman and colleagues (2015) also identified a lack of information sharing between the behavioral health and criminal justice systems and the development of financial resources as pivotal concerns. An already strained workforce shortage of mental health providers is now being spread even thinner with new people seeking services who now have Medicaid coverage to pay for the services. While the challenges to creating integrated responses for reentry are complex, successful programing has been achieved in many jurisdictions (Steadman et al., 2015).

Pre-release engagement with community based services, followed by immediate post-release support and intensive case management was found to be the most effective strategy for promoting successful reentry, per a recent evaluation of the *Second Chance Act of 2011* (Lindquist, Willison, Rossman, Walters, and Lattimore, 2015). The most common challenges to program implementation, according to the report, were staff turnover and barriers to effective collaboration between corrections and community partners. Also cited were problems with enrollment, recruitment and retention of participants in addition to service provision challenges. Among the recommendations for future programming, grantees suggested that initiatives should be administered as community rather than a law enforcement based programs. The need for cross-training of staff and hiring those who have criminal justice histories or a personal connection to incarceration were among the lessons learned highlighted in the report.

6. CH05-06: *Justice Involved Interventions.* Envisioning diversion and intervention services on a continuum emphasizes that each component is interdependent, with entry points into or out of the criminal justice system that can occur at any time. Justice system concerns involve both mental health needs and recidivism reduction to achieve its goals.

COMMUNITY CORRECTIONS AND COMMUNITY-BASED SERVICES

Almost all contemporary programs are designed to connect offenders with mental illness to community treatment services (Skeem et al., 2011). Community corrections and community-based services are complementary resources of support for ex-offenders with mental illness. More than 623,000 prisoners were released from state and federal prisons across the United States in 2013 (Lindquist et al., 2015). The sheer numbers in this population present enormous challenges to reintegration, particularly when complicating conditions such as mental disorders are considered. It is valuable to situate community corrections (probation and parole) in addition to community-based services within the *Sequential Intercept Model* so that the framework is complete.

Community Corrections and Support—Intercept Five

Community corrections itself is the largest component of corrections. During 2014, more than 4.5 million adults were under community supervision while on parole or probation (Bonczar, Kaeble, and Maruschak, 2015). Successful community reintegration and criminal deterrence for this population involves linkages to appropriate services and treatment. This population of offenders has substantial mental illness and treatment needs. There are three common approaches which are used to address the rehabilitation needs of offenders with serious mental illness suggests Matejkowski, Severson, and Manthey (2015). These include programs with the mental health approach (management of psychiatric symptoms), the risk reduction approach (reducing risks associated with recidivism), and the strengths promotion approach (achievement of positive life goals). Matejkowski and colleagues (2015) found that the probation and parole officers in their study, regardless of their exposure to specialized training, viewed mental health treatment as an effective component of offender supervision in combination with other approaches.

Prins and Draper (2009) maintain that six evidence-based mental health treatment programs have been shown to improve clinical outcomes for people with serious mental illness. These include *Assertive Community Treatment* (ACT), *Illness self-management and recovery*, *Integrated mental health and substance use services*, *Supported employment*, *Psychopharmacology*, and *Family psychoeducation.* Community-based programs that serve ex-offenders respond to a range of service requirements that are necessarily diverse and complicated. Housing, employment readiness, and mental health resources are among the service provision challenges.

EVALUATIONS OF COMMUNITY CORRECTIONS AND SUPPORT

While linking offenders to treatment is medially justifiable, there is evidence that mental health services alone are not successful in reducing the criminal involvement of offenders who experience the most severe forms of mental illness (Matejkowski, Severson, and Manthey, 2015; Prins and Draper, 2009). In other words, treatment may reduce psychiatric symptoms but are not particularly successful in reducing criminal justice involvement. Experts maintain that there is a lack of research on the effectiveness of combining the current models used in probation and parole, maintaining that evaluations are necessary to support or discount practice beliefs. Among the factors considered obstacles in a study of offenders under federal supervision are a lack of transportation, mental health problems, physical handicaps, homeless or unstable housing, reading and writing limitations, low intelligence, language, and child care (Cohen and Whetzel, 2014).

Reentry initiatives which start during incarceration as a direct link into community based support services is noted as a promising strategy for successful reintegration (Lindquist et al., 2015). Among the critical community support services, they maintain, are needs for affordable housing, employment opportunities, mental health services, health care, and family services. Identified gaps in community service include affordable housing options for sex offenders, clients with drug distribution charges, former gang affiliations, and mental health issues.

SUMMARY

From the earliest stages of its development and continuing through implementation, a diversion program must coordinate with the police, prosecutors, mental health clinicians, and community stakeholders. Breaking the cycle of repetitive contact with the criminal justice system requires substantial resources for an initial setup and a strong commitment for continued community mental health treatment options. Considerable variability exists between programs from state to state and at the federal level. Each program is unique and designed to meet the needs of the community it serves. Diversion initiatives commonly occur at every level of the criminal justice system prior to incarceration in prison. These are referred to as the first three intercept points in the Sequential Intercept Model. During reentry and community corrections, intercept four and five, diversion efforts are less common and generally support efforts to reduce recidivism.

Police officers traditionally have used informal diversion options prior to booking individuals with mental illness. Today, the diversion options are more formalized. Law enforcement officers have the discretion to divert individuals either prior to booking or after booking. While the prebooking option is considered the more desirable of the options, the postbooking is used most frequently. Most individuals that are diverted at the postbooking stage, which is after an arrest, will involve minor criminal acts.

Diversions in the pretrial/prosecution phase show greater variability in the criteria for inclusion and program goals. While many specialty mental health courts handle only defendants charged with minor offenses, the current trend is towards court-based alternative disposition programs that focus on individuals with serious felony charges. Sometimes, individuals who have already received a sentence to jail or prison are offered mental health services as a more effective therapeutic alternative. Numerous promising strategies have been introduced for reentry and community corrects. Evaluation and continued research is needed to determine which programs are most beneficial to promote mental health and reduce recidivism.

CHAPTER QUESTIONS FOR REVIEW

1. What is the purpose of the Sequential Intercept Model?
2. What is the difference between prebooking and postbooking diversion programs?
3. What is the primary goal(s) of diversion practices?
4. How is information sharing facilitated in court diversion?
5. What are some of the perceived benefits of mental health courts?

REFERENCES

Aldigé Hiday, V., Ray, B., and Wales, H. W. (2013). Effectiveness of a short-term mental health court: Criminal recidivism one year postexit. *Law and Human Behavior, 37*(6), 401–411.

America's Law Enforcement and Mental Health Project, codified as amended in scattered sections of 42 U.S.C. Cong. Rec. (2000).

Barr, H. (2003). Transinstitutionalization in the Courts: Brad H. v. City of New York, and the fight for discharge planning for people with psychiatric disabilities leaving Rikers Island. *Crime and Delinquency, 49*(1), 97–123.

Beck, A., Berzofsky, M., Caspar, R., and Krebs, C. (2013). Sexual victimization in prisons and jails reported by inmates, 2011–12 Washington, D.C.: Bureau of Justice Statistics.

Boccaccini, M. T., Christy, A., Poythress, N., and Kershaw, D. (2005). Rediversion in two postbooking jail diversion programs in Florida. *Psychiatric Services, 56*(7), 835–839.

Bonczar, T., Kaeble, D., and Maruschak, L. (2015). Probation and Parole in the United States, 2014. Washington, D.C.: Bureau of Justice Statistics.

Brad H. v. The City of New York, 779 N.Y.S. 2d 28 (N.Y. App. Div 2004).

Broner, N., Lamon, S., Mayrl, D., and Karopkin, M. (2003). Arrested adults awaiting arraignment: Mental health, substance abuse, and criminal justice characteristics and needs. *Fordham Urban Law Review, 30*, 663–721.

Camilletti, C. (2010). Pretrial diversion programs: Research summary. Arlington, VA: BJA.

Cohen, T., and Whetzel, J. (2014). The neglected "R"—Responsivity and the federal offender. *Federal Probation, September*, 11–18.

Cowell, A. J., Hinde, J. M., Broner, N., and Aldridge, A. P. (2013). The impact on taxpayer costs of a jail diversion program for people with serious mental illness. *Evaluation and Program Planning, 41*, 31–37.

Cowell, A. J., Hinde, J. M., Broner, N., and Aldridge, A. P. (2015). The cost of implementing a jail diversion program for people with mental illness in San Antonio, Texas. *Evaluation and Program Planning, 48*, 57–62.

Danjczek, L. (2008). The Mentally Ill Offender Treatment and Crime Reduction Act and its inappropriate non-violent offender limitation. *Journal of Contemporary Health, Law, and Policy, 24*(1), 69–117.

DeMatteo, D., LaDuke, C., Locklair, B. R., and Heilbrun, K. (2013). Community-based alternatives for justice-involved individuals with severe mental illness: Diversion, problem-solving courts, and reentry. *Journal of criminal justice, 41*(2), 64–71.

Estelle v. Gamble, 429 U.S. 97 (1976).

Fader-Towe, H., and Osher, F. (2015). Improving responses to people with mental illnesses at the pretrial stage: Essential elements. New York, NY: Council of State Governments Justice Center.

Fisher, W. H., Albert J. Grudzinskas, J., Roy-Bujnowski, K. M., and Wolff, N. (2011). Public policy and limits of diversion programs for reducing jail exposure of persons with serious mental illness. *Psychiatric Services, 62*(12), 1503–1505.

Fisher, W. H., Hartwell, S. W., Deng, X., Pinals, D. A., Fulwiler, C., and Roy-Bujnowski, K. (2014). Recidivism among released state prison inmates who received mental health treatment while incarcerated. *Crime and Delinquency, 60*(6), 811–832.

Heilbrun, K., DeMatteo, D., Yasuhara, K., Brooks-Holliday, S., Shah, S., King, C., . . . Laduke, C. (2012). Community-based alternatives for justice-involved individuals with severe mental illness: Review of the relevant research. *Criminal Justice and Behavior, 39*(4), 351–419.

IACP. (2010). Building safer communities: Improving police response to persons with mental illness. Alexandria, VA: International Association of Chiefs of Police.

Justice Center. (2008). Mental health courts: A primer for policymakers and practitioners. New York, NY: Council of State Governments.

Justice Center. (2015a). Mental Health Courts. Retrieved October 15, 2015, from https://csgjusticecenter.org/mental-health-court-project/

Justice Center. (2015b). The Mentally Ill Offender Treatment and Crime Reduction Act. Retrieved July 10, 2015, from http://csgjusticecenter.org/wp-content/uploads/2014/08/MIOTCRA_Fact_Sheet.pdf

Lamb, H. R., Weinberger, L. E., and DeCuir, W. (2002). The police and mental health. *Psychiatric Services, 53*(10), 1266–1271.

Lindquist, C., Willison, J., Rossman, S., Walters, J., and Lattimore, P. (2015). *Second Chance Act Adult Offender Reentry Demonstration Programs:* Implementation challenges and lessons learned. Washington, D.C.: U.S. Department of Justice.

Louden, J., and Skeem, J. (2013). How do probation officers assess and manage recidivism and violence risk for probationers with ent disorder? An experimental investigation. *Law and Human Behavior, 37*(1), 22–34.

Lurigio, A. (2011). Examining prevailing beliefs about people with serious mental illness in the criminal justice system. *Federal Probation, 75*(1).

Matejkowski, J., Severson, M., and Manthey, T. (2015). Strategies for postrelease supervision of individuals with serious mental illness: Comparing specialized community corrections officers to those not serving on a specialized team. *Journal of offender rehabilitation, 54*(7), 520–537.

McHugh, R., and Barlow, D. (2012). The reach of evidence-based psychological interventions. *Dissemination and implementation of evidence-based psychological interventions.* New York, NY: Oxford University Press.

Mellow, J., and Greifinger, R. (2008). The evolving standard of decency: Postrelease planning? *Journal of Correctional Health Care, 14*(1), 21–30.

Mental Health Weekly. (2015). Bipartisan bill reauthorizes mental health, criminal justice collaboration law. Retrieved December 5, 2015, from Wiley Periodicals, Inc wileyonlinelibrary.com

Mentally Ill Offender Treatment and Crime Reduction Act (2004).

Munetz, M. R., and Griffin, P. A. (2006). Use of the sequential intercept model as an approach to decriminalization of people with serious mental illness. *Psychiatric Services, 57*(4), 544–549.

NAPSA. (2008). Performance standards and goals for pretrial diversion/intervention. Washington, D.C.: National Association of Pretrial Services Agencies.

NAPSA. (2009a). Pretrial diversion in the 21st century. Washington, D.C.: National Association of Pretrial Services Agencies.

NAPSA. (2009b). Promising practices in pretrial diversion. Washington, D.C.: National Association of Pretrial Services Agencies.

Petrila, J., and Fader-Towe, H. (2010). Working with HIPPA and other privacy laws. In Council of State Governments Justice Center (Ed.), *Information sharing in Criminal Justice—Mental Health collaborations.* New York, NY: Bureau of Justice Assistance.

Prins, S., and Draper, L. (2009). Improving outcomes for people with mental illnesses under community corrections supervision (pp. 60). New York, NY: Council of State Governments Justice Center.

Redlich, A., and Han, W. (2014). Examining the links between therapeutic jurisprudence and mental health court completion. *Law and Human Behavior, 38*(2), 109–118.

Redlich, A., Steadman, H. J., Monahan, J., Petrila, J., and Griffin, P. A. (2005). The second generation of mental health courts. *Psychology, Public Policy, and Law, 11*(4), 527–538.

Rodriguez, P. (2014). Pre-conviction diversion is best for outcomes: TASC report. *Alcoholism and Drug Abuse Weekly, 26*(3), 3–4.

SAMHSA. (2015). Adult Mental Health Treatment Court Locator. Retrieved October 23, 2015, from http://www.samhsa.gov/gains-center/mental-health-treatment-court-locator/adults

Slate, R., Buffington-Vollum, J. K., and Johnson, W. W. (2013). *The criminalization of mental illness: Crisis and opportunity for the justice system* (2nd ed.). Durham, NC: Carolina Academic Press.

Skeem, J. L., Manchak, S., and Peterson, J. K. (2011). Correctional policy for offenders with mental illness: Creating a new paradigm for recidivism reduction. *Law and Human Behavior, 35*(2), 110–126.

Staton, M., and Lurigio, A. (2015). Mental health courts in Illinois: Comparing and contrasting program models, sanction applications, information sharing, and professional roles. *Federal Probation, 79*(1), 21–26.

Steadman, H., Deane, M. W., Borum, R., and Morrissey, J. P. (2000). Comparing outcomes of major models of police responses to mental health emergencies. *Psychiatric Services, 51*(5), 645–649.

Steadman, H. J., Morrissey, J. P., and Parker, T. W. (2015). When political will is not enough: Jails, communities, and persons with mental health disorders. Retrieved December 5, 2015 from *The Prison Journal*, http://metatoc.com/papers/46598-when-political-will-is-not-enough-jails-communities-and-persons-with-mental-health-disorders

Swanson, J. W., McGinty, E. E., Fazel, S., and Mays, V. M. (2015). Mental illness and reduction of gun violence and suicide: bringing epidemiologic research to policy. *Annals of Epidemiology, 25*(5), 366–376.

TASC. (2012). Cook county mental health court program: Outcomes and cost savings. Chicago, IL: Treatment Alternatives for Safe Communities.

The Center for Health and Justice at TASC. (2014). No entry: A national survey of criminal justice diversion programs and initiatives. Chicago, IL: TASC.

CHAPTER 6

Multi-Agency Collaborations

INTRODUCTION

Concerns regarding the overrepresentation of individuals with mental disorders in the criminal justice system has led to a rethinking of the law enforcement role. If only we could stop the flood of inappropriate incarcerations at the entry point of the criminal justice system! Decriminalizing mental issues is both compassionate and cost-effective, suggests the IACP (2010). Stakeholders in this effort took a huge leap forward towards understanding the perspectives and needs of each other's agencies. It hasn't been easy, but it shows that we have taken this next step together. Formal collaborations have been forged with mental health agencies to provide assessment and treatment for people with mental disorders who come to the attention of the police. The primary goal is to obtain services and treatment for this population instead of bringing them into the criminal justice system though an arrest. Many specialized programs and response models involving law enforcement and mental health have been developed in recent years, some of the more well-known programs are covered in this chapter.

To accomplish the goal of collaboration requires that we pool our resources and expertise. Sharing medical information between agencies is not as difficult as previously thought. Primary collaborations with medical facilities and mental health professionals HIPAA was never meant to create a barrier to disclosure to justice agencies, concern over violating confidentiality has resulted in a closed system which was not intended by the law. In fact, there is a legal duty of a psychiatrist or psychotherapist to warn an identifiable victim of a patient's serious threat of harm. In this chapter you will be introduced to the concept of collaborative policing, with examples of key partnerships specifically formed for serving the needs of people with mental illness.

Key Terms

COALITION

COLLABORATIVE POLICING

CO-RESPONSE MODEL

CRISIS INTERVENTION TEAM (CIT)

MEMPHIS MODEL

PEER SUPPORT SPECIALISTS

POST-CRISIS ASSISTANCE PROGRAM

Chapter Objectives

After completing this chapter, you should be able to:

- Define the concept of collaborative policing
- Describe the training and goals of *crisis intervention teams* (CIT)
- Explain models of multi-agency collaborations
- Discuss privacy concerns and the duty-to-warn concept

COLLABORATIVE POLICING

COLLABORATIVE POLICING has emerged as a model that embraces the philosophy of community responsiveness with an added emphasis on community building through agency partnerships. Collaborative policing does not seek to change the agency police partners with. Each retains its own identity and philosophy. It is important to understand that organizational goals will often be different. Differences should not stand in the way of working together for the population that both serve.

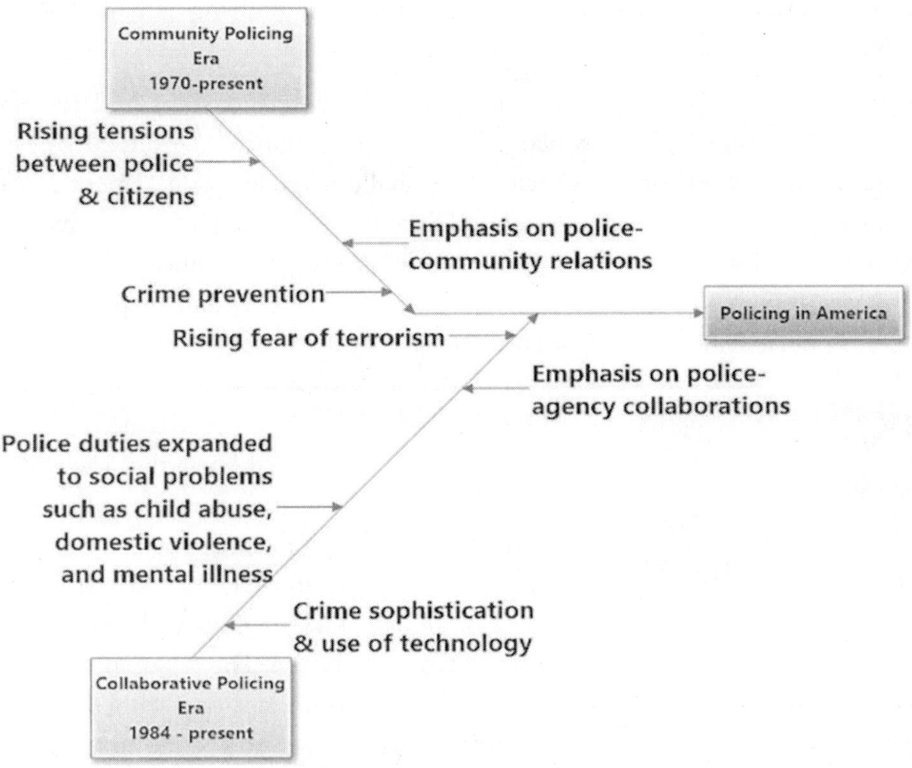

1. CH06-01: *Collaborative Policing* vs *Community Policing.* Collaborative Policing is the most recent policing era. It represents an emphasis on police-agency collaborations which have evolved in response to expectations that police duties include social problems such as child abuse, domestic violence, and mental illness in addition to crime control.

Arresting individuals with mental illness for minor crimes and disturbances is common practice when police officers cannot identify any other option to solve an immediate problem. The effect is short-term and often inappropriate since it places undue stress on the criminal justice system and harms the individual who needs treatment rather than incarceration. It also leaves open the probability of repeat calls for the same individual. The development of collaborative relationships is essential to finding answers to community problems (McCampbell, 2010). There are three primary goals necessary to accomplish a *Collaborative Policing Approach*: to work jointly with others, to cooperate with or willingly assist others, and to cooperate with an organization with which the police are not immediately connected. Identifying viable alternatives to incarceration for minor cases involving persons with mental disorders is a welcome approach which has been embraced by many police departments across the country. Over half of law enforcement officers are already employed in a department that actively encourages patrol officer involvement in community building activities (Reaves, 2015).

Collaborative policing offers options through relationships and resources that would not otherwise be available in these circumstances (Carter, 2015). Some common police collaborations include hospital emergency rooms, mental health professionals, community coalitions, and families. This is not an exhaustive list of possible collaborations; it is only a sample of the possibilities. Collaborative response programs assure access to mental health resources and keeps people out of the criminal justice system when criminal conduct is not the primary concern.

IN MY EXPERIENCE . . .

As a police officer, whenever I knew that I would be serving a warrant to search a home and arrest occupants where children lived, I would make prior arrangements to protect those children. A colleague from social services that was trusted not to give information on the location of the search would wait down the street from the house. The children would be safely escorted away from the home for temporary custody with the social worker. Doing this kept children from being exposed to the traumatic events of watching their parents and loved ones being arrested and having their home searched by the police. They were safe and could be reunited with the family when a non-offending member was identified by social services. It also helped me to focus on the search of the house. Everyone wins in with this simple collaboration!

Question for discussion: If a social worker was not available for this type of arrangement, can you think of another option that might work?

SPECIALIZED POLICING RESPONSE PROGRAMS

Specialized law enforcement response programs have evolved as a way to share the responsibility with the mental health community for the care of individuals in crisis who suffer from mental disorders (Reuland, Draper, and Norton, 2012). The distinguishing factor in this category of collaborative response is the direct involvement of law enforcement officers. To improve responses that prioritize treatment over incarceration, the mental health community, in addition to community stakeholders, need to be actively involved in the process. These specialized programs vary considerably to meet the needs and resources of specific communities. The educational component in each program addresses the police officers' level of awareness about community mental health resources and the characteristics of persons who need access to those services. This group of collaborative programs are also categorized as pre-booking diversion, which will be further explored in the next chapter.

Specialized law enforcement response programs are an excellent example of collaborative policing (Reuland, Draper, and Norton, 2012). The officers reach out to the community in a proactive way to become familiar with the individuals that have mental disorders. When agency relationships are formed for improved response, this becomes a collaborative policing effort. The belief is that police officers are better able to respond to a crisis event if they know the problems and needs of the people that require assistance. Reuland, et al. (2009) suggest that specialized law enforcement responses should strive for the following goals:

- To improve officer safety
- To increase access to mental health treatment, support and services
- To decrease the frequency of these individuals' encounters with the criminal justice system
- To reduce certain costs incurred by law enforcement agencies

Collaborative Responses to Persons with Mental Illness

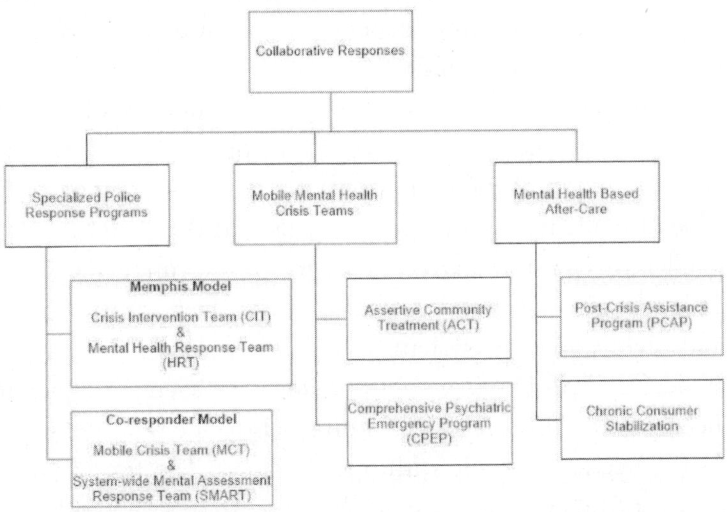

2. CH06-02: *Collaborative Responses to Persons with Mental Illness.* Note the three categories of collaborative relationship under which these programs have been developed to assist in responses to persons with mental illness at the street level of involvement with the criminal justice system.

The Memphis Model—CIT Response and HRT

The most well-known specialized police response programs are based on the Memphis Model. Considered a best practice model in law enforcement, the **MEMPHIS MODEL** includes a specialized police training program for officers who volunteer to work with the mental health community, along with community collaborations which involve mental health providers and stakeholders. The Memphis model was established in 1988 by the Memphis, Tennessee Police Department in response to a tragic incident in which a police officer killed a person who had mental illness. The Crisis Intervention Team (CIT) approach, the first example of the Memphis Model, is also an example of a prebooking diversion. Most encounters involving a Crisis Intervention Team Approach (CIT) result in a voluntary commitment or resolution at the scene (Lord, Bjerregaard, Blevins, and Whisman, 2011).

The Crisis Intervention Team (CIT) is an approach designed to improve safety during encounters with persons in crisis by enhancing officers' ability to de-escalate and providing community-based treatment alternatives to incarceration (Watson, Morabito, Draine, and Ottati, 2008). CIT International suggests that the model can be envisioned as a five-legged stool—training the police is only one "leg" of the program (CIT, 2016). To be strong, fully functional, and enduring, all five legs are needed. First, officers self-select to participate. Once approved, officers receive 40 hours of specialized training regarding mental illness. The range of specific topics offered differs depending on the department and community priorities but all programs include information on de-escalation techniques and education on mental illness. The second leg is community collaboration. Partners in in the community take on ownership of the program and become involved in its development and implementation. The IACP recommends that cross-training opportunities for mental health professionals and other stakeholders should be incorporated into CIT training curricula to nurture understanding and to help develop a common language (IACP, 2010). The third leg is critical; it requires a vibrant and accessible crisis system. For police to take a diversionary approach, quality services and providers need to be quick, efficient, and guaranteed. Police officers need priority for referrals of individuals to the behavioral health provider to address the needs of people with mental illness. The fourth leg is the training and education of behavioral health staff to foster positive working relationships with law enforcement. The fifth leg involves collaboration and education of family, consumers, and advocates. CIT is designed so that police are just one part of the response and are not solely responsible for addressing the needs of people with mental illness in the community.

The Cincinnati *Mental Health Response Team* (MHRT) team has operated as a modified Memphis Model since 2002 (Ratansi, 2004). Officers designated as MHRT in Cincinnati, Ohio are assigned to regular patrol but are available as primary responders to calls involving individuals with mental disorders. Using the CIT training as a model, this department selected the police officers who participated in the forty-hour training course (Ratansi, 2004). The topics covered in the training sessions include:

- Review of mental illness
- The Mental Health system
- Orientation/shadowing a mental health professional
- Police hotline and state mental hold
- MHRT interface with SWAT and Crisis Negotiation Teams
- Review of non-lethal force options
- Special Populations
- Role of Mobile Crisis Team
- Suicide
- Legal Issues
- Mediation
- Problem solving and community resources

Programs based on the Memphis Model establish partnerships between law enforcement and mental health systems, forcing the agencies to work together on common problems concerning mental health. These partnerships give police officers a better understanding about mental illness and community resources.

Co-Response Model—MCT and SMART

Law enforcement agencies in Los Angeles and San Diego, California were among the first to collaborate with the mental health community to form teams in which officers and mental health professionals respond together to a scene (Reuland and Schwarzfeld, 2008). The goal is to connect individuals in crisis with community based services more effectively. This has become known as the **Co-Response Model**. There are many variations of the *Co-Response Model*, the MCT and SMART programs are among these. Experts advocate the co-response approach because the presence of law enforcement provides safety to mental health professionals (Lamb, Weinberger, and DeCuir, 2004). An example of the co-response model is evident in *Mobile Crisis Team* (MCT). Team members can include case managers, social workers, nurses, mental health personnel, and addiction specialists, to name a few.

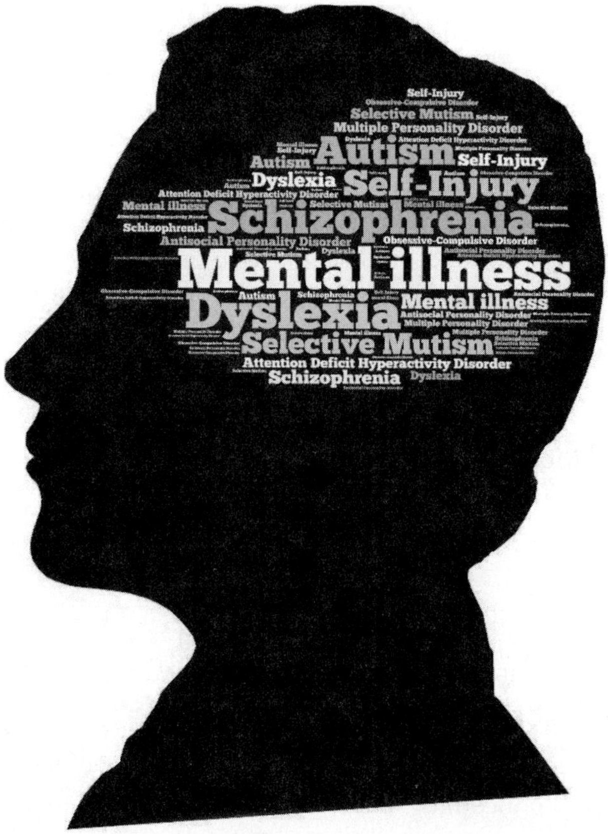

3. CH06-03: The common element in all programs to increase policing efficiency and response to individuals in mental health crisis is ***knowledge*** about mental disorders. In most situations, accurate determinations can be made about the level of risk a situation poses to the officer and others. Mental health professionals play a key role in providing healthy alternatives for individuals in crisis. Photo copyright mypokcik/Shutterstock.com

In Los Angeles, an additional layer of dispatch is in place to facilitate the co-response model. Law enforcement first responders can ask patrol dispatchers for a System-wide Mental Assessment Response Team (SMART) (Reuland, Draper, and Norton, 2010). The dispatchers then route their call to the "Triage Center" of the Mental Evaluation Unit (MEU) where an officer assesses when to send out teams. This triage officer can access the MEU database to gather information on the criminal justice history of the person who is the subject of the call for service. In this model, the forensic nurse located in the unit can access the Department of Mental Health (DMH) records to assist with the medical needs of the individual in crisis. The original program is modified for relevancy to first responders to assist them in developing tools that ensure safety when dealing with a person in crisis.

EVALUATIONS OF SPECIALIZED POLICE RESPONSE PROGRAMS

The movement to train law enforcement officers and educate them on the CIT approach has been very successful. Officers in the Chicago Police Department had positive attitudes towards the CIT program (Morabito, Watson, and Draine, 2013). At least eleven states have statewide CIT initiatives and many police departments across the country are adopting the model (NAMI, 2014). Experts evaluated the Memphis CIT model by comparing perceived preparedness, quality of response to persons with mental illness, diversion from jail, officer time spent on these calls, and community safety and found empirical support for the effectiveness of this approach (Borum, 2000). Additional researchers have provided further support for the Memphis CIT model with findings of higher response rates and fewer arrests (Steadman, Deane, Borum, and Morrissey, 2000). Components of the CIT program are the use of crisis intervention and active listening skills (e.g., paraphrasing, reflecting emotions, asking open-ended questions) which have been found beneficial for numerous applications in police work, including hostage negotiation and mental health response (Vecchi, Hasselt, and Romano, 2005).

There is some evidence that merely changing the method of policing does not alter the outcomes for people with mental illness, however (Morabito, Kerr, Watson, Ottati, and Angell, 2012). Intervention depends on access and availability of mental health services for individuals in need. On analyzing its effects on policing practice, some researchers find no evidence that CIT reduces the likelihood of arrest or that it has a direct effect on police use of force (Kerr, Morabito, and Watson, 2010). Others report that it is simply too difficult to evaluate CIT programs due to a lack of official data concerning CIT calls (Blevins, Lord, and Bjerregaard, 2014). An additional issue is that the program can be difficult for many police departments to implement due to the forty-hour training requirement (Cronin, 2015). Small law enforcement departments may lack the manpower and resources to provide this training for its officers.

The *mental health response team program* provides information and expertise to situations involving psychiatric crisis. According to Ratansi (2004), Cincinnati, Ohio formed a MCT program following a highly-publicized shooting of a suspect with mental illness in 2002. The police department increased training for all law enforcement officers to an additional five hours and hired a social work therapist to accompany police on mental health codes from 9 am to 5 pm on weekdays (Ratansi, 2004). Illustrating the need for empirical research to evaluate successes and failures of new programs, the Cincinnati MCT was not impressive. An evaluation of the collaboration found no decrease in the number of repeat calls and no reduction in the encounter time for the officers involved with persons with mental illness (Frank, Eck, and Ratansi, 2004). In fact, the authors found that repeat calls and response time both increased because of the collaboration. Additionally, they confirmed that in cases of police response to individuals with mental illness, injuries to citizens and officers had been low both prior and after the program. It was due to one sensationalized shooting that had prompted the change, the survey found. In most cases where injury was reported, they were associated with self-harm and suicide attempts prior to the police arrival. Only having a social worker available during the week from 9 am to 5 pm was not positively associated with increased response benefits.

MOBILE MENTAL HEALTH CRISIS TEAM

Multidisciplinary advisory groups have developed policies and protocols for emergency dispatchers that encourage calls for service involving individuals with mental illness who are not suspected of criminal conduct to mobile crisis teams comprised of mental health professionals rather than to law enforcement (IACP, 2010). Per the *International Chiefs of Police Association* (2010) 311 non-emergency call services are used in some jurisdictions for psychiatric emergencies that do not present a public safety risk. The availability of Mobile Mental Health Crisis Team responses is a fast-growing option. IACP recommends that these response teams be available 24/7 so that law enforcement does not become the default responder simply because there are no other crisis response resources available. Law enforcement remains an option for backup in these response efforts, when in rare cases it may be needed.

Assertive Community Treatment (ACT)

Assertive Community Treatment (ACT) is an example of a mobile crisis team with an intensive case management approach which offers treatment, rehabilitation, and support services to individuals that have been diagnosed with a severe and persistent mental illness (Burns and Santos, 1995; Morrissey, Meyer, and Cuddeback, 2007). ACT services also provide healthcare, vocational assistance, integrated dual disorder treatment, family education, wellness skills training, community linkages, and peer support. Services are provided to individuals by a mobile, multi-disciplinary team in community settings. ACT serves a small population of individuals with serious mental illness not engaged with traditional treatment services. The individuals often have significant inpatient and emergency psychiatric histories, involvement with the criminal justice system, and alcohol/substance abuse histories. The ACT plan of care evolves over time as the needs and goals of the individual change.

Comprehensive Psychiatric Emergency Program (CPEP)

As of 2013, the city of New York has mandated that all requests for a *Mobile Crisis Team* (MCT) which come from the community, i.e. family members, neighbors, friends, landlords, clergy, service providers to those who assist persons with a mental health issue, or other person concerned about an individual begins with a call to a LifeNet hotline, a Comprehensive Psychiatric Emergency Program (CPEP) (1-800-LifeNet, 2016). A LifeNet Crisis Counselor determines by phone if the situation meets criteria for the services of a MCT. Services provided include assessment, crisis intervention, counseling, information and referrals, and linkage with appropriate community mental health services. The team will make arrangements if emergency room transport is needed. If the person with mental illness presents a danger to self or others and is not willing to go voluntarily, however, law enforcement officers will be called for an involuntary transport. Similar mobile crisis intervention programs have been established across communities in the United States. In Massachusetts, the Behavioral Health Network, Inc provides similar emergency responses, known as *Mobile Crisis Intervention* (MCI). Availability is twenty-four hours a day, seven days a week for urgent psychopharmacology intervention, treatment, and assessment (BHN, n.d.).

EVALUATIONS OF MOBILE MENTAL HEALTH CRISIS TEAMS

Mobile crisis teams are cost-effective and reduce the use of emergency medical services and arrest. Research has suggested that Mobile Mental Health Crisis programs are effective, efficient, and have high satisfaction from consumers (Scott, 2000). The International Chiefs of Police (IACP) recommend the ACT model, stating that has proven to be more effective than traditional office-based mental health approaches (IACP, 2010).

HEALTH BASED AFTER-CARE

Police response to crisis does not address the long-term mental health issues of individuals with mental health disorders. An increasing amount of interest is being generated for *Health Based After-Care*, which may involve direct referrals from police officers who encounter persons with mental illness who are in need or present as high risk. This collaboration is a proactive approach to follow-up after someone has been identified as a person with mental health problems and who are likely to come to the attention of the police without intensive mental health involvement.

Post-Crisis Assistance

The **Post-Crisis Assistance Program** (PCAP) represents a program example which has evolved to reduce the likelihood of future crisis through prompt referral to a mental health organization following a mental health call for service (Bonkiewicz, Green, Moyer, and Wright, 2014). Follow-up from the organization to the individual is prompt and guaranteed. The authors of the Lincoln Police Department's PCAP study concluded that within six months following a police-involved mental health crisis the PCAP consumers generated fewer mental health calls for service. The individuals were less likely to be arrested and were also less likely to be taken into emergency protective custody than those without the PCAP assistance.

In another example of the PCAP approach, Los Angeles created the *Case Assessment and Management Program* (CAMP), which is a team strategy that focuses on proactive efforts to resolve the issues that generate repeat calls to police and other public services by employing mental health case management and rigorous follow-ups. The CAMP teams include detectives from the police department and mental health clinicians who work together to create customized plans for identified individuals. The CAMP team, which is located in the Mental Evaluation Unit area of the police department, receives referrals from many sources, including the Los Angeles Fire Department, school police, other city police officers, other LAPD detectives/investigators, and from mental health department personnel (Reuland, Draper, and Norton, 2010).

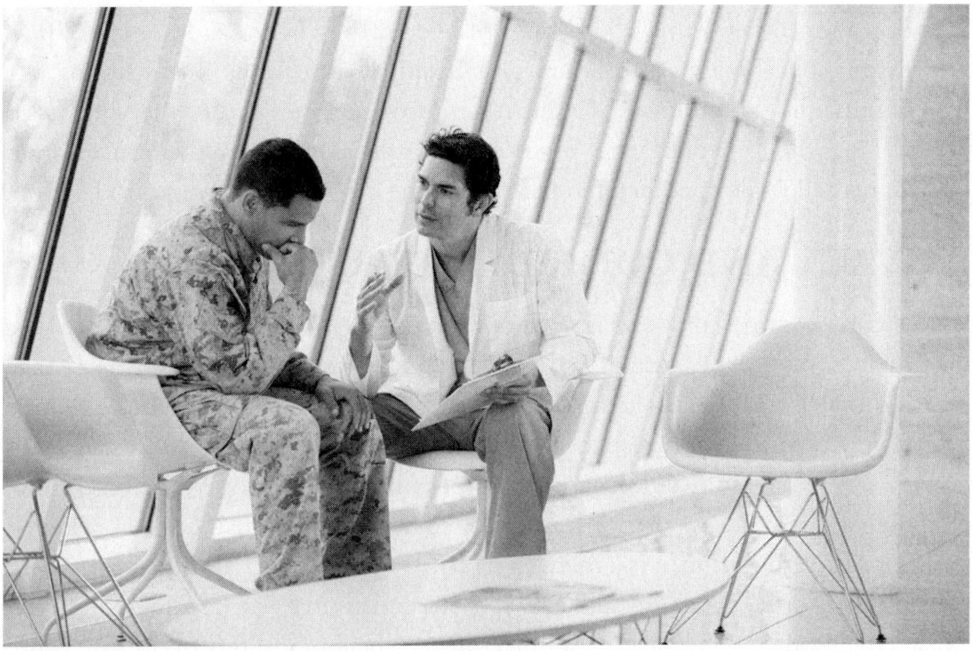

4. CH06-04: *Mental Health Based Aftercare.* For many individuals with mental health care problems, an aftercare program is necessary to prevent future crisis situations. Interventions in this category include caseworkers and mental health specialists that can provide follow-up and intensive interventions. They work closely with the clients in determining their medical and psychiatric needs and monitor their medication compliance. Photo copyright monkeybusinessimages/Bigstock.com

Chronic Consumer Stabilization

Concern over three deadly force encounters with individuals who had a history of severe mental illness, coupled with a sharp increase of repeat calls-for-service, the Houston Police Department in Texas developed the *Chronic Consumer Stabilization Initiative* which piloted for six months in 2009 (Houston Police, 2011). The police officers noted the cycle of their reactive response to situations involving the clear majority of mental health consumers in the city. An individual in crisis would be taken by the police for emergency mental health evaluations where he would be stabilized. Then, after twenty-four to seventy-two hours, the individual would be released back into the same environment where another crisis would often follow and the cycle would repeat. Forming a multi-agency collaboration between the City of Houston Health and Human Services Department, the Houston Police Department, and the Mental Health Mental Retardation Authority of Harris County, the city funded two licensed caseworkers to identify the needs of and provide services for the 30 most chronic consumers. After six months, results showed a 70 percent decrease in police contacts, a 76 percent decrease in emergency detention orders, and a 67 percent decrease in offenses committed by the population along with a cost savings of over $216,973 (Houston Police, 2011). Decreased police manpower hours and hospital admissions were among the benefits to the community. Caseworkers work closely with the clients in determining their medical and psychiatric needs along with their medication compliance, all while including families and home providers in their consideration.

PRIVACY AND CONFIDENTIALITY

In this current atmosphere of agency collaboration, the statement "I can't share medical information because of HIPAA" is being replaced with, "how can I make it easier to share medical information?" Collaborations between agencies require a clear understanding and respect for the rules of confidentiality and the laws of privacy. Even in circumstances that legally permit medical information disclosure, obtaining consent always demonstrates respect for an individual. Long considered a barrier to collaboration, it is a myth that HIPAA or 42 CFR Part 2 require patient consent for disclosures in judicial and administrative proceedings; for law enforcement purposes; to avert a serious threat to health or safety or for disclosure mandated under state abuse and neglect laws (Matz, 2014; Petrila, 2007).

Each state has law that further governs the confidentiality of medical records in addition to the federal mandates. Some state laws may require consent for release of medical information even when HIPAA does not. However, experts have suggested that misunderstanding the legal standards for information sharing can have serious negative consequences for individuals with mental health issues who are involved with the criminal justice system. The misunderstandings may compromise appropriate clinical care and public safety. Professionals that desire inter-agency collaboration need to research and fully understand their specific mandates to comply with state law. It appears that the greatest barrier to fully assisting those with mental health and substance abuse issues are based in myth rather than reality.

HIPAA Privacy Rule

At the federal level, the *Health Insurance Portability and Accountability Act* (HIPAA) sets standards for confidentiality and privacy of patient records. HIPAA, which was authorized by the U.S. Congress in 1996 to govern the security of individually identifiable health information in electronic form, was never meant to create a barrier to disclosure to justice agencies. The HIPAA Privacy Rule, also called the *Standards for Privacy of Individually Identifiable Health Information*, provided the first nationally-recognized regulations for the disclosure of an individual's health information. The Privacy Rule defines how covered entities use individually-identifiable health information or PHI (Personal Health Information). "Covered entities" is a term often used in HIPAA-compliant guidelines. The definition of a covered entity is specified in 45 CFR § 160.102 of the Privacy Rule: HIPAA covered entities do not include the courts, court personnel, accrediting agencies, and law enforcement officials such as police or probation officers (Matz, 2014; Petrila, 2007). Guidance from the federal Office for Civil Rights (OCR) under HHS clarifies a more permissive standard than has generally been understood pertaining to sharing information on mental health treatment (U.S. Department of Health and Human Services, 2014).

The Privacy Rule permits a HIPAA covered entity, such as a hospital, to disclose certain protected health information, including the date and time of admission and discharge, in response to a law enforcement official's request for locating or identifying a suspect, fugitive, material witness, or missing person. See 45 CFR § 164.512(f)(2). Under this provision, a covered entity may disclose the following information about an individual: name and address; date and place of birth; social security number; blood type and rh factor; type of injury; date and time of treatment (includes date and time of admission and discharge) or death; and a description of distinguishing physical characteristics (such as height and weight). The law enforcement official's request may be made orally or in writing.

42 CFR Part 2

The part of the Code of Federal Regulations, under the Public Health chapter, that deals with the confidentiality of alcohol and drug abuse patient records is known as 42 CFR Part 2. 42 CFR Part 2 regulates the release of information pertaining to alcohol or drug abuse diagnosis and restricts programs which are federally funded or whose primary function is providing substance abuse treatment. For example, an emergency room would not be held liable under 42 CFR Part 2 for information confidentiality, but a drug-abuse treatment "program" at the same hospital would (Petrila and Fader-Towe, 2010). For substance abuse treatment programs that fall under that definition, disclosures can only occur with the client's written consent. As noted earlier, HIPAA does not create a significant barrier to collaboration with law enforcement. 42 CFR Part 2 is a clear directive with little room for misunderstanding. Law enforcement officers are not bound by either federal mandate, meaning they too are free to provide information about an individual's mental health condition to a mental health professional or family member if needed (Petrila and Fader-Towe, 2010).

State Confidentiality Standards

State confidentiality standards vary greatly and are often more restrictive than HIPAA. The National Alliance of Mental Illness reports that two states have recently passed legislation that aligned state confidentiality standards with HIPAA to facilitate mental health services (NAMI, 2014). Hawaii enacted SB 2869, repealing stringent language governing the release of developmental disability and mental health records and replacing it with more permissive language to conform to HIPAA standards. Wisconsin has enacted AB 453, amending state health privacy laws to more closely match HIPAA regulations. The trend to simplify the terminology of HIPPA and educate individuals on its true purpose is acknowledged in both state and federal initiatives.

COLLABORATIONS WITH HOSPITAL EMERGENCY ROOMS

Emergency rooms are among the agencies overwhelmed by the rise of patients seeking treatment for mental health or substance use disorders. In a survey of over 6,000 emergency rooms, 70 percent reported holding patients in psychiatric crisis for days and even up to several weeks (Torrey, Fuller, Geller, Jacobs, and Ragosta, 2012). The security of hospital staff and other patients is a concern for those facilities dealing with historically high numbers of psychiatric patients. As emergency rooms are forced into becoming *de facto* psychiatric units, law enforcement officers generally must spend additional hours assisting hospital security staff manage emergency situations (Biasotti, 2011). Communities are struggling to find ways to balance resources through collaboration and program development. In an evaluation of a MCT program in Cincinnati, police officers reported that 96 percent of persons with mental illness were initially transported to the hospital, both prior to the MCT program and afterwards (Frank, Eck, and Ratansi, 2004).

Per the *Council of State Governments Justice Center*, an example of police-ER cooperation in dealing with the issue is evidenced in Fort Wayne, Indiana (Reuland et al., 2010). In Fort Wayne, three secure rooms of each local hospital have been dedicated to receiving the ambulance and law enforcement officers when an individual in crisis is brought to the emergency room. Patients are treated by a team of specially trained individuals. The patients in the care of officers get priority treatment and police talk directly with the mental health counselors in privacy and security. Once the physician determines the individual's medical condition is stable, the mental health clinicians assess the necessary level of care.

IN MY EXPERIENCE . . .

During an investigation into a homicide, it came to my attention that the suspect might have been in the emergency room of our local hospital. At the hospital I gave the administrator a description of the suspect and a time frame when he may have been treated for knife wounds. The name and address and other identifying information about the person was provided. Can the hospital give police officers the information in this situation under federal mandates? The answer is, yes.

Question for discussion: Is it a violation of privacy to say that a person was in a particular place?

The hospitals employ security staff to handle safety issues which enables officers to return to other duties. Clear policies on holding, restraining, and detaining patients were developed in conjunction with legal counsel to give guidance to the hospital security officers. Although the goal in these hospitals is to err on the side of protecting patients from harming themselves or others, reports the *Justice Center*, their care, dignity, and privacy were considered in developing these guidelines (Reuland et al., 2010).

COLLABORATIONS WITH MENTAL HEALTH PROFESSIONALS

It is difficult for many individuals to receive treatment due to the critical shortage of mental health professionals (NAMI, 2014). The situation is extreme in rural areas and among poverty-stricken populations. Communities are struggling to find new ways to improve their access to mental health services. One evidence-based practice gaining popularity is the cost-effective use of peer support specialists. **PEER SUPPORT SPECIALISTS** are individuals who are trained and credentialed to use their personal experience to help mental health clients navigate the challenges of daily life, link the person to appropriate services and provide emotional support. Peer support specialists have been employed effectively to defuse psychiatric crises, reach those who are hard-to-engage, and minimize the need for high-cost emergency and inpatient care. Wisconsin is among the states that have passed legislation to establish respite centers run by peer specialists (2013 Assembly Bill 455, 2014).

Proactive measures that keep people out of the criminal justice system are a promising approach towards addressing public safety while delivering services to adults with mental health disorders. Two examples of initiatives that partner law enforcement and behavioral health for early diversion are Project EDGE and the Knoxville Early Diversion Program (SAMHSA, 2015a). Project EDGE (Early Diversion, Get Engaged) in Boulder County, Colorado sponsors crisis intervention training for law enforcement and protocols for referring persons who meet the program criteria. Their peer support specialists provide case management, psychiatric or psychosocial rehabilitation, substance use and detoxification treatment. Additional assistance may include benefits enrollment for housing and employment. Mobile emergency response services are available to law enforcement to increase access to services for people when they are in crisis.

SAMHSA (2015a) explains that the Knoxville Early Diversion Program involves a diversion team made up of liaisons and case managers that are available during high-volume times to work side-by-side with law enforcement. The diversion team intervenes and diverts individuals that police encounter, thereby assessing and identifying possible treatment options. Those individuals who need further assistance are assigned to an early diversion case manager to assure that treatment options are identified and treatment is received. Project EDGE and the Knoxville Early Diversion Program are examples of innovative programs that received grant funding from the *Substance Abuse and Mental Health Services Administration* (SAMHSA, 2015a).

Information Sharing

Mental health professionals and social workers must abide by their professional codes of ethics which may not allow for health information to be shared, except under narrowly defined circumstances. The patient-client relationship is built on an establishment of trust (Petrila, 2010). Therefore, providers are often reluctant to share any information with the criminal justice system, particularly if doing so may subject the patient to sanctions or incarceration. Alleviating ethical concerns can be accomplished by obtaining a patient's knowing and voluntary consent to share information. Agencies that develop trusted relationships with criminal justice professionals may feel more comfortable in sharing necessary information that will be used to benefit rather than harm their clients. The ethical sharing of information assumes that the benefits outweigh the risks for the client (Petrila, 2010). Examples of benefits include intervention to avoid incarceration, better treatment for individuals in correctional facilities, and improved continuing care for clients. Criminal justice and health practitioners that are considering an information sharing initiative should also collaborate to determine which long and short term benefits specific to the population should be achieved. Interagency collaborations can be beneficial to the population that comes in frequent contact with the police due to mental disorders and substance abuse.

Duty-to-Warn

The legal duty of a psychiatrist or psychotherapist to warn an identifiable victim of a patient's serious threat of harm was established in the *Tarasoff v. Regents of the University of California* decision of the California Supreme Court ("*Tarasoff*," 1976). The *duty-to-protect* required of clinicians to warn potential victims varies from state to state, and may include a mandate to report to the police. The *Tarasoff* principle is the legal requirement for mental health professionals to warn victims of a risk or threat of violence and to provide criminal victims' warning mandated by statute (Felthous, 2006). The warnings are sometimes issued to the police departments who in turn would contact the victim.

In the wake of recent mass shootings, the duty-to-warn laws are receiving increased attention. The New York Mental Hygiene Law § 9.56, which was enacted in 2013, moved the state requirement from a permissive to a mandatory duty for mental health professionals, specifically giving police the authority to confiscate firearms owned by patients who are likely to be dangerous. California Welfare and Institutions Code § 8105 (c), which became effective in 2014, requires psychotherapists to report the patient's identity to police within 24 hours any time a patient meets the *duty-to-protect* criteria. Its primary purpose is to protect the victims and prevent the patients from possessing guns. Experts in California have suggested that clinicians notify the police and additionally warn the potential victim in order to comply with the law (Weinstock, Darby, Bonnici, Seroussi, and Leong, 2015).

Mental health practices in every state have been affected by legal requirements which govern therapists' duty to protect persons who are threatened by their patients. Some states maintain a *duty-to-warn* while others have a *duty-to-protect* standard. Some state laws require professionals to report danger to either the victim or to the police, while others mandate these reports be made by mental health professionals—refer to the map in Figure CH06-05 to see the variance between state laws (NCSL, 2015). Generally, these laws require clinical psychologists and other professionals to disclose information to relevant authorities if there are reasonable grounds to believe that a person may be in imminent danger of harming himself or others. State legislation is changing rapidly with respect to individuals with mental health problems. Therefore, criminal justice professionals should stay abreast of the current laws to maintain effective collaborations with the agencies and organizations that provide mental health care. These laws can be complex and difficult to understand, and police departments need to develop policies on officers' authority to act when reports are received. Trusting collaborations can be helpful to resolve specific case problems.

5. CH06-05: *Duty-to-Warn.* The *Tarasoff* principle is a legal duty which requires mental health professionals to report to potential victims and to the police, in certain circumstances, when a patient is a threat to himself or others. The *duty-to-warn* laws are receiving increased attention due to mass shootings across the country involving individuals that were known to have severe mental health issues.

In Colorado, House Bill 14-1271 has even broadened a physician's duty-to-warn to include situations where a patient communicates an imminent physical threat toward an institution or structure (NAMI, 2014). In Virginia, the duty-to-warn now includes public Colleges and Universities under HB 1268 (NAMI, 2014). The violence prevention committee of each public institution of higher learning must establish policies and procedures for faculty and staff to report threatening or aberrant behavior that might represent a threat to the community and to notify family members or guardians. Leon Rodriguez, Director of the Office for Civil Rights at the Department of Health and Human Services (Rodriguez, 2013), stated:

> "In light of recent tragic and horrific events in our nation, including the mass shootings in Newtown, CT, and Aurora, CO, I wanted to take this opportunity to ensure that you are aware that the Health Insurance

Portability and Accountability Act (HIPAA) Privacy Rule does not prevent your ability to disclose necessary information about a patient to law enforcement, family members of the patient, or other persons, when you believe the patient presents a serious danger to himself or other people."

COMMUNITY COALITIONS

Community coalitions are members of organizations bound together by common goals. Increasingly these are being used to nurture improvements in community health. The *Substance Abuse and Mental Health Services Administration* defines a **COALITION** as a group of individuals representing diverse organizations, factions, or constituencies who agree to work together to achieve a common goal (SAMHSA, 2015b). Community coalitions differ from other types of collaborations in that they include both professional and grassroots members committed to working together to influence long-term health and welfare practices in the areas in which they live and work. However, it is the problems they address, not geography, that define the scope of these groups. Their ability to leverage existing local resources and bring diverse groups of people together make community coalitions an attractive partnership opportunity for law enforcement. Crisis Stabilization Programs (CSP) and Mobile Crisis Services are examples of community coalitions that provide short-term psychiatric stabilization and 24/7 mobile crisis response.

Non-Traditional Coalitions

The Center for Mental Health Services (CMHS) of the Substance Abuse and Mental Health Services Administration (SAMHSA) within the U.S. Department of Health and Human Services estimates that approximately one third of the 744,000 homeless people in the United States have a serious mental illness. Homeless individuals with mental illness often have co-occurring disorders. Community coalitions that provide services in non-traditional settings such as soup kitchens, the streets, public parks and drop-in locations provide much-needed opportunities to build rapport with the homeless population. Without this relationship, it is unlikely that the person will agree to accept further services. Police collaborations with these community coalitions may be mutually beneficial.

The people with mental disorders that police encounter are frequently homeless. One study found that 74 percent of offenders that the police believed had a mental disorder were also homeless (Cordner, 2006). In another study, approximately two-thirds of psychiatric emergency patients evaluated by a police-mental health outreach team in Los Angeles were known to be serious substance abusers (Cordner, 2006). There is a wide range of services and support needed for effective outcomes in mental health, substance abuse, reduced victimization, and improved quality of life for these individuals. Law enforcement involvement in coalition efforts for alcohol and drug abuse interventions is a critical aspect of collaborative policing.

6. CH06-06: *Family members*. Among the most important collaboration is that which occurs between justice related responses and the families of individuals with severe mental disorders. Family members are often left out of the decision making care of their loved ones, yet they are the most likely to suffer the consequences when a crisis develops. Seek their input whenever possible, as families have often heard the cry for help.

COLLABORATING WITH FAMILIES

Medical confidentiality laws are intended to safeguard trust within the therapeutic relationship, yet families often need information to support the person's recovery and can provide information to facilitate care and manage crisis. Evidence indicates that when family members are involved in the care of individuals that have severe mental disorders, relapse rates can be cut in half, and treatment adherence, clinical symptoms, and consumer functioning also improve (Cohen et al., 2013). Still, overzealous application of health information privacy standards has resulted in frustration among families seeking help for their loved ones. Jurisdictions are attempting to address legal misunderstandings through legislation which specifically allows family members to be involved in the medical care of their loved ones. The Mental Health Reform Act of 2016 (S. 2680) is one of the most recent proposed acts of legislation at the federal level that is aimed at clarifying the circumstances in which HIPAA permits health professionals to communicate information to family members or other caregivers. The act also supports training health care providers about the circumstances in which information can be shared with caregivers.

The proliferation of data privacy laws across the United States continues to accelerate. Government and private entities collect and use information in its work on behalf of the public. Data privacy laws govern how information is stored, the conditions under which it may be released, and the persons who have access to it. By passing a law, legislatures can make data inaccessible. There are also federal laws that stipulate some data as inaccessible. Data privacy laws and their interpretation makes advocacy especially difficult (NAMI, 2010). To address the issue of information sharing without the written consent of the patient, NAMI Minnesota successfully advocated for a change in its data privacy laws to allow caregivers access to basic mental health information that will help them care for a person living with a mental illness. Diagnosis, admission to or discharge from treatment, and medication information (including dosage, side effects, consequences of not taking medications, etc.) can be provided to caretakers (NAMI, 2010).

SUMMARY

As our community needs have grown, so has the philosophy of community responsiveness towards individuals who have mental disorders. Forming agency partnerships shares the valuable resources and expertise of the many stakeholders that are concerned with the criminalization of mental illness. Recognition that the criminal justice system is overburdened with crisis response and lacking in alternative resources has provided a catalyst for multi-agency collaborations and program initiatives. Collaborations involve hospital emergency rooms, mental health professionals, community coalitions, and families, to name a few.

Three categories of multi-agency response have emerged which actively examine ways to share the responsibility and care of individuals with the mental health community. The first, specialized policing response programs, looks to improve policing options which prioritize treatment over incarceration. Programs based on the Memphis Model seek to educate police officers and the public to the needs of individuals with symptoms of mental illness and to address the police officers' level of awareness about community mental health resources. The second category are made up of the Mobil Mental Health Crisis Team responders. The unique aspect of this category is that the police are not the primary response agency involving individuals with mental illness. Mental health professionals are dispatched to respond to psychiatric emergencies which do not present a public safety risk with people that are not suspected of criminal conduct. The third category of multi-agency response is called Health Based After-Care. In this approach, the long-term mental health issues of individuals who had come to the attention of the police are given intensive supervision and follow-up by mental health professionals.

CHAPTER QUESTIONS FOR REVIEW

1. What is the Memphis model of CIT response?
2. What are some perceived benefits to a co-response collaborative program?
3. Explain the phrase "Duty-to-Warn."
4. Are there any benefits to a program involving post-crisis assistance? Who is responsible for these program developments?
5. Give examples of community coalitions.

REFERENCES

1-800-LifeNet. (2016). *Referral guide for providers and professionals: Mobile Crisis Teams* Retrieved from http://www.mhaofnyc.org/wp-content/uploads/2016/07/LifeNet-Provider-and-Professional-Referral-Guide-Mobile-Crisis-Teams-7-1-16.pdf

2013 Assembly Bill 455 (2014). An Act to create 46.48 (32) of the statutes relating to grants to counties to contract for peer-run respite centers. Retrieved from http://docs.legis.wisconsin.gov/2013/related/proposals/ab455.pdf

Biasotti, M. (2011). *The Impact of Mental Illness on Law Enforcement Resources.* Retrieved from http://www.prweb.com/releases/2011/12/prweb9053827.htm

Blevins, K. R., Lord, V., and Bjerregaard, B. (2014). Evaluating Crisis Intervention Teams: possible impediments and recommendations. *Policing: An International Journal of Police Strategies and Management, 37*(3), 484–500.

Bonkiwicz, L., Green, A. M., Moyer, K., and Wright, J. (2014). Left alone when the cops go home: evaluating a post-mental health crisis assistance program.

Policing: An International Journal of Police Strategies and Management, 37(4), 762–778.

BHN. (n.d.). BHN crisis services. Retrieved June 4, 2016, from http://bhninc.org/content/emergency-services

Borum, R. (2000). Improving High-Risk Encounters between People with Mental Illness and the Police. *The Journal of the American Academy of Psychiatry and the Law, 28*(3), 332–337.

Chamrd, S. (2006). *Partnering with Businesses to Address Public Safety Problems.* Washington, D.C.: Office of Community Oriented Policing Services.

CIT. (2016). CIT International. Retrieved June 2, 2016, from http://citinternational.org

Cohen, A. N., Drapalski, A. L., Glynn, S. M., Medoff, D., Fang, L. J., and Dixon, L. B. (2013). Preferences for family involvement in care among consumers with serious mental illness. *Psychiatric Services, 64*(3), 257–263.

Cordner, G. (2006). *People with mental illness.* Retrieved from http://www.popcenter.org/problems/pdfs/MentalIllness.pdf

Cronin, G. (2015). Forensic psychiatry in law enforcement. In R. L. Sadoff (Ed.), *The Evolution of Forensic Psychiatry: History, Current Developments, Future Directions* (pp. 282–293). New York, NY: Oxford University Press.

Felthous, A. R. (2006). Warning a Potential Victim of a Person's Dangerousness: Clinician's Duty or Victim's Right? *Journal of the American Academy of Psychiatry and the Law Online, 34*(3), 338–348.

Frank, J., Eck, J., and Ratansi, S. (2004). Mobile crisis team/police collaboration evaluation. Cincinnati, OH: University of Cincinnati.

Gibb, B. (2014). Mental Health First Aid for Public Safety—Three Case Studies. *The Police Chief, 81*(November), 56–59.

Houston Police. (2011). Chronic Consumer Stabilization Initiative. Retrieved from http://www.popcenter.org/library/awards/goldstein/2010/10–13(F).pdf

IACP. (2010). Building safer communities: Improving police response to persons with mental illness. Alexandria, VA: International Association of Chiefs of Police.

Kerr, A., Morabito, M., and Watson, A. (2010). Police Encounters, Mental Illness and Injury: An Exploratory Investigation. *Journal of Police Crisis Negotiation, 1*(10), 116–132.

Lamb, H., Weinberger, L., and DeCuir, W. (2004). Mentally ill persons in the criminal justice system: Some perspectives. *Psychiatric Quarterly, 75*(2), 107–126.

Lord, V. B., Bjerregaard, B., Blevins, K. R., and Whisman, H. (2011). Factors influencing the responses of crisis intervention team-certified law enforcement officers. *Police Quarterly, 14*(4), 388–406.

MacLeod, A., Pate, L., and Dempsey, C. (Presenters). (2012). Innovative law enforcement strategies for interacting with people with mental illnesses that frequently require emergency and crisis services. [webinar] Retrieved from https://csgjusticecenter.org/wp-content/uploads/2013/03/7_26_12_LE_Webinar.pdf

Matz,. K. (2014). *A Note on HIPAA and 42 CFR Part 2: Dispelling the Myths about Justice-Health Information Sharing* (Vol. 2015): American Probation and Parole Association.

McCampbell, M. (2010). The collaboration toolkit for community organizations: Effective strategies to partner with law enforcement. Washington, D.C.: COPS.

Mental Health Weekly. (2015). Bipartisan bill reauthorizes mental health, criminal justice collaboration law. Retrieved December 5, 2015, from Wiley Periodicals, Inc wileyonlinelibrary.com.

Morabito, M., Kerr, A., Watson, A., Ottati, V., and Angell, B. (2012). Crisis intervention teams and people with mental illness: Exploring the factors that influence the use of force. *Crime and delinquency, 58*(1), 57–77.

Morabito, M. S., Watson, A., and Draine, J. (2013). Police officer acceptance of new innovation: the case of crisis intervention teams. *Policing: An International Journal of Police Strategies and Management, 36*(2), 421–436.

Morrissey, J., Meyer, P., and Cuddeback, G. (2007). Extending assertive community treatment to criminal justice settings: Origins, current evidence, and future directions. *Community mental health journal, 43*(5), 527–544.

NAMI. (2010). Mental Health Crisis Planning. Retrieved from http://www.namihelps.org/Crisis–Booklet–Adults.pdf

NAMI. (2014). *State Mental Health Legislation 2014: Trends, Themes and Effective Practices.* Arlington, VA: National Alliance on Mental Illness.

NCSL (2015). Mental Health Professionals' duty to Warn. Retrieved from http://www.ncsl.org/research/health/mental-health-professionals-duty-to-warn.aspx

Petrila, J. (2007). *Dispelling the myths about information sharing between the mental health and criminal justice systems.* Delmar, NY: Policy Research Associates and CMHS National GAINS Center.

Petrila, J., and Fader-Towe, H. (2010). *Working with HIPPA and other privacy laws.* Retrieved from https://www.bja.gov/Publications/CSG_CJMH_Info_Sharing.pdf

Reaves, B. (2015). *Local Police Departments, 2013: Personnel, Policies, and Practices.* (NCJ 248677). Washington, D.C.: Bureau of Justice Statistics.

Ratansi, S. (2004). *Specialized response programs: Police handling of encounters involving persons with mental disorders.* (Electronic Dissertation). Retrieved from https://etd.ohiolink.edu/

Reuland, M., Draper, L., and Norton, B. (2010). Improving Responses to People with Mental Illness: Tailoring Law Enforcement Initiative to Individual Jurisdictions. New York, NY: Council of State Governments Justice Center.

Reuland, M., Draper, L., and Norton, B. (2012). Statewide law enforcement/mental health efforts: Strategies to support and sustain local initiatives. New York, NY: Council of State Governments Justice Center.

Reuland, M., and Schwarzfeld, M. (2008). Improving responses to people with mental illnesses: Strategies for effective law enforcement training. New York, NY: Council of State Governments Justice Center.

Rodriguez, L. (2013). Message to Our Nation's Health Care Providers from the U.S. Department of Health and Human Services. Retrieved from: http://news.unchealthcare.org/som-vital-signs/2013/Jan17/hipaa

SAMHSA. (2015a). Law enforcement and behavioral health partnerships for early diversion. Retrieved from http://www.samhsa.gov/gains-center/grants-grantees/early-diversion

SAMSA. (2015b). Prevention of Substance Abuse and Mental Illness. Retrieved from http://www.samhsa.gov/prevention

Scott, R. (2000). Evaluation of a Mobile Crisis Program: Effectiveness, efficiency, and consumer satisfaction. *Psychiatric Services, 51*(9).

Steadman, H. J., Deane, M. W., Borum, R., and Morrissey, J. P. (2000). Comparing outcomes of major models of police responses to mental health emergencies. *Psychiatric Services, 51*(5), 645–649.

Tarasff v. Regents of the University of California (1976).

Torrey, E., Fuller, D., Geller, J., Jacobs, C., and Ragosta, K. (2012). *No room at the inn: Trends and consequences of closing public psychiatric hospitals*. Retrieved from http://tacreports.org/storage/documents/no_room_at_the_inn–2012.pdf

U.S. Department of Health and Human Services. (2014). HIPAA Privacy rule and sharing information related to mental health. Retrieved from http://www.hhs.gov/ocr/privacy/hipaa/understanding/special/mhguidance.html

Watson, A. C., Morabito, M. S., Draine, J., and Ottati, V. (2008). Improving police response to persons with mental illness: A Multi-level conceptualization of CIT. *International Journal of Law and Psychiatry, 31*(4), 359–368.

Weinsock, R., Darby, W. C., Bonnici, D. M., Seroussi, A., and Leong, G. B. (2015). The Ever-Evolving Duty to Protect in California. *Journal of the American Academy of Psychiatry and the Law Online, 43*(2), 262. Retrieved from http://www.jaapl.org/content/43/2/262.1.short

Vecchi, G., Hasselt, V. V., and Romano, S. (2005). Crisis (Hostage) Negotiation: Current strategies and issues in high risk conflict resolution. Aggression and Violent Behavior, 10, 533–551.

CHAPTER 7

Civil Commitment

INTRODUCTION

Changing times affect the enforcement of laws and court adjudication. Think back to the history of mental illnesses and the treatments which influenced how society acted towards individuals with mental disorders. Remember that in the recent past, institutionalism was the primary method of handling individuals with mental disorders. Individuals with minor disorders lived under the care of their families. In situations where families were not able to provide care, people were institutionalized in state or private facilities. Committing an individual to an institution was done by court order, typically at the request of a family member or doctor. Civil commitment is still achieved by court order, but the laws and processes have changed significantly. It is widely acknowledged that the majority of individuals with mental disorders are not dangerous or in need of judicial or court intervention.

Concern over the individual rights and the coercive nature of involuntary commitment is a primary complaint of those who oppose the practice. Advocates point to the inhumanity of allowing individuals who have severe mental illnesses to deteriorate to the point of near death before intervention is available. Court action varies in different states, as communities have differing ideas on justice itself. Despite the lack of agreement, there does exist a similar court process across the United States. The minimum acceptable standards are continually argued and agreed upon in order to establish the rules that make up procedural and substantive law. This chapter will focus on practices and court remedies which exist under civil commitment law.

Key Terms

ASSISTED OUTPATIENT TREATMENT (AOT)

BURDEN OF PROOF

CIVIL COMMITMENT

CRIMINAL COMMITMENT

INPATIENT CIVIL COMMITMENT

PSYCHIATRIC HOLD

Chapter Objectives

After completing this chapter, you should be able to:

- Describe in detail the four categories of involuntary civil commitment
- Define the burden of proof needed for court action in civil commitment
- State the purpose of Assisted Outpatient Treatment (AOT)
- Compare and contrast current controversies in civil commitment

CIVIL COMMITMENT STATUTES

CIVIL COMMITMENT is court-ordered involuntary treatment during evaluation or confinement, either on an inpatient or outpatient basis. In order to be committed, all states require that the respondent have a mental illness and that the person must be a danger to themselves or others as a result of that mental illness. Civil commitment laws establish the criteria for determining when involuntary treatment is appropriate for individuals with severe mental illness who cannot or will not seek care voluntarily. These laws also stipulate the process and procedures that must be followed for an involuntary commitment to occur. The United States Constitution guarantees that no person will be deprived of liberty without due process of law. Civil commitment serves two goals: (1) the rehabilitation or care of people who are mentally ill and (2) the protection of society from the potential harms the person may cause (Levy and Rubenstein, 1996).

Individuals with severe mental disorders pose a challenge to the application of due process. Asserting the doctrine of *parens patriae,* which grants the power and authority to the state to protect persons who are legally unable to act on their own behalf, is sometimes required to ensure their safety (Schug and Fradella,

2015). The state's intrusion is limited to reasonable and necessary treatment. States and the federal government attempt to apply *parens patriae* power with due process in addressing the rights of individuals with mental illness. Another justification for the state's commitment power is found under its police power. Under the police power, individuals may be committed if they are dangerous to others.

While *parens patriae* was the primary focus in early commitment codes, "dangerousness" must be established and police power asserted for modern commitment to occur (Schug and Fradella, 2015). Dangerousness itself has become a controversial standard on which to base medical intervention and treatment. Procedural safeguards, including court oversight for every civil commitment petition, attempt to balance the right of the state with the use of its police power to protect society and an individual's right to liberty. The Supreme Court is the arbitrator between these contradictory goals.

Refusing care or refusing to acknowledge one's illness may at one time have been attributed to a person being "in denial" or to a conscious decision on the part of the patient. It is now recognized as a biological condition of the illness itself. The significant role this condition, which is termed anosognosia, plays in the treatment of severe mental illness has only recently become widely recognized. This is an important recognition since lack of insight is one of the main reasons why many individuals fail to take their medication and repeatedly become caught up in a cycle of hospitalization, incarceration, and homelessness (Jaffe, 2014).

MODERN CIVIL COMMITMENT

Four general categories of civil commitment exist today. Each category allows for different options of treatment for an individual with severe mental illness: Psychiatric Hold, Inpatient Civil Commitment, Outpatient Civil Commitment, and Criminal Commitment. Placing the approaches into these broad categories can help to eliminate some confusion about crisis intervention and mental health treatment options, since states use different names to describe each form. All states, as well as Washington D.C. and Puerto Rico, have at least three of the four categories, and most states have laws that allow for all four. Since the program names vary from state to state, one should look at the description in each category in addition to the approach that is associated with it. You should be able to distinguish among your state options by looking at the approach and the law that permits mental health intervention. A common thread to each is that they are involuntary treatments ordered by court action.

There is a growing movement to bring back the asylum as the best option to care for severe and treatment-resistant psychotic disorders, and those who are too unstable or unsafe for community based treatment (Sisti, Segal, and Emanuel, 2015). The promise of community care for individuals with the most severe of mental illness is unfilled. Regardless, involuntary commitment is controversial. It occurs when someone calls authorities to override the constitutional liberty interests of an individual by detaining him or her against their will for evaluation and/or treatment. This can occur when a mental health provider determines that a person is unable to care for themselves due to illness or in cases where a treatment plan is not followed. Civil commitment appears to be making a comeback under various law reforms in many states, evidenced by the legislative enactment of the "gravely disabled" standard, outpatient commitment statutes, and the increased criminal incarceration of persons with mental illness. There is growing recognition that the inability to understand that treatment is needed can be a condition of severe mental illness. Remember that involuntary commitment is appropriate only to help severely disordered individuals who are unable to care for themselves, seek treatment, or live safely in the community. Experiencing mental illness is not uncommon. The vast majority of individuals with mental disorders live and work successfully without the types of intervention presented in this chapter.

PSYCHIATRIC HOLD

The first category of civil commitment is a **PSYCHIATRIC HOLD** or an "emergency hospitalization for evaluation," which may also be called "pick-up" or referred to by the color of the form required, such as "pink slip". The legal provision may be a stand-alone law in your state, or it may be the first part of a law that defines the process for both psychiatric hold and inpatient treatment. All states have a provision for psychiatric hold, but how often it is used depends on many factors. A common problem is the difficulty in finding a mental health professional to make an assessment and finding a bed that is available for the individual to use if an evaluation becomes necessary. Typically, the law only allows for a psychiatric hold of around seventy-two hours so that a short assessment can be conducted at an emergency facility. If no bed is available for needed inpatient care, the person may be released after the initial seventy-two hours without having received treatment.

The Blue Form in Maine

The process for an involuntary psychiatric hold is typically initiated by a police officer, but family members, mental health professionals and others who are allowed by law can start this process of medical intervention for someone in crisis, though this varies by state. The stated legal procedure must be followed exactly for the individual to be evaluated, and this is, again, different from state to state.

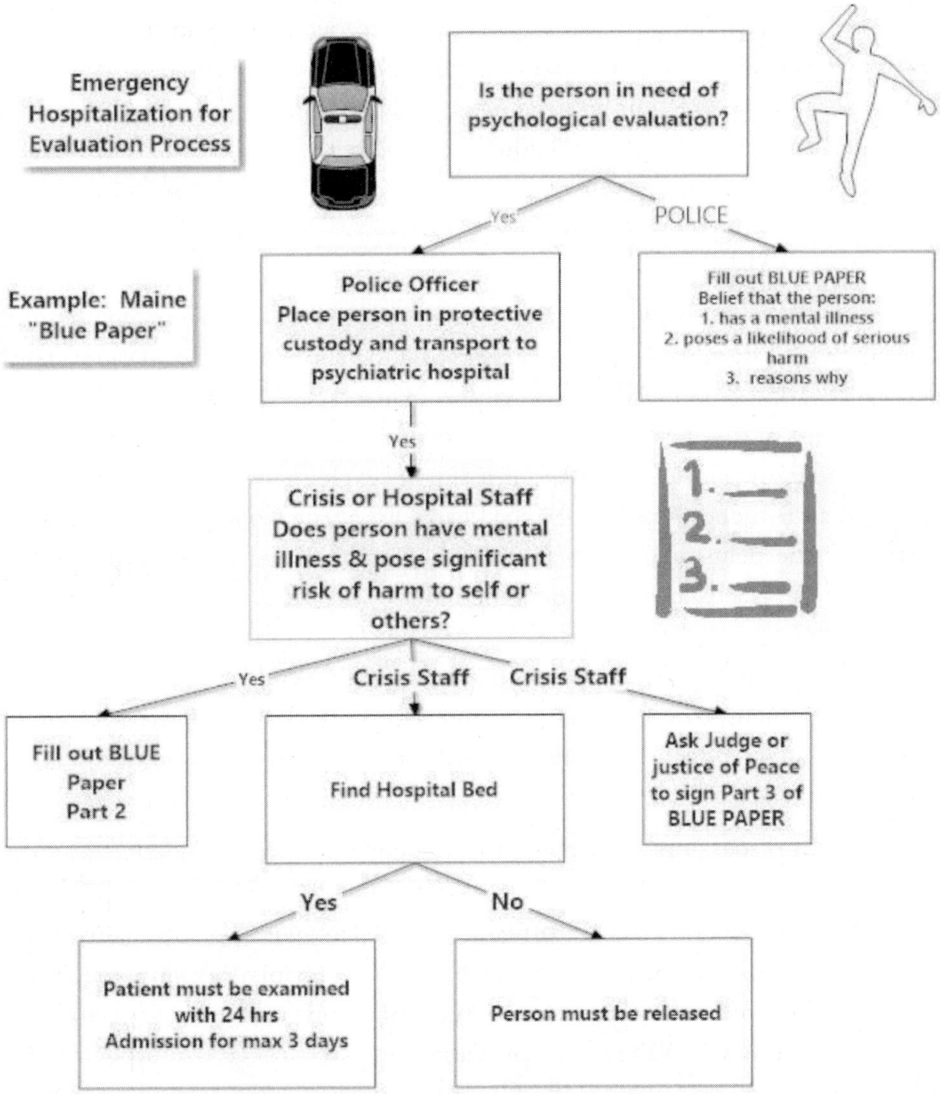

1. CH07-01: The "psychiatric hold process" is illustrated here in the Maine example. It is commonly referred to as the "Blue Paper"—reflecting the color of the form needed for the process. The statute in Maine is entitled the *Emergency Hospitalization for Evaluation.*

An example of "emergency hospitalization for evaluation" is provided in figure CH07-01, which illustrates how it is done per Title 34B, C. 3 § 3863 of Maine's Revised Statutes. In Maine, the psychiatric hold is referred to as "blue paper" because the process involves a three-step blue form. The applicant (typically the law enforcement officer) who takes a person into protective custody under this statute fills out part one and takes the individual in crisis to the hospital or crisis center. The hospital staff fill out part two and ask a judge to certify (by signing part three of the blue form) that the proper procedure was followed. If the hospital determines that the evaluation is needed, they find a bed for the person in a psychiatric facility person in a psychiatric facility. The patient must be examined within twenty-four hours and may only be held on a blue paper for three days. After the three days, the individual must be released, signed into the facility voluntarily, or a court order must be obtained for continued treatment.

IMAGINE THAT . . .

Virginia State Senator, Creigh Deeds can be seen in countless newspaper stories, on television, and on the internet speaking about his son and the system that failed him. Gus Deeds is the young man responsible for the scars the senator bears across his face. They are a constant reminder of the son he lost to mental illness and a state without a single psychiatric bed. Gus, a talented musician and student who was on the dean's list at the College of William and Mary, became delusional and was diagnosed as bipolar disorder. One day in 2013, Creigh Deeds became concerned that Gus might kill himself, so he obtained a court order for his son's psychiatric evaluation and temporary emergency commitment. There was no bed available and Gus was sent home without treatment. The following morning, Gus attacked his father, stabbing him in and around his face ten times. Gus committed suicide as his father was being taken to a hospital.

Question for discussion: How could this tragedy have been avoided?

What gives law enforcement officers the right to take a person against his or her will to a medical examination or psychiatric hospital? Using the Maine example, police officers are given the statutory power to take a person into protective custody when they have probable cause to believe that a person may be mentally ill through Title 34B, C. 3(4)(1) § 3862. This section specifically explains the circumstances for the custody as well as what an officer must do. It also states the situations when the person must be released from protective custody. This is not an arrest; this is a statutory power for detainment.

All states that allow law enforcement officers to take an individual into custody for psychiatric hold or commitment are given this authority by law and under specific circumstances. It is this power that also creates a responsibility for law enforcement. When called to an emergency involving an individual in mental health crisis, law enforcement officers are tasked with transporting individuals to hospitals and treatment centers for care and mental health services. Although the transportation to emergency civil commitment is typically left to law enforcement, there is widespread agreement that this is not an ideal strategy. A few states have pilot programs underway that involve protected transport using non-law enforcement personnel in unmarked vehicles. One of the obstacles to this approach is the failure of Medicaid to reimburse non-law enforcement modes of transportation for individuals with mental illness (NAMI, 2014).

2. CH07-02: Law enforcement officers are given the power to detain individuals for transportation by specific legal authority. Even though the individual is not free to go, this is a detainment. It is not an arrest since it is authorized by law. Photo copyright Nosnibor137/Bigstock.com

INPATIENT CIVIL COMMITMENT

The second category of civil commitment is an "inpatient" or "involuntary inpatient" placement. Labeled differently in different states, **INPATIENT CIVIL COMMITMENT** is a process whereby the judge orders a person with symptoms of mental illness to be held in a hospital for treatment beyond the emergency detention period. The process of inpatient civil commitment is necessarily lengthy or complex since there must be numerous legal safeguards to protect the rights of the individual. The patient must meet all the state's legal criteria in order that he or she be involuntarily committed to hospital care. This form of civil commitment exists in all states, but the requirements that must be met for inpatient commitment to occur vary from state to state. It is essential to know the standards for civil commitment in your own state.

The Baker Act in Florida

The process for civil commitment in Florida is referred to as the *Baker Act,* named after Maxine Baker, a former State representative from Miami who sponsored the Act while serving as chairperson of the House Committee on Mental Health. Since the *Baker Act* became effective in 1972, several legislative amendments have been enacted to protect persons' civil and due process rights.

Involuntary Inpatient Placement - Florida CH 65E-5.290, F.A.C.

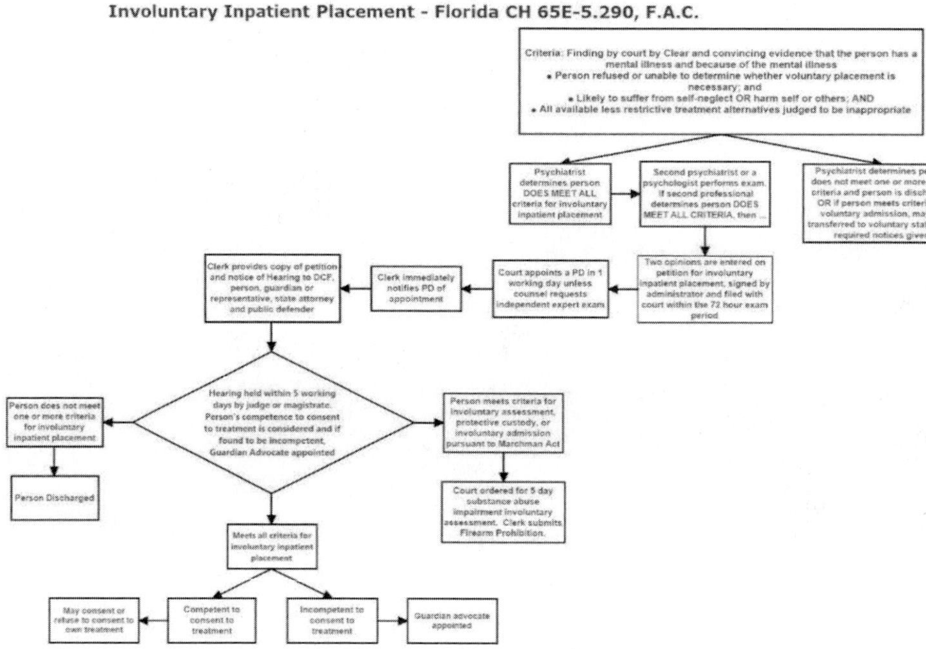

3. CH07-03: An inpatient civil commitment is very complex, as illustrated here. Among the checks and balances are requirements for oversight from a judge and two psychiatrists who agree that all criteria have been met for an involuntary inpatient placement. This example represents the major steps in the process that required under the *Baker Act* in the state of Florida. Source: Mental Health Program Office and Department of Mental Health Law and Policy (2014).

The most recent major revision was when Involuntary Outpatient Placement (AOT) was added by the Legislature effective January 2005. Refer to figure CH07-

03 for a flow chart which illustrates the complexity of involuntary inpatient placement and the numerous procedural safeguards that are in place (Mental Health Program Office and Department of Mental Health Law and Policy, 2014).

The Law in Arizona

In Arizona, the law and procedure governing "inpatient civil commitment" and "outpatient assisted treatment" are the same and are simply called *Court Ordered Mental Health Treatment.* This approach makes a distinction on inpatient versus outpatient civil commitment based on the needs of the individual in need of treatment. The legal emphasis of the Arizona legislation is referred to as the need-for-treatment standard. The need-for-treatment standard recognizes that the deterioration of general health, psychiatric damage and loss of ability to function independently when severe mental illness goes untreated are unacceptable harms per se. *Court ordered mental health treatment* is for a person who meets the established criteria and is unwilling or unable to accept voluntary treatment. The court order for inpatient treatment is limited to ninety, 180, or 365 days depending on the criteria that is determined by the court. The court order may include inpatient treatment, outpatient treatment, or a combination of both, but the treatments cumulatively cannot exceed 365 days. According to research from the Treatment Advocacy Center, the need-for-treatment law based on the Arizona standard represents a position that best addresses the needs of a person whose health and severe suffering place him or her at risk (Stettin, Geller, Ragosta, Cohen, and Ghowrwal, 2014).

ASSISTED OUTPATIENT TREATMENT (AOT)

ASSISTED OUTPATIENT TREATMENT (AOT) also called "involuntary outpatient treatment," "outpatient commitment" or "mandated outpatient treatment," is a court-ordered, community-based treatment for people with untreated severe mental illness, such as bipolar disorder or schizophrenia, who meet strict legal criteria. AOT is a form of civil commitment because it allows individuals to be ordered into treatment, which may consist of as little as prescribing medication. There is a loss of liberty in AOT even though it does not include physically being held somewhere, like a hospital—it does, however, include the mandate to physically adhere to a court-ordered treatment plan. Typically, the individuals in an AOT plan are too ill to recognize they need medical care and have a history of medication and treatment noncompliance. The Treatment Advocacy Center reports that AOT laws have been passed in forty-five states. The states that do not have assisted outpatient treatment statutes are Connecticut, Maryland, Massachusetts, New Mexico and Tennessee (Stettin et al., 2014).

Assisted outpatient treatment is the third of the four types of modern civil commitment. The goal of AOT is to provide treatment to individuals with severe mental illnesses before they require psychiatric hospitalization. Proponents of AOT laws believe they reduce psychiatric hospital admissions, homelessness, and violence and improve treatment compliance. Those who are opposed feel that such laws remove an individual's civil right to choose where and how to receive treatment.

Someone from a legally defined group of individuals petitions the court, and only a judge can mandate an AOT program for an individual's treatment and medication. The petition must give the reasons why the petitioner believes the individual meets the criteria and the petition must be accompanied by an affidavit from a physician who has examined or tried to examine the person. Once the court receives the petition and the physician's affidavit, it will schedule a hearing and give notice to the appropriate parties. The patient is provided with free legal representation and extensive due process protections throughout the assisted outpatient treatment process. In the hearing, the court hears testimony and takes evidence from all the parties, including a doctor who has examined the patient.

If the court finds that the individual meets all the criteria for placement in an assisted outpatient treatment, it will have a treatment plan developed and order the patient to comply with it. Compliance with the court's order is monitored through case managers. If an individual does not meet the terms of his or her treatment plan, interventions are triggered which can ultimately result in the individual's re-hospitalization for seventy-two hours for treatment and an evaluation to determine if he or she meets the inpatient commitment criteria. Initial AOT orders are for a minimum of one year and each renewal can be for up to two years.

Kendra's Law in New York

Kendra Webdale, a woman who died in January 1999 after being pushed in front a New York City subway train by a man with a history of mental illness and hospitalizations, became the namesake of *Kendra's Law*. The law became effective in November of 1999 and was renewed in June of 2005. In comparison with *Laura's Law*, this assisted outpatient treatment law required that each county in New York State and New York City establish a local AOT program to implement the statute's requirements. *Kendra's Law* is somewhat unique in that it allows family members and other interested professionals to act as petitioners to the court for a person in need of treatment (New York State Office of Mental Health, 2006). Refer to figure CH07-04 for an illustration of those relationships.

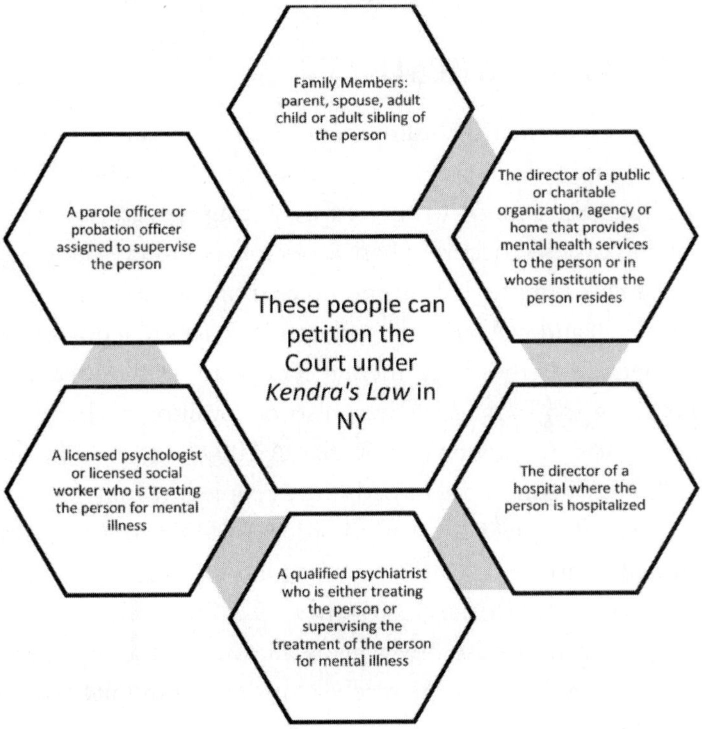

4. CH07-04: State statutes vary on the individuals who may be allowed to file petitions for civil commitment. *Kendra's Law* in New York is particularly inclusive since it allows family members and others that have knowledge of the individual's level of functioning and need of treatment to file.

Laura's Law in California

Laura's Law was passed in California in 2002. It was named after Laura Wilcox, a nineteen-year-old who was killed in 2001 while working in a mental health facility. This AOT program requires that participants be eighteen-years-old, suffering from a mental illness, and unlikely to survive safely in the community without supervision, based on a clinical evaluation. California Code requires that individuals also have a history of repeated hospitalization or incarceration related to their mental illness or a history of violence to self or others along with a history of noncompliance which includes two hospitalizations in the previous thirty-six months or an act/threat/attempt of violence to self/others in the forty-eight months immediately preceding petition filing. *Laura's Law* is available to every one of California's fifty-eight counties, but must be adopted by a county to be implemented. As of 2014, *Laura's Law* had only been implemented in the city of San Francisco in addition to the counties of Los Angeles, Nevada, Orange, Placer, and Yolo (NAMI, 2014; Treatment Advocacy Center, 2014).

CRIMINAL COMMITMENT

The fourth type of modern civil commitment is criminal commitment. Individuals under criminal commitment come to the attention of the court due to criminal wrong-doing, but are found to be experiencing severe mental disorders. **CRIMINAL COMMITMENT** occurs when a person is either found not guilty of criminal responsibility but mentally ill and in need of care and treatment, or found guilty and mentally ill and will receive psychiatric services in a prison. A significant number of individuals with severe mental illness are committed to psychiatric services in this category. Individuals may also be awaiting trial and are receiving treatment to become competent to stand trial. A 2009 *Task Force Report* noted that about one third of civil commitment beds are occupied by individuals confined in forensic psychiatric hospitals due to a court-ordered pretrial evaluation or following criminal court adjudication as not guilty by reason of insanity (Hoge, Buchanan, Kovasznay, and Roskes, 2009). In *United States v. Salerno*, the Court held that pretrial detention of accused persons is allowed in the event that it can be shown that they pose a danger to themselves or the community (*Salerno*, 1987).

An alarming number of individuals with severe mental illnesses are also represented in the general corrections population after being found guilty of criminal conduct regardless of their mental disorder. These general population inmates with mental illness represent another large population that must be considered alongside the corrections-diverted and pre-sentenced individuals referred to in the preceding paragraph. More than one half of all corrections inmates are believed to experience mental illness. Approximately six in ten inmates have a substance use disorder and more than a one third meet criteria for having both mental illness and a substance use problem (James and Glaze, 2006). The men and women who are adjudicated guilty of a crime and also present with issues of mental illness are not included in the category of civil commitment. The corrections population will be discussed in a later chapter.

Following the repeal of indeterminate sentencing laws in 1990, state and federal governments have passed civil commitment laws for the confinement of sexually violent predators (Miller, 2010). Washington was among the first states to pass a bill addressing sex offenses. The bill included sex offender registry and community notification programs in addition to the civil commitment law for sexually violent predators. As with all civil commitment statutes, the specific criteria vary from state to state. Generally, sexual predator statutes refer to sexual offenders as having a mental illness and being unable to control the urges to sexually offend.

Sexually Violent Persons in Illinois

To prevent a convicted sex offender from being released from prison under the *Sexually Violent Persons Commitment Act*, the State of Illinois must file a petition no more than ninety days before an inmate is to be released from a Department of Corrections correctional facility and no more than thirty days after release into parole, per the Illinois Act, codified at 725 ILCS 207. To be eligible for civil confinement, the person must have been convicted or been found delinquent for a sexually violent offense or found not guilty by reason of insanity. The individual must have a mental disorder and be considered dangerous to others because the mental disorder creates a substantial probability that he or she will engage in acts of sexual violence in the future.

The Illinois Act requires that the individual be evaluated by a psychologist and afforded a probable cause hearing and subsequent trial to determine if he or she is sexually violent. During trial, the individual is given most of the rights and protections as one would have during a criminal proceeding. The standard of proof is a finding that the individual is a sexually violent person beyond a reasonable doubt. If found sexually violent, civil commitment to a secure institution or conditional release will occur. Treatment and services are mandated and must be offered to the offender.

The Federal Adam Walsh Act

The *Adam Walsh Child Protection and Safety Act of 2006* established the federal law for civil commitment of dangerous sex offenders under TITLE III Sec. 301. The language of the Act requires that dangerous sex offenders be held in secure civil confinement and receive treatment. The Adam Walsh Child Protection and Safety Act of 2006 authorized the federal government to institute a civil commitment program for federal sex offenders ("Jimmy Ryce State civil commitment programs for sexually dangerous persons," 2006). The Act also authorizes the Attorney General to make grants to jurisdictions for the purpose of establishing, enhancing, or operating effective civil commitment programs for sexually dangerous persons. Twenty states (Arizona, California, Florida, Illinois, Iowa, Kansas, Massachusetts, Minnesota, Missouri, Nebraska, New Hampshire, New Jersey, New York, North

Dakota, Pennsylvania, South Carolina, Texas, Virginia, Washington, and Wisconsin) and the District of Columbia have enacted laws permitting the civil commitment of sexual offenders (ATSA, 2010). The statute defines sexually dangerous as: a person suffering from a serious mental illness, abnormality, or disorder, as a result of which the individual would have serious difficulty in refraining from sexually violent conduct or child molestation.

IN MY EXPERIENCE . . .

A pedophile is an adult who is sexually attracted to children. The dangerousness is that the person knows that it is undesirable and even criminal to have sexual relations with a child, but personally believes that it is not harmful or wrong. The urges are uncontrollable in a sexually dangerous person. I have investigated many sexual child abuse cases during which the offender explained to me that he felt love for the child(ren) and took care of them in sharing that love. In one case, I identified over 100 child victims of one man. There were likely more. He was sexually indiscriminate, meaning he had no sexual preference by age or gender. He actively sought out any child for sex, including his own. During a warranted search of the room in which he lived, sexually explicit photos of children were found, along with things he used to lure children into his room. He was found guilty of numerous counts of child abuse and was committed to a psychiatric hospital until cured.

Question for discussion: Does society have the right to protect children at the expense of this man's liberty? What do you think?

To illustrate the different requirements in civil commitment, it should be noted that the federal standard for a finding of "sexually dangerous" is less rigorous than that of the state of Illinois. The standard of proof is that the court finds by clear and convincing evidence that the person is a sexually dangerous person. The statute provides that when he is no longer sexually dangerous to others he may be released under a prescribed regimen of medical, psychiatric or psychological treatment. The *Adam Walsh Act* also established a sex offender registry and notification (SORNA). Historically, states have been slow in implementing these provisions. The National Conference of State Legislatures reports that only seventeen states, three territories and sixty-three tribes had substantially implemented SORNA as of April 2014 (NCSL, 2014).

CIVIL COMMITMENT STANDARDS

As you have noticed, it is common to have state variation on the process of civil commitment and the titles of these laws. In *Jones v. United States*, the Court held that a person found not guilty by reason of insanity may be committed after the finding until such a time as he can be reasonably considered sane and is no longer a danger to himself or others (*Jones*, 1983). Nine years later, the Court clarified that the commitment cannot be an automatic consequence of an acquittal by reason of insanity (*Foucha*, 1992). To safeguard due process rights, it must be established in front of a fact-finder, designed by state law in a civil proceeding, that the requirements for civil commitment in each case has been met.

Civil Commitment Criteria

Regardless of variation, each state's civil commitment criteria must also reflect standards set forth in *Connor v. Donaldson,* an important Supreme Court case (*O'Connor v. Donaldson*, 1975). This case involved a man named Kenneth Donaldson who was diagnosed with paranoid schizophrenia and was held in a psychiatric hospital against his will for fifteen years. When his release was repeatedly denied by the psychiatrist in charge of his care even though he had not shown any evidence of suicidality or intentions to harm others, Donaldson argued to the court for restoration of his freedom.

5. CH07-05: Every step of every petition for inpatient and outpatient civil commitment must follow a process that has been approved by law with oversight from the court. The court determines if the legal criteria for commitment is clearly present and whether the burden of proof for commitment has been met before any person can be committed. Photo copyright wavebreakmedia/Shutterstock.com

The Donaldson case was eventually heard by the Supreme Court, who determined that he should be released. The Supreme Court laid out acceptable criteria for holding patients against their will. Justices stated that a mentally ill individual must either present a known risk of harm to themselves or others, be in such a state that he or she would be "hopeless to avoid the hazards of freedom," or be in need of psychiatric treatment. The court seemed to embrace the dangerousness model for civil commitment; however, they did also find that individuals with mental disorders could not be kept in institutions "without more." The word "more" is not explained, but is typically believed to refer to treatment. Additional standards can exist that satisfy dangerousness from different perspectives.

✓ "Danger to other" Standard

Often referred to as dangerousness, "danger to other" reflects the need to protect the public from dangerous individuals. An assessment of dangerousness includes identifying the person's risk factors that are often associated with violent behavior towards others, such as past violent history and recent substance abuse. Risk assessments are generally required within seventy-two hours of the time a petition for civil commitment being made to the court. Additional relevant risk factors for violence include medication noncompliance, young age, psychopathy, and recent unemployment. The type and frequency of past violent behavior may be considered as well as intervention and treatment options being prescribed when evaluating an individual's dangerousness.

✓ "Danger to Self" Standard

Danger to self refers to the possibility that the person is in jeopardy of self-harm, such as not meeting their basic needs of food, shelter, hygiene and/or security, or by engaging in intentional suicidal or self-injurious behavior. Historically, an attempt to commit suicide was a criminal act. By 1990, these criminal statutes had been repealed. In some states, however, suicide is still considered a crime under common law, as stated in Blackstone's Commentaries (*Wackwitz v. Roy*, 1992).

✓ "Capable of surviving safely in freedom" Standard

The most important phrase used by the Supreme Court in the O'Connor decision reads: "A finding of 'mental illness' alone cannot justify a State's locking a person up against his will and keeping him indefinitely in simple custodial confinement. . . . In short, a state cannot constitutionally confine, without more, a non-dangerous individual who is capable of surviving safely in freedom by himself or with the help of willing and responsible family members or friends" (*O'Connor*, 1975). Experts maintain that the decision itself is reasonable, but that the interpretation of this paragraph is not (TAC, 2015). The mental health bar has argued that a person is "surviving safely" until he or she is on the point of death. The unintended consequence of this case has been its role in massive deinstitutionalization and an overall decline in treatment for individuals with severe mental illness. The modern trend is towards a more liberal interpretation of this standard.

✓ "Gravely Disabled" Standard

The gravely disabled standard authorizes court-ordered treatment when inability to access food, shelter or other basic needs was judged to imperil physical safety. States maintain this standard while broadening its meaning to incorporate, at a minimum, the inability to make informed medical decisions or to seek psychiatric care.

✓ "Obviously Ill Patient in Need of Treatment" Standard

In 1995, the Wisconsin Legislature amended its civil commitment statute to permit the commitment of individuals who, due to mental illness, are unable to understand the advantages, disadvantages, or alternatives to a particular treatment or is unable or unwilling to apply them to their own situation and require such treatment to prevent severe mental, emotional, or physical harm. This is referred to as the fifth standard of dangerousness, and is a clear departure from previous standards for civil commitment as it does not require that the alleged mentally ill person pose a substantial direct risk of harm to themselves by their own actions (Erickson, Vitacco, and VanRybroek, 2005). The court recognized that the state has a well-established interest under its *parens patriae* power to provide care for persons unable to care for themselves in addition to its inherent authority under its police power to protect the community from mentally ill persons determined to be dangerous. The Supreme Court of Wisconsin upheld the constitutionality of the standard against numerous challenges (*In re Dennis H.*, 2002).

Burden of Proof

Civil commitment proceedings are required to meet a specific legal **BURDEN OF PROOF**, which is the degree to which the evidence presented convinces the trier of fact that their decision is correct. Considered the highest standard of proof, "beyond a reasonable doubt" requires that the trier of fact be convinced of their decision without any reservations that would be expected of a reasonable person. This standard applies in all criminal cases. The next lower standard allows decisions to be based on "clear and convincing evidence." Considered the lowest standard of proof is "preponderance of the evidence," which requires that the trier of fact be certain that the decision is more likely to be correct than incorrect. This is the standard that is used in civil law suits.

The Supreme Court in *Addington v. Texas* clarified the burden of proof required for involuntary commitment (Addington, 1979). The Court recognized that twenty states at the time used the standard of "clear and convincing" evidence; three states used "clear, cogent, and convincing" evidence; and two states required "clear, unequivocal and convincing" evidence for civil commitments. This case proved that not only was it acceptable for states to have different standards, the more stringent criminal law standard of "beyond a reasonable doubt" was not necessary and "preponderance of the evidence" was not enough. A "clear and convincing" standard was enough to adequately balance the rights of the individual and the public safety concerns of the state.

IN MY EXPERIENCE . . .

While we generally consider arrest to be punitive, there may be circumstances when it is done to help someone. I know of a trooper who made an arrest of a man who attempted suicide. When we talked about it, the trooper claimed that it was the only way to get the man some psychiatric care. It was the third unsuccessful suicide that the man had attempted. He was deeply depressed and had no family or loved ones that lived in the area. By making an arrest, the trooper was able to request that the local judge commit the man for psychiatric evaluation and treatment. There was no other way. . . .

Question for discussion: Why would a police officer arrest in this type of situation?

CURRENT CONTROVERSIES

The primary concern regarding involuntary commitment has always focused on the coercive nature of this approach. There can be little argument of that fact. All forms of the involuntary civil commitment approach to treatment employ options only after the individual refuses or is unable to engage in treatment voluntarily. As such, the debate turns to the imperative of the state to properly balance its police power and *parens patriae* right to interfere with an individual's personal liberty. Positions regarding self-determination versus state intervention are strong on both sides, providing valuable insights on persistent issues. In a review of civil commitment cases world-wide, most patients reported that in retrospect, their admission was correct or necessary and their forced hospitalizations were justified (Katsakou and Priebe, 2006).

Additional controversies surround criticisms that involuntary commitment is coercive treatment, therefore it is anti-therapeutic and stigmatizing. An anti-therapeutic concern is raised in studies which indicate that feelings of coercion may damage the relationship between the patient and the provider. It is also argued that involuntary civil commitment contributes to the stigma associated with mental illness. International programs such as Mental Health First Aid attempt to educate the public about mental illness and thereby reduce the stigma associated with mental illness.

A staunch opposition to compulsory intervention among some professionals lingers. In one national study on psychiatrist opinions about civil commitment, professional respondents often gave inaccurate responses about the grounds for commitment in their states or whether assisted outpatient treatment was allowed in their states (Brooks, 2007). Misunderstandings about legal options along with the lack of services that are humanely provided, contribute to the problem. Among groups that strongly advocate treatment for individuals with severe mental illness, the availability of mental health services is driven by funding. The significance of an older study still resonates; the availability of detention beds in the community, rather than the person's diagnosis, is a significant predictor of whether a person will be detained through involuntary commitment (Engleman, Jobes, Berman, and Langbein, 1998). According to the Council of State Governments, the AOT programs are "in name only" in most of the forty-six states that have them, in part because taxpayers and politicians have been unwilling to spend the money to get the programs off the ground (Edwards, 2015).

Assisted outpatient treatment (AOT) is a new trend in the United States. Most professionals believe that it is the least objectionable option of involuntary treatment. A major benefit of outpatient commitment is the monitoring of committed individuals in the community with the requirement that they adhere to mental health visits. Recall that as an alternative to inpatient care, AOT first came about in 1999 in New York as *Kendra's Law. Kendra's Law* has been evaluated by two empirical studies since its passage. These studies found the *Kendra's Law* AOT program successful with the following outcomes (Treatment Advocacy Center, 2015):

- Helps the mentally ill by reducing homelessness (74 percent); suicide attempts (55 percent); and substance abuse (48 percent).
- Keeps the public safer by reducing physical harm to others (47 percent) and property destruction (43 percent).

- Saves money by reducing hospitalization (77 percent); arrests (83 percent); and incarceration (87 percent).
- Results in beneficial structural changes to local mental health service delivery including enhanced accountability and improved access to services; improved treatment plan development, discharge planning, and coordination of services.
- The studies also thoroughly debunk the predictions of some that *Kendra's Law* would lead to increased stigma or perceived "coercion" among AOT recipients.

When individuals with severe mental illness do become violent, family members are most often the victims (Copeland and Heilemann, 2008). Research supports anecdotal evidence that families are frustrated by the lack of available services for a family member with mental disorders. Rarely do state policies and funding support the efforts of families to care for their loved ones. AOT presents an avenue of hope for these families. Despite the controversies regarding civil commitment, there is an unprecedented wave of interest in outpatient commitment programs (Appelbaum, 2001). In part, the stream of highly publicized acts of violence by persons with severe mental disorders confirms beliefs that the system has failed the individuals who need care and treatment. As a society we can no longer ignore this small subset of individuals who represent our most needy citizens. A strong impetus for the creation of outpatient commitment programs is the frustration of doctors, mental health workers, and families who continuously witness the failure of outpatient treatment and fruitless attempts to have someone admitted to a psychiatric facility (Erickson et al., 2005).

Sexual Offender Commitment Statutes

The sexual predator laws are controversial, in part because they confine individuals after they have already been incarcerated for criminal sexual acts. Additionally, there is disagreement as to whether there is any cure for this type of offender; therefore, the laws appear more punitive- than treatment-oriented. The American Psychiatric Association is formally opposed to sexual offender commitment laws (Kernberg, 1999). Those who support the civil commitment of sexual offenders emphasize that the laws impact a small group of highly dangerous sexual offenders found to have mental disorders that render them an unacceptable risk to public safety. The U.S. Supreme Court has ruled on three cases with direct bearing on the constitutionality of the sexual predator commitment laws. In every case, the constitutionality of the statutes has been upheld.

In 1994, Kansas enacted the *Sexually Violent Predator Act*, which established procedures for the civil commitment of persons who, due to a mental abnormality or a personality disorder, are likely to engage in predatory acts of sexual violence. Leroy Hendricks, an inmate with a long history of molesting children was the first to be committed under the Act. His challenge to the commitment was the assertion that his "substantive" due process rights were violated since his condition was not a mental illness and he also made a double jeopardy claim that he had could not be tried twice for the same crime. In *Kansas v. Hendricks* the Court upheld the Act due to its requirement of previous sexual offending and inability to control oneself as proof of sexual dangerousness (*Hendricks*, 1997). The Court stated that Hendricks' diagnosis as a pedophile, which qualifies as a "mental abnormality" under the Act, plainly suffices for due process purposes (e.g., id, at 360). Further, the Court determined that civil confinement was neither punitive nor a deterrent. The Supreme Court upheld the state's police power rights and legitimized the constitutionality of civil commitment of sexually violent persons.

The second case that fell under the Sexually Violent Predator Act was *Kansas v. Crane,* wherein Crane argued that he retained some control over his sexual impulses and behavior and was therefore ineligible for civil confinement. The U.S. Supreme Court, once again, upheld the Act (*Crane*, 2002). The U.S. Supreme Court then heard a challenge to the federal sex offender civil commitment law on a number of grounds, including the less-stringent standard of "clear and convincing" and the right of Congress to legitimately enact a civil commitment statute (*Comstock*, 2010). In *U.S. v. Comstock* the Court upheld the right of the U.S. Government to enact the *Adam Walsh Act* and the standard of proof, finding it neither punitive nor a denial of due process.

Funding

Amid complaints that funding is insufficient to establish treatment programs, indications are that funding is available. Recall that in 2004 Congress authorized the *Justice and Mental Health Offender Treatment and Crime Reduction Act* (MIOTCRA). Between 2006 and 2015, $82.9 million has been allocated through grants administered by the Justice's Bureau of Justice Assistance as *Justice and Mental Health Collaboration Project* (JMCHCP) grants (Justice Center, 2015). The grants are broad in nature and may be used for specialized law enforcement training, mental health courts, mental health or substance use treatment for incarcerated individuals, community reentry services, and cross-training of criminal justice and mental health personnel.

According to NAMI, states cut $4.35 billion from their mental health budgets between 2009 and 2012, literally decimating access to services for many people living with mental illness. The damage from these policies is lasting, and in some cases it is devastating to organizations that provide services (NAMI, 2014). Further, while twenty-two states and the District of Columbia increased mental health spending in 2013 and 2014, six states cut it in both those years. Four states increased mental health spending in 2013, but then cut it in 2014. Five states increased mental health spending in 2013, but their spending stayed level in 2014. Five states kept mental health spending level in 2013 and managed to increase it in 2014. Indiana stayed level in both years.

A recent study, entitled *Fraud, Waste and Excess Profits: The Fate of Money Intended to Treat People with Serious Mental Illness,* calculates that $4 to 8 billion in public mental health funds are lost annually to fraud, waste, and excess profits that go mainly to managed care companies (Torrey, Jaffe, Geller, and Lamb, 2015). Examples in the report show that a simple internet search of Medicare fraud convictions point to losses that total $1 billion; WellCare, a for-profit mental health program in Florida, kept 50 percent of the Medicaid premiums rather than the contracted 20 percent. In California, $1 out of $5 from a special tax allocated specifically to help individuals diagnosed with serious mental illness was diverted to programs such as yoga, line-dancing, and other wasteful initiatives. While the deterioration in mental health services is often blamed on reductions in funding, the authors note that when comparing 1981 to 2012, the amount of money designated for mental health in constant dollars has increased by 36 percent. According to lead author, Dr. E. Fuller Torrey, those wasted, diverted, and stolen funds could provide:

- Three months of state hospitalization for 112,000 individuals
- One year of Assertive Community Treatment for 267,000 individuals
- One year of Assisted Outpatient Treatment for 800,000 individuals
- One year of a clubhouse rehabilitation program for 364,000 individuals
- One year of supported housing for 333,000 individuals
- One year of standard antipsychotic medication for 6.7 million individuals
- One year of clozapine treatment for 667,000 individuals

SUMMARY

An unintended consequence of applying strict dangerousness criteria for civil commitment is that the medical system will not intervene against a person's wishes until they become suicidal, physically violent, or grossly unable to perform activities of daily living. While the movement was based on the noble intentions of protecting the rights of individuals with mental illness and ensuring that they receive appropriate treatment, there has been a significant increase in Americans with mental illnesses who are living on the street or in our jails and prisons. The high numbers of individuals with mental disabilities that are being held in federal and state corrections facilities indicate a crisis that cannot be ignored.

Involuntary civil commitment is mandated treatment. There are three distinct categories of intervention which is court ordered and court supervised. This approach to intervention for individuals with severe mental illness may have different names in different states, but some form of civil commitment law is evident in all states and in federal law. The laws that establish civil commitment practices have been scrutinized and found constitutionally appropriate. Where states have mandated implementation of involuntary outpatient commitment (AOT), these programs have shown remarkable success for reducing homelessness, suicide attempts, and substance abuse. Arrest and incarceration of individuals with severe mental illness is also a noted outcome of AOT.

CHAPTER QUESTIONS FOR REVIEW

1. How would you describe the four categories of involuntary civil commitment? Use examples of laws from the book or from your own state statutes.
2. Compare the burden of proof needed for court action in civil commitment with the criminal court requirement.
3. State the purpose of Assisted Outpatient Treatment (AOT). How do we know if this form of treatment is successful or not?
4. Compare and contrast two or more current controversies in civil commitment.
5. Explain the pros and cons of civil commitment laws that involve sexually violent predators.

REFERENCES

Addington v. Texas, 441 U.S. 418 (1979).

Appelbaum, P. (2001). Thinking carefully about outpatient commitment. *Psychiatric Services, 52*(3), 347–350.

ATSA. (2010). Civil commitment of sexually violent predators. Retrieved October 10, 2015, from http://www.atsa.com/civil-commitment-sexually-violent-predators

Brooks, R. (2007). Psychiatrist's opinions about involuntary civil commitment: results of a national survey. *Journal of American Academy of Psychiatry and the Law, 35*(2), 219–228.

Copeland, D. A., and Heilemann, M. V. (2008). Getting to "The Point:" The experience of mothers getting assistance for their violent, mentally ill, adult children. *Nursing research, 57*(3), 136–143.

Edwards, H. S. (2015). Should mentally ill people be forced into treatment? Retrieved October 20, 2015, from http://csgjusticecenter.org/mental-health/media-clips/should-mentally-ill-people-be-forced-into-treatment/

Engleman, N. B., Jobes, D. A., Berman, A. L., and Langbein, L. I. (1998). Clinicians' decision making about involuntary commitment. *Psychiatric Services, 49*(7), 941–945.

Erickson, S., Vitacco, M., and VanRybroek, G. (2005). Beyond overt violence: Wisconsin's progressive civil commitment statute as a marker of a new era in mental health law. *Marquette Law Review, 89*(359).

Foucha v. Louisiana, 504 U.S. 71, 80 (1992).

Hoge, S., Buchanan, A., Kovasznay, B., and Roskes, E. (2009). Outpatient services for the mentally ill involved in the criminal justice system *A Report of the Task Force on Outpatient Forensic Services*: American Psychiatric Association.

Levy, R. M., and Rubenstein, L. S. (1996). The rights of people with mental disabilities: The authoritative ACLU guide to the rights of people with mental illness and mental retardation.

Jaffe, D. (2014). The real mental health crisis in America. *Ripon Forum, 48*(1), 6.

James, D., and Glaze, L. (2006). Mental health problems of prison and jail inmates *BJS Special Report.* Washington, D.C.: U.S. Department of Justice, Office of Justice Programs, Bureau of Justice Statistics.

Jimmy Ryce State civil commitment programs for sexually dangerous persons, 42 U.S. § 16971 (2006).

Jones v. United States, 463 U.S. 34, 370 (1983).

Justice Center. (2015). The Mentally Ill Offender Treatment and Crime Reduction Act. Retrieved July, 2015, from http://csgjusticecenter.org/wp-content/uploads/2014/08/MIOTCRA_Fact_Sheet.pdf

Kansas v. Crane, 534 U.S. 407 (2002).

Kansas v. Hendricks, 521 U.S. 346 (1997).

Katsakou, C., and Priebe, S. (2006). Outcomes of involuntary hospital admission: A review. *Acta Psychiatrica Scandinavica, 114*(232–241).

Kernberg, O. (1999). *Dangerous sex offenders: Task Force Report of the American Psychiatric Association*. Washington, D.C.: American Psychiatric Association.

Mental Health Program Office and Department of Mental Health Law and Policy. (2014). *Baker Act User Reference Guide: The Florida Mental Health Act* (Vol. 2015). Tallahassee, FL: Department of Children and Families, Mental Health Program Office; Tampa, FL; University of South Florida, Louis de la Parte Florida Mental Health Institute.

Miller, J. A. (2010). Sex offender civil commitment: The treatment paradox. *California law review, 98*(6), 2093–2128.

NAMI. (2014). *State mental health legislation 2014: Trends, themes and effective Practices.* Arlington, VA: National Alliance on Mental Illness.

NCSL. (2014). Adam Walsh Child Protection and Safety Act. Retrieved October 12, 2015, from http://www.ncsl.org/research/civil-and-criminal-justice/adam-walsh-child-protection-and-safety-act.aspx

New York State Office of Mental Health. (2006). An explanation of Kendra's Law. Retrieved October 10, 2015, from http://bi.omh.ny.gov/aot/about?p=kendras-law

O'Connor v. Donaldson, 422 U.S. 563 (1975).

Schug, R., and Fradella, H. (2015). *Mental illness and crime.* Los Angeles, CA: Sage.

State v. Dennis H., 647 NW 2d 851 (2002).

Stettin, B., Geller, J., Ragosta, K., Cohen, K., and Ghowrwal, J. (2014). Mental health commitment laws: A survey of the states (pp. 29). Arlington, VA: Treatment Advocacy Center.

TAC. (2015). O'Conner v. Donaldson (1975). Retrieved October 15, 2015, from http://www.treatmentadvocacycenter.org/component/content/article/341

Torrey, F., Jaffe, D., Geller, J., and Lamb, R. (2015). Fraud, waste and excess profits: The fate of money intended to treat people with serious mental illness. New York, NY: Mental Illness Policy Org.

Treatment Advocacy Center. (2014). Laura's Law. Retrieved October 10, 2015, from http://www.treatmentadvocacycenter.org/lauras-law/2651#what-is

Treatment Advocacy Center. (2015). Kendra's Law: Results from New York's first ten years with AOT. Retrieved October 20, 2015, from http://www.treatmentadvocacycenter.org/solution/assisted-outpatient-treatment-laws/kendras-law-successes

United States v. Salerno, 481 U.S. 739, 747 (1987).

US v. Comstock, 560 U.S. (2010).

Wackwitz v. Roy, 418 SE 2d 861 (1992).

PART III

Criminal Justice Responses

Photo copyright Catalin Petolea /Shutterstock.com

The following chapters are covered in PART III

A crucial question is:
How does criminal justice assure public safety and security?

The criminal justice system enforces law, determines guilt and incarcerates individuals found guilty. Chapter 8 looks at law enforcement through a public safety lens. Chapter 9 deals with the criminal court terminology and processes. Chapter 10 deals with the incarceration of offenders. These are the three components of the criminal justice system. The goal is to avoid the incarceration of people whose mental illness is the reason for confinement; criminals may be incarcerated due to crimes not associated with their mental disorders.

CHAPTER 8

Law Enforcement

INTRODUCTION

Law enforcement encounters fall within a discretionary continuum defined by law and policy, from making accommodations to the use of de-escalation techniques or making an arrest. The expanding role of law enforcement in response to persons needing psychiatric care has left police officers themselves to wonder what the current law enforcement response is when a crime has been committed and the suspect appears to have severe mental illness. The quandary is understandable. Police encounters with individuals who suffer from mental illness rely on the ability of the officer to distinguish between disability and danger. Making the determination between disability and danger is not a choice between the two, but a constant reevaluation during an encounter. Geoffrey Albert suggests that the interpretation is a subjective process, one that requires an officer to differentiate among many reasons to explain the same behavior (Alpert, 2015). The skill to make such a distinction is critical, since the consequences of misreading or misunderstanding the cues of an individual can have dire consequences.

Given the complex world in which law enforcement officers must operate, it is important to take note that police officers will have contact with people who have mental disorders under a variety of conditions. A mental disorder may be minor or severe; the officer may not even know that the person has an illness. Even in situations that go beyond diversion, officers are aware that one's perception is his or her own reality. They may not share that reality.

Key Terms

ARREST RELATED DEATHS

CONVICTION INTEGRITY UNITS

EXCLUSIONARY RULE

EXCITED DELIRIUM

MENTAL HEALTH FIRST AIDS

PURPOSEFUL INTERROGATION

TOTALITY OF THE CIRCUMSTANCES

Chapter Objectives

After completing this chapter, you should be able to:

- Explain the connection between violent victimization and violent offending
- Discuss the issues surrounding police use of force
- List numerous techniques for de-escalation during crisis
- State the reasons for officer wellness programs

Mission of Law Enforcement

The International Chiefs of Police Association (ICAP) argues that the only persons with mental illness who should encounter law enforcement are those who are suspected of committing crimes or who are a danger to themselves or others (IACP, 2010). Additionally, people with mental disorders who are victims, witnesses, and complainants will also come to the attention of the police. Previous chapters have outlined the programs and initiatives which law enforcement has taken to address the issues of nuisance behaviors and the diversion of people whose illness causes unusual behaviors which typically are not crimes. The primary mission of law enforcement remains that of maintaining public safety. All police actions conform with that mission, regardless of individual characteristics. Crime control remains an important aspect of that mission. At the street level, police officers have discretion on how best to maintain public safety within the parameters of the law. If a person is a danger to himself or others, or has committed a crime for which the police have the legal right of arrest, those options may be exercised.

1. CH08-01: *Policing.* Policing functions include responding to dangerous situations which ordinary citizens are not equipped to handle, to investigate crimes, and to act as protectors. These multiple roles will bring police officers in contact with victims, suspects, witnesses, and complainants on any given day.

VIOLENT VICTIMIZATION

Law enforcement officers are likely to encounter people with mental illness who have been victims of crime. There is a small but growing amount of literature on victimization that suggests mental disorder and its related symptoms increases the risk of violent victimization (Silver, Piquero, Jennings, Piquero, and Leiber, 2011). From a major study conducted in Chicago, researchers found that psychiatric outpatients were 11 times more likely to be victimized by violent crime than the group without mental disorders (Teplin, McClelland, Abram, and Weiner, 2005). Silver et al. (2005) suggest that compared to people without mental disorders, individuals with anxiety disorders experienced more sexual assaults; people with schizophreniform disorders experienced more threatened and completed physical assaults; and those with alcohol dependence disorders experienced more attempted physical assaults. A recent study found that among 826 observed individuals three variables are positively and significantly related to victimization are: having personality or adjustment disorder along with substance abuse disorders; exhibiting behavioral symptoms of psychopathy; and exhibiting a high degree of psychiatric symptomatology (Silver et al., 2011).

Victimization and Perpetration Overlap

There is evidence to suggest an overlap between victimization and perpetration among people with mental disorders who commit crime. Authors of the 2011 Silver study found a significant correlation between violent offending and violent victimization. Identified variables that were common to both violent offenders and violent victims include substance abuse diagnosis, psychopathy, perceived stress, and residential moves (Silver et al., 2011). The authors suggest that the link may be due to provocation or retaliation, or chronic relationship conflict.

Silver et al. (2011) also suggest that *The Dangerous Mentally Ill Offender Program* (DMIO) is a promising multi-agency strategy which may address both risks of offending and victimization among violent ex-prisoners. The DMIO program was established by the 1999 Legislature to identify mentally ill prisoners who pose a threat to public safety and provides them opportunities to receive mental health treatment and other services up to five years after their release from prison. An analysis indicates that the program is successful at reducing overall new felony recidivism rates by 42 percent and reduces new violent felony recidivism by 36 percent (Washington State Institute for Public Policy, 2009).

CRIME RATES

It is a common perception that people with mental disorders are disproportionately involved in violent crime. As stated earlier in the chapter, most calls for service that involve an individual with mental disorder are for minor or nuisance offenses. Evidence exists that mental disorders might serve as a protective factor from arrest. This means that formal action such as an arrest is less likely to occur for an individual with mental disorders in cases of minor offending (Kerr et al., 2010). By not arresting all the individuals involved in crime who have mental illness, it may appear as though the most offenders commit serious crimes.

A widespread concern is that there may be an increase in crime associated with the closing of the psychiatric hospitals since deinstitutionalization. Per Torrey and colleagues (2010), an analysis on state closures of psychiatric beds found a statistical trend between public hospital bed populations and certain violent crimes, including homicide. States that closed more public psychiatric beds between 2005 and 2010 have experienced higher rates of violent crime generally and of aggravated assault in particular (Torrey, Fuller, Geller, Jacobs, and Ragosta, 2012). An association between lower per capita hospital expenses and higher rates of aggravated assault was also revealed in a recent study (Torrey et al., 2012). Co-occurring mental disorders, drug and alcohol use and noncompliance with medication requirements are thought to be among the factors associated with an increase in violent behavior (Steadman et al., 1998). Approximately one out of every 59 assaults on police officers and one out of every 42 felonious officer deaths are associated with a suspect known to have mental disorders (Cordner, 2006).

IN MY EXPERIENCE . . .

In their work, police officers endure periods of boredom, moments of panic, and a touch of fear. They are expected to possess a thorough knowledge of law, first aid, mental health, and to be excellent marksmen and good swimmers. Officers must have a high level of self-control even in the face of verbal or physical attacks. A high standard of ethics and moral responsibility are necessary personal attributes. Law enforcement officers work shifts and overtime by department need and not necessarily by personal choice. They are required to work during holidays, birthdays, and family events. In some jurisdictions, they must cut their hair, shave their beards, be free of tattoos, and avoid wearing jewelry, perfumes or scents. When shots are fired, people scatter in the opposite direction while the police must run toward the shots. They must run faster than a speeding bullet and jump higher than the tallest building. . . ok, I got carried away on the last one. . . .

Question for discussion: Would you become a police officer? Why or why not?

Some experts suggest that only a small proportion of crime can be directly linked to symptoms of mental illness. In one study, researchers examined 429 crimes committed by 143 offenders and found that only 3 percent of those crimes were directly related to symptoms of major depression, 4 percent to symptoms of schizophrenia disorders and 10 percent to systems of bipolar disorder (Peterson, Skeem, Kennealy, Bray, and Zvonkovic, 2014). It was very difficult to distinguish between symptoms of mental illness and common risk factors for committing crime, such as anger and impulsivity, suggesting that intervention would be needed to improve criminal justice outcomes that extend beyond symptoms.

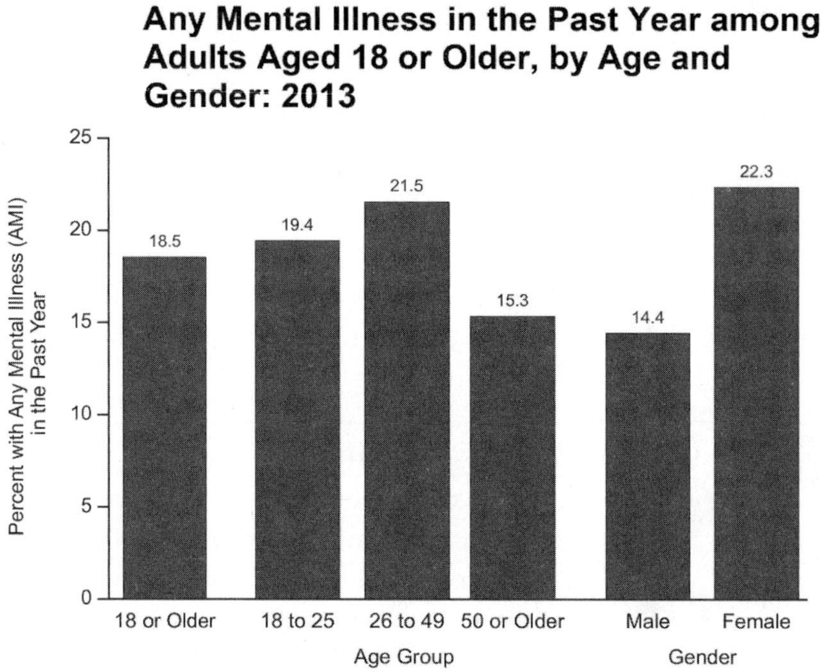

2. CH08-02: *Any Mental Illness 2013.* Given the high rates of mental disorders among the general population, it is not surprising that police officers would have many contacts with individuals who suffer from mental illness. Note that females experience higher overall rates of mental disorders when to compared men. The age group at the highest rates of experiencing mental disorders is between ages 26 to 49. Source: Substance Abuse and Mental Health Services Administration. (2014).

POLICE USE OF FORCE

While police encounters with individuals in crisis who have mental disorders can be dangerous, according to some researchers, they usually are not (Reuland, Schwarzfeld, and Draper, 2009). Law enforcement officers report that the typical call involves cooperative subjects, with only occasional individuals that resist law enforcement authority (Kerr, Morabito, and Watson, 2010). When injury does occur, it is most likely to be the reaction of the individual with mental illness that influences injury (Kerr, Morabito, and Watson, 2010). In other words, research discovered that a relationship exists between the amount of force used by law enforcement officers and the resistance from the offender. Higher resistance was found to increase the likelihood of physical harm to the person with the mental disability. Finding a way to safely reduce resistance and take control of situations without force can be a challenge. Vigilance to dangerousness is not a one-time assessment however. It is a process of constant concern in police encounters, whether the individual is thought to be mentally disordered or not. The officer does not know when or if a suspect will perceive that they are being threatened. Additionally, a willingness to violate the law and resist police authority is demonstrated by the actions of some citizens (Gallo, 2006). Co-occurring mental disorders, drug and alcohol use and noncompliance with medication requirements are thought to be among the factors associated with an increase in violent behavior (Steadman et al., 1998).

Research has consistently shown that police officers seldom use force against citizens (Alpert, 2015). When force is used, it typically involves low-level tactics and minor injury. When a suspect is violent or threatening, encounters with the police are more likely to involve an increase in the police use of force. Deadly interactions between the police and citizens are occurring with alarming frequency, however, and there is significant concern as to the reasons.

It can be difficult to verify an often-invisible population, but advocates say at least one in four fatal police incidents involves an individual with severe mental illness (Fuller, Lamb, Biasotti, and Snook, 2015). A recent audit of the government databases tasked with tracking the number of fatal law enforcement encounters in the U.S. cited a significant underestimation and potentially biased picture of arrest-related deaths in the United States. In some cities, the numbers may be even higher. One study reported that nearly 75 percent of those shot in 2010 and 2011 in New Mexico suffered from mental illness (Santos and Goode, 2014).

If police officers seldom use force during citizen encounters, how do we explain the fact that so many of the individuals shot and killed by the police have serious mental disorders? A commonly accepted explanation is that law enforcement officers lack the training or resources to cope with people living with untreated schizophrenia, bipolar disorder, or other acute mental health conditions. Training police officers to recognize and respond appropriately to cases involving individuals having mental disorders is therefore a high national priority. There is a difference between angry behavior and violent behavior or acting menacingly and threatening violence. Developing community partnerships with mental health professionals and community coalitions is an active mandate in all cities and towns as a method of sharing resources and reducing harm. In past years, communicating between agencies was informal and uncomplicated. Due to the changing needs of the population who have mental health problems, there is a growing trend towards more formal partnerships designed to promote appropriate medical and psychological intervention, as well as case diversion.

An alternate explanation to the use of force by police in their encounters is that mentally disordered suspects are more likely to act violently, resist the police, and possess a weapon (Johnson, 2011). When the violence, resistance and weapon were controlled in the Johnson study, results indicated that mentally disordered suspects were not more likely than non-disordered suspects to be treated with physical force by the police. It is difficult to understand what is behind the police-related deaths that are occurring, as no national data on the mental state of the deceased is collected that would provide answers. From all directions, people want to know why more complete and detailed information on justifiable homicides by law enforcement is not available.

Research has suggested that between 36 percent to 46 percent of officer-involved shootings are purposeful suicide-by-cop incidents initiated by the victim (Mohandie, Meloy, and Collins, 2009). Another concern is the noted increase of suicide-by-cop situations in recent years (Mohandie et al. 2009). Justifiable homicides by police had declined by 5 percent between 1980 and 2008, but those resulting from an attack on a law enforcement officer increased by 67 percent—from an average of 153 to 255 homicides per year due to attacks on police (Torrey, 2013; NAMI, 2010). More information is necessary to understand why more individuals may be attacking law enforcement officers.

Less-than-Lethal Technology

Law enforcement officers are amenable to using less-than-legal technology when it is available. A reduction of injury rates is achieved with the reduced need to physically intervene with a person. In a study of 24,000 use-of-force cases, a decrease in injuries to civilians and police was found to be as high as 62 percent when Tasers are used (MacDonald et al., 2009). While the use of Tasers as a less-than-lethal option enjoys a high level of public acceptance, there is a growing concern about the safety and aggressive use of the technology. Amnesty International urges stronger limits on police use, claiming that the Taser has been a contributing factor in 500 United States deaths (Trimel, 2012). Sudden deaths, injuries, and adverse health effects may be linked to Taser use in those with high blood pressure, obesity, cardiac and respiratory disease, and among people with severe mental illness and substance use (O'Brien and Thom, 2014). More information is needed to determine if Taser use is directly or indirectly related to the increase of injuries and death of individuals with medical issues, including mental illness.

What happens if police officers use the Taser to avoid harming someone and it results in severe injury or death to the individual? The Supreme Court has consistently recognized that police officers are entitled to some form of immunity from suits for damages when reasonable force is used. Thus, police officers are immune from suit under 42 U.S.C. § 1983 unless they have violated a statutory or constitutional right that was clearly established at the time of the challenged conduct. The Court has recognized that government officials may make reasonable though mistaken judgements.

Reasonableness is analyzed by the Court from the **TOTALITY OF THE CIRCUMSTANCES** standard, which means that the whole situation must be studied and considered when determining if police action was reasonable or not to determine criminal liability. Reasonableness includes that police officers are often forced to make split-second judgments in circumstances that are tense, uncertain and happen quickly. The question of whether law enforcement officers are required to provide accommodations to an armed, violent, and mentally ill suspect while bringing the suspect into custody has not specifically been addressed by the Court (*City and County of San Francisco, California, et al. v. Sheehan*, 2015). Recall that civil liability under the American with Disabilities Act has been established by the Court in *Hainze v. Richard* (2000), which held that ADA standards do not require that police officers comply in the presence of exigent circumstances and prior to securing the safety of themselves, other officers, and any nearby civilians, when doing so might pose an unnecessary risk to innocents.

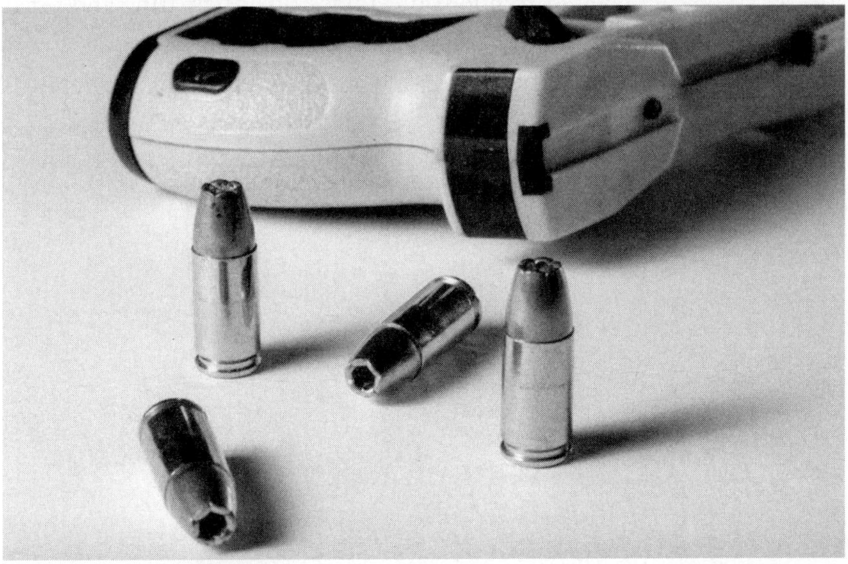

3. CH08-03; *Tasers.* Less-than-lethal weapons enjoy wide public support for police use since they reduce the need to physically intervene with a person. However, there is growing concern about the safety of Taser use against some individuals. Taser use has been associated sudden deaths, injuries and adverse health effects. More research is needed on the cause of these tragedies and how they might be avoided in the future. Photo copyright John Roman/Bigstock.com

Arrest Related Deaths

Loss of an individual through death is a horrific ordeal for any family. News reports are full of media coverage on shootings and other deaths that are occurring among the severely mentally ill population during encounters with the police. Each situation is different and must be studied on a case-by-case basis so that we can learn from them. Early intervention by the mental health community and easier access to mental health care are high priority. There is no easy answer on the horizon. Education and training is helpful for recognizing and responding to the unique challenges this population poses during crisis.

ARREST-RELATED DEATHS *(ARD)* typically involve a highly-charged encounter involving agitated and intoxicated suspects aggressively struggling with police prior to being subdued (Ho et al., 2013). Individuals have been described by police as super-strong, requiring the use of multiple tools and techniques in attempts to control the subjects. The use of CEW's or a Taser is sometimes associated with the death and has drawn scrutiny. These are not deaths at the hands of law enforcement officers, but deaths due to physical vulnerabilities of the individual that may be exacerbated during struggle and confinement.

The criminal justice community is very concerned about any death that occurs within police custody. While they don't know the exact reasons behind these deaths, medical experts provide some advice on anticipating and preventing them. Some experts question whether sedatives or calmative agents might be a viable option for police officers to more safely respond to crisis situations (Weiss, 2008). Others are suggesting that high levels of acidosis caused by physical exertion may cause physiologic imbalances in subjects at high risk for ARD (Ho et al., 2013).

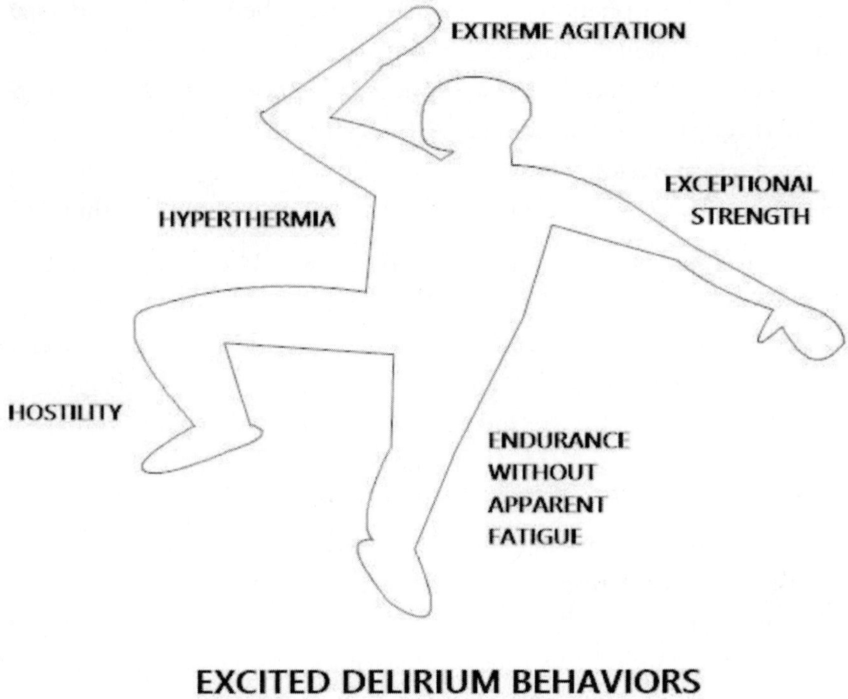

4. CH08-04: *Excited Delirium.* These are the characteristics of an individual exhibiting signs of ExDS according to Department policy in Seattle, Washington (Seattle Police Department, 2013). If recognized, this constitutes a true emergency requiring immediate medical response.

Excited Delirium

Excited delirium *(ExDS)* is a serious psychotic disorder that can be fatal if police officers and emergency response personnel fail to recognize its symptoms. The syndrome was described more than 150 years ago by Dr. Luther Bell and named as Bell's Mania (Takeuchi, Ahern, and Henderson, 2011). Reports of deaths due to this acute exhaustive mania slowed during the 1950s as antipsychotic medications came into use, and increased during the 1980s due to widespread cocaine use (Roach, Echols, and Burnett, 2014). **Excited delirium** is recognized as a state of extreme mental and physiological excitement characterized by sudden bizarre and/or violent behavior that may be accompanied by combativeness, confusion, hallucinations, incoherent shouting, paranoia and even sudden death. Approximately two thirds of *ExDS* victims die at the scene or during transport by paramedics or police (Takeuchi et al., 2011).

Recognized by the American College of Emergency Physicians (ACEP) as a syndrome on a continuum of delirium, it is believed to be linked with drug use, mental illness, certain metabolic disorders, and alterations of brain neurochemistry

(Hoffman, 2009). The phenomenon is being researched to fully understand its association with individuals who die without injury sufficient to cause fatality, but who have been handcuffed or tasered during altercations with the police (Strote, Walsh, Auerbach, Burns, and Maher, 2014). Sudden deaths of individuals with *ExDS* have been reported within an hour after struggling with police officers, being tasered, or handcuffed (Special Panel Review of Excited Delirium, 2011).

The syndrome itself is considered controversial. Although delirium is a mental disorder described in the DSM-5, neither the American Psychiatric Association (APA, 2015) nor the International Classification of Diseases (ICD-10, 2016) currently recognizes *excited delirium* as a psychiatric diagnosis. The syndrome is recognized by the medical profession and within criminal justice (Hoffman, 2009). Continued research is needed to determine its cause and effect, however. Researchers maintain that a lack of recognition of the condition in the context of law enforcement activities does not negate the significance of the behavioral and physical signs referred to as *ExD*S (Takeuchi et al., 2011). Takeuchi and colleagues argue that while there has been speculation over the years of police brutality being the underlying cause, most of deaths occur suddenly prior to capture, in the emergency department (ED), or unwitnessed at home.

In police departments with established policy on responding to *ExDS*, dispatchers are being trained to ask key questions to determine if a person has any signs or symptoms of *ExDS* (Roach et al., 2014). Law enforcement officers are also being trained to assess cases for behaviors consistent with *ExDS* along with the need to call for immediate paramedic backup.

IN MY EXPERIENCE . . .

Shortly after the closing of the Northampton State Hospital in Massachusetts came a complaint that a woman recently released had been raped. I learned that she had severe anxiety as well as a significant learning disorder. Conducting an interview with Sandy was difficult. It took immense concentration on my part to understand what she was saying. As with any crime the elements of the offense had to have been satisfied for a crime to have been committed. Rape requires a penetration, no matter how slight. She would have to tell me that penetration had occurred without any prompting or suggestions. To preserve the forensic integrity of the interview it was conducted in a room specifically designed for interviewing, and the entire statement was videotaped and audiotaped. In this situation, I used a set of anatomically correct dolls which I also used in interviewing children who had been abused and neglected. Asking Sandy to show me what happened to her by using the doll proved to very helpful. Once I was satisfied that she could explain the crime in sufficient detail I gathered enough information to locate the suspect and continue the investigation. Medical evidence was not available in this case, unfortunately. The offender was identified and arrested. Sandy testified in Grand Jury and the video tape was shown also. The offender pled guilty and was sentenced to prison.

Question for discussion: Knowing that an individual with a mental disorder may have difficulty communicating with others can you think of any other way to help in a similar interview?

DE-ESCALATION TECHNIQUES

There is evidence that an officer may be able to influence the perceptions of a person with mental illness to improve outcomes (Bahora, Hanafi, Chien, and Compton, 2008). Officers may be called to de-escalate the situation when an individual is armed with a weapon, threatening violence, or has reached the point where medical intervention is needed. A person in crisis may not be taking prescribed medication or taking medication that may be causing a psychotic condition to worsen, or their condition may have deteriorated due to co-occurring disorders. During a mental health crisis, the individual cannot always communicate his feelings, thoughts, or emotions clearly. NAMI (2010) suggests that he may find it difficult to understand what others are saying. It is important to empathize with the person, to stay calm and try to de-escalate the crisis. Try to think of the person as he is—someone in need of help. Here are some de-escalation techniques that may help resolve a crisis (NAMI, 2010):

- Avoid overreacting—an angry person is not the same as a violent person!
- Be patient—very patient!
- Don't argue or try to reason with the person—at this point their thinking is disordered!
- Express support and concern—the person is likely fearful of what they are experiencing!
- Avoid continuous eye contact—and avoid touching the person unless restraint is needed!

Attempts to defuse a potentially violent situation takes a show of respect and calm, non-threatening approach to communication. Always avoid touching a person with a disability in crisis, since it could be perceived as an invasion of personal space and evoke a violent response. An individual that is "touch toxic" may become upset. A person with a cognitive disorder may not feel able to deal with the invasion.

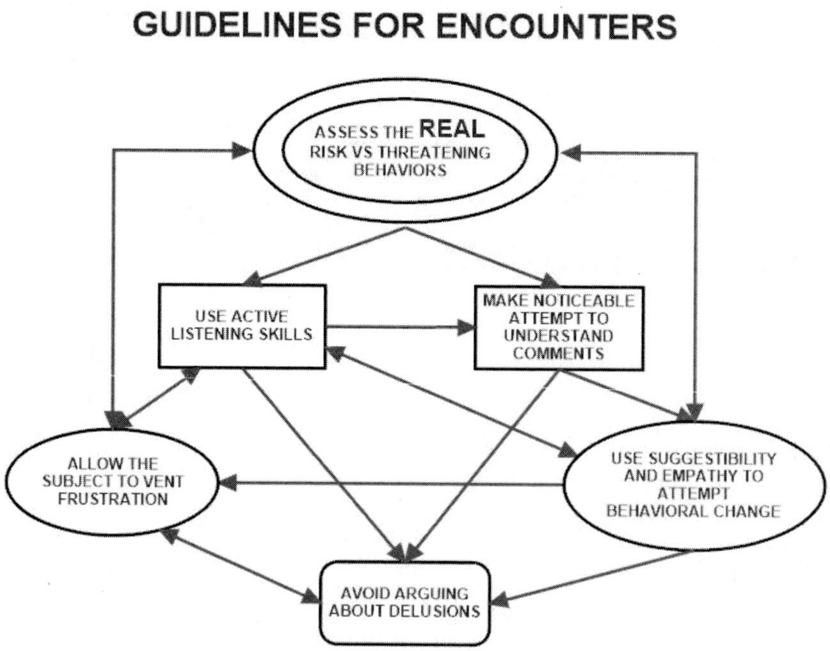

5. CH08-05: *Potentially Violent Confrontations.* Police officers attempt to deescalate potentially violent confrontations. Here are some guidelines suggested by Mohandie and Duffy (1999).

INTERROGATION OF SUSPECTS

Individuals who have mental disorders do commit crimes; accusations must be investigated like allegations against any other perpetrator. But what happens when the police officer is investigating a crime committed by someone who has a psychiatric disability? The ability to obtain a confession has always been recognized as one of the most valuable skills of a criminal investigator. A suspect's admission of guilt carries great weight in a court of law, sways the judge and jury, and often leads to a conviction. Strict adherence to the mindset of purposeful interrogation are necessary to protect the rights of the accused, preserve the integrity of the case, and avoid false confessions when the offender is thought to have a mental illness. However, a confession does not amount to an investigation. The approach to use is purposeful interrogation.

PURPOSEFUL INTERROGATION refers to the realization that the goal of obtaining a confession is secondary to obtaining the truth (Gosselin, 2007). Purposeful interrogation is not a method but a process incorporated into an investigation. Generally, the process moves the focus of investigation away from the interrogation as a central feature of the case. Interrogation is merely a tool of the investigation. The interrogation of a suspect should not provide the primary evidence of the guilt of a suspect. Instead, information gained through an interrogation should confirm evidence, as well as prove the involvement of the person being interrogated. As a process, purposeful interrogation requires a mindset which acknowledges that there may be multiple suspects to interrogate and evidence logically pointing to others needs to be explored.

Law enforcement professionals are mindful of the potential dangers and over-reliance on confessions without corroborating evidence. **CONVICTION INTEGRITY UNITS**, also known as post-conviction review programs, are entities located within District Attorneys' offices that have been designed to investigate claims of wrongful convictions. Many of these units have also developed policies designed to reduce future false convictions that are based on false confessions. Conviction integrity units find law enforcement personnel initiating or cooperating in a substantial portion of all exonerations (The National Registry of Exonerations, 2015). At a minimum, the standards for interrogating individuals who may also have mental disorders involves the protection of the constitutional rights of the suspect, is mindful of the integrity of the case, and seeks to reduce the possibility of a false confession.

Protect the Rights of the Accused

One of the most important mandates to law enforcement in any investigation is strict adherence to upholding the Constitution, including the protection of all rights belonging to the accused. Taking shortcuts in order to obtain evidence may result in a tainted investigation and a statement that is subject to the exclusionary rule or worse. The **EXCLUSIONARY RULE** is a principle based on Constitutional law which states that evidence seized in violation of an individual's constitutional right cannot be used to prove the guilt of that person in a court of law (*Mapp v. Ohio*, 1961). Purposeful disregard for the rights of the accused subjects an officer to possible criminal and civil court action and liability.

IN MY EXPERIENCE . . .

In the case of a multiple stabbing death, the perpetrator told my partner during the interrogation that the devil had infiltrated the body of his mother, the deceased. He had to rid her of the demon, which was why he stabbed his victim 106 times. The suspect was under doctor's care and on medication for psychiatric illness. There was no doubt of his guilt, yet the prosecutor declined to bring the man to trial. Instead, he was committed to a psychiatric hospital for treatment. The prosecutor made this decision for many reasons. First, it was clear that the offender was not responsible for his actions due to his mental condition and secondly, it would be safer for him to be in a hospital and receive treatment for his psychosis.

Question for discussion: Do you think justice was accomplished in this case?

To assure that the suspect can knowingly and voluntarily waive the protection against self-incrimination, the officer makes a determination based on the individual's level of functioning. Prior to questioning, ask the suspect a few simple questions such as their age, name, and address. Determine the suspect's level of education completed and ability to read. The law allows some flexibility as it is not required that *Miranda* warnings be given verbatim (*Miranda v. Arizona*, 1966). It may be helpful to give the warnings verbally to the person and explain them in a way that is simple and easy to understand. It should be noted that individuals with intellectual disability often do not understand *Miranda* warnings even if they say they do (Gosselin, 2007). Follow department rules and regulations that may exist relative to interrogating potentially vulnerable persons. The law enforcement officer is not a mental health specialist and is not qualified to diagnose a suspect's mental health. The officer is responsible for accurately documenting the status of the accused so that the prosecutor can decide on the appropriateness of a criminal trial and gauge the evidentiary weight of any confession. Video and audio recording of interrogations is now a widely accepted practice so that a review of the suspect questioning can occur.

Integrity of the Case

Protecting the integrity of a case refers to assurance of the reliability of the evidence. Justice is not served if the wrong person is arrested. An interrogation takes time and patience to ensure trustworthiness. Even so, many attempts at obtaining confessions will fail. There is some evidence that the chances of obtaining a confession can increase 25 percent for every hour of interrogation, up to four hours (Vessel, 1998). In the well-known landmark case of *Miranda* (id 446), the Court expressed concern over "sustained and prolonged questioning" (*Miranda v. Arizona*, 1966). Lengthy confessions (over four hours) are more likely to be associated with cases of false confessions, and should therefore be avoided whenever possible.

Two important issues impact interrogation trustworthiness: tunnel vision and contamination. Tunnel vision on the part of the investigator is an overwhelming confidence in the suspect's guilt to the point that evidence to the contrary is not investigated. Experts claim this to be misclassification of guilt. Tunnel vision can occur when police officers falsely believe that they can distinguish truth from deception based on body language, demeanor, and behavioral symptoms (Leo, 2013). The second hazard to avoid is interrogation contamination. All police officers are aware of the problems of contaminating physical evidence at a scene, but may not be as careful in safeguarding the details of the crime during the interrogation (Trainum, 2014). Statements given by the suspect that are suggestive of guilt must be followed up by asking for details of the event. Non-leading questions should elicit key details without prompting or suggesting. No photos or case files should be shown to the suspect.

False Confessions

It sounds counter-intuitive to think that someone might confess to something that they did not do; only recently have we realized that false confessions can occur. Individuals who have intellectual or mental disorders are more likely to confess to something that they did not do (Leo, 2013). Identifying those with special needs during questioning should be a major focus for the interrogator. Individuals with intellectual or cognitive disorders, those with severe mental illness, and juveniles may be easily confused about the criminal justice process and "confess" even when they are innocent. At high risk during interrogation are individuals with *Autism Spectrum Disorders* whose condition may present behavioral indicators of guilt such as a lack of eye contact or an apparent aloof and indifferent manner which may be misinterpreted.

Individuals with some cognitive disorders and intellectual disabilities are conditioned throughout their lives to be compliant and submissive and are at risk of falsely incriminating themselves to please the interrogator (Gosselin, 2007). Police officers should check for understanding by asking the individual easy questions, for example, what a lawyer is and how a lawyer might help the individual, or asking the individual for an example of a Constitutional right. Using simple language or pictures and symbols, speaking slowly and clearly, and asking concrete questions are all ways to ensure clear communication. The person may not be able to understand the questions, but may repeat things as if they do understand. When in doubt, be sure to re-direct questions to determine whether the person understands what is being said. Avoid asking questions that require a yes or no answer. It is deplorable for the police to accept a confession if the person does not understand what he or she has admitted to doing.

Between 1989 and 2015, 1,614 exonerations have occurred (The National Registry of Exonerations, 2015). False confessions are a factor that contributed to a wrongful conviction in 13 percent of the exonerations. A review of the false confession factors reveals that most individuals suffered from some form of mental disorder. Individuals with mental disorders are more prone to falsely confess in situations that are psychologically overbearing and stressful. The highest number of false confessions occurs in homicide cases (The National Registry of Exonerations, 2015), those in which interrogators have a high stake in solving the crime.

LAW ENFORCEMENT OFFICERS

The primary response to people with mental disorders has fallen, by default, to the criminal justice system. Meeting this obligation is one of the biggest challenges to modern policing. Who are the law enforcement officers that confront the challenges of today's crisis? The modern law enforcement officer is more diverse now than at any other time in history. The Bureau of Justice Statistics reports that 27 percent of police officers are members of a racial or ethnic minority, and 12 percent are women (Reaves, 2015).

Police Training

Meeting the needs of those with mental disorders are complex and the outcomes of police encounters has been less than optimum. To address these critical law enforcement issues, policy makers, leaders, former patients, family members and others met in 2009. The resulting plan to improve interactions between police and people with mental disorders came from the International Chiefs of Police (IACP) in association with the Bureau of Justice Assistance and numerous stakeholders ("IACP Initiative: Building Safer Communities: Improving Police Response to Persons with Mental Illness," 2010). The initiatives set forth included recommendations for law enforcement training and education. Further recommendations included the development and sustaining of collaborations between law enforcement, mental health professionals, communities, families, and advocates. Finding alternatives to the criminalization of the mentally ill became the stated goal of the summit.

The IACP Initiative recommended that law enforcement training should reduce stigma and decrease the perception of danger to law enforcement officers. To meet these goals, police academy training should educate peace officers on the behaviors associated with the DSM categories of serious mental illness and developmental disability, psychotropic medications and their side effects as well as the mental health resources available in the local community. To prevent the unnecessary use of force officers should also learn effective communication and de-escalation techniques and issues unique to youth with mental disorders.

The most common training for law enforcement officers on mental health and disorders is associated with a CIT. Recall from previous chapters that *Crisis Intervention Team* (CIT) training is a pre-booking jail diversion program. It is intended to improve the outcomes of police interactions with people with mental illness by de-escalating crisis situations, decreasing the use of force by officers and increasing access to community treatment options. Some of the training is planned and delivered by mental health consumers and family members. Some departments may only train volunteer police officers, while others mandate training only for police officers that carry electronic control devices such as Tasers. An increasing number of jurisdictions require the full forty-hour CIT course for all officers.

Another training option is Mental Health First Aid. More than 10,000 police officers, corrections officers, and other public safety professionals have embraced the training known as *Mental Health First Aid for Public Safety*, according to a press release from the National Council for Behavioral Health (Cobb, 2014).

> "*Mental Health First Aid* is the help offered to a person developing a mental health problem or experiencing a mental health crisis . . . to preserve life when a person may be a danger to self or others; provide help to prevent the problem from becoming more serious; promote and enhance recovery and provide comfort and support (Mental Health Association of Maryland, 2013)."

MENTAL HEALTH FIRST AID is a program designed to educate adults about mental illness with goals of modifying attitudes and perceptions, including how to respond to individuals who are experiencing mental health crises. The standardized program was developed at the Australian National University in 2001 and first used in the United States in 2007. First offered at the Rhode Island Municipal Police Academy, instructors with a background in law enforcement or corrections often teach the program to first responder audiences and in police academies (Gibb, 2014). Topics of the specialized program include depression, suicide, anxiety disorders, psychosis, substance abuse disorders, and legal issues. The goal is to provide public safety officers with more options to help de-escalate incidents and better understand the risk factors and warning signs of mental illness. Still in its infancy, the attractiveness of this program is the 8-hour training time and relatively low cost, making this option viable for most police departments. Acquiring empathic listening skills is a core component of the course model. Since its inception the program has been implemented internationally in seventeen countries and in all American states, Washington D.C., and Puerto Rico (NREPP, 2015).

Policing courses on mental disorders designed to meet the requirements of CALEA may range from a few hours to a few days. A common complaint is that police academies spend hundreds of hours training individuals to defend themselves against the public, then at graduation hand them a badge with instructions to go out and develop community relationships. Some states have begun to address this void in training. The State of Illinois, for example, recently passed legislation mandating a standard certified training program in crisis intervention addressing specialized policing responses to people with mental illnesses offers a substantial 12-hour basic police course which includes instruction on how to identify common mental illnesses and other disabilities in a law enforcement context in addition to appropriate law enforcement responses to suicide ("Mental Health and Disabilities," 2006).

IN MY EXPERIENCE . . .

When I heard of the *Mental Health First Aid* program I was intrigued and decided to take the course myself. The instructor was knowledgeable and sensitive about the issues surrounding mental health problems. The course offered information that would help most people in identifying levels of risk and safe intervention options for individuals in crisis situations. For the minimal time commitment and the importance of the course material, it was well worth becoming certified! Not just for police officers, it is a great course for everyone.

Question for discussion: Do you have a *Mental Health First Aid* program on campus? What would it take to start such a program?

POLICE OFFICER WELLNESS

While it may seem simplistic, it is important to note that law enforcement officers are just people doing a job. Some will do the job better than others and some will excel. Some law enforcement officers have high personal standards and others don't. They have the same issues, problems, and concerns as any other person in society. They are not exempt from paying bills, caring for children and elders, and having marital problems. However, law enforcement officers typically lack concern for their own mental health and well-being. Mental health issues and threats of officer suicide are often concealed in this profession where strength, bravery, and resilience are revered (IACP, 2014). Law enforcement officers are not immune to developing post-traumatic stress disorder, stress, anxiety, or depression.

Working in public safety, whether as a government employee or in the private sector, carries with it an increased risk of workplace violence and suicide. The U.S. Department of Justice has found that government employees working in law enforcement and security occupations (140 per 1,000 U.S. citizens) and private sector organizations (102 per 1,000) have the highest annual average rate of violent victimization occurring in the workplace (Harrell, 2013). The category includes law enforcement officers, prison or jail guards, security guards, and other law enforcement occupations. Most of the workplace violence against government employees occurred at the state, county, and local levels. According to the Federal Bureau of Investigation (FBI), almost 50,000 law enforcement officers were assaulted in 2013. In 2014, fifty-one law enforcement officers were killed in line-of-duty incidents in addition to forty-four officers who were killed accidentally while performing their duties (FBI, 2015).

Post-Traumatic Stress Disorder

It is widely accepted that post-traumatic stress syndrome is a common affliction among law enforcement officers. Stressors that affect law enforcement officers include exposure to horrific events, relationship issues including divorce or loss of a loved one, serious or terminal illness, financial strain, significant change in routine and domestic violence. Research suggests that as many as 33 percent of law enforcement officers may suffer from post-traumatic stress syndrome at some point during their career (Kates, 2010). Qualified mental health intervention from peer support personnel and employee assistance programs is necessary to provide intervention for work related stress issues among police officers. Protocols to effectively and consistently address mental wellness after critical incidents should be established in addition to intervention programs that address the daily chronic stress of the job. Training on the recognition of signs and symptoms of emotional distress, PTSD or other mental illness, or suicidal behavior among colleagues is imperative for the well-being of those who are tasked with our protection.

6. CH08-06: Policing can be a dangerous job. Officers experience high levels of post-traumatic stress syndrome, and are at higher risk of experiencing violent workplace injury and suicide compared to individuals working in private sector jobs. Approximately twice the number of officers killed in the line of duty die by suicide. Wellness among law enforcement officers is a national priority which involves meeting the challenges of mental disorders and breaking down barriers of health seeking. Photo copyright Straight 8 Photography/Shutterstock.com

Roughly 25 percent of law enforcement officers have served in the military, some of whom have been deployed to combat (IACP, 2010). The psychological effects of combat duty have been well documented. One common illness that follows a traumatic event such as combat is PTSD. Symptoms may include anxiety attacks, depression, nightmares, aggressive behavior, flashbacks, sensitivity to noises and movement, and a numbing of emotions. PTSD can make it difficult for veterans to get along with family and friends. If untreated, these "invisible injuries" can lead to problems including alcoholism, drug abuse, and even suicide.

Rates of PTSD run high among combat veterans compared to the civilian population, and likely run higher for veterans with multiple deployments (IACP, 2010). Future police recruits will undoubtedly include some of the military service members who are active in combat now, in addition to the men and women deployed to combat from within the law enforcement ranks. Although much remains to be learned about the effects of combat zone deployment on police officers specifically, clearly some officers and their families will need professional services to successfully deal with the changes in their lives, and all will need some form of support, including support in the workplace.

The International Chiefs of Police point out that many mental health problems are like psychological "injuries." Just as with many physical injuries, most eventually heal and the person makes a full recovery. Law enforcement officers with mental health issues should not be judged as flawed or weak. The negative stigma often attached to seeking mental health treatment does a great disservice to all law enforcement officers, including the returning combat veterans who could benefit from such treatment.

Suicide Among Police Officers

It is estimated that twice as many law enforcement officers take their own lives than are killed in the line of duty (IACP, 2014). The stigma associated with having mental health problems in law enforcement and seeking professional help is strong in police culture. The IACP identified three barriers to achieving mental health parity in law enforcement:

- Fear of consequences for seeking help for emotional problems or mental illness
- Officers are not generally trained to respond to emotional trauma, mental illness, or suicidal behavior that they experience
- Departments with limited resources may lack the time and capacity to provide the necessary and confidential mental wellness program

SUMMARY

Law enforcement officers are in contact with citizens in our diverse American culture daily. People with mental disorders will be represented among victims, offenders, witnesses, and complainants. Some individuals will require service and protection. Determining the real risk that an individual may pose to the public is an important direction for improved policing efforts. Successful intervention for thousands of individuals in crisis has become a reality, but continuing that trend requires resources and commitment. The future of policing must involve heightened understanding of these behaviors and include techniques to de-escalate crises whenever possible. Research on medical conditions and their relation to ARD and other tragedies is evolving in a way that is similar to any other investigation. Purposeful interrogation techniques include ways to avoid false confessions and bolster the integrity of the case when a vulnerable person is involved without overreliance on a confession. Of concern is the compromised wellness of police officers and those who work in public safety occupations.

CHAPTER QUESTIONS FOR REVIEW

1. Under what circumstances is there a connection between violent victimization and violent offending?
2. Is crime linked to mental illness? Explain both sides of the debate.
3. What are the issues surrounding police use of force?
4. List numerous techniques for de-escalation during crisis.
5. What is purposeful interrogation?

REFERENCES

Akins, S., Burkhardt, B., Lanfear, C., Stevens, K., and Amorim, M. (2014). *Law enforcement response to people with mental illnesses in Benton County: Executive Summary*. Oregon State University. Corvallis, OR. Retrieved from https://www.co.benton.or.us/sites/default/files/fileattachments/district_attorney039s_office/page/2025/osufinalexecsummaryreport.pdf

Akins, S., Burkhardt, B. C., and Lanfear, C. (2016). Law Enforcement response to "Frequent Fliers": An examination of high-frequency contacts between police and justice-involved persons with mental illness. *Criminal Justice Policy Review, 27*(1), 97–114.

Akins, S., Burkhardt, B., Lanfear, C., Stevens, K., and Amorim, M. (2014). *Law enforcement response to people with mental illnesses in Benton County: Executive Summary*. Oregon State University. Corvallis, OR. Retrieved from https://www.co.benton.or.us/sites/default/files/fileattachments/district_attorney039s_office/page/2025/osufinalexecsummaryreport.pdf

Alpert, G. (2015). Police use of force and the suspect with mental illness. *American Society of Criminology, 14*(2), 277–283.

APA. (2015). *Understanding mental disorders: Your guide to DSM-5*. Washington, D.C.: American Psychiatric Association.

Bahora, M., Hanafi, S., Chien, V. H., and Compton, M. T. (2008). Preliminary evidence of effects of crisis intervention team training on self-efficacy and social distance. *Administration and Policy in Mental Health and Mental Health Services Research, 35*(3), 159–167.

Biasotti, M. (2011). The Impact of Mental Illness on Law Enforcement Resources. Arlington, VA: Treatment Advocacy Center.

City and County of San Francisco, California, et al. v. Sheehan (575 U.S. ___ 2015).

Cobb, H. (2014). Mental Health First Aid for Public Safety Officers [Press release]. Retrieved from http://www.thenationalcouncil.org/press-releases/national-council-members-congress-convene-briefing-mental-health-first-aid-public-safety-officers/

Coleman, T., and Cotton, D. (2014). TEMPO: A contemporary model for police education and training about mental illness. *International Journal of Law and Psychiatry, 37*(4), 325–333.

Cordner, G. (2006). People with mental illness *Problem-Specific Guides for Police*. Washington, D.C.: U.S. Department of Justice.

FBI. (2015). FBI Releases 2014 Preliminary Statistics for Law Enforcement Officers Killed in the Line of Duty Retrieved May, 2015, from https://www.fbi.gov/news/pressrel/press-releases/fbi-releases–2014–preliminary-statistics-for-law-enforcement-officers-killed-in-the-line-of-duty

Fuller, D., Lamb, R., Biasotti, M., and Snook, J. (2015). Overlooked in the undercounted: The role of mental illness in fatal law enforcement encounters. Arlington, VA: Treatment Advocacy Center.

Gallo, F. (2006). *Defensive Tactics*. Cranston, RI: L.E. Press.

Gosselin, D. K. (2007). *Smart talk: Contemporary interviewing and interrogation*. Upper Saddle River, NJ: Pearson Education.

Green, T. (1997). Police as frontline mental health workers: The decision to arrest or refer to mental health agencies. *International Journal of Law and Psychiatry, 20*, 469–486.

Hainze v. Richards, 207 F.3d 795, 801 (2000).

Harrell, E. (2013). *Workplace Violence against Government Employees, 1994–2011.* (NCJ 241349). Washington, D.C.: U.S. Department of Justice.

Ho, J. D., Dawes, D. M., Nystrom, P. C., Collins, D. P., Nelson, R. S., Moore, J. C., and Miner, J. R. (2013). Markers of acidosis and stress in a sprint versus a conducted electrical weapon. *Forensic Science International 233*(1), 84–89.

Hoffman, L. (2009). ACEP Recognizes Excited Delirium as Unique Syndrome. *Emergency Medicine News, 31*(11), 4.

Houston Police Department. (2010). A multi-agency collaboration between the city of Houston health and human services department and the mental health retardation authority of Harris County. *Chronic consumer stabilization initiative.* Retrieved from: http://www.popcenter.org/library/awards/goldstein/2010/10–13(F).pdf

IACP. (2010). Law Enforcement Leader's Guide on Combat Veterans: A Transition Guide for Veterans Beginning or Continuing Careers in Law Enforcement. Alexandria, Virginia: International Association of Chiefs of Police.

IACP. (2014). IACP National Symposium on Law Enforcement Officer Suicide and Mental Health: Breaking the Silence on Law Enforcement Suicides. Washington, D.C.: Office of Community Oriented Policing Services.

IACP Initiative: Building Safer Communities: Improving Police Response to Persons with Mental Illness. (2010). Retrieved June14, 2015, from http://www.theiacp.org/portals/0/pdfs/ImprovingPoliceResponsetoPersonsWithMentalIllnessSummit.pdf

ICD-10. (2016). International classification of diseases. Retrieved March 10, 2016, from http://www.who.int/classifications/icd/en/

Johnson, R. R. (2011). Suspect Mental Disorder and Police Use of Force. *Criminal Justice and Behavior, 38*(2), 127–145.

Kates, A. (2010). *CopShock: Surviving Post-Traumatic Stress Disorder.* Tucson, AZ: Holbrook Street Press.

Kerr, A., Morabito, M., and Watson, A. (2010). Police encounters, mental illness and injury: An exploratory investigation. *Journal of Police Crisis Negotiation, 1*(10), 116–132.

Leo, R. (2013). False confessions and the Constitution: Problems, possibilities and solutions *The Constitution and the future of criminal justice in America.* Retrieved July, 2015, from http://ssrn.com/abstract=2104416

MacDonald, J. M., Kaminski, R. J., and Smith, M. R. (2009). The Effect of Less-Lethal Weapons on Injuries in Police Use-of-Force Events. *American Journal of Public Health, 99*(12), 2268.

Mapp v. Ohio, 367 U.S. 643 (1961).

Miranda v. Arizona, 384 U.S. 436, 86 S. Ct. 1602, 16 L. Ed. 2d 694 (1966).

Mental Health and Disabilities. (2006). Retrieved June 14, 2015, from http://naminc.org/nn/blet/oregon-lesson-plan.pdf

Mental Health Association of Maryland. (2013). *Mental Health First Aid USA.* Lutherville, MD: Missouri Department of Mental Health and National Council for Behavioral Health.

Mental Health Training. (2010). Retrieved June 16, 2015, from http://www.calea.org/content/mental-health-training

Mohandie, K., and Duffy, J. (1999). Understanding subjects with paranoid schizophrenia. *FBI law enforcement bulletin, 68*(12), 8.

NAMI. (2010). Mental Health Crisis Planning. St. Paul, MN: NAMI Minnesota.

NAMI. (2015). Risk of Suicide. Retrieved from http://www.nami.org/Learn–More/Mental–Health–Conditions/Related–Conditions/Risk-of-Suicide

NREPP. (2015). Mental Health First Aid. Retrieved from http://www.nrepp.samhsa.gov/ViewIntervention.aspx?id=321

O'Brien, A. J., and Thom, K. (2014). Police use of TASER devices in mental health emergencies: A review. *International Journal of Law and Psychiatry, 37*(4), 420–426.

The National Registry of Exonerations. (2015). Exonerations in 2014. Ann Arbor, Michigan: University of Michigan Law School.

Torrey, E., Entsminger, K., Geller, J., Stanley, J., and Jaffe, D. (2012). The shortage of public hospital beds for mentally ill persons (pp. 17). Arlington, VA: Treatment Advocacy Center.

Torrey, E., Kennard, A., Eslinger, D., Biasotti, M., and Fuller, D. (2013). Justifiable Homicides by Law Enforcement Officers: What is the Role of Mental Illness? Arlington, VA: Treatment Advocacy Center.

Trimel, S. (2012). Amnesty International Urges Stricter Limits on Police Taser Use as U.S. Toll Reaches 500. London: Amnesty International.

Peterson, J., Skeem, J., Kennealy, P., Bray, B., and Zvonkovic, A. (2014). How Often and How Consistently do Symptoms Directly Precede Criminal Behavior Among Offenders with Mental Illness? *Law and Human Behavior, 38*(5), 439–449.

Reaves, B. (2015). Local Police Departments, 2013: Personnel, Policies, and Practices. Washington, D.C.: Bureau of Justice Statistics.

Reuland, M., Draper, L., and Norton, B. (2010). Improving Responses to People with Mental Illness: Tailoring Law Enforcement Initiative to Individual Jurisdictions. New York, NY: Council of State Governments Justice Center.

Reuland, M., Schwarzfeld, M., and Draper, L. (2009). Law enforcement responses to people with mental illnesses: A guide to research-informed policy and practice. New York, NY: Justice Center.

Ruiz, J. (2003). Policing persons with mental illness: The Pennsylvania experience. Middletown, PA: Institute of State and Regional Affairs.

Roach, B., Echols, K., and Burnett, A. (2014). Excited Delirium and the Dual Response: Preventing In-Custody Deaths. *FBI Enforcement Bulletin* (July).

Santos, F., and Goode, E. (2014). Police confront rising number of mentally ill *New York Times, Late Edition (East Coast) ed.*

Seattle Police Department. (2013). Excited Delirium. *Policy 16.135*. Retrieved July 7, 2015, from http://www.seattle.gov/police-manual/title–16——patrol-operations/16135——excited-delirium

Silver, E., Piquero, A., Jennings, W., Piquero, N., and Leiber, M. (2011). Assessing the violent offending and violent victimization overlap among discharged psychiatric patients. *Law and Human Behavior, 35*(1), 49.

Special Panel Review of Excited Delirium. (2011). Executive Summary. Retrieved July 2, 2015, from Pennsylvania State University at https://www.justnet.org/pdf/ExDS–Panel–Report–FINAL.pdf

Steadman, H., Mulvey, E., Monahan, J., Robbins, P., Appelbaum, P., Grisso, T., . . . Silver, E. (1998). Violence by people discharged from acute psychiatric inpatient facilities and by others in the same neighborhoods. *Arch Gen Psychiatry, 55*, 393–401.

Strote, J., Walsh, M., Auerbach, D., Burns, T., and Maher, P. (2014). Medical conditions and restraint in patients experiencing excited delirium. *The American Journal of Emergency Medicine, 32*(9), 1093–1096.

Takeuchi, A., Ahern, T. L., and Henderson, S. O. (2011). Excited delirium. *Western Journal of Emergency Medicine, 12*(1), 77–83.

Teplin, L., McClelland, G., Abram, K., and Weiner, D. (2005). Crime victimization in adults with severe mental illness: Comparison with the National Crime Victimization Survey. *Arch Gen Psychiatry, 62*, 911–921.

Torrey, E. (2012). *Bedlam Revisited: Jails, Police, and Mental Health Courts as the New Psychiatric Care System.* Paper presented at the APA, Philadelphia.

Torrey, E., Fuller, D., Geller, J., Jacobs, C., and Ragosta, K. (2012). No room at the inn: Trends and consequences of closing public psychiatric hospitals. Arlington, VA: Treatment Advocacy Center.

Trainum, J. (2014). 'I Did It'—Confession contamination and evaluation. *The Police Chief.* 81. Retrieved July 5, 2015, from http://www.policechief magazine.org/magazine/index.cfm?fuseaction=displayandarticle_ id=3366andissue_id=62014

Vessel, D. (1998). Conducting successful interrogations. *FBI Enforcement Bulletin, 67*(10).

Washington State Institute for Public Policy. (2009). The dangerous mentally ill offender program: Four-year felony recidivism and cost effectiveness. Retrieved from: http://wsipp.wa.gov/ReportFile/1036

White, M., Goldkamp, J., and Campbell, S. (2006). Co-occurring mental illness and substance abuse in the criminal justice system: Some implications for local jurisdictions. *The Prison Journal, 86*, 301–325.

Weiss, D. (2008). Calming down: Could sedative drugs be a less-lethal option? *National institute of justice journal, 261*(NCJ 224090).

CHAPTER 9

Criminal Court

INTRODUCTION

Until recently, the criminal court did not routinely concern itself with psychological variables when dealing with ordinary offenders. Most accused offenders are assumed to be rational people with sufficient capacity to survive the ordeal of trial and face punishment if found guilty. Most of the individuals with mental disorders who are diverted out of the criminal justice system have committed minor, nonviolent crimes and are in great need of treatment rather than punishment. A small minority are so severely disordered that prosecution could not reasonably occur. These individuals come to the attention of law enforcement, prosecution, and the courts due to severe mental illnesses that impair their ability to live safely in society because they are a danger to themselves or others, or because clinical intervention is necessary due to a crisis.

A certain threshold level of mental impairment must be exceeded before the court will make exceptions. Typically, the criminal justice system does not judge that threshold to have been crossed unless the disability and impairment is severe. Once a form of incapacity is identified as an aspect of a mental disorder which justifies diversion, the court system presumes that all other offenders are free of that type of impairment. By using established criteria to identify and divert abnormal offenders from traditional court processing, the criminal justice system is also affirming the normality of the offenders who are not identified or diverted. Hearings for competency, diminished capacity, and pleas of insanity are among the ways in which the criminal court system identifies individuals that require differential treatment.

Key Terms

COMPETENCY TO STAND TRIAL DOCTRINE

COURT JURISDICTION

FORENSIC PSYCHOLOGIST

INSANITY DEFENSE

PRESUMPTION OF INNOCENCE

PRESUMPTION OF SANITY

Chapter Objectives

After completing this chapter, you should be able to:

- Define and describe the elements that must be present for a crime to have been committed
- Explain the factors that determine court jurisdiction
- Compare and contrast competency and insanity
- Describe the insanity defenses and the legal rules involved

CRIMINAL CONDUCT

Crimes are committed for many complex reasons: potential for personal gain, the influence of poverty, and substance abuse are among the many factors that can lead to criminal activity. Some research suggests that there may be a modest increase in violence among those with serious mental illness as compared to those without disorders, particularly when substance abuse is co-occurring (Swanson, McGinty, Fazel, and Mays, 2015). However, many individuals that suffer from mental disorders commit crimes for the same reasons that others do. Criminal responsibility rests on the fact that all persons are considered responsible for their behavior, except for certain categories of individuals: children and those who are incapable of understanding the societal rules of responsible behavior because of serious mental illness or intellectual disability.

Our criminal justice system has a difficult time determining when an offenders' mental illness limits them enough that the process cannot determine their innocence or guilt. Psychological variations, such as dangerousness within groups of mentally ill offenders, are often shared by other criminal offenders that are not identified as having mental disorders. Fairness dictates that a line must be drawn between mentally disordered and all other offenders, however. This chapter deals with that process of determining how criminal offenders may be handled differently within the court phase of the criminal justice system when their criminal responsibility is in question.

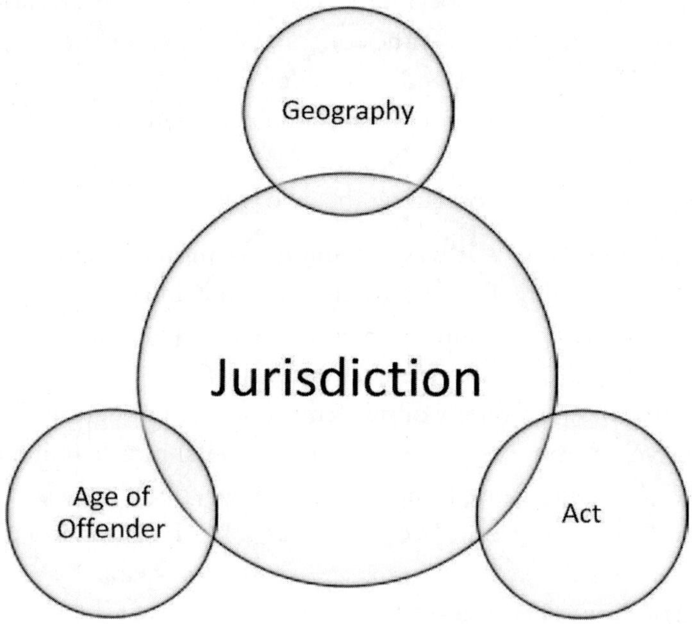

1. CH09-01: *Jurisdiction.* The power of a court to hear its case is based on multiple factors which are determined by constitutional authority and defined legislatively by state statutes. Consider the overlapping nature of geography, act, and age of the offender to understand the way jurisdiction is determined.

COURT JURISDICTION

A court is an agency of the judicial branch of government with one or more judicial officers who have the authority to decide cases, controversies in law, and disputed matters of fact. Each court across the United States acts within legally defined statutory and constitutional authority and limitations. When a crime has been committed and a person is identified as the individual likely to have committed the crime, the goal of the court system is to determine their guilt or innocence. When guilt is adjudicated, the court specifies an appropriate sanction. Decisions made within a legally recognized court compel individual compliance to the orders of the court.

The power of the court, its scope and authority, is called its jurisdiction. Three conditions typically determine a court's jurisdiction: geography, act, and age. Geography affects the court since a case is usually tried in the place where the crime was committed, or in cases of continuing crimes, where it began or ended.

An example of a continuing offense would be where a person is kidnapped from one city and taken across state lines to another city where the person is then murdered. This crime might be tried at the location where the kidnapping occurred or where the death occurred. The jurisdiction would also include a choice between the state courts (either one) or the federal court. America's dual court system separates federal and state courts. The federal court system has jurisdiction over crimes committed across multiple state lines in cases where a federal law also prohibits the act. As a point of practicality, the jurisdiction that has the greatest interest in prosecuting the case will agree to do so.

The act, or the crime that was committed, is another factor in determining which court has the jurisdiction to determine the innocence or guilt of the individual charged. There are numerous jurisdictional levels of court based on the type of crime. Courts of general jurisdiction in either the federal or state systems can hold a trial to hear any felony or misdemeanor case put before it that does not belong exclusively to another court. Courts of general jurisdiction are known by various names, including felony, superior, supreme, county, and circuit courts. A felony is a criminal offense punishable by death or incarceration in a prison facility for at least one year. A misdemeanor is an offense punishable by incarceration in a jail, typically for one year or less.

State courts of limited jurisdiction usually hear misdemeanor criminal violations, violations of municipal ordinances, traffic violations and civil court cases that involve damages limited to a certain amount of money. They are known as municipal courts, county courts, district courts, and metropolitan courts, to name a few. There is a growing trend in the United States toward the creation of specialty courts that have a more limited jurisdiction. These specialty courts usually focus on misdemeanor crimes that involve a pressing social issue or concern. Court personnel in a specialty court are trained with a greater level of expertise in the issue being resolved. Mental health courts, domestic violence courts, drug courts and veteran's courts are examples of specialized courts across America. As you learned in an earlier chapter, mental health courts are a diversion from traditional court processing. A court that has jurisdiction over the crime alleged to have occurred must give up its jurisdiction to the specialized court for the case to be moved to another court docket. Individuals that meet the criteria for diversion to the specialty courts are given a choice, and they must agree to have their case handled by the specialty court.

The third factor that determines jurisdiction is the age of the offender. Traditional general jurisdiction courts only have the power to hear cases involving an adult defendant. The age at which a person is considered an adult for the purposes of trial does vary state by state and by the crime that is alleged to have occurred—the act. Eighteen is the most common age at which states and the federal system consider a person to be an adult. Some states have responded to serious violence committed by juveniles through a punitive approach which changes the age of adult court processing for certain crimes, such as murder and gun violations.

Appellate courts do not have the jurisdiction to try a case to determine guilt or innocence. The role of an appellate court is to review the trial process in cases where the constitutionality of a law or procedure is in question or when an error is suspected to have been made in the lower court. In cases where the appellate court determines that an error has been made, or a person's constitutional rights were violated, it can order a new trial or even allow the defendant to go free.

FOUNDATIONS OF CRIMINAL LAW

The criminal justice system recognizes that the law should take into consideration a variety of situations in which a person's ability to function within the laws' mandate is impaired. Yet it struggles on how to respond to offenders whose behavior is severely affected by mental disorder. The foundations of American criminal justice rest on the *actus reus* and *mens rea* of the accused individual. *Actus reus* is the Latin term for "wrongful act." Unless an act (or action) is expressly designated as a crime or forbidden by law, either as a voluntarily wrongful act or the absence of an act, a person cannot be held responsible in a criminal court. The criminal omission of an act occurs when a person has a legally defined duty and fails to perform that duty. An example would be crimes involving child abuse and neglect that result from a parent's failure to feed or properly clothe a child who suffers because of that neglect.

Mens rea, a Latin phrase that means "guilty mind," refers to the legal requirement that, in order for a person to be held criminally liable for having committed an act that is a crime, that person must have had the ability to choose to commit the criminal act. Simply stated, a person must have the mental capacity to be able to choose to do something and know that it was wrong. This does not mean that a person necessarily meant for the results of his or her action; rather, there was an act, or failure to act, that was made voluntarily, and which resulted in the crime. *Mens rea* may be inferred from a person's actions and from all circumstances that surround those actions. This analysis may include studying past behaviors of the individual to determine their ability to act by independent thought. Being reckless or negligent in one's actions may also constitute grounds for prosecution. For example, driving a car recklessly and causing the death of another by accident. Strict liability offenses do not require *mens rea*, a mental state, as an element of the offense. To obtain a conviction for a strict liability crime, the state must only prove that the defendant committed the prohibited act. An example of a strict liability case is driving under the influence; strict liability cases are about determining cause and effect, not rationale. *Mens rea* and motive are not the same. A motive is a person's reason for committing a crime.

OFFICERS OF THE COURT

The judge is the most senior officer of the court. The duties of the judge are primarily concerned with oversight of the trial process. The judge controls the demeanor in the courtroom, settles questions of evidence and procedure, and guides the questioning of witnesses. In cases that are tried before a jury, the judge gives instructions to the jury members about the law that governs the case. In cases when a jury is waived, the judge determines guilt or innocence. When the defendant is found guilty, the judge must decide the sentence. The judge controls and influences the court personnel with the responsibility for safeguarding the rights of the accused and treatment of the witnesses. To accomplish these goals, judges work closely with prosecution and defense attorneys, court security officers, probation officers, and many others that are directly employed by the court to streamline access and coordinate services while preserving the court's safety.

The prosecutor is the chief law enforcement officer overseeing a specific jurisdiction that is defined by law. The prosecutor may be known as a district attorney, county attorney, state's attorney, or U.S. attorney, depending on the jurisdiction. The prosecutor has the power to execute search and arrest warrants, impanel a grand jury, and determine whether criminal charges will be filed. He represents the state in plea negotiations, pretrial motions, and bail hearings. The prosecutor is responsible for building the criminal case against a defendant and offering evidence through witnesses to the judge and jury. The prosecution must prove a criminal case against the accused beyond a reasonable doubt.

The defense attorney is the person who represents the rights and best interests of a person accused of a criminal offense. As an officer of the court, the defense attorney represents the defendant in competency hearings, plea negotiations, pre-trial and post-trial hearings, and bail hearings. Each defendant has the constitutional right to be represented by an attorney at critical times during the criminal justice process. Indigent defendants are entitled to have an attorney provided to them by the court if they cannot afford one. Depending on the resources of the jurisdiction, the court will assign private counsel or a public defender if an individual is found to be indigent. It should be noted that the court makes the determination on indigence. The probation office will usually take a financial statement from the defendant to inform the judge when indigence is claimed.

The courtroom clerk serves the judge and the jury and helps maintain order in the courtroom. The clerk typically administers the oath or affirmation to prospective jurors and to witnesses. The clerk oversees physical exhibits introduced into evidence and maintains a record of the papers, exhibits, orders and rulings of the judge as well as the verdict.

A court reporter, also known as a short hand reporter, is always present during court proceedings. The court reporter is responsible for creating written records of everything that is said at trials, word-for-word or verbatim. Records include the testimony of witnesses, objections made by the lawyers, and the judge's rulings on those objections. The court reporter uses a stenographic or electronic machine to record what is said in court and prepares an official written transcript of the proceeding.

Many other professionals work in and around the courtroom as well. Probation officers and court security officers, or bailiffs, are essential to the workings of the criminal court system. Some jurisdictions employ victim advocates, forensic child interviewers, and mental health professionals to meet the needs of the diverse defendants, victims, and witnesses involved in the court process. Law enforcement officers and forensic examiners are frequent witnesses to criminal proceedings. Jurisdictions may invite experts and develop specialized programs to assist in administering justice. Some notable advances are evident in mental health, public defense and forensic examiner initiatives.

2. CH09-02: *The Mental Health Public Defender*. Specialized training in mental health issues along with a daily commitment to addressing the needs of this special population are the hallmarks of the Mental Health Public Defender approach. Forensic social workers are an integral component for collaborative relationships in the community and linking clients with services. Copyright Nosnibor137/Bigstock.com.

Mental Health Public Defenders

In 2007, Travis County in Texas became the first county in the nation to implement a stand-alone Mental Health Public Defenders Office (MHPDO) (Mills and Calkins, 2012). Mental health public defenders concentrate full-time on advocacy for people with mental disorders, unlike public defenders or defense counsel appointed by typical randomized appointment. The mission of the MHPDO in Travis County is to:

1. Minimize the number of days a person with mental illness spends in jail
2. Increase the number of dismissals among defendants with mental illness
3. Reduce recidivism by providing intensive case management services

4. Enhance legal representation by providing attorneys with the specialized knowledge necessary to defend persons with mental illness

The value of the MHPDO approach is that it provides greater familiarity with relevant state law than do most private practice attorneys due to special training, and because their defenders deal with criminal issues related to mental illness daily. Forensic social work services are another key feature of MHPDO assistance. A social worker identifies aspects of the mental illness which may be relevant to a defense strategy, links defendants to social services, and monitors compliance throughout the pretrial period. During its first assessment period, the MHPDO program in Travis County served 1,236 clients and 1,762 case management referrals (Mills and Calkins, 2012). The assessment report quantified cost savings of almost $2 million through a reduction in jail bed days, an increase in dismissals, and a reduction in recidivism during its first five years. Similar MHPDOs are now functioning successfully in other counties in Texas and within specialized mental health units in Arizona, California and New Jersey.

Forensic Psychologists

Forensic psychology is a relatively new and developing specialty within the field of psychology. Changes in mental health law require more specialized and professionalized services at different stages during the judicial process. Forensic psychologists apply clinical specialties and research to areas of law. Per the American Psychological Association guidelines, a **FORENSIC PSYCHOLOGIST** refers to a psychologist who examines the psychological condition of a person whose psychological condition is in controversy or at issue (APA, 2013). Forensic examiners are increasingly present within the criminal court system to conduct evaluations in a wide range of legal contexts at every stage of the criminal trial, to testify as expert witnesses, and to direct treatment plans. Most psychological assessments for the criminal court involve three critical stages during the judicial process:

1. Competency to stand trial
2. Insanity evaluation
3. Prediction of dangerousness

3. CH09-03: *The Forensic Examiner.* The expanded legal criteria of the mental health assessment in various stages of the criminal trial has led to an increased role for forensic examiners. These professionals must adhere to similar standards of legal responsibility and accountability which closely resemble other professionals in the criminal justice system. Copyright Kasia Bialasiewicz/Bigstock

The Supreme Court's rulings on competency, insanity, and dangerousness since the 1960s have expanded the legal criteria of the forensic assessment. Forensic examiners are subjected to standards of legal responsibility and accountability which closely resemble those of other professionals in the criminal justice system. For example, some states require Miranda-like warnings to be given by forensic examiners to the defendant that inform them about the limitations of confidentiality that may apply (Roesch, Zapf, Golding, and Skeem, 1999). Forced treatment, competency restoration, and other issues related to insanity and sentencing require predictions of dangerousness as assessed by an examiner according to case law (*Washington v. Harper*, 1990). As the new officers of the court, forensic examiners have a dual role of conducting psychological assessments that will inform the court, while at the same time protect the rights of the defendant who may be mentally disordered. Specialized knowledge of the law and an ability to perform a thorough mental illness assessment are required to accomplish the goals of this profession.

PRETRIAL CONSIDERATIONS

The **PRESUMPTION OF INNOCENCE** is a cornerstone of the American legal system meaning that all individuals accused of a crime are legally presumed to be innocent. Therefore, the prosecution bears the burden of proving that the person is guilty beyond a reasonable doubt, which is the standard for proof in a criminal court. Another important legal presumption is that every person accused of a crime is sane, referred to as the **PRESUMPTION OF SANITY**. Sanity is an important issue in two different capacities: whether the person is sane at the time of the trial, or competency, and whether the person was sane at the time of the offense.

Competency to Stand Trial Doctrine

To be tried in a criminal court, defendants must be able to understand the nature of the charges against them and be able to assist counsel in their own defense during their trial. This is referred to as the **COMPETENCY TO STAND TRIAL DOCTRINE.** Incompetence is an absolute bar to a criminal trial. While the doctrine dates to early English common law, modern standards on the right to effective counsel and due process confirm this rule as an essential part of the American legal system. The Sixth Amendment to the U.S. Constitution is interpreted to guarantee the right to the effective assistance of counsel to all felony defendants (*Gideon v. Wainwright*, 1963) and to most misdemeanor defendants (*Argersinger v. Hamlin*, 1972). Effective assistance of counsel rests on the defendants' ability to participate in the criminal trial process. The Due Process clause of the Fifth Amendment to the U.S. Constitution is interpreted to guarantee a fair trial. Procedural fairness requires that the defendant can understand the criminal justice process and the nature of the charges, in addition to being able to participate meaningfully in his or her own defense. This includes the right to effective assistance of counsel, the rights to summon, confront, and cross-examine witnesses, and the right to testify on one's own behalf or to remain silent without penalty for doing so.

As stated earlier, it is presumed in law, unless proved by evidence to the contrary, that the defendant being tried is sane at the time of the trial. Every state now uses some variation of the definition known as the *Dusky Standard* to determine competency (Zapf, 2013). The standard requires that the defendant have a current ability to consult with his lawyer, possess a reasonable degree of rational understanding and a factual understanding of the proceedings against him. In *Dusky*, the Supreme Court held:

> It is not enough for the district judge to find that "the defendant is oriented to time and place and has some recollection of events," but that the test must be whether he has sufficient present ability to consult with his lawyer with a reasonable degree of rational understanding—and whether he has a rational as well as factual understanding of the proceedings against him (p.402). (*Dusky v. United States*, 1960)

The prosecution or defense will usually raise the issue of competency in front of the judge prior to the beginning of the trial, although a failure to do so does not keep either from bringing it up as a consideration later during the proceedings (*Pate v. Robinson*, 1966). The American Bar Association standards on mental health states that the judge has a continuing obligation, separate and apart from that of counsel for each of the parties, to raise the issue of incompetence to stand trial at any time the Court has a good faith doubt as to the defendant's competence, and may raise the issue at any stage of the proceedings on its own motion (ABA, 2015). A defense attorney has the obligation to move for evaluation regardless of the client's objection if there is a good faith doubt of competence.

A motion for evaluation should be made in writing with the reasons why competence is in question. Once the issue is raised, the defendant has a constitutionally-based due process right to a hearing to determine his or her competency to stand trial. The judge will order a forensic psychological evaluation of the person, which can take place in the jail, an outpatient facility or in an institutional setting. The defendant will usually be examined by a single psychiatrist or psychiatric team. This examination team may include psychologists, social workers, psychiatric nurses or other relevant professionals. In rare cases, when the incompetence appears beyond remedy, such as severe mental retardation, a dangerousness assessment is made and the patient is returned to court for disposition. If the person is found mentally incompetent, the court then must determine the best way to resolve the case. In most jurisdictions, defendants that are deemed incompetent to stand trial are required to be held in an appropriate mental health facility and provided treatment to restore his or her competency.

The Due Process Clause permits a state to require a defendant claiming incompetence to stand trial to bear the burden of proving so by a "preponderance of the evidence" (*Medina*, 1992). The Fifth Amendment Due Process Clause permits the government to involuntarily administer antipsychotic drugs to a mentally ill defendant facing serious criminal charges to render that defendant competent to stand trial. This is allowed only if the treatment is medically appropriate, substantially unlikely to have side effects that may undermine the fairness of the trial, and, taking account of less intrusive alternatives, significantly necessary to further important governmental trial-related interests (*Sell v. United States*, 2003).

Questions of incompetency place a hold on all further stages of adjudication. Approximately 60,000 competency evaluations are court-ordered each year, and around 80 percent result in findings of competence (The National Judicial College, 2012). Competency evaluations, hearings, and restoration take up most forensic mental health dollars and account for approximately 10 percent of inpatient psychiatric beds in the majority of jurisdictions (Golding, 2015). Although the rates vary from state to state, of those defendants referred for issues of competency, an estimated 90 percent are diagnosed with a mental health disorder and 10 percent are diagnosed with a cognitive disorder or developmental disability (Zapf, 2013). Researchers have discovered that when defendants were treated with medication, in addition to being provided instruction and videos on courtroom procedures, 43 percent were more likely to be found competent on reevaluation, compared to only 15 percent with medication alone (Siegel, Schmalleger, and Worrall, 2015). Those who are restored to competency, typically with medication, are returned for trial.

4. CH09-04: *Competency to Stand Trial Doctrine.* Approximately 60,000 competency evaluations are court-ordered each year by the defense attorney, prosecuting attorney, or judge. While the vast majority of individuals referred are diagnosed with a mental health disorder, 80 percent are found competent to stand trial. Having a mental health disorder is a medical finding while competence is a legal category, having a mental illness does not mean a person also incompetent. Copyright Kamira/Bigstock.com

THE TRIAL

The criminal trial begins with opening statements where the prosecutor and defense attorney summarize the arguments that they will be making. The prosecution first presents their case by presenting evidence through witness testimony. The defense cross-examines (or challenges) the prosecutions' witnesses to attack their credibility, after which the prosecution has an opportunity to make another recross-examine to clarify or add information as needed. The second part of the trial begins with the defense's case. Defenses such as insanity may be presented at this stage through witness or expert testimony, or by the defendant directly. The prosecution has the right of rebuttal, if warranted. Final motions and closing arguments signal the end of the trial. Afterward, the judge addresses the jury and provides them with instructions. If the jury reaches a consensus after deliberations, a verdict is announced. If no consensus if reached, a hung jury results and a mistrial is declared.

The government has the burden to prove that an individual charged with a criminal offense has committed the illegal act beyond a reasonable doubt. This is the entire reason for a criminal trial. The presumption of innocence means that the prosecution must prove the case against the defendant, who does not have to do or say anything if he or she chooses. Considering the evidence, the accused will offer defenses and provide contrary evidence that calls into question their guilt. **DEFENSES** are justifications or excuses, defined by law, under which a defendant may be released from prosecution or punishment for a crime. With a justification defense, the defendant acknowledges responsibility for the act but argues that it was necessary and therefore reasonable behavior under the circumstances. An example of the justification defense would be a killing in self-defense. The excuse defense is used when the defendant admits what he did was wrong but claims that some condition kept him from forming criminal intent. There are many examples of defenses. Relevant here are the excuses of insanity and diminished capacity.

INSANITY DEFENSES

An **INSANITY DEFENSE** is a legal claim by a defendant that he or she was suffering from a disease or mental defect that caused them to not understand the difference between right and wrong at the time the criminal act was alleged to have occurred. In 1984 following public outrage over the acquittal of John Hinckley by reason of insanity for attempting to assassinate John Hinckley, the United States passed the Comprehensive Crime Control Act (18 U.S. Code § 20). Renumbered in 1986, the CCA provides that it is an affirmative defense to all federal crimes that, at the time of the offense, "the defendant, as a result of a severe mental disease or defect, was unable to appreciate the nature and quality of the wrongfulness of his acts. Mental disease does not otherwise constitute a defense" (18 U.S. Code § 17). The Supreme Court has never held that the insanity defense is constitutionally required by due process, yet forty-six states and the federal criminal code allow insanity as a defense (Morse, 2011). Insanity must be pled at the time of arraignment or else that defense is waived and cannot be considered later in the trial. Recall that insanity is not the same as competency. Insanity involves the mental state of the defendant at the time the crime was committed, so it might still be a condition from which the person suffers during the trial. Competency is only concerned with the defendant's abilities during the trial.

Assessing insanity requires a retrospective examination that may encompass the defendant's entire life to determine if the person is capable of willful intent (Simon, 2008). Willful intent is an essential part of most offenses. Therefore, a person who is not of sound mind at the time of the alleged offense is not capable of forming such intent. The role of the forensic examiner at trial is to offer assessment and opinion on the sanity of the defendant. It is the jury, or sometimes the judge, who ultimately gives weight to the evidence and makes a determination. The issue of insanity may also be relevant during the sentencing phase.

IMAGINE THAT . . .

The jury rejected an insanity plea in the case of the 2013 slaying of "American Sniper" Chris Kyle and his friend, Chad Littlefield. Despite the strange statements that "pigs [were] taking over the world," and his reasoning for killing the two men because he got angry when Kyle didn't shake his hand, Eddie Ray Routh did not meet the legal requirement of insanity. According to the ABA journal, the prosecutor's case was strengthened by a statement of knowledge of wrongdoing that Routh gave to a Texas ranger during questioning (Weiss, 2015). The ranger asked, "You know what you did today is wrong, right?" and Routh answered, "Yes, sir."

Routh's legal team did not dispute that he carried out the killings but hoped to convince the jury to return a verdict of not guilty by reason of insanity. They argued that he was a paranoid schizophrenic who was having a psychotic episode when he shot and killed the men. However, Routh has been found guilty and sentenced to life in prison without parole for the killings.

Question for discussion: Is it possible that Routh suffers from mental disorders? If so, why can he still be held criminally responsible?

Not Guilty by Reason of Insanity

Based on British common law and legal precedents, the American legal system in most states allows individuals with severe mental disorders or disability to plead *not guilty by reason of insanity* when charged with a criminal offense. Suffering from a mental disorder does not mean that a person is also insane. To prove the claim of insanity, defendants are required to prove that their mental capacity at the time of the crime was not sufficient enough to establish culpability and responsibility for their actions. Proving insanity is a difficult task, requiring that defendants confess to the crime, convince a jury or judge of their insanity, and pass independent psychological evaluations before they can be declared insane (Simon, 2008). Unlike TV court cases, the insanity defense is rarely raised as a defense in the United States (Robinson, 2014). When insanity is raised as a defense it is rarely successful, only a fraction of 1 percent of felony cases results in an acquittal due to insanity (Pasewark, 1981).

An insanity defense generally requires a three-pronged assessment: first, that the defendant is or was suffering from a serious mental disease or defect; second, whether there was a significant impaired practical functioning at the time the crime was committed, and third, there is a link between the impairment and the disease or defect. Mental impairments fall into two categories: cognitive and volitional (Simon, 2008). The volitional category of the insanity defense appraises the degree of impairment relative to an ability to conform conduct to the requirements of the law. It is generally accepted that the volitional aspect is the more difficult to assess (Simon, 2008). The cognitive category gauges the defendant's ability to appreciate the wrongfulness of the conduct. Most jurisdictions, including the Federal government, have eliminated the volitional prong from consideration as part of the insanity defense because of how difficult it is to assess objectively.

5. CH09-05: *The Judge.* With the responsibility for safeguarding the rights of the accused, the judge must instruct the jury on the available verdicts that are available in the jurisdiction where the trial is being held. As you can see, this is no simple task. Copyright Nosnibor137/Bigstock.com

Diminished Capacity Doctrine

Insanity is a very difficult standard to prove in court. In some cases, an individual is severely mentally ill but still knows the difference between right and wrong and therefore does not meet the legal requirements for insanity (Simon, 2008). Case law and statute law of some states recognize this dilemma through the doctrine of "diminished capacity," but it is not constitutionally required that they do so. "Diminished capacity" differs from the insanity defense and other affirmative defenses because it is not an actual defense (Robinson, 2014). If a state allows the claim, then a defendant is permitted to assert that she lacks lack the *mens rea* for the crime—which requires that the prosecutor overcome that claim to prove guilt (Robinson, 2014). *Federal Sentencing Guidelines* explicitly adopt this principle by providing a reduced sentence if a significantly reduced mental capacity contributed substantially to the commission of the offense ("U.S. Sentencing Guidelines," 2004).

Guilty-but-Mentally-Ill Verdict

In 1975, Michigan was the first state to offer a *guilty-but-mentally-ill* (GBMI) verdict as a way to ensure lengthy confinement of an individual found to be insane. Since the 1970s, a substantial minority of jurisdictions have adopted the verdict. Typically, the verdict is used as an alternative rather than a replacement for legal insanity, though a few states have replaced the insanity defense with the GBMI verdict (Morse, 2011). To prove that the defendant is *guilty-but-mentally-ill* in Michigan, the three criteria that must be met and determined beyond a reasonable doubt are as follows ("Michigan Comprehensive Laws," 1975):

1. The defendant is guilty of an offense;
2. The defendant was mentally ill at the time of the commission of the offense;
3. The defendant was not legally insane at the time of the commission of the offense.

Having the GBMI verdict allows juries to convict those who are not clearly insane, but who suffered from a mental illness at the time of the commission of a criminal offense. Typically, a traditional "guilty" finding or GBMI verdict provides the same sentencing options. GBMI offenders must be examined by psychiatrists prior to serving the sentence, and if in need of treatment, they would be imprisoned in a criminal mental health facility. While it may seem that the verdict is designed to help mentally ill offenders, the practical outcome is that GBMI convicts tend to serve longer sentences than sane convicts (Robinson, 2014). Concerns have been raised that its use constitutes a form of civil commitment without adhering to commitment law requirements.

DEVELOPMENT OF THE INSANITY DEFENSE

In one form or another, the idea that insanity provides a defense to criminal conduct goes back to at least the sixth century and the Justinian Code (Rabin, 2004). Considered to be the first legal test of insanity, the *Wild Beast Defense* was articulated in 1256 by the English Judge Henry de Bracton (Platt and Diamond, 1965). Judge Bracton excused the crimes committed by madmen since they "lack sense and reason and can no more do wrong or commit a felony than a brute animal." In England, the first recorded case of a defendant being acquitted due to insanity occurred in 1505 when a man who had murdered an infant was found to be of unsound mind; he was allowed to go free (Moran, 1985). The insanity defense has been revised numerous since it was first conceived. The *Wild Beast* test was abandoned and replaced by the *M'Naghten Rule* in England, which to this day considers insanity as a mitigating factor that exempts the accused from punishment. There are currently five different tests used by the American courts to make legal determinations of insanity. Each is explained in the following section.

M'Naghten Rule and the Irresistible Impulse Test

The most commonly used test of sanity in the United States judicial system comes from an acquittal due to insanity in an 1843 case in which Daniel M'Naghten tried to kill the English Prime Minister and instead killed his secretary (*M'Naghten's Case*, 1843). A defendant must prove, by clear and convincing evidence, that due to his mental illness, he did not know his actions were wrong (Ellis, 2014). Under the M'Naghten rule, insanity is a viable defense if, because of the defendant's mental illness:

1. He did not understand the "nature and quality" of his acts, or
2. If he did, he did not understand why they were wrong.

Through the first half of the twentieth century, the insanity defense was expanded to include recognition of the *irresistible impulse test.* The states of New Mexico, Texas, and Virginia use a combination of the M'Naghten rule and the irresistible impulse test, thereby covering both cognitive and volitional insanity. The irresistible impulse test is used when the defendant knows what he has done and may even know that his actions were wrong, but he was irresistibly driven to a criminal act by an overpowering impulse resulting from a mental condition (Gordon, 2015). No state relies exclusively on the irresistible impulse test.

Durham Rule

The *Durham Rule* excuses a defendant "if his unlawful act was the product of mental disease or mental defect" (*Durham v. United States*, 1954). The *Durham Rule* has been applauded by some for being the most permissive standard and criticized by others for placing too much trust in the opinions of mental health professionals. The expectation of the Durham Rule is that the psychiatric expert would be able to accurately differentiate a mentally ill offender who committed his crime because of his psychopathology from a mentally sound offender who committed his crime for more usual reasons (Diamond, 1973). Experts suggest that the rule reduced mental diseases and defects to justifications for criminal acts, which made criminal responsibility avoidable (Harrison, 2015). The inexactness of the psychiatric evaluation and the body of scientific knowledge has failed to meet the challenge set forth by the Durham decision. New Hampshire is currently the only state that uses the Durham Rule standard.

Model Penal Code Affective Test for Insanity (ALI)

The *Model Penal Code Affective Test for Insanity* was formulated in 1962 by an American Law Institute team of judges, lawyers, and scholars from law and related disciplines. It is commonly referred to as the *ALI test.* It states that:

> A person is not responsible for criminal conduct if, at the time of the offence, the defendant suffered from a mental disease or defect (other than antisocial personality disorder or any other abnormality manifested only by repeated criminal or otherwise antisocial conduct) that caused the defendant to lack either:
>
> a) The substantial capacity to appreciate the criminality (wrongfulness) of his or conduct or
>
> b) The substantial capacity to conform his conduct to the requirements of the law.

The goal of the Model Penal Code Affective Test for Insanity was to provide a reliable measure of criminal insanity that would incorporate the use of scientific evidence to determine if a defendant is mentally insane (Harrison, 2015). The model expects that the defendant's symptoms had to have been exhibited though various aspects of the defendant's life and not merely evidenced by their criminal conduct. It is a much broader test than the M'Naghten Rule or the Irresistible Impulse Test. Currently, twenty states use the *ALI* standard (Harrison, 2015). Under this measure, a criminal defendant must be found guilty by reason of insanity if (1) he is diagnosed with a relevant mental defect such as severe mental retardation or schizophrenia disorder, or (2) he lacked substantial capacities to understand the law or conform his conduct to the requirements of law at the time of the incident.

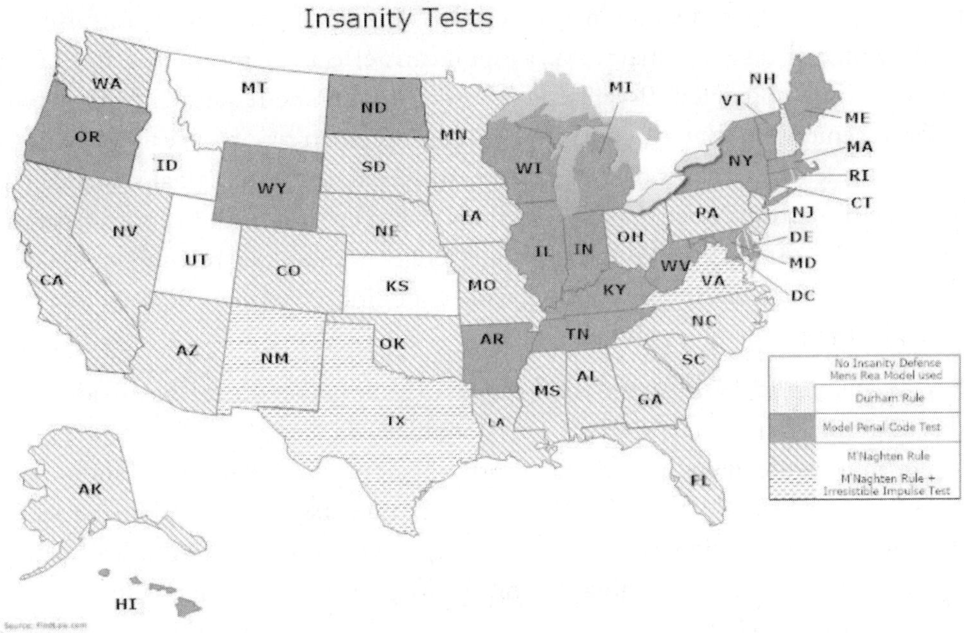

6. CH09-06: *Insanity Tests.* The most frequently used insanity test among the states is the M'Naghten Rule, followed by the Model Penal Code Test, which is sometimes referred to as the ALI test. Source: (FindLaw, 2016).

Mens Rea Model

Some states have abolished insanity as a defense altogether and instead use a *Mens Rea Model.* Idaho, Kansas, Montana, and Utah are the four states that do not have an insanity defense per se, but do allow a defendant to introduce evidence of mental disease or defect to rebut the prosecution's claim that he or she possessed the mental state of *mens rea*, a necessary component of the crime (Ellis, 2014). Using this approach, defendants only need to raise a reasonable doubt that, because of their mental illness, they did not have the requisite mental state that is an element of the offense (Ellis, 2014). The Supreme Court in 2012 refused certiorari to consider whether the Due Process Clause and the Eighth Amendment to the Constitution required all jurisdictions to retain some form of the insanity defense (*Delling v. Idaho*, 2012). This means that each state can determine whether or not they will include a defense of insanity in their court system.

POST-TRIAL ISSUES

Having a mental illness short of "insanity" does not affect one's responsibility for having committed a crime. The law requires those suffering from mental illnesses to be judged to the same criminal standards as everyone else. However, suffering from a mental disorder may have a significant effect on the sentencing of an offender once convicted. Psychiatric reports will often be requested by the court prior to sentencing. Based on psychologist examination reports, treatment orders can be made as a condition of probation or used to mitigate a final sentence. If, after hearing from a doctor, the judge finds that there is a risk of serious harm to others if the offender were released, the judge can also set restrictions on the offender's future discharge. Release with conditions typically requires that the defendant remain under court supervision.

Beginning in 1978 with *Lockett v. Ohio*, the Supreme Court has made clear that the defendant can introduce any potentially mitigating evidence at capital sentencing proceedings whether or not it supports a statutorily authorized mitigating factor (*Lockett v. Ohio*, 1978). It is universally accepted that mental disorder is a mitigating factor and many jurisdictions specifically list mental abnormality alone as a mitigating factor. Although only a minority of states make "dangerousness" per se a statutorily aggravating factor, dangerousness is incorporated implicitly or explicitly in lists of other factors.

Dangerousness

A balance must be made between a defendant's individual rights and the need for treatment, as well as public safety. Although practices vary from state to state, three categories of offenders may require treatment within a criminal justice context: those who are acquitted as not guilty due to insanity are often placed in mandatory outpatient treatment as conditional release programs; persons found incompetent to stand trial; and individuals who fall under the jurisdiction of laws regarding dangerous mentally ill offenders. Typically, psychiatric treatment focuses on alleviating symptoms, however, a primary concern in the outpatient treatment of defendants is any mental condition that may indicate dangerousness (Lamb, Weinberger, and Gross, 1999). The risk of harm is therefore addressed first in the treatment of this population. In all jurisdictions, a defendant acquitted by reason of insanity may be automatically civilly committed. The commitment may be for an evaluation that will be followed by formal civil commitment or by formal commitment itself without a prior evaluation. Although not punishment for crimes, these civil commitments have been justified because the defendant is found to be dangerous and not responsible for that dangerousness. The terms of such possible commitments vary across jurisdictions, and some states even limit the duration of the commitment to the maximum potential sentence that would have been given if the defendant had been convicted of the offense. In other jurisdictions the term may be indefinite with periodic review. In *Jones*, the Supreme Court upheld both an automatic commitment for evaluation and a potentially indefinite commitment (*Jones*, 1983).

IMAGINE THAT . . .

Under common law, a prisoner sentenced to death could not be executed if he was incompetent because he did not understand what penalty was being imposed or why. The Supreme Court in *Panetti* reaffirmed that the common-law practice has constitutional status under the Eighth Amendment (*Panetti v. Quarterman*, 2007). This suggests that if the incompetent offender could not recognize the gravity of his crime, his execution would not allow the community to affirm its judgment that the prisoner's culpability was so serious that he deserved the death penalty.

In 1992, Scott Louis Panetti shaved his head and went to the home of his estranged wife, shooting both of his in-laws in front of his wife and daughter. Diagnosed with schizophrenia, Panetti was found guilty and sentenced to death in 1995. Although Panetti's long history of mental illness is well documented, the state of Texas insists he is malingering and clearly understands that the state intended to kill him and why (Carasik, 2014). Hours before his scheduled execution in December 2014, the fifth U.S. Circuit Court of Appeals issued a stay for Panetti (Carasik, 2014). The Texas Department of Criminal Justice reports that Panetti is still on death row (TDCJ, 2016).

Question for discussion: Do you think the courts should have discretion to determine on a case by case basis if a person with mental illness is criminally responsible and therefore eligible for the death penalty or should the death penalty be abolished for all persons with mental illness?

DEATH PENALTY AND MENTAL ILLNESS

The *Death Penalty Information Center* website informs us that thirty-one states, the U.S. Military, and the Federal Government permit the use of the death penalty (DPIC, 2015). There have been 1,430 executions since 1976. A total of thirty-five executions were carried out in 2014 alone (Snell, 2014). Between 1973 and 2015, there have been 156 death row exonerations. Three groups of individuals are constitutionally protected from facing the death penalty: individuals who are intellectually disabled, those who are declared to be insane, and juveniles under the age of 18. Inmates who are mentally ill, but not insane, are not exempted from execution (DPIC, 2015).

Inmates who are insane, so out of touch with reality that they do not know right from wrong and cannot understand their punishment or the purpose of it, are exempt from execution. The Supreme Court has held that the Eighth Amendment prohibits states from inflicting the penalty of death upon a prisoner who is insane (*Ford v. Wainwright*, 1986). Prior findings of competency do not prohibit a prisoner from proving he is incompetent to be executed because of his current mental condition. Under *Ford*, once a prisoner makes the requisite preliminary showing that his current mental state would bar his execution, the Eighth Amendment, applicable to the States under the Due Process Clause of the fourteenth Amendment, entitles him to an adjudication to determine his condition. If an individual's mental competency is restored, then the execution may commence.

Inmates who are intellectually disabled represent one group of individuals who cannot be executed. "Mentally retarded" has the same meaning and is the term that has often been used in court decisions. An intellectual disability is a disability originating prior to the age of 18 that is characterized by significant limitations both in intellectual functioning and in adaptive behavior, which covers daily social and practical skills (aaidd, 2013). In the landmark case of *Atkins*, the Court held that it is a violation of the Eighth Amendment ban on cruel and unusual punishment to execute death row inmates with mental retardation (*Atkins v. Virginia*, 2002). The criteria for determining that an inmate is intellectually disabled varies from state to state; clinical methods and IQ tests are examples of methods used in making that determination.

More recently the Court ruled that it is unconstitutional to execute individuals who committed their crime prior to the age of 18 (*Roper v. Simmons*, 2005). The Court recognized that society's "evolving standards of decency" made executions of such defendants inappropriate. The Court ruled that because of their reduced judgment, understanding, and self-control as compared to others convicted of murder, defendants with mental retardation and defendants under the age of 18 lack the level of culpability that would warrant the most severe sanction, and so should be exempt from the death penalty.

SUMMARY

Age-old concepts of law are at the heart of the American justice system, alongside the competing interests of a growing mentally ill population within the courts. Modern court practices are supplemented by traditional approaches with a view towards improving services and streamlining access to address the mental health crisis. Recent cases have firmly established that the constitutional right to council can be compromised by severe mental illness—it is of the utmost importance that competency hearings conform to the requirements established by case law. Insanity defenses may be of little help in maintaining due process rights since they are rarely successful even on the rare occasions when they are used. Although insanity has been recognized since the beginning of recorded law, the rules that test modern insanity are fairly new and still in flux. Four states have abolished the insanity defense altogether and we can expect further changes to our methods of assessment in the future. Finally, the Supreme Court has expressly excluded from execution those who are of diminished capacity due to age, incompetency, or intellectual disability. The question remains whether the trend will continue.

CHAPTER QUESTIONS FOR REVIEW

1. What are the criminal law elements that must be proven for a crime to have been committed and a particular person held responsible for the crime?
2. How would you explain the factors that determine court jurisdiction?
3. What is the difference between showing competency and proving insanity?
4. Compare and contrast the tests for insanity.
5. Which categories of person have the Supreme Court decided are ineligible for the death penalty in the United States? Explain.

REFERENCES

aaidd. (2013). Definition of intellectual disability. Retrieved October 29, 2015, from http://www.aamr.org/content_100.cfm?navID=21

ABA. (2015). Standard 7-4.2. Responsibility for raising the issue of incompetence to stand trial. Retrieved November 1, 2015, from http://www.americanbar.org/publications/criminal_justice_section_archive/crimjust_standards_mentalhealth_blk.html

APA. (2013). Specialty guidelines for forensic psychology. *American Psychologist, 68*(1), 7–9.

Argersinger v. Hamlin, 407 U.S. 25 (1972).

Atkins v. Virginia, 536 U.S. 304 (2002).

Carasik, L. (2014). Federal Appeals Court spares mentally ill man from execution—for now. Retrieved June 5, 2016, from http://america.aljazeera.com/opinions/2014/12/scott-panetti-usappealscourtmentalillnessdeath penalty.html

Delling v. Idaho, 133 S. Ct. 504 (2012).

Diamond, B. (1973). From Durham to Brawner, A futile journey. *Washington University Law Review, 109*. Retrieved from: http://openscholarship.wustl.edu/law_lawreview/vol1973/iss1/8

DPIC. (2015). Facts about the death penalty. Retrieved October 29, 2015, from http://www.deathpenaltyinfo.org/documents/FactSheet.pdf

Durham v. United States, 214 F. 2d 862 (1954).

Dusky v. United States, 362 U.S. 402 p. 402 (1960).

Ellis, T. (2014). Mental illness, legal culpability, and due process: Why the Fourteenth Amendment allows states to choose a *Mens Rea* insanity defense over a *M'Naughten* approach. *Mississippi Law Journal, 84*(215).

FindLaw. (2016). The Insanity Defense among the states. Retrieved from http://criminal.findlaw.com/criminal-procedure/the-insanity-defense-among-the-states.html

Ford v. Wainwright, 477 U.S. 399 (1986).

Gideon v. Wainwright, 372 U.S. 355 (1963).

Golding, S. (2015). Learning forensic examinations of adjudicative competency. In R. Jackson and R. Roesch (Eds.), *Learning forensic assessment: Research and practice.* New York, NY: Routledge.

Gordon, J. (2015). The current state of the insanity defense in Virginia. *The Kabod, 2*(1). Retrieved from: http://digitalcommons.liberty.edu/kabod/vol2/iss1/2/

Harrison, J. (2015). Idaho's abolition of the insanity defense—An ineffective, costly, and unconstitutional eradication. *Idaho Law Review, 51*(575).

Jones v. United States, 463 U.S. 34, 370 (1983).

Lamb, R., Weinberger, L., and Gross, B. (1999). Community treatment of severely mentally ill offenders under the jurisdiction of the criminal justice system: A review. *Psychiatric Services, 50*(7), 907–913.

Lockett v. Ohio, 438 U.S. 586 (1978).

M'Nahten's Case, 8 Eng. Rep. 718 (1843).

Medina v. California, 505 U.S. 437 (1992).

Michigan Comprehensive Laws, § 768.36(1) (1975).

Mills T., and Calkins, E. (2012). Mental health public defender office cost-benefit analysis. Austin, TX: Justice and Public Safety.

Mora, R. (1985). The origin of insanity as a special verdict: The trial of James Hadfield (1800). *Law and Society Review, 19*(3), 487–519.

Morse, S. J. (2011). Mental disorder and criminal law. *Journal of criminal law and criminology, 101*(3), 885–968.

Panetti v. Quarterman, 127 S.Ct. 2842 (2007).

Pate v. Robinson, 383 U.S. 375, 86 S. Ct. 836, 15 L. Ed. 2d 815 (1966).

Platt, A. M., and Diamond, B. L. (1965). The origins and development of the "wild beast" concept of mental illness and its relation to theories of criminal responsibility. *Journal of the History of the Behavioral Sciences, 1*(4), 355–367.

Rabin, D. (2004). *Identity, crime, and legal responsibility in eighteenth-century England.* New York, NY: Springer.

Robinson, P. (2014). The effect of mental illness under U.S. Criminal Law. *Northern Ireland Legal Quarterly, 65*, 229.

Roesch, R., Zapf, P., Golding, S., and Skeem, J. (1999). Defining and assessing competency to stand trial. *The handbook of forensic psychology, 2*, 327–349.

Roper v. Simmons, 543 U.S. 551 (2005).

Sell v. United States, 539 U.S. 166 (2003).

Siegel, L., Schmalleger, F., and Worrall, J. (2015). *Courts and Criminal Justice in America* (2 Ed.). Upper Saddle River, NJ: Pearson Education.

Simon, R. (2008). Retrospective assessment of mental states in criminal and civil litigation: A clinical review. In R. Simon and D. Shuman (eds.), *Retrospective assessment of mental states in litigation: Predicting the past.* Washington, D.C.: American Psychiatric Publishing, Inc.

Skeem, J. L., Manchak, S., and Peterson, J. K. (2010). Correctional policy for offenders with mental illness: Creating a new paradigm for recidivism reduction. *Law and Human Behavior*(2), 110.

Snell, T. (2014). Prisoners executed under civil authority in the United States, by year, region, and jurisdiction, 1977–2014. Washington, D.C.: Bureau of Justice Statistics.

Swanson, J. W., McGinty, E. E., Fazel, S., and Mays, V. M. (2015). Mental illness and reduction of gun violence and suicide: bringing epidemiologic research to policy. *Annals of Epidemiology, 25*(5), 366–376.

The National Judicial College. (2012). Mental competency: Best practices model. Retrieved November 1, 2015, from http://www.mentalcompetency.org/

U.S. Sentencing Guidelines, § 5K2.13 (2004).

Washington v. Harper, 494 U.S. 210 (1990).

Weiss, D. (2015). Jurors reject insanity defense, convict veteran in 'American Sniper' slaying. *ABA journal.* Retrieved October 30, 2015, from http://www.abajournal.com/news/article/jurors_reject_insanity_defense_convict_veteran_in_american_sniper_slaying/

Zapf, P. (2013). *Standardizing protocols for treatment to restore competency to stand trial: Interventions and clinically appropriate time periods.* (Document No. 13-01-1901). Olympia, WA: Washington State Institute for Public Policy.

CHAPTER 10

Corrections

INTRODUCTION

Most Americans tend to think of corrections as either a prison or a jail. These facilities are the institutions of incarceration where convicts are housed. While a substantial number of people are held in prisons and jails, convicts represent only 30 percent of the individuals who are under the supervision of the correctional system (Glaze and Kaeble, 2014). Convicted felons are incarcerated in long-term state or federal prisons with sentences typically longer than one year. Jails are administrated by local law enforcement and they hold offenders with shorter sentences and those awaiting trial. Most people under correctional supervision, however, are those who are living in the outside community and are on probation or parole. This chapter is concerned with the mission of the prison system and the impact of a large special needs population within that traditional correctional setting.

The corrections system is the third prong of the American justice system. Simply stated, law enforcement identifies crime that has been committed and brings the accused individuals to the attention of the courts. If the court determines an individual to be guilty they are sentenced to a correctional institution or to probation. The mission of the institution is to provide a safe and secure environment during incarceration and to offer opportunities for convicted criminals to change their behavior. The three prongs of the justice system work independently and also cooperatively. Their duties and responsibilities frequently overlap and they influence one another.

Key Terms

MISSION OF CORRECTIONS

NON-SUICIDAL SELF-INJURY

OBJECTIVE CLASSIFICATION

RIGHT TO TREATMENT

SOLITARY CONFINEMENT

TELEMEDICINE

Chapter Objectives

After completing this chapter, you should be able to:

- Explain the mission and goals of corrections
- Define the *right to treatment* in correction facilities
- Describe the connection between mental disorders and self-injury
- Explain the debate regarding solitary confinement

THE MISSION AND GOALS OF CORRECTIONS

The **MISSION OF CORRECTIONS** is two pronged: to protect citizens from crime by safely and securely handling criminal offenders while providing opportunities for inmates' self-improvement and reintegration back into society as law-abiding citizens. Corrections officials have a clear duty to control inmate behaviors to assure the success of the first prong of its mission, maintaining the safety and security of the inmates and staff (Carlson, 2011). The duty of corrections has changed very little since the founding of our nation. To accomplish this primary goal, jails and prisons are highly structured with strong central authority and clear behavioral rules.

The second prong of the corrections mission is to provide opportunities that will increase the chances that the inmate will become a productive and law-abiding citizen upon release. To this end, the four justifications for incarceration are focused on deterrence, incapacitation, rehabilitation, and retribution. While these four concepts have always been evident in the field of corrections, the priority given to each has changed numerous times based on the philosophical approach that was prominent at that time in history. Influenced by the support of elected officials and public sentiments, correctional philosophies have gone through many different stages in history. They, in turn, influence the management of the institution.

1. CH10-01: Alcatraz Island is perhaps the most well-known examples of the containment model in corrections. This federal prison operated for 29 years (1934–1963) during which time it held an average of 270 prisoners, including Al Capone and George "Machine-Gun" Kelley. Thought to be escape-proof, violent and dangerous prisoners and those considered as an escape risk might be sent to this maximum-security penitentiary. The daily routine of inmates was highly structured and monotonous. Photo copyright f11photo/Bigstock.com

Throughout most of American correctional history, the managerial focus was almost exclusively centered on the punishment of offenders; rehabilitation was only occasionally the top priority. Models of correctional development at different times placed emphasis on moral rehabilitation, on education and self-reliance, or on industrialization. The 1970s saw the rise and fall of the medical model of inmate treatment aimed at reducing recidivism (MacNamara, 1977). Unfortunately, nothing seemed to work and correctional facilities entered the age of responsibility. Custodial priorities have now shifted to a model which emphasizes maintenance of the offender's ties to family and the community, in recognition that the offender will be returning to the community.

AMERICAN INMATE POPULATION TRENDS

The United States inmate population is over 2.3 million people. This represents the largest rate of incarceration in the world (ACLU, 2012; Carson, 2015). In the

United States, one in every eleven prison inmates are incarcerated on a life sentence (Ax, 2011). At the end of 2014, the number of prisoners held by federal and state correctional facilities declined by 1 percent for a second consecutive year, the second largest decline in thirty-five years. According to the Bureau of Justice Statistics (BJS), the decline was due to the decrease in numbers of persons on probation and those held in local jails. The prison and parole population experienced a modest increase (Glaze and Kaeble, 2014).

Prison Rates

Violent offenders account for more than half of the male prison population within the state prison population and 40 percent of those held under military jurisdiction. The small decline in the prison population of 2014 refers only to male incarceration (Carson, 2015), as the rate of female incarceration is growing. Females accounted for 7 percent of the total state and federal prison population in 2014 (Carson, 2015). While women make up the minority of prison populations, studies indicate that the mental health needs of female inmates are more severe than their male counterparts (Ross and Lawrence, 2009).

Most prisons are operated by state and federal authorities. The federal prison system is the largest correctional system in the United States, housing 197,672 at the end of 2012 (Motivans, 2015). Felony offenders from the District of Columbia and defendants from other federal jurisdictions are committed to the Federal Bureau of Prisons (BOP) system. Some are under private contract to the government. To provide the complete picture on incarceration, the military also its own system for trying and confining offenders, as do Native American Tribal Courts. Additional U.S. facilities include the U.S. Immigration and Customs Enforcement Agency (ICE) and prisons in foreign countries.

Jail Rates

Most jails are operated by local authorities or private enterprise. Many local and state police departments also have temporary holding cells for individuals under arrest. There are approximately 11.4 million admissions to U.S. jails each year (Minton and Zeng, 2015). Local jails range in size from very small, with a capacity of less than twenty-five inmates, to more than 1,000 inmates. Jail sentences average twenty-three days (Subramanian, Delaney, Roberts, Fishman, and McGarry, 2015). The Bureau of Justice Statistics reports that the female inmate population increased 18.1 percent between midyear 2010 and 2014, while the male population declined 3.2 percent. At mid-year 2014, the Indian country jail facilities housed 2,380 (Minton, 2015).

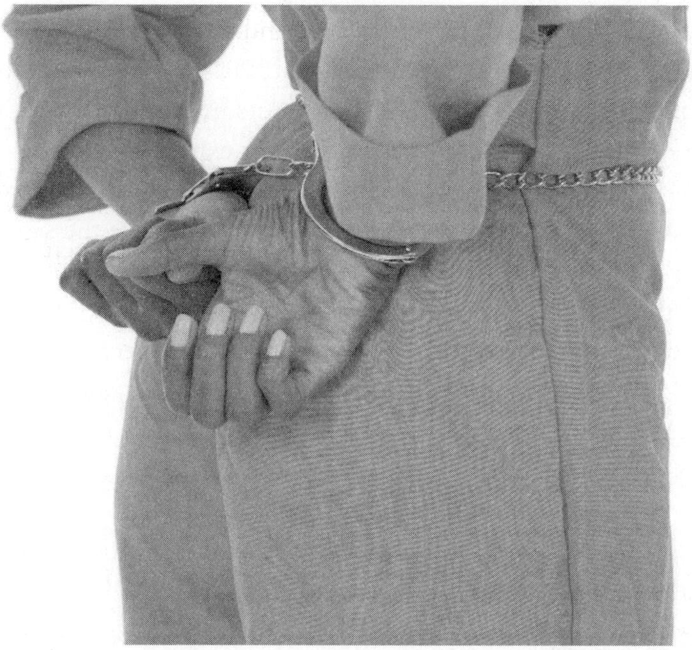

2. CH10-02: Women make up less than 10 percent of the prison population, but their numbers are still growing even while the rate of men is trending downwards. The mental health needs of women are more severe than men due to histories of victimization and abuse. Photo copyright Alan and Vicena Poulson/Bigstock.com

MENTAL ILLNESS IN CORRECTIONS SETTINGS

One of the most urgent problems faced by society today concerns the mass incarceration of offenders that are diagnosed with mental illness. Despite the strides made during the penal reform era of the 1800s, the present correctional conditions for mentally disordered individuals have greatly worsened. The past has repeated itself and society has failed to learn from its previous lessons. In 1955, an estimated .3 percent of the U.S. population was mentally disordered and living in a mental institution; by 1999 an estimated .3 percent of the U.S. population was mentally ill and in the criminal justice system (Borum, 2000).

> *It is deplorable and outrageous that this state's prisons appear to have become a repository for a great number of its mentally ill citizens. Persons who, with psychiatric care, could fit well into society, are instead locked away, to become wards of the state's penal system. Then, in a tragically ironic twist, they may be confined in conditions that nurture, rather than abate, their psychoses.*
>
> —Judge William Wayne Justice (*Ruiz v. Johnson*, 1999)

An estimated 20 percent of inmates in jails and 15 percent of inmates in state prisons have a serious mental illness (Torrey et al., 2014). In large jail facilities, the population of inmates with serious mental disorders may be as high as 30 percent (AbuDagga et al., 2016). A well-known corrections expert concludes that the *jail as asylum model* is fully entrenched in urban jails (Kerle, 2016). Treatment issues in corrections facilities are complex because no two inmates have the same needs or expectations. Prisons and jails were never intended to become psychiatric institutions, so the transition to provide adequate services has not been easy. The people that work there are not trained to make the difficult decisions on diagnosis and treatment which are typically handled by psychiatrists and psychologists. Institutions were initially unprepared to meet the level of care necessary for some of the severely disordered population. They often act defensively to avoid the litigation that parallels their transition from care-and-custody to care-and-treatment facilities. For better or worse, correctional institutions today are the primary mental health providers in America (Torrey et al., 2010).

IN MY EXPERIENCE . . .

Over the years I had put a lot of people who were under arrest into the cell at the barracks. This particular suspect was different than others in the past. His demeanor and statements seemed exaggerated beyond the reality of what was happening. He was under arrest for operating a motor vehicle while under the influence of alcohol. He did not hurt anyone and he was uninjured. As I locked the cell door, he was moaning that his life was over . . . gasping and blurting out over and over "I can't stand it—don't leave me here." Yes, this arrest seemed very different. The man was getting overanxious and depressed. My next move seemed like the best insurance against him hurting himself. I locked my gun in the station gun cabinet and informed the desk officer what I was going to do so that it would be monitored by camera. I went into the cell and sat down with the man under arrest. We talked for about twenty minutes, about his wife and family and those who loved him. I explained the process for bail and what would happen if he did not make bail. When I left, I told him that I had to get back to work, but that I would return to talk some more later.

Question for discussion: How might this communication reduce the risk of suicide?

CLASSIFICATION DECISIONS

An objective offender **OBJECTIVE CLASSIFICATION** system is a formal process used to identify the level of risk presented by newly admitted inmates. This classification is used to make appropriate housing and program assignments based on the inmate's needs and potential risk to staff, other inmates and to himself or herself. In contrast to subjective models of classification that relied on informal criteria prior to the 1970s, the objective method is based on a narrow set of legal factors and personal characteristics with greater emphasis on fairness, consistency, and transparency. Classification decisions include determining the appropriate security level: maximum, medium, or minimum. The offender program and treatment needs are also considered.

Classification stages occur at least three times for each prisoner. A needs assessment evaluates prisoners for program needs and services, including a correctional mental health screen (Goldberg and Higgins, 2006). For inmates that test positive on the mental health screening during the first screening, qualified professionals such as psychiatrists, psychologists, and psychiatric social workers perform an in-depth mental health evaluation. An internal classification, in the second stage of classification, verifies objective data for placement in inmate housing. The third classification occurs thirty to ninety days later, when the initial classification is re-evaluated so that inmate behavior and other variables that might change the classification may be considered.

Non-Classified Disordered Offenders

Those who work in corrections must deal with the reality that many disturbed offenders are never formally categorized as having mental illnesses (Halleck, 1987). These persons may have the same characteristics as those who are formally classified. The failure to classify individuals occurs for several reasons, according to Halleck (1987). Among them is that some inmates may not recognize that they are ill at all. Offenders may perceive mental illness as a weakness and want to avoid being diagnosed. Others will try to disguise their symptoms while in prison to avoid being medicated. Prisoners may hesitate to provide information to corrections authorities. Without proper diagnosis, these individuals will be managed differently by the justice system. If identified, however, there are opportunities for treatment. They may receive brief treatments, crisis intervention, or counseling, regardless of their classification status if behavior problems bring them to the attention of corrections officers.

3. CH10-03: Classification of offenders is a complicated process that is used to identify the level of risk of an inmate and to make appropriate housing program assignments based on the inmate's needs. The supervision of inmates begins with the physical security of the institution. Prisons and jails are designed according to security levels. Walls, towers, and wire fencing are physical signs of the level of inmate security within. Photo copyright Tilita Nicolielo/Bigstock.com

SUPERVISION

Inmate supervision begins with the physical security of prisons and jails. The wall or fence surrounding the facility must be monitored from strategically placed towers or by mobile patrols. Increasingly, electronic detection devices monitor jail and prison perimeters. The next layer of security, for many institutions, is an area that the prisoners are not allowed to cross. The forbidden zone is known as an internal perimeter. Maximum security prisons often use interior fencing with razor wire, making it difficult for inmates to go outside the interior perimeter. Physical features within the institution make it easy to visually supervise inmates, including cells that are typically located on open floors that face a center hallway.

Another form of supervision is administrative segregation, a term that refers to both a classification and a type of unit within the corrections facility. There are at least three distinct types of segregation in corrections facilities: administrative segregation, disciplinary segregation, and protective custody (Cloud, Drucker, Browne, and Parsons, 2015; Shames et al., 2015). Any of these types of segregation might involve a period of solitary (or near solitary) confinement. Institutional misbehavior is the primary basis for segregation. Significantly, it is the increased use of solitary confinement, not segregation per se, that troubles those with concerns about contemporary correctional practice (Frost and Monteiro, 2016).

Solitary Confinement

SOLITARY CONFINEMENT involves locking inmates into a small single cell for long periods of time; it prohibits an inmate from being in contact with other prisoners, participating in programs, or engaging in prison work. Some institutions may view rule violations as indications of mental illness and mandate counseling instead of isolation. Typically, however, most institutions make no distinction between mentally disordered inmates and non-disordered inmates when it comes to its use of segregation. There are few options available in the corrections facility to keep assaultive inmates from harming themselves or others.

In a study of Colorado prisons, almost half of the placements were for inmate-on-inmate assaults or fighting (49 percent); riotous activity, often comprised large-scale yard fights (15 percent); weapons possession (12 percent); assaults on staff (11 percent); and staff intimidation or threats (10 percent) (O'Keefe, 2008). In the Colorado study, a third of the assaults on corrections staff involved a weapon or resulted in serious injury. Additional reasons for administrative segregation (17 percent) was for committing multiple disciplinary infractions, an average of sixteen per inmate; possession of drugs or drug paraphernalia; security threat group activity or recruitment; and refusing housing, most of these did so because they feared for their safety in the general population. A small proportion of the population over a two-year period was due to escapes (3 percent). Note that the percentages do not add up to 100 percent because it is a combination of behaviors that result in an offender's placement.

The use of solitary confinement for the mentally disordered population of inmates is controversial, despite its widespread use. Some studies indicate that the conditions of mental illness are exacerbated by prolonged isolation (Metzner and Fellner, 2010). This has led to an ethical dilemma for medical professionals in recent years. Some argue that solitary confinement is used excessively and has damaging effects on inmates (Cloud et al., 2015). Recent research, however, has challenged that assumption, finding that solitary confinement has little to no effect on the deterioration of inmate mental health (Gendreau and Theriault, 2011; O'Keefe et al., 2013; O'Keefe, Klebe, Stucker, Sturm, and Leggett, 2010). O'Keefe (2008) maintains that administrative segregation is a necessary tool for correctional supervision and management which is used to promote safety for those who work and live in the prisons.

The trend appears to favor a restriction on the amount of time that prisoners can be confined in isolation. Metzner and Fellner (2010) cite isolation as psychologically harmful depending on the individual, the duration, and the specific conditions of the confinement. The adverse effects may be significant for persons with serious mental illness (Metzner and Fellner, 2010). The National Commission on Correctional Health Care (NCCHC), the nation's leading authority on health care systems in jails, prisons, and juvenile detention recently released a position statement calling for an end to solitary confinement for periods more than 15 consecutive days (NCCHC, 2016).

DISRUPTIVE INMATES

Each institution usually has a small subset of inmates whose behaviors endanger themselves, or others, and threaten the safety, security and long term stability of the correctional system in which they live (Helfand, 2011). The management of chronically disruptive offenders presents challenges to the mental health, medical, and correctional staff. Behaviors may include cell-flooding or fire-setting; refusing to exit cells; self-harm; physically assaulting others; throwing feces or urine; or spitting at others. The question of whether these chronic disrupters are acting out of control due to mental illness, or out of anger and volatility by choice, are important distinctions as it will influence the management reaction.

The assumed choice to act violently in these situations has led some to suggest that these sometimes-bizarre behaviors are a means of creating a sense of control within restrictive environments (Skeem, Miller, Mulvey, Tiemann, and Monahan, 2005). Violence potential in similar circumstances may be associated with a generally suspicious attitude towards others along with anger and impulsiveness (Skeem and Mulvey, 2001). Among the most violence-predictive items, according to Skeem et al. (2005), are poor behavioral controls (which describes people who are easily angered, often manifesting sudden outbursts and impulsivity), is meaningfully associated with antagonism (combativeness and aggression) and low conscientiousness (poor impulse control). From a national study sample of 16,000 inmates from state and federal institutions, evidence suggests that psychosis and major depression have strong effects on infractions involving aggression (Felson, Silver, and Remster, 2012). The authors found that paranoid thinking is the best predictor of aggressive offending while incarcerated. Helfand (2011) states that traditional correctional strategies, such as behavioral management programs, are unlikely to be effective in the supervision of the disruptive subset of inmates.

IN MY EXPERIENCE . . .

In a conversation with a local sheriff, I asked about the most difficult part of his work day. Without hesitation, he described an inmate who was being held pending trial. The young man could not be allowed to wear clothes because he had taken them off and tried to hang himself with his pants. Naked in the cell, he would paint his walls with his own feces or alternately throw it through the bars at the sheriffs or urinate on them when they checked on him. This constituted a health risk to the officers and to the inmate. The man would not voluntarily come out of the cell and would hit and bite any sheriff who came close to him. A group of corrections officers in hazmat suits would periodically go in and forcibly remove him in order that he and his cell could be washed. They quickly learned he could not be given a bar of soap in the shower because he would swallow it. This inmate did not think he had any mental illness and repeatedly refused treatment and medication. Corrections officers do not have any control over who receives medication and who does not.

Question for discussion: Do you think that the officers would feel a loss of control over this situation? Do you have any suggestions on what you might do under similar circumstances?

Personality Disorders

Traits of impulsivity and self-injury behaviors are often related to antisocial and borderline personality disorders (as described in Chapter 3). Antisocial and borderline personality disorder (ASPD and BPD) represent two of the most frequent disorders among prison inmates (Coid, Yang, Tyrer, Roberts, and Ullrich, 2006). Antisocial personality disorder (the older term is sociopath) in the community is about 5.5 percent for males and 1.9 percent for females (overall 3.6 percent of the general population), which represents more than 8.5 million Americans (Black, 2013). Studies which document the prevalence of antisocial personality disorder within the prison population find significantly higher numbers, with estimates between 43 percent and 66 percent of the population (Fazel and Danesh, 2002; Ogloff, Talevski, Lemphers, Wood, and Simmons, 2015).

Borderline personality disorders among the corrections population is also significantly higher than are found in the community. Among jail inmates Trestman et al. (2007) found rates of 16.6 percent. This is compared to less than

2 percent prevalence rate for BP in the community, 75 percent of those diagnosed with BP are women (APA, 2015). In a study of male and females entering the prison system, 26.8 percent of men and 54.5 percent of women met the criteria for BPD (Black et al., 2007). Additionally, more than half of the offenders with borderline personality disorder met criteria for antisocial personality disorder in the Black study (2007). Research findings suggest that that persons with BPD respond aggressively to provocative behavior by another person (New et al., 2009).

Non-Suicidal Self-Injury

While individuals with personality disorders can cause disruption in the corrections setting, self-injury behaviors are particularly disconcerting, even though they occur regularly in correctional settings among a subset of inmates (DeHart et al., 2009). Examples of behaviors include burning, cutting, head-banging, scratching, and forcing objects under the skin. Self-injurious behavior is also known as **NON-SUICIDAL SELF-INJURY** (NSSI), which is defined as a deliberate self-directed tissue damage without the intent to die (Dixon-Gordon, Harrison, and Roesch, 2012). NSSI is not recognized as a mental disorder within the DSM-5, but self-injury is associated with borderline personality disorder (APA, 2015).

From a review of the literature, Dixon-Gordon and colleagues found estimates of NSSI as high as 48 percent among offenders, 61 percent among offenders with mental illness, and rates of 3 percent among non-incarcerated adults (2012). The authors state that although NSSI is frequently seen as a manipulative behavior in the correctional setting, it is more appropriately viewed as a robust predicator of suicide. There are few interventions to NSSI, the most promising involves a fourteen-week *Emotion Regulation Group Therapy* treatment for patients with borderline personality disorder and co-occurring NSSI (Gratz and Gunderson, 2006).

LEGISLATION AND COURT ACTION GOVERNING TREATMENT

In 1984, Congress enacted comprehensive provisions addressing the treatment and evaluation of mentally ill offenders. Title 18 U.S.C. Chapter 313, §§ 4241–4247, describes necessary judicial procedures which must be followed when an offender appears to be, or is, suffering from a mental disease or defect. Hearing requirements and procedures to determine competency, delay trial, and for civil commitment are contained with these sections of Chapter 313. The Adam Walsh Child Protection and Safety Act of 2006 (Walsh Act), Pub. L. No. 109–248, provides for the civil commitment of a sexually dangerous person after the completion of the term of incarceration, as codified in § 4248. Additionally, compliance with the Americans with Disabilities Act is being forced through civil litigation efforts. The right of filing complaints under ADA provisions was clarified in *Yeskey* when the Supreme Court failed to exclude corrections from ADA mandates (*Pennsylvania Department of Corrections v. Yeskey*, 1998). The Court stated that state prisons fall squarely within the Title II statutory definition of "public entity."

Right to Mental Health Treatment

Dr. Morton Birnbaum was among the first to advocate for therapeutic and rehabilitative services in public institutions for people with disabilities (Birnbaum, 1960). His influential article published in the American Bar Association Journal detailed, from a legal standpoint, the problem of whether the institutionalized mentally ill person receives adequate medical treatment so that he may regain his health. An inmate's right to mental health treatment progressively evolved from that point onward. Though disability rights litigation the courts recognized the right to treatment as a constitutional guarantee. Early cases involved the right to treatment during periods of involuntary civil commitment.

The first right to treatment case was *Rouse v. Cameron,* where eighteen-year-old Charles Rouse was found not guilty by reason of insanity and committed to a psychiatric hospital without a hearing. After having been committed for four years as the result of a crime that was punishable by one year had he been found guilty, Rouse petitioned the court for his release (*Rouse v. Cameron*, 1966). The court agreed that involuntary hospitalization is for treatment, not punishment. Judge Bazelon became the first appellate judge to say that the government, when holding people involuntarily, had an obligation to provide psychiatric care. Psychiatric hospitals were emptied during the period of deinstitutionalization and most are now closed. It did not take long after that for the right to treatment issue to turn towards correctional institutions.

The **RIGHT TO TREATMENT** in a correctional environment was established when the Supreme Court formally recognized that the Eighth Amendment to the Constitution required the correctional environment to provide a standard of care for inmates that should not differ from the community standard (*Estelle v. Gamble,* 1976). Additionally, the Court held in *Estelle* that where prison officials are "deliberately indifferent" to serious medical needs, they cause the kind of "wanton infliction of pain" that gives rise to liability under federal civil rights statutes. The courts have consistently included mental health needs in defining what constitutes necessary and appropriate medical care (Moore, 2003).

Individuals suffering from severe mental disorders may have a legal claim if treatment is delayed or denied under *Bowring v. Godwin* (*Bowring*, 1977). Inmates also have the right to refuse treatment. In *Washington v. Harper* (1990), the Court found that a prisoner had "a significant liberty interest in avoiding the unwanted admission of antipsychotic drugs under the Due Process Clause of the 14th Amendment." Id. at 221–22. However, the Court also recognized that prison officials may need to involuntarily medicate a mentally ill inmate with psychotropic medication if the inmate is dangerous to himself, either actively or by being gravely disabled, or to others, if such treatment is in the prisoner's medical interest (*Washington v. Harper*, 1990). Treatment is permissible after the inmate has received notice and a hearing before an administrative panel. In a psychiatric emergency, psychotropic medication may be administered involuntarily if the medication is an appropriate treatment for the mental illness and other alternatives would not be effective. Inmates given emergency treatment of this type are then considered for referral to a psychiatric referral center. In challenges to the right of the inmate to refuse, the court has consistently upheld the constitutional right of a prison or jail inmate to refuse psychiatric medication (Torrey et al., 2014).

HIPAA

Misguided and exaggerated fears surrounding the sharing of medical information between criminal justice and health organizations due to HIPAA and 42 CFR Part 2 are commonplace even though federal regulations do not prohibit information sharing. Per the Council of State Governments (CSG), HIPAA's *Lawful Custody Exception* explicitly allows correctional institutions to access an inmate's health information without consent if the information is needed to provide health care to the individual. Access is also permitted to ensure the safety and security of the inmate and others housed or working in the facility (Matz, 2014). It is also possible that clinical staff at a correctional facility might be considered "covered entities," but their status must be independently assessed (Petrila and Fader-Towe, 2010).

MEDICAL CARE

Inmates receive essential medical, dental, and psychiatric services in all federal and state institutions. There is no medical condition that would preclude admission to a corrections facility, therefore all medical needs are met within the commitment facility, a specialized institution, and if necessary, at appropriate community facilities (BOP, 2014). While both the processes for obtaining care and the quality of medical care vary from state to state and among institutions, they are governed by state and federal law and policy. Courts have interpreted the Fourteenth Amendment of the Constitution to require correctional facilities to provide inmates with essential dental, medical, psychiatric and psychological care (*Bowring*, 1977). Yet less than half of the jails in a recent study reported offering some sort of mental health treatment for seriously mentally ill inmates inside the jail facilities (AbuDagga, Wolfe, Carome, Phatdouang, & Torrey, 2016).

Housing inmates in corrections facilities is not a cost-saving initiative. For a variety of reasons, the costs associated with mentally ill inmates are higher than for inmates without mental illness (Torrey et al., 2010). In a state-by-state survey of mental health issues among inmates in corrections, Torrey et al. (2010) concluded that increased staffing, program needs, and psychiatric medication are among the reasons for greater costs. Examples include Broward County, Florida, where the cost is $80 a day for a traditional inmate and $130 a day for an inmate who has mental illness. In Texas, for example, the average prisoner costs the state about $22,000 a year, but expenses for those with mental illness range from $30,000 to $50,000 a year. Psychiatric exams, which are required for admissions, pose a substantial financial burden on the institutions.

The influx of inmates with special needs has resulted in significant changes in the corrections system. Cook County Jail in Chicago is now referred to as the largest mental health facility in America (Ford, 2015). There are over 6,900 sworn officers in the sheriff's department and all of them receive sixty hours of advanced mental illness training. Cook County Jail provides mental health services to a high percentage of its inmates; three out of four offenders are expected to be suffering from ADHD, bipolar disorder, severe depression, personality disorders, or schizophrenia, to name a few (Ford, 2015). Some personality disorders are characterized by impulsive acting out with no regard for the rights of others. These inmates may have very little understanding of the consequences of his or her actions that are sometimes volatile, including both harming others and self-harm.

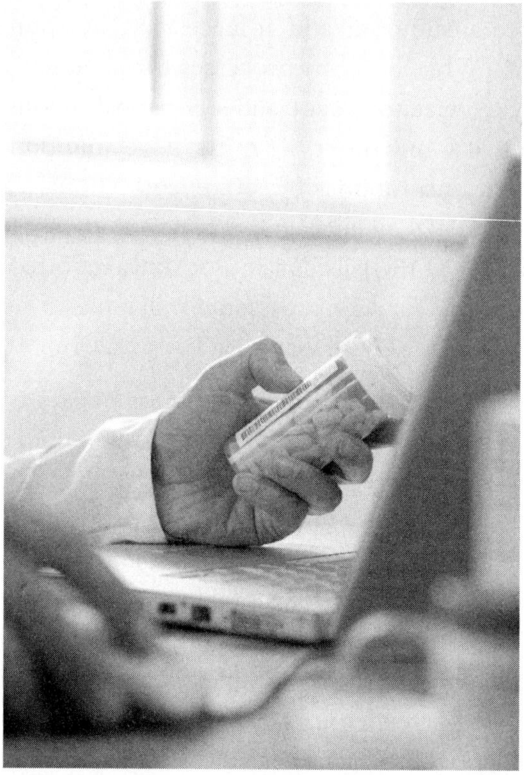

4. CH10-04: More than half of states have turned to telemedicine in efforts to improve inmate access to health care. The approach is very useful for mental health treatment. Photo copyright 18 percentgrey/Bigstock.com

Telemedicine

Skyrocketing healthcare costs for the inmate population has driven some facilities to use electronic communications and information technology. **TELEMEDICINE** is the use of technology to deliver health care, health information or health education at a distance. Video conferencing and technology that transmits data, images, sounds, or video from the institution to the evaluation site is among the most promising advances to institutional health care. The American Correctional Association reports that in 2010 more than half of the states were using some form of telemedicine to deliver medical services to inmates. Telemedicine initiatives, combined with other measures, have contributed to lower average blood sugar rates for diabetic inmates and a reduction in AIDS-related deaths (Pew Charitable Trusts, 2013). Triage and treatment of inmates with psychological service needs represent a growing use of this technology. The Federal Bureau of Prisons relies on both telemedicine and on-site evaluations for psychiatric treatment of federal inmates (BOP, 2014).

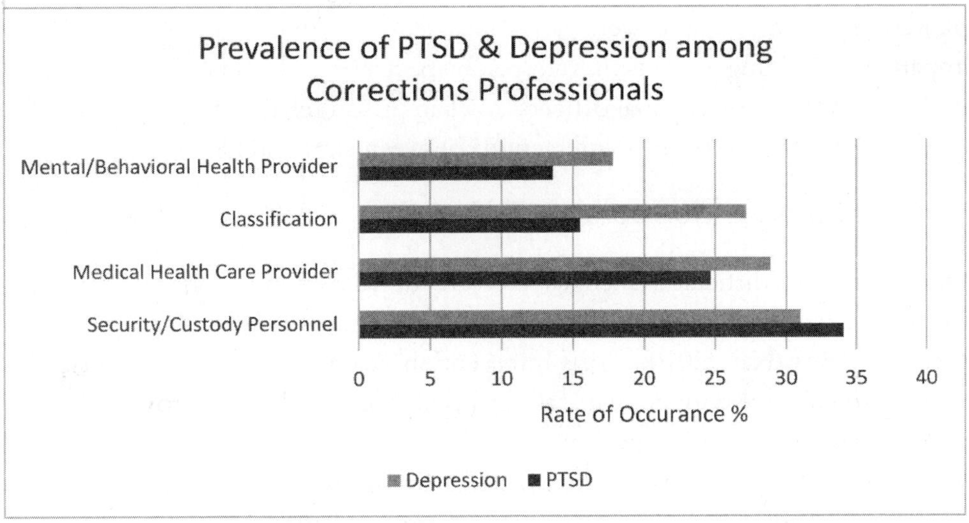

5. CH10-05: *Depression and PTSD Among Corrections Officers.* Corrections officers are the front-line worker in the jails and prisons. They are exposed to violence, injury, and death as an occupational hazard. The mental health needs of these officers is of vital importance to the institution. Maintaining a healthy life-style and supportive relationships can help to balance the demands of this work environment. Source: Denhof, M., and Spinaris, C. (2013).

THE RELATIONSHIP BETWEEN INMATE AND CORRECTIONAL OFFICER

Corrections staff have a critical role in the functioning of the corrections facility beyond that of supervision and management duties. Once thought to be merely custodial staff, contemporary correctional officers are skilled professionals who are called on to use communication and human service skills to reduce tension, defuse crises, and conduct daily business. The change from authoritarian to helper occurred with the recent philosophical emphasis on rehabilitation coupled with judicial intervention.

The key to understanding how correctional officers maintain order is knowing that they work with inmates rather than merely using coercive measures to control them (Galanek, 2015). In a study of the relationships between mentally disordered inmates and the corrections officers at the Pacific Northwest Penitentiary, inmates talked about their relationships with corrections officers in terms of trust and honesty, according to Galanek (2015). Inmates acknowledged that when mental illness was not displayed through exaggerated symptoms, it allowed correctional officers to use discretion in disciplinary matters and to assist them in accessing mental health services. Officers, in turn, did not rely on rigid roles or responses to disordered behaviors when they knew an inmate was cognitively disordered. Galanek concluded that inmate safety and the maintenance of inmates' mental health were not contradictory within that prison. Fair and impartial upholding of prison rules, a respect for individual dignity and an understanding of correctional officers' roles in prison rehabilitation contribute to an environment with positive interactions between staff and inmates.

Training for Corrections Officers

One of the most difficult challenges for correctional personnel today is in meeting the urgent demands for response, services, and the care of inmates suffering from mentally illness (NIC, 2010). Crisis Intervention Team (CIT) provides an effective training to enhance correctional staff knowledge and skill for improving the care and management of this population. The National Institute of Corrections (NIC) Maine chapter of the Alliance for the Mentally Ill (NAMI) was the first state to introduce the forty hour CIT training to corrections officers in 2011. The NIC reports that in 2014 the *Crisis Intervention Training* (CIT) was officially revised for corrections settings (NIC, 2015). Within two days of training completion, an officer in the South Carolina Department of Corrections used the training to de-escalate a situation involving a mentally ill offender, preventing harm to himself and to staff members. There exists a significant amount of research on the CIT method used by police officers and for criminal justice diversion programs, but relatively little on its application in corrections settings (Tucker, VanHasselt, Mendez, Palmer, and Browning, 2012). Citing the example of the CIT implementation experience in Adams County Sheriff's Office in Colorado, Tucker et al. (2012) concluded that CIT training holds considerable promise in jail and corrections settings due to wide acceptance and support of the model. Improved collaborations with community mental health treatment facilities and a notable cultural shift within the facility are early indications of its success in Adams County.

CORRECTIONS PROFESSIONALS

Corrections professionals perform a variety of different jobs. Classification staff conduct intake screenings and classify inmates using a variety of criteria, including behavioral and mental health issues. Corrections officers in jails and prisons provide security and maintain inmate custody. Health providers are often contract agencies that work within the facilities. Medical personnel and mental health experts are among those professionals who may work under contract within the corrections facilities.

Job Stress

Prison and jail facilities in some jurisdictions lack the resources to meet the needs of stressed and overtaxed doctors, nurses, psychologists, and prison guards. Corrections professionals experience high rates of burnout as they are exposed to violence, injury, and even death as an occupational hazard. Most of their work is done indoors where they are locked inside the corrections facilities. Professionals must maintain heightened vigilance for their safety and the safety of inmates while adhering to strict security protocols. Corrections officers work day and night with some of the most hardened and dangerous individuals in the county to keep the community safe and to protect inmates from each other. Theirs is one of the most important jobs in criminal justice and among the least appreciated.

Researchers estimate that over 30 percent of corrections officers who work in direct custody of inmates' experience PTSD and depression (Denhof and Spinaris, 2013). This PTSD rate is three times higher than that of the general public and it rivals even that of wartime military personnel (Spinaris, Denhof, and Kellaway, 2012). Correctional officers working in security/custody roles demonstrate the highest rates among corrections personnel—over 40 percent of the population suffers from PTSD, stress, or a combination of the two. Additionally, corrections officers have one of the highest rates of occupational injuries due to assaults and violent acts committed against them (Bureau of Labor Statistics, 2015). The Bureau also reports that being exposed to contagious diseases results in corrections officers having one of the highest rates of illnesses of all occupations, according to the Bureau of Labor Statistics. PTSD and depression contribute to suicidal behavior. Although the state has one of the lowest suicide rates in the nation, a study by the New Jersey Police Suicide Task Force found the suicide rate for male police officers to be more than double the rate of the general public. Astoundingly, the risk of suicide among corrections officers is 50 percent higher than with police officers ("New Jersey police suicide task force report," 2009).

Working within corrections has long been regarded as stressful employment. Corrections medical health care providers, mental health workers, and classification personnel also exhibit high PTSD and stress symptoms. The professionals who work in the corrections field are at increased risk of experiencing negative effects on their overall health, as well as personal and social relationships. The importance of wellness training cannot be underestimated among these professionals. Exercise, and both social and spiritual activities appear to reduce the negative effects of work among corrections professionals.

SUMMARY

The two-pronged mission of corrections is to protect citizens while providing inmates with opportunities for self-improvement and reintegration back into society. The priorities of corrections have shifted over the years, and currently the trend is towards a model of reintegration. Throughout the chapter many of the challenges facing corrections have been noted. In particular, is the dual responsibility of acting as the asylum and the correctional system for people that have been found guilty of committing crimes who have severe mental illness. It is no simple task to establish the wide variety of services for this population, but the transition is being made. It must be made. The Courts have mandated that inmates have a constitutional right to treatment, including the treatment for mental disorders. At a minimum, the standard in the corrections facility must meet the standard of care in the community. While community health care is not held responsible, the corrections industry is liable for court damages for failure to provide adequate services.

Increased numbers of inmates are being incarcerated, many of whom have substantial mental health care needs. The costs associated with the overpopulation of prisons and jails call into question the realities of what can be accomplished in a prison or jail setting. A growing population of elderly inmates threatens a potential crisis as administrations look to meet the mental health needs of that population. Providing adequate mental health services and medical care is a complex and expensive undertaking. Increased use of technology and improved cooperation between agencies are approaches that continue to ease the strain and show promise for the future.

It is stressful and can be dangerous for any person that works within corrections. Higher than normal rates of PTSD have been documented for employees who work in the correctional institutions, in any position. Additionally, corrections officers experience high rates of depression and suicide because of their stressful employment. Programming to improve the lives of corrections staff needs to take higher priority than is currently evidenced.

CHAPTER QUESTIONS FOR REVIEW

1. What are the primary missions and goals of corrections?
2. How was *the right to treatment* in corrections formally recognized?
3. What are the two sides of the debate regarding solitary confinement?

4. Explain the connection between mental disorders and self-injury.
5. Explain the factors that are associated with job stress experienced by employees who work in corrections?

REFERENCES

AbuDagga, A., Wolfe, S., Carome, M., Phatdouang, A., & Torrey, E. F. (2016). *Individuals with serious mental illness in county jails: A survey of jail* staff's *perspectives.* Retrieved from Washington, D.C.: http://www.citizen.org/documents/2330.pdf

ACLU. (2012). At America's expense: The mass incarceration of the elderly. New York, NY: American Civil Liberties Union.

APA. (2015). Understanding mental disorders: Your guide to DSM-5. Washington, D.C.: American Psychiatric Association.

Ax, R. (2011). Correctional mental health. In T. Fagan and R. Ax (eds.), Correctional Mental Health: From Theory to Best Practice (pp. 353–378). Los Angeles, CA: Sage.

Birnbaum, M. (1960). The right to treatment. *American Bar Association Journal, 46*(May), 499–504.

Black, D. (2013). Bad boys, bad men: confronting Antisocial Personality Disorder (Sociopathy). New York, NY: Oxford University Press.

BOP. (2014). Legal resource guide to the Federal Bureau of Prisons. Washington, D.C.: U.S. Department of Justice, Federal Bureau of Prisons.

Borum, R. (2000). Improving High-Risk Encounters between People with Mental Illness and the Police. *The Journal of the American Academy of Psychiatry and the Law, 28*(3), 332–337.

Bowring v. Godwin, 551 F.2d 44 (1977).

Bureau of Labor Statistics. (2015). Occupational Outlook Handbook. 2014–15. Retrieved November 9, 2015, from http://www.bls.gov/ooh/protective-service/correctional-officers.htm

Carlson, P. (2011). Managing the mentally ill from a correctional administrator's perspective. In Thomas Fagan and R. Ax (eds.), *Correctional Mental Health* (pp. 57–76). Thousand Oaks, CA: Sage

Carson, A. (2015). Prisoners in 2014. (NCJ 248955). Washington, D.C.: U.S. Department of Justice.

Cloud, D. H., Drucker, E., Browne, A., and Parsons, J. (2015). Public health and solitary confinement in the United States. American Journal of Public Health, 105(1), 18–26.

Cloyes, K. (2010). Time to prison return for offenders with serious mental illness released from prison: A survival analysis. *Criminal Justice and Behavior, 37*(2), 175–187.

Coid, J., Yang, M., Tyrer, P., Roberts, A., and Ullrich, S. (2006). Prevalence and correlates of personality disorder in Great Britain. The British Journal of Psychiatry, 188(5), 423–431.

DeHart, D. D., Smith, H. P., and Kaminski, R. J. (2009). Institutional responses to self-injurious behavior among inmates. Journal of Correctional Health Care, 15(2), 129–141.

Denhof, M., and Spinaris, C. (2013). Depression, PTSD, and comorbidity in United States corrections professionals: Prevalence and impact on health and functioning. Retrieved November 9, 2015, from Desert Waters Correctional Outreach.

Dixon-Gordon, K., Harrison, N., and Roesch, R. (2012). Non-suicidal self-injury within offender populations: a systematic review. International Journal of Forensic Mental Health, 11(1), 33–50. http://desertwaters.com/wp-content/uploads/2013/09/Comorbidity_Study_09–03–131.pdf

Estelle v. Gamble, 429 U.S. 97 (1976).

Fazel, S., and Danesh, J. (2002). Serious mental disorder in 23,000 prisoners: A systematic review of 62 surveys. The Lancet, 359(9306), 545–550.

Felson, R. B., Silver, E., and Remster, B. (2012). Mental disorder and offending in prison. Criminal Justice and Behavior, 39(2), 125–143

Ford, M. (2015). America's largest mental hospital is a jail. Retrieved November 10, 2015, from http://www.theatlantic.com/politics/archive/2015/06/americas-largest-mental-hospital-is-a-jail/395012/

Frost, N., and Monteiro, C. (2016). Administrative segregation in U.S. prisons (NCJ 249749). Washington, D.C.: U.S. Department of Justice.

Galanek, J. D. (2015). Correctional officers and the incarcerated mentally ill: Responses to psychiatric illness in prison. *Medical Anthropology Quarterly, 29*(1), 116–136.

Gendreau, P., and Theriault, Y. (2011). Bibliotherapy for cynics revisited: Commentary on One Year Longitudinal Study of Psychological Effects of

Administrative Segregation. Corrections and Mental Health: An Update of the National Institute of Corrections.

Glaze, L., and Kaeble, D. (2014). Correctional populations in the United States, 2013. Washington, D.C.: Bureau of Justice Statistics.

Goldberg, A., and Higgins, B. (2006). Brief mental health screening for corrections intake. *Corrections Today, August.*

Gratz, K. L., and Gunderson, J. G. (2006). Preliminary data on an acceptance-based emotion regulation group intervention for deliberate self-harm among women with borderline personality disorder. Behavior Therapy, 37(1), 25–35.

Halleck, S. (1987). The mentally disordered offender. Washington, D.C.: American Psychiatric Press.

Helfand, S. (2011). Managing disruptive offenders: A behavioral perspective. In T. Fagan and R. Ax (eds.), Correctional Mental Health: From Theory to Best Practice. Los Angeles, CA: Sage.

Kerle, K. (2016). The mentally ill and crisis intervention teams, reflections on jails and the U.S. mental health challenge. The Prison Journal, 96(1), 153–161.

MacNamara, D. E. J. (1977). The medical model in corrections. *Criminology, 14*(4), 439–448.

Matz, A. K. (2014). *A Note on HIPAA and 42 CFR Part 2: Dispelling the Myths about Justice-Health Information Sharing* (Vol. 2015): American Probation and Parole Association.

Metzner, J., and Fellner, J. (2010). Solitary confinement and mental illness in U.S. prisons: A challenge for medical ethics. *American Academy of Psychiatry and the Law, 38*(1), 104–108.

Minton, T. (2015). Jails in Indian Country, 2014. (NCJ 248974). Washington, D.C.: U.S. Department of Justice.

Minton, T., and Zeng, Z. (2015). Jail Inmates at Midyear 2014. (NCJ 248629). Washington, D.C.: U.S. Department of Justice.

Moore, J. M. (2003). *Management and administration of correctional health care*: Civic Research Institute, Inc.

Motivans, M. (2015). Federal justice statistics, 2012—Statistical tables. (NCJ 248470). Washington, D.C.: U.S. Department of Justice.

NCCHC. (2016). New position statement provides guidance on solitary confinement. Retrieved from http://www.ncchc.org/solitary-confinement-position-statement

New, A. S., Hazlett, E. A., Newmark, R. E., Zhang, J., Triebwasser, J., Meyerson, D., . . . Goodman, M. (2009). Laboratory induced aggression: a positron emission tomography study of aggressive individuals with borderline personality disorder. Biological Psychiatry, 66(12), 1107–1114.

New Jersey police suicide task force report. (2009). Retrieved November 9, 2015, from http://www.nj.gov/oag/library/NJPoliceSuicideTaskForceReport-January-30-2009-Final(r2.3.09).pdf

NIC. (2015). *Report to the nation FY14*. Retrieved from https://s3.amazonaws.com/static.nicic.gov/Library/031512.pdf

O'Keefe, M. (2008). Administrative segregation from within a corrections perspective. *The Prison Journal, 88*(1), 123–143.

O'Keefe, M., Klebe, K. J., Metzner, J., Dvoskin, J., Fellner, J., and Stucker, A. (2013). A Longitudinal Study of Administrative Segregation. *Journal of the American Academy of Psychiatry and the Law Online, 41*(1), 49–60.

O'Keefe, M., Klebe, K. J., Stucker, A., Sturm, K., and Leggett, W. (2010). *One year longitudinal study of the psychological effects of administrative segregation*: Colorado Department of Corrections, Office of Planning and Analysis.

Ogloff, J. R., Talevski, D., Lemphers, A., Wood, M., and Simmons, M. (2015). Co-occurring mental illness, substance use disorders, and antisocial personality disorder among clients of forensic mental health services. *Psychiatric Rehabilitation Journal, 38*(1), 16.

Pennsylvania Department of Corrections v. Yeskey (1998).

Petrila, J., and Fader-Towe, H. (2010). Working with HIPPA and other privacy laws. In Council of State Governments Justice Center (Ed.), *Information sharing in Criminal Justice—Mental Health collaborations.* New York, NY: Bureau of Justice Assistance.

Pew Charitable Trusts. (2013). Managing prison health care spending. (NCJ 247358). Retrieved November 10, 2015, from http://www.pewtrusts.org/~/media/legacy/uploadedfiles/pcs_assets/2014/pctcorrectionshealthcarebrief050814pdf.pdf

Ross, P. H., and Lawrence, J. (2009). Women in jail: Mental health care needs and service deficiences. In R. Gido and L. Dalley (eds.), *Women's mental health issues:*

Across the criminal justice system (pp. 117–128). Upper Saddle, NJ: Pearson/Prentice Hall.

Rouse v. Cameron, 373 F.2d 451 (1966).

Ruiz v. Johnson, 37 F. Supp.2d 855 (1999).

Shames, A., Wilcox, J., and Subramanian, R. (2015). *Solitary confinement: Common misconceptions and emerging safe alternatives.* New York, NY: Vera Institute of Justice.

Skeem, J. L., Miller, J. D., Mulvey, E., Tiemann, J., and Monahan, J. (2005). Using a five-factor lens to explore the relation between personality traits and violence in psychiatric patients. Journal of Consulting and Clinical Psychology, 73(3), 454.

Spinaris, C., Denhof, M., and Kellaway, J. (2012). Posttraumatic Stress Disorder in United States corrections professionals: Prevalence and impact on health and functioning. Retrieved November 9, 2015, from http://desertwaters.com/wp-content/uploads/2013/09/PTSD_Prev_in_Corrections_09–03–131.pdf

Subramanian, R., Delaney, R., Roberts, S., Fishman, N., and McGarry, P. (2015). Incarceration's front door: The misuse of jails in America. New York, NY: Vera Institute of Justice.

Torrey, E., Kennard, A., Eslinger, D., Lamb, R., and Pavle, J. (2010). More mentally ill persons are in jails and prisons than hospitals: A survey of the states. Arlington, VA.

Torrey, E., Zdanowicz, M., Kennard, A., Lamb, H., Eslinger, D., Biasotti, M., and Fuller, D. (2014). The treatment of persons with mental illness in prisons and jails: A state survey. Arlington, VA: Treatment Advocacy Center.

Trestman, R. L., Ford, J., Zhang, W., and Wiesbrock, V. (2007). Current and lifetime psychiatric illness among inmates not identified as acutely mentally ill at intake in Connecticut's jails. Journal of the American Academy of Psychiatry and the Law Online, 35(4), 490–500.

Tucker, A., VanHasselt, V., Mendez, J., Palmer, L., and Browning, S. (2012). Crisis Intervention Team (CIT) training in the jail/detention setting: A case illustration. *International Journal of Emergency Mental Health, 14*(3), 209–216.

Washington v. Harper, 494 U.S. 210 (1990).

Williams, B., Sudore, R., Greifinger, R., and Morrison, R. (2011). Balancing punishment and compassion for seriously ill prisoners. *Annals of Internal Medicine, 155*(2), 122–126.

PART IV

Alternatives to Incarceration

Photo copyright Karich/Bigstock.com

The following chapters are covered in PART IV

11. REENTRY

12. COMMUNITY CORRECTIONS

13. JUVENILE JUSTICE

A crucial question is: How does the criminal justice system assure that programming meets its intended goals?

Major changes have recently occurred within the criminal justice system that have a focus on reducing recidivism outside of incarceration. Programing and needs assessment begin at the time an offender enters the corrections institution and far beyond reentry into the community. Chapter 11 looks at reintegration from a new lens, called reentry. Chapter 12 redefines community corrections as a continuation of reentry initiatives. Chapter 13 examines the mental health initiatives that are specific to meet the needs of young people within the juvenile justice system.

CHAPTER 11

Reentry

INTRODUCTION

Prisoner reentry is an important national and local policy issue. Reentry has been reconceived as a process which begins when the offender is first incarcerated. Corrections has extended its responsibility from the jail and prison into the community. The movement is driven by high rates of incarceration and the high rates of recidivism among men and women who are released from our jails and prisons. Most individuals who are incarcerated will be released. Reentry is born from that realization. These contemporary reentry programs attempt to address the considerable deficits of most prisoners that return to the community: limited education, few marketable job skills, no stable home, chronic health issues, substance abuse needs and mental health needs.

Hundreds of programs have been developed across the country with intentions to offer interventions in line with the criminalization hypothesis that are successful in keeping people out of psychiatric hospitals or homeless shelters. Case management interventions aim to reduce psychiatric hospitalizations and decrease symptoms. Other programs deal with dual disorders and offer treatment adapted for persons with mental illnesses involved in the criminal justice system. Developing interventions consider both individual level factors such as criminogenic risk. Reentry is in its infancy; therefore, programs are being evaluated to find out what works and what does not work. While programming is varied across the nation, they all have one thing in common, the need for collaboration.

Key Terms

CRIMINOGENIC RISK

PROGRAMMING

REENTRY

RELEASE PLANNING

REINTEGRATION MODEL

TRAUMA-INFORMED CORRECTIONAL CARE

Chapter Objectives

After completing this chapter, you should be able to:

- Explain the concept of reentry
- Describe the barriers to successful reentry
- Define the reintegration model of corrections
- State the purpose for forensic assertive community treatment

CRIME AND MENTAL ILLNESS

Some researchers now suggest that the relationship between mental illness and crime is weak, meaning that offenders who have mental disorders vary in the degree to which they are motivated by their symptoms (Peterson, Skeem, Kennealy, Bray, and Zvonkovic, 2014). There may be two groups of offenders with mental illness, Peterson and colleagues suggest. A larger group whose symptoms and crimes are not directly related and the smaller group of offenders whose mental health treatment may reduce recidivism. These experts suggest that the most effective approach to reduce recidivism is to think past the psychiatric symptoms and address criminogenic traits.

We have the assessment ability to make distinctions among offenders with different probabilities of offending by focusing on the risk factors that are directly relate to criminal behavior. Commonly referred to as **CRIMINOGENIC RISK** are the eight factors outlined by Andrews and Bonta (2006) that are the most likely to accurately and reliability predict the risk of criminal behavior:

1. history of antisocial behavior;
2. antisocial personality patterns;
3. criminal thinking and antisocial attitudes;

4. antisocial associates;
5. family and/or relationship circumstances;
6. school and/or work functioning;
7. leisure and/or recreational activities;
8. and substance abuse.

Offenders at high risk have multiple risk and need factors, therefore, programs that target only one need may not produce the desired effect (Latessa and Lowenkamp, 2005). Experts argue that the failure to address these criminogenic risk factors may continue to limit the effectiveness of mental health treatment on improving both mental health and criminal justice outcomes (Epperson et al., 2014). Accordingly, they suggest that for people with serious mental illness, ignoring their co-occurring criminogenic needs may inhibit treatment effectiveness. The (still) emerging approach is to provide treatment efforts which focus on both criminogenic and mental health factors, with emphasis on treating substance use disorders.

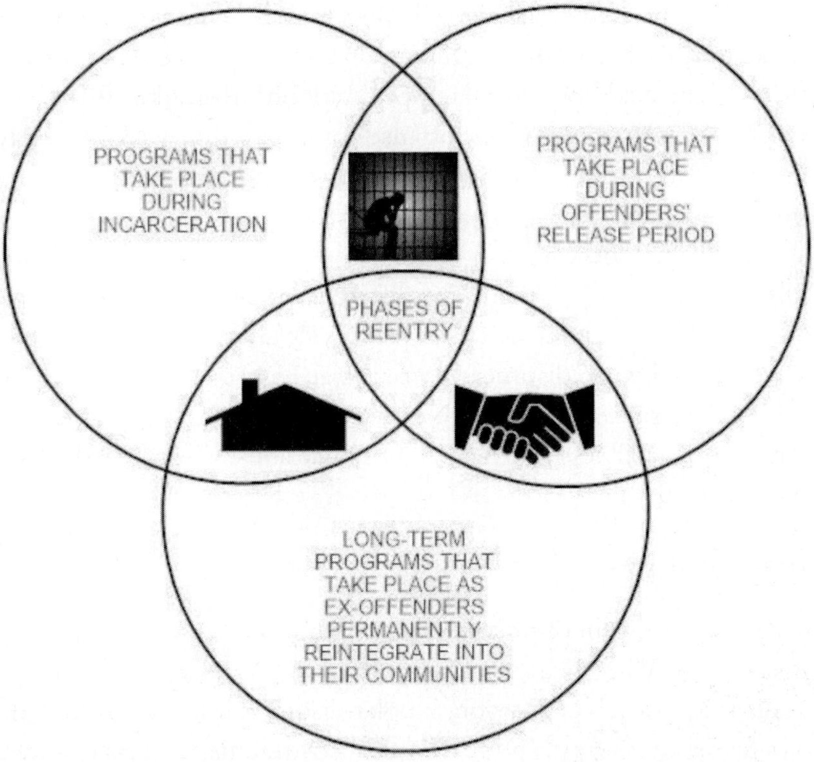

1. CH11-01: *Phases of Reentry*. Reentry is a philosophy which consists of three phases. It actually begins at the time an inmate is incarcerated and continues after release back into the community. Source: James (2015).

RATES OF MENTAL DISORDERS IN CORRECTIONS

Approximately 14 percent to 16 percent of the 7.3 million people under correctional supervision have been diagnosed with serious mental illness such as schizophrenia, bipolar disorder, or major depression (Peterson et al., 2014). Of significance is that the rate is of incarcerated mentally ill is at least ten times larger than the population of individuals with severe mental illness who are being treated in state psychiatric hospitals (Torrey et al., 2014). A major concern is the extent to which psychiatric symptoms directly relate to crime. An estimated 15.4 percent of prisoners reported taking prescription medication for a behavioral health condition at the time of the offense for which they were currently being held (Substance Abuse and Mental Health Services Administration, 2014). Over a third of inmates reported that they receive counseling or therapy for mental health problems in correctional institutions (Beck, Berzofsky, Caspar, and Krebs, 2013).

Jail Inmates

Approximately 17 percent of jail inmates (2 million) have active symptoms of SMI when booked into jail (Steadman, Dupius, and Morris, 2009). An estimated 19.7 percent of jail inmates reported taking prescription medication for a behavioral health condition at the time of the offense for which they were currently being held. (Substance Abuse and Mental Health Services Administration, 2014). Yet an estimated 43.7 percent of jail inmates reported in the National Inmate Survey (NIS-3) that they had been told by a mental health professional that they had a mental disorder (Beck et al., 2013). The difference in prevalence rates may be due to the use of assessment at intake where previously untreated mental disorders are diagnosed. Substance use disorders co-occur at high rates among persons with mental illness, regardless of gender. Nearly three out of every four jail detainees with a serious mental illness also have a substance abuse disorder (Abram, Teplin, and McClelland, 2003).

Prison Inmates

An estimated 36.6 percent of prison inmates in the National Inmate Survey (NIS-3) reported that they had been told by a mental health professional that they had a mental disorder (manic depression, bipolar disorder, other depressive disorder, schizophrenia or another psychotic disorder, posttraumatic stress disorder, or an anxiety or personality disorder) (Beck et al., 2013). More than a third of inmates, 35.8 percent in prisons, reported that they received counseling or therapy for these problems. Challenges to reentry programming include concerns of reoffending among this population. Research also suggests that inmates with major psychiatric disorders (major depressive disorder, bipolar disorders, schizophrenia, and nonschizophrenic psychotic disorders) have substantially increased risks of multiple incarcerations (Baillargeon, Binswanger, Penn, Williams, and Murray, 2009). During the six-year study period Baillargeon et al. (2009) found that the greatest increase at risk of multiple incarcerations was observed among inmates with bipolar disorders, who were 3.3 times more likely to have had four or more previous incarcerations compared with inmates who had no major psychiatric disorder. Prison reentry program components address the mental health needs of offenders during incarceration and after release.

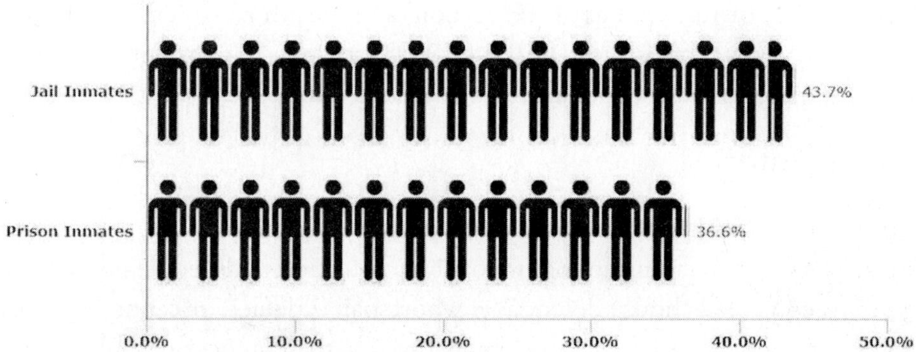

2. CH11-02: *Percentage of Inmates with a History of Mental Disorders.* More jail inmates than prison inmates reported in the National Inmate Survey (NIS-3) that they had been told by a mental health professional that they had a mental disorder including: manic depression, bipolar disorder, other depressive disorder, schizophrenia or another psychotic disorder, posttraumatic stress disorder, or an anxiety or personality disorder (Beck, Berzofsky, Caspar, and Krebs, 2013).

REENTRY

The process of planning for release from the correctional facility to prepare inmates for long-term post release success is called **Reentry**. Traditionally reentry has been thought of as pre-release planning, more recently, it is conceptualized as an approach which begins during an admission into a prison or jail. What does that mean? Essentially, anything that could influence an inmate's potential for success as a law-abiding citizen upon release could be called a reentry program. From this perspective, every educational, vocational, or treatment program offered by the Department of Corrections (DOC) is a reentry program (LaVigne, Davies, Palmer, and Halberstadt, 2008). Reentry planning is a complicated process that involves knowledge of the population who will be transitioning from corrections back into the community, their needs, and the best evidence-based practices for treatment both inside and outside of the institution.

Reentry therefore is not a program, but a philosophy that connects programing with the goal of total reintegration to meet the needs of offenders and reduce recidivism. There are many different forms of reentry and hundreds of program examples that fit into the general picture of reentry. Generally, reentry programs fit into three phases of the corrections reintegration process (James, 2015). Programs which occur during incarceration intend to prepare offenders for their eventual release; during the release period connections are made with the various services which are needed; the final phase are programs that provide support and supervision to sustain successful reintegration into the community. Reentry as a concept is supported by the U.S. Government and funded through the Departments of Justice, Labor, Education, and Health and Human Services. The Second Chance Act (P.L. 110–199) of 2008 expanded the existing offender reentry grant program at the Department of Justice (James, 2015).

Jail Reentry

Jails are difficult places to offer significant mental health services other than crisis intervention due to the transient nature of the population and people going back and forth to court. Jails house defendants whose bail is denied or cannot be paid; misdemeanants found guilty, typically individuals with sentences of one year or less; defendants who could not make bail pending and during a trial; individuals found guilty waiting for sentencing; and probation or parole violators pending a dispositional hearing. Jails also house individuals that have been arrested under a warrant from another state, pending extradition. Rural jails which vary culturally, socially, and economically, make up a substantial share of the nation's 3,365 jails (Solomon, Osborne, LoBuglio, Mellow, and Mukamal, 2008). An Alaskan model of jail reentry programming begins with a reduction of the number of misdemeanor offenders cycling in and out of jails using five strategies:

a) Identify the laws, rules, policies and practices that lead to the incarceration of individuals who pose no substantial risk to public safety.

b) Expand prosecutorial diversion programs for misdemeanor offenses.

c) Expand the ADOC Electronic Monitoring Program for misdemeanants.

d) Make good use of halfway house stays by assessing sentenced misdemeanants for behavioral health and criminogenic risks and needs. Make good use of halfway house placements by screening sentenced misdemeanants for behavioral health and criminogenic risks and needs and assessing and referring for services as appropriate.

e) Expand therapeutic courts and other problem-solving courts for misdemeanants such as the Mental Health and Addiction Therapeutic Courts, Operating Without License (OWL) Courts, and Anchorage adjudication/disposition courts.

The process of jail reentry is different if one is being released from jail or being released from prison. The transitory nature of the jails has prompted initiatives which strongly encourage collaborative programing for community reentry (Steadman, Morrissey, and Parker, 2015). One complication of jail reentry is that with the shorter and more narrow window to provide treatment it may be difficult to engage individuals into post release treatment. Since jails are also community institutions where prisoners live, however, it is easier to stay connected to families. In areas where community-based treatment providers are not in place to facilitate reentry, jails may consider being a part of the network to establish partnerships among existing agencies such as departments of health, family and welfare services, and workforce development (Solomon et al., 2008). In 2011, King County, Washington in collaboration with key stakeholders created a plan for offender reentry to include evidence-based strategies designed to improve public safety and enhance the community (Department of Community and Human Services, 2011). Refer to figure CH11-03 for an illustration of the objectives, strategies and proposed activities for that plan.

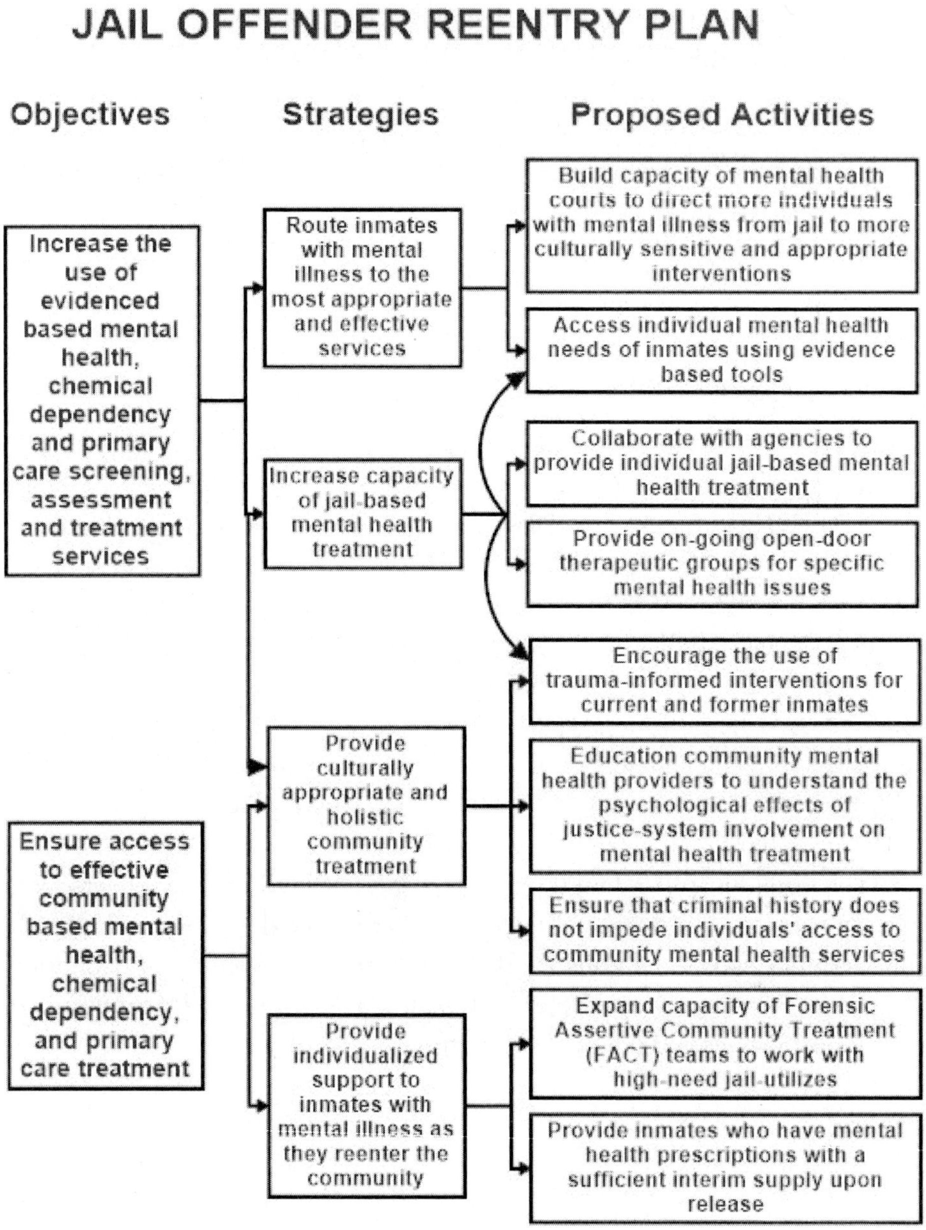

3. CH11-03: *Jail Reentry Plan.* Given the high rates of mental disorders among the transient jail population this reentry plan creates a framework to guide coordinated policies and services. The goal is to include individuals released directly to the community with the general outcome goals of reducing recidivism and improving public safety. Source: King County, 2011.

Prison Reentry

Prisons are geographically distant from families, making it difficult for people to keep in contact over long periods of time. Because of the geographical isolation, those released from prison often have no home and may, as a result, end up homeless. Within the first two weeks of leaving prison, ex-convicts face a thirteen times higher risk of dying from heart disease, overdose, suicide, or homicide than similarly situated persons who were not in prison (Binswanger et al., 2007). A high prevalence of mental illness and the psychological stress of reentry may contribute to the excess risk of suicide in addition to difficulty obtaining care and medications from community providers after the medications provided by prisons run out (Binswanger et al., 2007). Disproportionate levels of poverty, mental illness, substance abuse, and lack of education compound the difficulties and may affect their risk of reoffending, particularly during the first several months following release from prison. Improved transitional planning for inmates may help to reduce these risks.

CORRECTIONAL MENTAL HEALTH SERVICES

The contemporary corrections movement which involves treatment inside and outside of the institution to facilitate reentry in collaboration with the community is known as the **REINTEGRATION MODEL**. Given the large numbers of offenders with mental illness and co-occurring disorders, a growing policy focus of this approach is on the involvement and delivery of mental health services in correctional settings (N. James, 2015; Solomon et al., 2008). To better understand the purpose of correctional mental health, Thomas Fagan proposed an enduring conceptual model in which three levels of services are described (Fagan, 2003). Refer to figure CH11-04. At level 1, per Fagan, services typically involve the identification and treatment of mental disorders, particularly those that may lead to suicidal and/or homicidal behavior; level 2 are services that are offered to specific targeted groups such as substance abusers; level 3 involve organizational or staff directed behavioral science interventions, training and consultation. Achieving level 3 is the optimum for correctional mental health services involving interagency collaborations which are supportive of long-term reintegration back into the community.

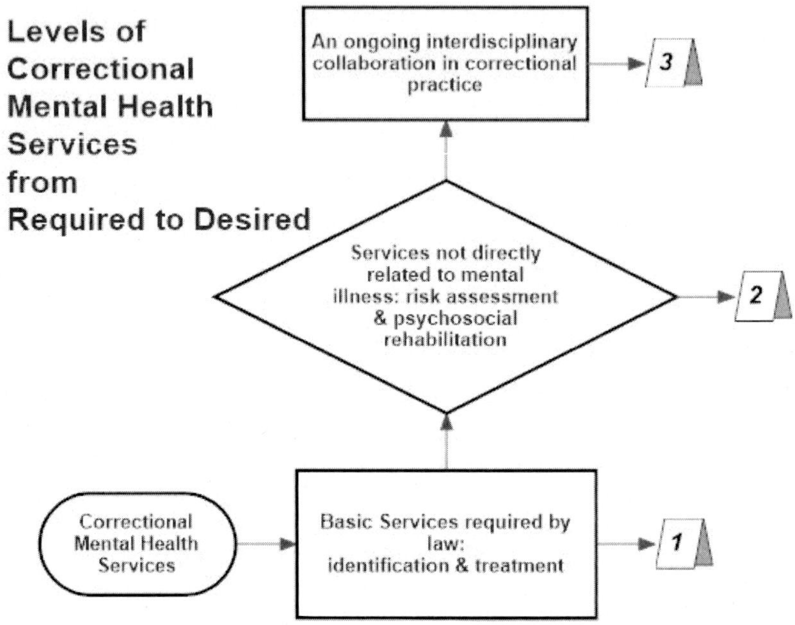

4. CH11-04 *Correctional Mental Health Services*. Three levels of mental health services exist in corrections. The basic or level #1 are those services which are concerned with identification and treatment of mental disorders, typically these are required by law. To improve services for offenders with mental illness, level #2 adds risk assessment and psychosocial services which are rehabilitative and aimed at reducing recidivism. Achieving level #3 requires an orientation change in the corrections facility that includes interagency community collaborations to provide a range of services for reintegration. Adapted from Fagan (2003).

Trauma-Informed Correctional Care

An important aspect of trauma-informed care is the recognition and identification of offenders who are affected by trauma. **TRAUMA-INFORMED CORRECTIONAL CARE** aims to identify trauma and its symptoms among inmates, train staff to understand the impact of trauma, minimize re-traumatization, maintain sensitivity to triggers of trauma, and identify how traumatic dynamics may, without intent, repeatedly play out in prisons (Miller and Najavits, 2012). Sexual or physical victimization is a highly relevant issue for people with serious mental illness who are involved with the criminal justice system (Epperson et al., 2014). Numerous studies have found a significant association between trauma history and the criminal justice system. In one study, most 209 female inmates interviewed reported experiencing victimization through at least one type: of crime related (58 percent), general disaster (98 percent), and/or interpersonal (87 percent) trauma, and most (74 percent) reported a childhood history of sexual or physical trauma

(Wolff et al., 2011). The psychological consequences of trauma are potentially severe and may include fear, anxiety, depression, anger, guilt, substance abuse, suicidal ideation, and post-traumatic stress disorder (PTSD) (Breslau, Davis, Andreski, and Peterson, 1991; Bryant, 2010).

Some correctional facilities have recently augmented staff training on trauma, including programs on techniques to respond effectively to trauma symptoms, the trauma-recovery approach, and trauma-specific interventions (Seeking Safety, 2016). During training, staff learn ways to minimize triggers, stabilize offenders, reduce critical incidents, deescalate situations, and avoid measures that may repeat aspects of past abuse (e.g., restraint and seclusion). This approach not only enhances effective behavior management but also creates safer facilities and greater job satisfaction.

Suicide Risk Assessment

Mental disorders greatly increase the risk of suicide. Research has consistently shown that 90 percent or more of those who died by suicide had a mental disorder at the time of their deaths (AFSP, 2015). The Centers for Disease Control and Prevention (CDC) collects data about mortality in the U.S., including deaths by suicide. In 2013, 41,149 suicides were reported, making suicide the tenth leading cause of death for all Americans. Risk factors that increase the likelihood that a person may try to take her life include substance abuse and mental health disorders such as depression, bipolar disorder, schizophrenia, antisocial personality disorder, conduct disorder, psychotic disorders and anxiety disorders. Depression is the most common mental health risk factor. In 2013, adults aged 18 or older who were on parole or a supervised release from jail in the past twelve months were more likely to have serious thoughts of suicide than their counterparts who were not on parole or a supervised release from jail during this period (10.7 vs. 3.9 percent) (NSDUH, 2014).

PROGRAMMING

The terms rehabilitation and treatment are rarely used today in corrections to describe the activities designed to improve the well-being of inmates. Correctional terms commonly used include *programs, activities*, and *correctional interventions*. This difference in terminology reflects a philosophical change from the 1970s-medical model, which sought to cure inmates through rehabilitation. The current era is one that places greater emphasis on the inmates' responsibility for making change and the role of the institute as the facilitator. **PROGRAMMING** refers to the opportunities that are provided to inmates for self-improvement and behavioral change to improve conditions during incarceration and as preparation for re-entry to society. There are many different types of correctional programs offered both in prison and jail settings. These opportunities generally include educational, vocational, and psychiatric services. Prerelease programs are job readiness initiatives designed to help inmates prepare to enter the workforce. Most prisons provide vocational training in specific job categories such as carpentry, electronics, food service or landscaping. Student inmates earn certificates of completion at the end of their training, which is focused on obtaining entry-level positions in a chosen vocation. Research has generally found that vocational training reduces recidivism.

Education programs are frequently offered in prisons and jails. They are highly regarded to improve literacy and lead to improved job opportunities. The Federal Bureau of Prisons (BOP) requires participation for those who lack a high school diploma or General Educational Development credential (GED) and for individuals who are functionally illiterate (BOP, 2014). Non-English-speaking individuals unable to perform at the eighth-grade level who are in the care of the BOP are also required to attend an English as a Second Language program. The results of a recent study concluded that earning a secondary degree in prison significantly improves employment opportunities upon re-entry to society after release (Duwe and Clark, 2014). Individuals who can obtain a job and work regularly are less likely to commit crimes.

At all stages of the criminal justice process, offenders report high levels of drug and alcohol use. Approximately 50 percent of individuals with a mental health concern report having a substance use disorder at least one time in their life (Substance Abuse and Mental Health Services Administration, 2013). Persons with substance use disorders have significantly higher rates of major depressive episodes. Individuals with co-occurring mental illness and substance use disorders are 40 percent more likely to be re-arrested after release from jail than those who have mental illness alone (Blank Wilson, Draine, Barrenger, Hadley, and Evans, 2014). It is not surprising, then, that programing dedicated to drug and alcohol abuse rehabilitation is frequently offered in both jail and prison settings.

Inmate programming that focuses on skill building rather than specific problematic behaviors is gaining popularity. Numerous recent studies suggest that some of the characteristics of individuals who commit crimes are similar, regardless of whether they experience mental illness or not (Peterson et al., 2014). Based on the perspective of positive psychology, one such treatment model involves skill building in positive emotions, engagement, relationships, positive meanings and feelings of accomplishment. Offenders that were introduced to these positive psychological principles through a Positive Re-Entry in Corrections Program (PCP) in Washington experienced measurable changes in gratitude, life satisfaction, and hope (Huynh, Hall, Hurst, and Bikos, 2015). The program is unique because of its focus on changing the way that an offender thinks, and to nurture a person's strengths and values, as a way to affect recidivism.

Programs that incorporate behavioral interventions for self-improvement also show great promise. Another model involves cognitive behavioral therapy that is specifically designed for inmates with mental health issues. Known as *Beyond the Bridge*, the focus in this New York jail program is to bring treatment into the living areas of mentally ill inmates and to provide additional clinical support to identify individuals that need intensive therapy. Evaluation of the program found there were significant reductions in time spent on suicide watch and in recidivism among the offenders that participated (Glowa-Kollisch et al., 2014). A reduction in violent incidents and fights involving the participants, along with fewer incidents of self-injurious behavior, was also noted in the study.

RELEASE PLANNING

Researchers from the Urban Institute argue that the actual time of release from prison represents a critical juncture for the success or failure of reintegration; as such it requires preparation independent of the broader reentry planning (LaVigne et al., 2008). **RELEASE PLANNING**, also called discharge planning, is a focus on short-term needs including an individualized assessment to identify what an inmate will need to be released and any problems that might occur with meeting the conditions of release. For example, a release plan would address long-term employment needs by providing in-prison training and education and might involve looking for a job and a place to live. In addition to a written discharge assessment of medical and treatment needs, the plan might include contact names, phone numbers and addresses of resources (LaVigne et al., 2008). The Urban Institute suggests that release planning activities might include pre-release classes for two months prior to the actual release to identify the basic immediate needs of shelter, food, transportation, civilian clothes to wear out of the institution and some minimal cash to fulfill the most pressing needs.

BARRIERS TO SUCCESSFUL REENTRY

Nally et. al (2012) boldly state that inmates are often characterized as economically poor, educationally lacking, illiterate, and disproportionally unemployed, both pre- and post-incarceration. They are also thought to be re-incarcerated at high rates. These unfortunate characterizations have resulted from extensive research on prisoner reentry. Studies have also consistently confirmed that individuals experiencing mental disorders have an even more difficult reentry experience than others. There are many reasons why this is occurring. A study by Mallik-Kane and Visher (2008) found that the consistent lack of health care access, housing, and employment could all be significant barriers to the successful reentry into society. Offenders classified on the higher end of the risk continuum are more likely to struggle with inadequate transportation, lack of interest in program participation, mental health, and residential issues compared to their lower risk counterparts. Among the 1,341 high-risk offenders surveyed, approximately a fifth did not have adequate transportation (22 percent) or lacked any desire to participate in interventions (20 percent). In addition, 18 percent of those high-risk offenders had mental health issues and 13 percent had residential problems serious enough to hinder successful supervision. Among the largest obstacles for successful completion of federal probation is mental illness (Cohen and Whetzel, 2014). For the disordered population, supervision planning must be individualized and comprehensive to maximize the probability of successful completion of the program.

Access to Health Care

Medical information should be released to community providers shortly before an inmate is released on parole or assigned to probation. Those with serious mental disorders, substance abuse problems, or co-occurring disorders need a summary of needs diagnosis, current medication, and recent history of treatment prior to leaving an institution or beginning a probationary sentence. Having a supply of medication that will last a few days beyond their first appointment with health care providers is identified as essential to continued use of prescribed medications. Securing a fixed appointment with a health care provider should be arranged by the community supervision officer at the beginning of the community corrections period.

It bears repeating that there are many inaccurate assumptions about sharing health care information due to state and federal laws. Probation and parole departments are not classified as "covered entities" and are not subjected to the provisions of HIPAA. Neither are probation or parole agencies held to the standards of 42 CFR Part 2, since these agencies do not publicly identify as substance abuse/mental health treatment providers that receive federal funds for substance abuse services. State laws may bar some information sharing in certain circumstances, however. It is important for professionals to become familiar with the laws in their state which govern community corrections and health care information sharing. Protected health information (PHI) can be received by probation and parole officers in the following circumstances (Abernathy, 2014):

- Information is provided voluntarily to the officer
- A legally compliant consent form is voluntarily signed to permit the service provider to release the desired information
- As a condition of supervision, the client forfeits his right to refuse consent to the release of information
- A court order authorizes the disclosure and is combined with a subpoena to compel the service provider to relinquish the information

Employment

Employment may well be the most important predictor of recidivism. The risk of unemployment is high among the community corrections population. One study found that the unemployment rate among released offenders reached 65 percent during the years of 2008–2009 (Nally, Lockwood, and Ho, 2011). Struggling with mental health problems can make it even more difficult to find employment after release. Only 36 percent of men and 26 percent of women with mental health conditions had found any employment within the first two to three months out of prison, and within ten months after release their employment rates were still significantly lower than the rates reported by other offenders (Mallik-Kane and Visher, 2008).

A consistent finding in the literature is that unemployment after release from prison is linked to inadequate education. Nally et. al (2012) conducted a five-year follow-up longitudinal study on recidivism in Indiana and found that 38 percent of the released offenders, most of whom were under age 30, had an education below high school. The undereducated offenders had a consistently higher post-release recidivism rate at over 50 percent and a lower post-release employment rate—regardless of whether they were violent offenders, sex offenders, or non-violent offenders. The authors concluded that undereducated offenders are likely to be re-incarcerated after release from prison due to their inability to gain employment (Nally, Lockwood, Ho, and Knutson, 2012).

Housing

There is no easy way to fix the problem of homelessness among individuals with mental illness. It is widely acknowledged that permanent sustainable housing is necessary for community reintegration. However, returning offenders with mental disorders are less likely to have long-term support from family members for housing and are more likely to experience homelessness. As many as two-thirds of the homeless population nationwide are individuals suffering from mental illness (Torrey, Fuller, Geller, Jacobs, and Ragosta, 2012). In a Massachusetts forensic transition program, 39 percent of released offenders with mental illness reported histories of homelessness (Hartwell, 2001). Among jail diversion offenders in Cincinnati, females were more likely than males to have a history of homelessness, 48 percent vs. 27 percent (Cuddeback, Wright, and Bisig, 2013). Some professions see mental health treatment as the means of stabilizing the lives of homeless individuals.

OVERCOMING BARRIERS

Developed by the National Institute of Corrections (NIC) in 2014, the *Desistance Model* is a positive way to work with offenders to build skill and leverage their strengths to encourage them to give up criminal lifestyles. Key elements of the model include the use of cognitive behavioral therapy, an emphasis on coordinated services to address criminogenic needs of the offender, and an intensive supervision and case management. Typically, moderate to high risk offenders for re-offending are included in the project. Case management is improved through parole officer training. A unique aspect of the approach is its motivational enhancement therapy.

Education programs are frequently offered in prisons and jails. They are highly regarded to improve literacy and lead to improved job opportunities. The Federal Bureau of Prisons (BOP) requires participation for those who lack a high school diploma or General Educational Development credential (GED) and for individuals who are functionally illiterate (BOP, 2014). Non-English-speaking individuals unable to perform at the eighth-grade level who are in the care of the BOP are also required to attend an English as a Second Language program. The results of a recent study concluded that earning a secondary degree in prison significantly improves employment opportunities upon reentry to society after release (Duwe and Clark, 2014). Individuals who can obtain a job and work regularly are less likely to commit crimes.

Prerelease programs are job readiness initiatives designed to help inmates prepare to enter the workforce. Most prisons provide vocational training in specific job categories such as carpentry, electronics, food service, or landscaping. Student inmates earn certificates of completion at the end of their training, which is focused on obtaining entry-level positions in a chosen vocation. Research has generally found that vocational training reduces recidivism.

While the success rates of alcohol and drug abuse programs vary, the results are generally positive. One study that examined recidivism among a cohort of formerly incarcerated people released from a therapeutic community model of prison-based drug treatment found a 15 percent lower likelihood of recidivism more than six years later (Olson and Lurigio, 2014). The therapeutic community model is designed to provide a total treatment environment in which substance abusers are taught through repetition and reinforcements the daily regimen of community roles and community life to create a new substance-free lifestyle. This resocialization approach stresses self-help through changes in behavior, attitudes, emotions, and values that had contributed to the substance use. Olson and Lurigio (2014) found that prison-based drug treatment followed by aftercare programing resulted in a 44 percent reduction in recidivism. They concluded that aftercare was essential to reentry success for the treatment population.

JAIL REENTRY PROGRAMS

Assertive Community Treatment (ACT) and (FACT)

Assertive Community Treatment (ACT) is an example of a case management approach that has been shown to reduce psychiatric hospitalizations and decrease symptoms in many research trials (Morrissey, Meyer, and Cuddeback, 2007). A promising practice in providing treatment for the population of severely disabled persons due to mental illness is called assertive community treatment (ACT). ACT is a high intensity strategy for providing multidisciplinary mental health services to clients with severe mental health issues. With assertive community outreach available on a twenty-four-hour basis, this multidisciplinary model provides psychiatric outpatient treatment, rehabilitation and support programs for persons with severe mental illness (Substance Abuse and Mental Health Services Administration, 2008). Based on the ACT model, *Forensic Assertive Community Treatment* (FACT) is designed to prevent criminal recidivism through mental health and criminal justice collaborations using intensive services to ensure successful community reentry from prison or diversion from jail. FACT uses a multidisciplinary team approach that may include psychiatrists, nurses, and case managers that receive referrals directly from the criminal justice system. A nationwide study found that almost 60 percent of the FACT programs specifically involved collaboration with probation departments (Lamberti, Deem, Weisman, and LaDuke, 2011). Services provided to FACT probationers include mental health and substance use treatment, medication management, educational support, housing assistance, and crisis services.

Boston Reentry Initiative (BRI)

The Boston Reentry Initiative (BRI) is a multiagency initiative implemented in 2001 that was designed to ease the transition process for especially high-risk and violent male inmates released to Boston neighborhoods from the Suffolk County House of Correction. Braga and colleagues (2009) describe the BRI program as a two-stage reentry that provided services for high risk offenders. The first stage of the program involves a sit down between social service agencies, faith-based organizations, law enforcement and participants. Available resources are described. After taking part in the panel session, program participants work with jail-based caseworkers and mentors from faith-based organizations to develop individual transition plans that detail the services to be provided both during incarceration and after release. Available services include mental health and substance abuse treatment, career counseling, job placement, education, identification/driver's license assistance, housing, and transportation. Faith-based mentors work with participants both within the institution and for a period of twelve to eighteen months after release. A mentor or family member meets participants outside of the jail upon release. To be eligible for the program, participants must be between 18 and 32 years of age and considered to be at a high risk of committing violent crimes upon release.

Evaluations of Jail Initiatives

Some experts maintain that the evidence of jail programs reducing recidivism is weak, particularly for the mental health-based models such as FACT programs (Skeem, Manchak, and Peterson, 2011). In contrast, other studies have shown that compared to those without intensive intervention, the FACT participants have fewer psychiatric hospitalizations, more contact with community treatment providers, and a higher probability of avoiding jail (Cuddeback et al., 2013).

Evaluation of the BRI concluded that the treatment group exhibited significantly lower rates of recidivism than the comparison group, although both group rates were high (Braga, Piehl, and Hureau, 2009). The authors found that was not surprising given the high-risk nature of both groups. The treatment group rearrest rate was 31.1 percent lower than that of the comparison group. Differences between rates of arrest among the treatment and comparison groups grew progressively smaller over the three-year follow-up period. While 36.1 percent of BRI participants had been rearrested at one year after release, compared to 51.1 percent of the comparison group (a difference of 15 percent), this difference shrank to 9.9 percent after three years, at which time 77.8 percent of the treatment group had been rearrested, compared to 87.7 percent of the comparison group.

PRISON REENTRY PROGRAMS

Mentally Ill Offender Community Transition Program (MIOCTP)

This program was implemented in 1998 in Washington state as a collaboration between the Department of Corrections and the Department of Mental Health. Theurer and Lovell (2008) describe MIOCTP as a collaborative venture which involves corrections and mental health staff who work together to provide mentally ill prisoners with care management and coordinated services, including risk assessment, treatment planning, service referrals, and applications for entitlements that are provided three months prior to release. The post-release services are delivered through a multidisciplinary approach which includes a mental health case manager, psychiatrist, nurse practitioner, registered nurse, substance abuse counselor, community corrections officer, and residential house manager. Later years of program operation also include a period of voluntary confinement to the residential site after release to address substance abuse and the tendency of individuals released from custody to abuse drugs soon after release. This team works together to ensure that seriously mentally ill offenders continue their psychotherapy and pharmaceutical course of treatment; have access to housing, drug treatment, and other basic services; and report as required to their parole officers. The post-release program includes structured programming, access to daily contact with team members.

Transition from Prison to Community (TPC)

Several states have adopted the National Institute of Correction's *Transition from Prison to the Community* (TPC) model. The TPC model is an example of the *Integrated Case Management Approach* which differentiates itself from the control and surveillance approach, embracing behavior change, risk reduction and reduction of recidivism (Burke, Herman, Stroker, and Giguere, 2010). It builds on collaborative team building to facilitate programs and interventions to address the offenders' risk and needs, bringing about change through the use of incentives for goal attainment. This reentry initiative begins at intake through discharge (and beyond). Collaborative teams involved in TPC set additional goals, including building stronger communities and families through enhanced employment, treatment of mental illness and educational attainment (Burke et al., 2010). Plans for individual offenders are designed to target an offender's risk and criminogenic need during each phase into the community.

5. CH11-05: *Aging Inmates.* Long prison sentences, including life-sentences has contributed to the elderly prison population crisis. Mental health needs among this population is high. Copyright oscarcwilliams/Bigstock.com

In the TPC model, the release planning is the second phase of reentry which begins from six months to twelve months before release through the first six months after release (Burke et al., 2010). During this period the inmate completes any remaining programing and makes plans for community services such as applying for benefits and addressing identification needs. The third stage of reentry in the TOC model is the community phase, beginning from six months after release through discharge from community supervision (Burke et al., 2010). Designed to establish the long-term stabilization of offenders it includes the completion of required risk-reduction programing. An important component for continued success is the transition from criminal justice supports towards community-based networks such as family, employers, a faith community and agencies that serve the broader community.

Evaluations of Prison Initiatives

Theurer and Lovell (2008) examined the effectiveness of the MIOCTP with a sample consisting of a high percentage of women (44 percent) and drug offenders (47 percent). Primary diagnoses among sample members included 56 percent psychotic disorders, 20 percent with severe depression, 20 percent with bipolar disorder, and 3 percent with other conditions. Nearly 90 percent of the sample had co-occurring chemical dependency issues, and 52 percent suffered from a personality disorder. The treatment group was matched to a comparison group (N = 64 in each group) based on a number of factors, including past felonies, past misdemeanors, whether the individual was a first-time sex offender, infraction rate, mental health residential time, age at release, ethnicity, and gender. During a two-year follow-up period, program participants showed a recidivism rate of 19 percent, measured as felony conviction for any new offense, compared with 42 percent for matched controls. The treatment group's rate of conviction of any new offense was 22 percent less than the comparison group. The researchers concluded that the treatment group's rate of recidivism, defined as both re-conviction for any new offense and re-conviction for a felony offense, was significantly lower than that of the comparison group over the two-year follow-up period. The Urban Institute selected this program as "promising" (Kim, Becker-Cohen, and Serakos, 2015).

The TPC model *Integrated Case Management Approach* became the basic approach for a National Serious and Violent Offender Reentry Initiative (SVORI). According to the Justice Center (2016), a collaborative federal initiative provided resources to sixty-nine grantees in all fifty states as well as the District of Columbia and the U.S. Virgin Islands to develop or expand integrated programs offering services to juveniles and adults at high risk of recidivating in their communities. SVORI supported system-level change by requiring cross-agency collaboration and centered program services around a case management model. The initiative intentionally gave sites significant flexibility to design and implement programs targeted to the specific needs of their reentering populations. As a result, implementation varied significantly by site but generally focused on addressing criminal justice, employment, education, health, mental health and/or housing outcomes. According to Veeh and colleagues (2015), their evaluation yields mixed findings about the impact of SVORI on recidivism. No significant difference was found between groups in the rate of return to prison, yet program participants had significantly lower rates of reconviction. Over the course of the study, 35.3 percent of those in the treatment group and 37 percent of the comparison group returned to prison. There was no significant difference between groups in the hazard of returning to prison.

AGING INMATES IN PRISON

The population of aging prisoners is rapidly changing the face of the typical American inmate. Approximately 10 percent of the U.S. prison population is age 55 or older (Carson, 2015). Between 2001 and 2008, the elderly inmate population rose by 94 percent. In 2011, the number of state and federal prisoners aged 55 and older stood at more than 120,000 and is projected to exceed 400,000 by 2030 (Pew Charitable Trusts, 2013). This aging trend presents a potential crisis that concerns policy makers, practitioners, and human rights advocates (Maschi, Sutfin, and O'Connell, 2012).

Relatively little research has examined the mental health of elderly imprisoned Americans (Maschi et al., 2012). In addition to the normal aging processes, research suggests that about half of the incarcerated elderly are diagnosed with serious mental illness such as major depression, dementia, and schizophrenia (James and Glaze, 2006). Researchers suggest that the rate of dementia among the prison population may be two to three times higher than in the community due to high risk lifestyles, poor health, and an absence of protective factors (Wilson and Barboza, 2010). Based on projected estimates, this equates to a range from 127,130 to 381,391 of inmates that have dementia by 2050. Wilson and Barboza point out that dementia is progressive, without cure, and no treatments are effective in halting the decline. Individuals diagnosed with dementia tend to live approximately six years after diagnosis and the clear majority eventually require full-time institutional nursing care. Some states have responded by opening corrections facilities exclusively to meet the needs of older inmates. Florida is among them and has dedicated four corrections facilities for older inmates (Jones, n.d.).

THE CORRECTIONS MENTAL HEALTH WORKER

One of the most difficult challenges in ensuring adequate access to mental health care for inmates is the difficulty in finding qualified and motivated clinicians who are willing to work inside of a correctional facility (Carlson, 2011). Another obstacle is that some of the correctional facilities are in isolated rural areas where psychiatrists, psychologists, social workers and other mental health workers may not wish to live. Carlson argues that practitioners in the mental health field are in great demand and typically command the ability to earn salaries greater than government institutions are authorized to pay. Of no small concern are the security and safety issues involved in the day-to-day operations of a corrections facility.

Adding to the problem of increased demands for mental health specialists in correctional settings is an acknowledged high rate of professional burnout. Among mental health professionals burnout comes from persistent work stress, emotional exhaustion, depersonalization, and strain (Lanham, Rye, Rimsky, and Weill, 2012). Offender interactions with special needs and exposure to manipulative offender behavior within corrections facilities negatively impacts the health and work attitudes of corrections officers as well as nurses, psychologists, and educators employed within corrections facilities (Brough and Biggs, 2015).

SUMMARY

Prisoner reentry as a concept of continuation of services to improve the changes of successful reintegration back into the community is still in its infancy. Programs are being designed and implemented across the nation to test the ideas of coordinated services and collaborations as means to reduce recidivism. These are programs are particularly relevant to people who have mental illness and substance abuse co-occurring disorders. Programming is being designed to improve outcomes for individuals with special needs while addressing criminogenic traits.

CHAPTER QUESTIONS FOR REVIEW

1. What is does reentry mean for offenders being released from prison and jail?
2. What are the most common barriers to successful reentry and reintegration back into the community following incarceration?
3. What are some of the common elements of a jail reentry program?
4. What is the difference between jail and prison reentry?
5. Why is there concern over aging inmates?

REFERENCES

Abernathy, C. (2014). *Corrections and reentry: Protected health information privacy framework for information sharing.* Retrieved from Lexington, KY.

Abram, K., Teplin, L., and McClelland, G. (2003). Co-morbidity of severe psychiatric disorders and substance use disorders among women in jail. *American Journal of Psychiatry, 150*, 1007–1010.

Andrews, D., and Bonta, J. (2006). The psychology of criminal conduct (4th ed.). Newark, NJ: Anderson Publishing Co.

Baillargeon, J., Binswanger, I. A., Penn, J. V., Williams, B. A., and Murray, O. J. (2009). Psychiatric disorders and repeat incarcerations: the revolving prison door. *American Journal of Psychiatry, 166*(1), 103–109.

Beck, A., Berzofsky, M., Caspar, R., and Krebs, C. (2013). *Sexual victimization in prisons and jails reported by inmates, 2011–12* Retrieved from Washington, D.C..

Binswanger, I. A., Stern, M. F., Deyo, R. A., Heagerty, P. J., Cheadle, A., Elmore, J. G., and Koepsell, T. D. (2007). Release from prison—a high risk of death for former inmates. *New England Journal of Medicine, 356*(2), 157–165.

Boccaccini, M., Christy, A., Poythress, N., and Kershaw, D. (2005). Rediversion in two postbooking jail diversion programs in Florida. *Psychiatric Services, 56*(835–839).

Breslau, N., Davis, G., Andreski, P., and Peterson, E. (1991). Traumatic events and posttraumatic stress disorder in an urban population of young adults. *Arch Gen Psychiatry, 48*, 216–222.

Brough, P., and Biggs, A. (2015). Job demands× job control interaction effects: Do occupation specific job demands increase their occurrence? *Stress and Health, 31*(2), 138–149.

Bryant, R. (2010). Treating the full range of posttraumatic reactions. In G. Rosen and B. Frueh (eds.), *Clinicians guide to posttraumatic stress disorder* (pp. 205–234). Hoboken, NJ: John Wiley and Sons.

Burke, P., Herman, P., Stroker, R., and Giguere, R. (2010). *TPC Case Management Handbook: An integrated case management approach*. Retrieved from Washington, D.C.: National Institute of Corrections.

Carlson, P. (2011). Managing the mentall ill from a correctional administrator's perspective. In T. Fagan and R. Ax (eds.), *Correctional Mental Health* (pp. 57–76). Los Angeles, CA: Sage.

Carson, A. (2015). Prisoners in 2014. (NCJ 248955). Washington, D.C.: U.S. Department of Justice.

Department of Community and Human Services. (2011). *Offender reentry plan* (pp. 28). Retrieved from http://www.kingcounty.gov/~/media/health/MHSA/

documents/2011–RPT0042_A__Offender_Reentry_Plan_March_2011. ashx?la=en

Epperson, M., Morgan, R., Fisher, W., Frueh, C., and Huening, J. (2014). Envisioning the next generation of behavioral health and criminal justice interventions. *International Journal of Law and Psychiatry*, 37, 427–438.

Fagan, T. (2003). Mental health in corrections: A model for service delivery. In T. Fagan and R. Ax (eds.), *Correctional Mental Health* (pp. 1–19). Thousand Oaks, CA: Sage Publications.

James, D., and Glaze, L. (2006). *Mental health problems of prison and jail inmates.* Retrieved from Washington, D.C.: U.S. Department of Justice.

James, N. (2015). *Offender reentry: Correctional statistics, reintegration into the community, and recidivism.* Congressional Research Services. Library of Congress, Washington, D.C..

Jones, J. (n.d.). Florida Department of Corrections Facilities. Retrieved 2015, November 6, from http://www.dc.state.fl.us/oth/inmates/elderly.html

Justice Center. (2016). What Works. Retrieved from https://whatworks.csgjustice center.org/program/serious-and-violent-offender-reentry-initiative-national

Kim, K., Becker-Cohen, M., and Serakos, M. (2015). *The processing and treatment of mentally ill persons in the criminal justice system: A scan of practice and background analysis.* Retrieved from Washington, D.C..

Lanham, M. E., Rye, M. S., Rimsky, L. S., and Weill, S. R. (2012). How gratitude relates to burnout and job satisfaction in mental health professionals. *Journal of Mental Health Counseling, 34*(4), 341.

Latessa, E., and Lowenkamp, C. (2005). What are criminogenic needs and why are they important? *Community corrections: Research and best practices.* Retrieved from http://ojj.la.gov/ojj/files/What_Are_Criminogenic_Needs.pdf

LaVigne, N., Davies, E., Palmer, T., and Halberstadt, R. (2008). *Release planning for successful reentry: A guide for corrections, service providers, and community groups.* Retrieved from Washington, D.C..

Louden, J., and Skeem, J. (2013). How do probation officers assess and manage recidivism and violence risk for probationers with mental disorder? An experimental investigation. *Law and Human Behavior, 37*(1), 22–34.

Maschi, T., Sutfin, S. L., and O'Connell, B. (2012). Aging, mental health, and the criminal justice system: A content analysis of the literature. *Journal of Forensic Social Work, 2*(2–3), 162–185.

Miller, N., and Najavits, L. (2012). Creating trauma-informed correctional care: A balance of goals and environment. *European Journal of Psychotraumatology, 3.*

Morrissey, J., Meyer, P., and Cuddeback, G. (2007). Extending assertive community treatment to criminal justice settings: Origins, current evidence, and future directions. *Community mental health journal, 43*(5), 527–544.

NSDUH. (2014). *Results from the 2013 National Survey on Drug Use and Health: Mental health findings.* (HHS Publication No. 14-4887). Rockville, MD: Substance Abuse and Mental Health Services Administration.

Peterson, J. K., Skeem, J., Kennealy, P., Bray, B., and Zvonkovic, A. (2014). How often and how consistently do symptoms directly precede criminal behavior among offenders with mental illness? *Law and Human Behavior, 38*(5), 439–449. doi:10.1037/lhb0000075.

Pew Charitable Trusts. (2013). Managing prison health care spending. (NCJ 247358). Retrieved November 10, 2015, from http://www.pewtrusts.org/~/media/legacy/uploadedfiles/pcs_assets/2014/pctcorrectionshealthcarebrief050814pdf.pdf

Seeking Safety. (2016). Summary of evidence on Seeking Safety. Retrieved from http://www.treatment-innovations.org/cdevid-summary-ss.html

Skeem, J. L., Manchak, S., and Peterson, J. K. (2011). Correctional policy for offenders with mental illness: Creating a new paradigm for recidivism reduction. *Law and Human Behavior, 35*(2), 110–126. doi:10.1007/s10979-010-9223-7.

Solomon, A., Osborne, J., LoBuglio, S., Mellow, J., and Mukamal, D. (2008). *Life after lockup.* Washington, D.C.: Urban Institute.

Steadman, H., Dupius, S., and Morris, L. (2009). *For whom does jail diversion work? Results of a multi-site longitudinal study.* Paper presented at the American Psychology-Law Society, San Antonio, TX.

Steadman, H. J., Morrissey, J. P., and Parker, T. W. (2015). *When political will is not enough jails, communities, and persons with mental health disorders.* Delmar, NY: Policy Research Associates, Inc.

Theurer, G., and Lovell, D. (2008). Recidivism of offenders with mental illness released from prison to an intensive community treatment program. *Journal of offender rehabilitation, 47*(4), 385–406.

Torrey, E., Zdanowicz, M., Kennard, A., Lamb, H., Eslinger, D., Biasotti, M., and Fuller, D. (2014). The treatment of persons with mental illness in prisons and jails: A state survey. Arlington, VA: Treatment Advocacy Center.

Veeh, C., Severson, M., and Lee, J. (2015). Evaluation of a serious and violent offender reentry initiative (SVORI) Program in a Midwest State. *Criminal Justice Policy Review*, 1–17.

Wilson, J., and Barboza, S. (2010). The looming challenge of dementia in corrections. *CorrectCare, 24*(2).

Wolff, N., Frueh, B., Shi, J., Gerardi, D., Fabrikant, N., and Schmann, B. (2011). Traumatic and stressful even exposure and behavioral health characteristics of incarcerated females self-referred to specialty PTSD treatment. *Psychiatric Services, 62* (954–958).

CHAPTER 12

Community Corrections

INTRODUCTION

The clear majority of the corrections system population is made up of persons who are in community corrections. Community corrections is an umbrella term within the corrections system for the distinctly different approaches of probation and parole. In contrast to jail and prison incarceration, the individuals living under probation or parole are supervised in traditional community areas. In fact, an estimated 70 percent of individuals under the supervision of the corrections system live in the community under probation or parole (Glaze and Kaeble, 2014). They live by rules which govern their behaviors. These are known as the "conditions" for their release back into society. Some of the conditions are individually developed to meet the reentry needs of the offender. General requirements like keeping away from illegal drug use and crime, are standard. Probation and parole rules may be as broad as a requirement to attend school, get an apartment, or find employment; they may be as specific as orders to stay away from named individuals and places. Typically, problematic and risky behaviors such as substance abuses, smoking, and interaction with negative social influences are restricted through mandates of probation or parole program requirements.

The corrections system is challenged to create fair supervision practices for individuals serving time in the community. A federal or state judge may sentence an individual to probation and community supervision. In cases where parole is discretionary, it is the parole board that determines whether an inmate will be granted early release to parole and community supervision.

Key Terms

COMMUNITY CORRECTIONS

DISCRETIONARY PAROLE

INTENSIVE PROBATION SUPERVISION

MANDATORY PAROLE

PAROLE

PROBATION

Chapter Objectives

After completing this chapter, you should be able to:

- Describe community corrections
- Compare probation and parole
- Explain the common goals of specialized probation programming
- Discuss the effectiveness of probation and parole on reducing recidivism

TRENDS IN COMMUNITY CORRECTIONS

COMMUNITY CORRECTIONS, also called to as community supervision, refers to the supervision of criminal offenders in the mainstream population, as opposed to confinement in secure correctional facilities. A significant increase in the prison and jail populations, along with mandatory supervision policies after release, has created considerable challenges and commitment of resources must be addressed. Most inmates will return to society under the conditions of community supervision. Millions of offenders will serve community sentences under probation supervision. After four decades of steady growth, the Bureau of Justice Statistics (2015) reports that between 2008 and 2014 the number of people under correctional community supervision in the United States has finally decreased, by 10 percent overall. Yet there are still over 4.7 million adults under the supervision of community corrections through probation or parole, most are males between the ages of eighteen and forty-four (BJS, 2015).

The two main types of community corrections are probation and parole. While probation and parole are typically studied together, they are very different concepts. **PROBATION** is a court-ordered sentence with conditions of release that allows the offender to remain in the community under the supervision of a probation officer. The origin of modern probation can be traced to John Augustus, known as the Father of Probation. In 1841, Augustus bailed out a drunkard and returned the man for his three-week hearing as a sober and changed man. Augustus spent the next eighteen years in Boston courts as a volunteer "probation" officer, a term he coined for his method of treating offenders. The first statute to legally recognize probation was passed in Massachusetts in 1859 and soon the practice spread across the country. Today, probation is the most widely used sanction in the criminal justice system. Probation officers take custody of individuals who are placed on probation, and if the terms of probation are violated, the officer returns the person to the custody of the court for further action. The administrative structure of probation varies greatly from state to state. There are state-administered probation systems and locally-administered systems. In some states, probation and parole are combined and they share the same administration. The Bureau of Justice Statistics reports that probationers account for more than 80 percent of the community corrections population. An estimated 3.8 million people were under probation in 2014 (Bonczar, Kaeble, and Maruschak, 2015).

PAROLE is a prison release mechanism that requires correctional supervision in the community with conditions that the parolee must meet. The concept of parole was developed in the mid-1800s in Australia, England, and Ireland. The United States followed their lead, and by 1922, the use of parole existed in forty-four states, the federal system, and Hawaii (NIC, 2010). Parole was created for two reasons. The first was that prison bed spaces were expensive and parole conserved limited criminal justice resources. Second, it was believed that serving a portion of one's sentence was sufficient to satisfy the goal of punishment. Releasing the inmate back into society with the remaining portion of the sentence suspended acted as a deterrent to committing further crime.

Parole came under attack in the 1970s and 1980s when the public outcry for truth-in-sentencing and get-tough-on-crime policies sparked significant parole reform. As a result, at least fifteen states and the federal government have abolished discretionary parole as an early release mechanism in favor of a fixed-sentence structure. **DISCRETIONARY PAROLE** is the release of an offender, decided by a Board of Paroles, to serve the remainder of a sentence in the community while under supervision. The practices of parole vary from state to state. Some states that have restricted the use of early release through discretionary parole have instituted a mandatory supervised parole period following release from incarceration. **MANDATORY PAROLE** is a legislatively mandated release of a prisoner to parole supervision when the combination of actual calendar time and good conduct time equal the sentence. Good conduct time is credited to an offender for participating in work and self-improvement programs. States that did not abolish the use of parole have established guidelines that standardize the decision-making process in cases where parole is considered. An estimated 856,900 prisoners were on parole at the end of 2014, they represent less than 20 percent of the community corrections population (Bonczar, Kaeble, and Maruschak, 2015).

THE MISSION AND GOAL OF COMMUNITY CORRECTIONS

The primary mission of community corrections is to protect society by deterring crime. The strategies of community corrections fall into two general categories: the rehabilitation approach and the surveillance and control approach. There is an overlap between the two models; both share the goal of altering probationers' criminal dispositions by emphasizing the consequences of revocation. The surveillance and control approach involves an enforcement role of monitoring conditions and the requirement of rigorous rule adherence. The rehabilitation approach involves supportive casework with programming and services that are aimed at reducing recidivism. There is disagreement on the best overall approach to reduce recidivism.

If a person who is released on probation or parole does not follow the rules of his community release, it may be revoked, which means it could be taken away altogether or the conditions may be changed. There are two ways that a person might have his community supervision revoked. A person under supervision can be returned to custody for committing a new crime or for a technical violation, which is when the offender breaks any of the conditions under which they were released. A technical violation can include any number of general requirements, such as failing to maintain employment or attend school, associating with known felons, or missing an appointment with the supervising officer. Most revocations involve technical violations rather than new crimes.

Compliance with the conditions for release is overseen by probation and parole officers. If a person on probation or parole violates the conditions of their release the probation or parole officers may revoke the community sanction and surrender him to the court. A revoked probation does not automatically mean the probationer will be sent to jail. Since probation is a sentence, a judge can alter that sentence. For instance, upon a revoked probation, a judge may extend the duration of the probation, impose additional fines, or require counseling or other treatment programs. Parole revocation is more complex than probation revocation since it typically involves incarceration and the loss of liberty. The administrative procedures for parole vary between states, but must conform to constitutional requirements. In 1972, the U.S. Supreme Court established "due process" requirements for revoking parole, which involves an administrative Hearing process before a neutral and detached officer (*Morrissey v. Brewer*, 1972).

IN MY EXPERIENCE . . .

If a person violates their parole by failing to comply with a condition of release, a warrant may be issued for his or her arrest. The arrest warrant states the original charge from which they were paroled. Police officers who make the arrest of a parolee typically have information about that original charge, but may not have information on the violation for which the warrant is issued. Unless the parole officer for the person is directly involved with the arrest, officers do not have any of the information on whether the person has mental illness or substance use disorders. Information is also not available on dangerousness or proclivity to violence.

While on duty, I received a call that a man who was just seen in the local church was wanted on an arrest warrant. The warrant was for parole violation—murder. We did not know the nature of the current violation. With guns drawn, my partner and I searched the church and found only one person in the basement. His back was to us, so I called out his name and instructed him to put his hands in the air and turn around. To our surprise it was a very old man with a cup of coffee in his hand. He was placed under arrest and taken to the station where his parole officer was notified. We later found out that the violation which had resulted in his arrest was that he moved out of his apartment and had failed to notify his parole officer about his new place of residence.

Question for discussion: Could this lack of information affected the arrest of this suspect?

One of the ways society judges whether probation or parole have been successful in meeting their goals is by examining the rates of recidivism. Recidivism is measured by criminal acts that result in re-arrest, re-conviction or return to prison with or without a new sentence anytime during a three-year period following the prisoner's release. Research over the past ten years has documented alarmingly high rates of re-arrest among released prisoners. The National Institute of Justice maintains that recidivism rates are as high 67 percent in some states. With so many people under corrections supervision, the high rates of recidivism are of considerable concern to policy makers, practitioners, and academics.

MENTAL ILLNESSES IN COMMUNITY CORRECTIONS

Reducing recidivism and promoting recovery among the population of community corrections is increasingly difficult given that many on probation and parole have problems linked to substance abuse, mental illness, or both. Individuals that have mental disorders are overrepresented among parole and probation populations. Experts estimate the rate of mental disorders range from two to four times higher among those on community corrections than for individuals in the general population (Osher, D'Amora, Plotkin, Jarrett, and Eggleston, 2012). The *National Survey on Drug Use and Health* (NSDUH) found that adults on probation and parole experience higher rates of any mental illness including serious mental illness, compared to people who are not on community corrections (NSDUH, 2014). Collaborations with mental health agencies is among the highest priorities in designing treatment protocols and establishing conditions for individuals with severe mental illnesses.

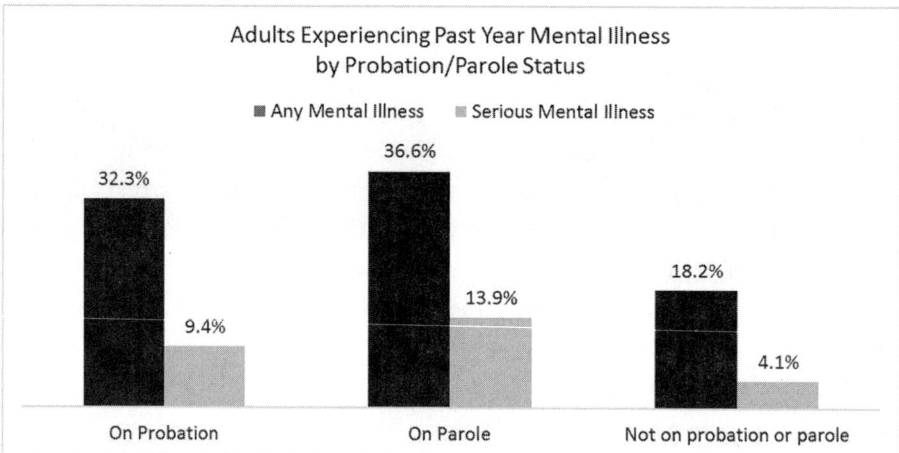

1. CH12-01: *Adults on Probation.* The percentage of adults in 2013 with past year mental illness and on probation was higher than that among adults who were not on probation or parole. Similarly, among adults on parole or supervised release in the past year, the percentage having mental illness was higher than the percentage having mental illness among adults who were not on parole or supervised release in the past year. Source: *NSDUH*, 2014

Probationers with Mental Illness

An estimated half a million adult probationers in the United States struggle with mental health disorders (Babchuk and Lurigio, 2012). The percentage of adults with SMI is higher among adults on probation or parole (9.4 percent and 13.9 percent) in the past year versus those who were not on probation or parole (4.1 percent both) (NSDUH, 2014). Community treatment of individuals with severe mental illnesses occurs for those who receive mandatory outpatient treatment as a condition of probation. Probationers who have mental disorders require more services and are at a higher risk of recidivism and technical violations than are non-disordered probationers. Compared to the population without mental illness, they are more likely to fail under supervision and to have their community term revoked for either a technical violation or a new offense (Louden and Skeem, 2013). Re-arrest rates as high as 54 percent have been documented among this population (Babchuk, 2012). Probation officers are recognized as having an important gate keeping responsibility for individuals at risk to sink further into the criminal justice system.

Parolees with Mental Illness

Based on a sample of 44,987 offenders, experts found that parolees with mental illness (52–62 percent) were about two times more likely than parolees without illness to return to prison within one year of release (30 percent) (Louden and Skeem, 2013). Given the high rate of recidivism among parolees who have mental illness, in cases where the paroling authority has discretion over the timing of release it may be used as an incentive for offenders to participate in appropriate mental health and risk reduction programming (NIC, 2010). Other studies have reported that parolees with mental illness have a 70 percent higher risk of committing technical violations compared to parolees without mental disorders (Grattet, Petersilia, and Lin, 2008). Continuity of care is an important aspect of reentry to which parole officers participate. Their facilitation for continued treatment on release is important for continued stabilization of people who have mental illness.

VICTIMIZATION

Many probationers and parolees with mental disorders live in poverty, are unemployed, and have few social supports, making it difficult for them to meet supervision requirements. Additionally, they may have functional impairments and experience relapses that further complicate their ability to meet supervision conditions. A review of the literature on violence perpetration and violent victimization of people with serious mental illness suggests that individuals with severe mental illness are victimized more often than they commit crime (Choe, Teplin, and Abram, 2008). These authors suggest that violent victimization is a greater public health concern than perpetration.

Female probation and parole populations are at risk of victimization. As many as 40 percent of women with mental health conditions and who are released from custody self-report having been victimized by a family member prior to incarceration (Mallik-Kane and Visher, 2008). Women abused prior to incarceration are not likely to receive the support they need after release due to the lack of sustained family relationships. They are also vulnerable to further abuse. Generally, adult women with mental disorders receive less financial and emotional support from their families after release when compared to other women who do not experience mental illness (Mallik-Kane and Visher, 2008). Since the rates of mental disorders experienced by female probationers and parolees is roughly double that of women in the general population, according to Mallik-Kane and Visher (2008), the challenge for community corrections professionals is to develop appropriate interventions for this population.

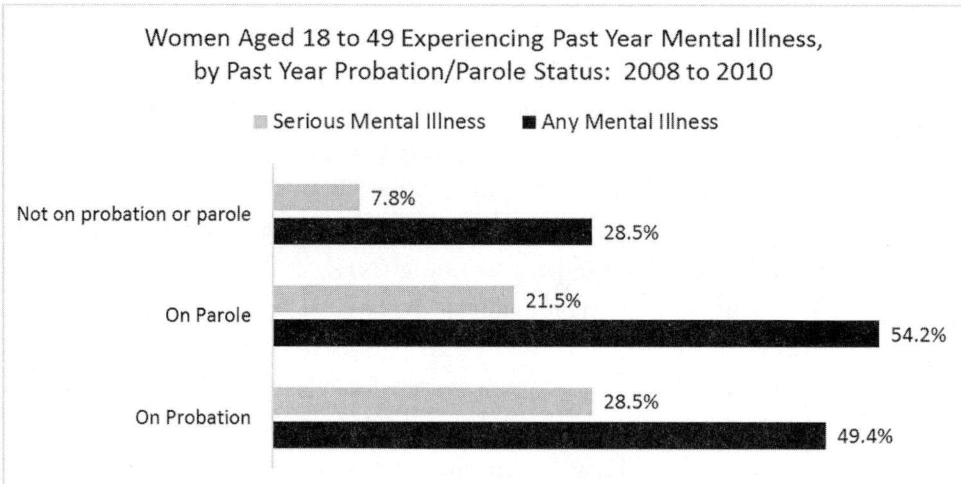

2. CH12-02: *Women on Probation.* Women on probation or parole are almost twice as likely to experience mental illness as other women. Rates of serious mental illness (i.e., mental illness that substantially limits major life activities) were three times higher for women who had been on probation or on parole than for women who had not been on probation or parole. Source: 2008 to 2010 *National Surveys on Drug Use and Health,* SAMHSA, 2012.

PROBATION PRACTICES

The practice of probation varies between states and in the federal system. In some jurisdictions, probation can be a combined sentence of incarceration followed by a period of community supervision. Approximately eight out of ten people in community corrections supervision are on probation (Glaze and Kaeble, 2014). The incarceration rate among probationers at risk of violating their conditions of supervision remained stable at 5.4 percent in 2013 following what had been a four-year period of gradual decline.

There are a variety of intermediate sanctions in use in the United States that fall into the classification of probation. **INTENSIVE PROBATION SUPERVISION**, used since the 1970s, involves strict control, surveillance, and monitoring of high-risk offenders who typically have not been successful under standard probation conditions. In need of more supervision and intervention, offenders in intensive probation supervision (IPS) programs have more frequent contact with the probation officer. Specialty mental health probation programs are a form of IPS.

A higher level of security and supervision for some offenders who remain in the community comes in the form of house arrest. Offenders avoid a prison sentence in this model and can continue working or participating in approved activities outside of their home. The monitoring system can be active or passive. The active system sets off an alarm when the probationer leaves the approved location, typically a home. The passive system involves random telephone calls that require the offender to place the receiver against the transmitter which provides the location of the offender at that time. First introduced as a means of improving supervision during the 1980s, research evaluations suggest that successful house arrest probation programs continue among a range of 57 percent to 92 percent of participants (Roy, 2013). Consistent with prior research, Roy found that employed offenders were more likely to complete the program successfully. House arrest is commonly used in conjunction with electronic monitoring. Electronically monitored home detention (EMHD) is used to enforce the conditions for release as well as improve the ability of corrections officers to supervise offenders in the community. Electronic monitoring requires offenders to wear a tamper-proof bracelet around their ankles that acts as a receiver. Those with prior offense records and prior community corrections placement were the least likely to be successful in EMHD programs.

3. CH12-03: *Electronic Monitoring.* Technology has made surveillances of individuals on community corrections easier. Electronically-monitored home detention (EMHD) shown here is a form of control used in both probation and parole. Copyright Tagging/Bigstocck.com

In the 1980s a new form of probation was devised that is typically reserved for young offenders, called "boot camp." The first boot camps were built in Georgia in 1983 and Oklahoma in 1984 and spread across the country over the next ten years. A boot camp is operated similar to a military boot camp; offenders must keep a clean living space and maintain their appearance, including shined shoes and short hair. Daily routines are marked by extensive physical exercise, strict discipline, and hard work to gain self-control and master leadership skills. Behavior modification through reinforcement of positive behavior and immediate punishment of negative behaviors requires a higher ratio of staff to offenders. As an alternative to incarceration, the boot camp can be a less expensive option. Boot camps are viewed by some as more punitive than prison. In an interesting study on offenders' perceptions of criminal sanctions, May and Wood (2010) interviewed offenders in Indiana, Kentucky, and Oklahoma. The offenders in their research frequently expressed a preference for a one-year prison term over relatively short stays in a county jail or boot camp, although the results varied by age, race, and other factors (May and Wood, 2010). The costs associated with boot camps in these states were higher than the costs of ordinary incarceration, and recidivism rates were disappointing. Many states have discontinued the use of boot camps as a probation option.

Another form of enhanced probation is called "shock incarceration." Designed to provide specific deterrence to reduce recidivism, probationers experience a combination of a short incarceration period, typically thirty to 120 days, followed by release into the community under probation. The idea is to expose an offender to a short confinement in an institution, the type of punishment that he would receive for additional crimes. Typically, this approach is used for nonviolent offenders, the short stay avoids the negative aspects of long-term exposure to correctional institutions.

The U.S. Sentencing Guidelines Manual provides the general framework for sentencing in federal courts (BOP, 2014). The U.S. Probation Office monitors offenders that are sentenced to terms of probation in federal court. The most common forms of federal probation include community confinement, intermittent confinement, and home detention. Community confinement refers to residence in a community treatment center, halfway house, restitution center, mental health facility, alcohol or drug rehabilitation center or other community facility. The court may also place an offender in a community corrections facility in lieu of revocation of probation or supervised release for technical violations. The intermittent confinement option refers to weekend terms and other forms of intermittent confinement that may be imposed as a special condition of probation or supervised release. Federal sentencing guidelines also allow home detention as a condition of probation or a condition of supervised release as a substitute for imprisonment in certain instances. Typically, inmates on home detention are electronically monitored.

SPECIALTY MENTAL HEALTH PROBATION PROGRAMS

The primary goal of probation is to keep communities safe and to provide probationers with rehabilitative tools that they need to lead productive and law-abiding lives. The supervision and custodial responsibilities of the criminal justice system are more complicated when applied to individuals with mental disorders. In response to increasing numbers of persons on probation who have mental health and substance use disorders, specialty probation programs have developed to form collaborative community mental health options along with intensive probation supervision. Specialty probation officer programs are characterized by high-quality care-oriented relationships, strengthened by social service and treatment collaborations (Lurigio, Epperson, Canada, and Babchuk, 2012). Three common goals of specialized probation programming are to assess the offender's criminal risk to the community; target the offender's needs which are served by criminal activity; and identify appropriate treatment and other resources to impact the criminal behavior. Recognizing that co-occurring disorders of mental illness and substance abuse greatly increase the probability that probationers will fail in traditional probation program efforts, specialty probation programs target both issues.

Unlike traditional probation practices, specialized mental health probation officers are specifically trained in mental health issues and carry reduced caseloads that consist only of probationers who meet the diagnostic criteria for psychiatric disorders. Reduced caseloads are necessary to meet the unique needs of this population with services that are not typically coordinated through traditional probation practices. Developing treatment options and finding housing and employment for the probationer are among a range of services that require an extraordinary level of community collaboration and personal commitment. Providing incentives rather than punitive measures for assuring client compliance to conditions of probation is a part of the treatment-oriented approach to specialized court programs. While standardization of programs has yet to be achieved, smaller probation caseloads and greater access to community healthcare services are the hallmarks of successful programs. Specialty probationers are slightly less likely to be arrested, and less likely to be revoked during the first year (Skeem, Manchak, and Peterson, 2010). High rates of recidivism following traditional community corrections have provided the impetus for states to devise specialty probation programs based on interventions that address the high-risk needs of offenders with mental illness. Studies on the effectiveness of specialized mental health probation programs are encouraging (Wolff et al., 2014).

Hawaii's HOPE Program

Hawaii's Opportunity Probation with Enforcement (HOPE), which began in 2004, is an example of a program that uses intensive probation supervision, treatment-focused services, and the certainty of punishment rather than the severity of it to target co-occurring disorders. In traditional programs, offenders may fail to attend mandated programming for substance abuse problems and avoid taking drug tests numerous times before facing revocation. In the HOPE model, probationers are required to call in daily to learn if they are required to report for a drug test on that day. Failure to comply results in certain and almost immediate revocation of probation, a condition that probationers must acknowledge to be accepted into the program. Evaluations of the HOPE program showed an 80 percent reduction of missed probation appointments, failed drug tests, and revocations (Hawken and Kleiman, 2009). As a result, the HOPE probationers spent less time in prison than those who did not participate in the program. Per the National Institute of Justice, HOPE is not just a drug-offender-supervision model. In Hawaii, the concept is applied to a broad range of offenders, including felony sex offenders and domestic violence offenders. At least forty similar programs have sprung up in eighteen states across the United States. Texas has the oldest version of a HOPE style program and Washington State has the largest. To find out whether the successes of the HOPE model can be duplicated nationwide, the National Institute of Justice has set up programs in four jurisdictions that will be closely monitored with outcome evaluations and cost assessments. These monitored programs are underway in Clackamas County, OR; Essex County, MA; Saline County, AK; and Tarrant County, TX. (Pearsall, 2014).

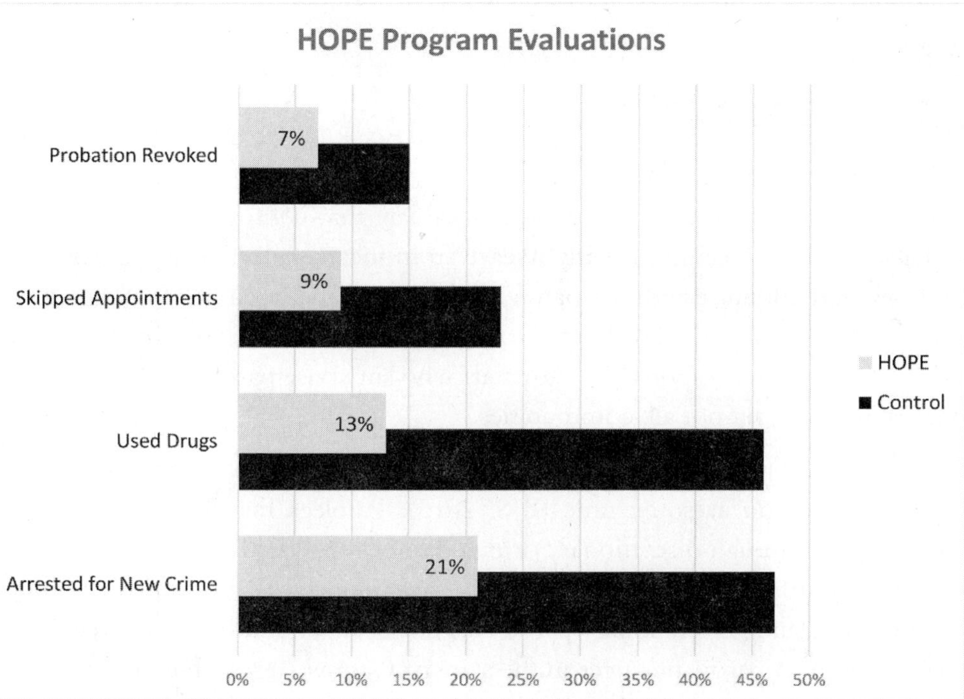

4. CH12-04: *HOPE Program Evaluations.* Results from the NIJ-funded quasi-experimental evaluation show that HOPE probationers were less likely to have their probation revoked, compared to a group of offenders who did not participate in HOPE. The group also had fewer missed appointments with probation officers and decreases in positive drug tests. They were much less likely to be arrested for a new crime. Source: Hawken and Kleiman, 2009.

Kentucky's SMART Program

In an example of programming based on the HOPE model of intensive supervision and swift sanctions, the legislature in Kentucky approved pilot programs in six jurisdictions. Evaluators Shannon, et. al (2015) report that the implementation of the *Supervision, Monitoring, Accounting, and Treatment* program, called SMART, does differ from the original model in some respects. The SMART program uses random drug testing, a move that was thought to be more cost effective than the HOPE model. Preliminary evaluations suggest that increased contact with probation officers and higher accountability of probationers are key components to this approach. The increased number of collaborations and stronger relationships between stakeholders and involved agencies is an unintended consequence that benefited the probationers as well as the criminal justice system. The probationers who were not on the SMART program test positively for drugs at a rate that was three times higher than the SMART probationers (Shannon, Hulbig, Birdwhistell, Newell, and Neal, 2015). An important conclusion based on this statistic is that swift and certain consequences promote program compliance.

PAROLE PRACTICES

Per the National Institute of Corrections, the word parole has come to mean an inmate promise to conduct themselves in a way that conforms to the law and certain rules in exchange for early release from incarceration. The organization, location, and administration of parole varies greatly between states. Some have autonomous parole boards while others may be part of the executive branch of government. Direct responsibility for staff who supervise parolees falls on parole boards in some, but not all, communities.

Almost 80 percent of the state prisoners are expected to be released under parole supervision at some time (BJS, 2015). Parolees may be released from incarceration through discretionary or mandatory supervised release from prison or through other types of post-custody conditional supervision. The move towards abolishing discretionary parole has not been without consequences. In a study examining parole practices in the state of Georgia, research confirmed that since the incentive of early release was removed, the inmate disciplinary infractions rose and fewer prison rehabilitation programs were completed (Kuziemko, 2013).

Parole revocations are central to the parole debate in California. California has a mandatory parole release system which allows offenders to earn day-for-day "good time" for up to a 50 percent reduction in time served. For most California prisoners, there is no appearance before a parole board to determine whether they are fit to return to the community; instead, they are automatically released (Grattet, Petersilia, and Lin, 2008). Once released, virtually all prisoners are placed on formal parole supervision, usually for three years. The sheer number of individuals on parole under this scheme has put strains on the state's ability to properly supervise its parolees. California's recidivism rate is 66 percent, compared to the national average of 40 percent (Grattet et al., 2008). On any given day, six out of ten admissions to California prisons are returning parolees.

Medical Parole

While the clear majority of states have medical parole statutes for inmates, few utilize the practice due to restrictive policies and opposition from policymakers and citizens. Medical parole is also known as compassionate release and humanitarian parole. There is a downward trend in granting release for medical reasons. Some states have established hospice programs and medical units for inmates with terminal illnesses, so it may be a simpler alternative to transfer the inmate to a special unit rather than file the paperwork and request release. The inmate himself is responsible for filing for medical release, an overwhelming requirement for those who may be close to death. A major problem identified by researchers is the requirement that physicians predict limited life expectancy as a condition of release, since this requirement excludes inmates with dementia (Williams, Sudore, Greifinger, and Morrison, 2011).

A medical parole law in California went into effect in 2011 under the auspices of a cost saving initiative. A review board makes the decision on which prisoners will be released under the state's law, by determining if the level of risk that the offender represents to the public is reasonable. The process has already saved over $20 million in correctional health care costs to California by granting medical parole to inmates (Pew Charitable Trusts, 2013). Typically state statutes and policies allowing medical or geriatric parole for elderly inmates contain strict release terms and eligible inmates must be found to pose little or no threat to public safety. These statutes may, in fact, be too restrictive.

Federal Parole Practices

Since the Sentencing Reform Act of 1984 was enacted on November 1, 1987, offenders sentenced to federal prison are no longer eligible for discretionary parole, but are required to serve a term under supervision following release from prison (BOP, 2014). Individuals sentenced to prison prior to the Act continue to be eligible for parole, in addition to those individuals who violate laws of the District of Columbia, military offenders, and foreign treaty transfer offenders. The Sentencing Reform Act also requires the adoption and use of sentencing guidelines.

PAROLE BOARDS

There are roughly 325 parole board members in the United States. They make up a very small proportion of the employees in the state correctional system (NIC, 2010). While their numbers are relatively low, they have extraordinary influence on public safety and the use of public resources. Each year they make thousands of decisions about the timing and release from prison of a significant number of inmates. They also set conditions of release and respond to violations of post-release supervision for many thousands of individuals. Parole release is a privilege and not a right, therefore, parole boards typically have wide discretion in making their decisions. Parole guidelines make clear that they are advisory in nature and that the Board is free to grant or deny that privilege, based on the exercise of their discretion and regardless of the guidelines. Decisions for parole are expected to relate directly to the offense for which a person had been convicted.

COMMUNITY CORRECTIONS PROFESSIONALS

Despite promising practices, numerous studies have found little effect of either probation or parole on recidivism rates. Charges have been made that the community corrections model relies heavily on control strategies to supervision rather than focusing on the underlying causes of criminal behaviors. The accusation rang true considering a 0 percent reduction in violent recidivism evidenced among probationers and parolees in recent years (Bonta, Rugge, Scott, Bourgon, and Yessine, 2008). In response to the dismal outcomes, a model of intervention has emerged which is attempting to change the community corrections approach. Appropriately named the *principles of effective intervention*, is a model focusing on three core principles known as risk—need—responsibility or RNR. These principles are being incorporated into programs such as the *Staff Training Aimed at Reducing Rearrest* or STARR program, which is a training course for federal community supervision officers who provide direct service to clients. The STARR curriculum includes a discussion of the theory and research behind the RNR model and it offers opportunities for officers to practice skills and receive feedback. Specific strategies for active listening, effective use of authority, effective reinforcement, and problem solving are among the skills taught as part of the training. The RNR model, as explained by the National Institute of Justice, constitutes the following principles (NIJ, 2012):

- *Risk principle*: The level of services should be matched to the level of the offender. High-risk offenders should receive more intensive services; low-risk offenders should receive minimal services.

- *Need principle*: Target those factors that are associated with criminal behavior. Such factors might include substance abuse, pro-criminal attitudes, criminal associates, and the like. Do not target other, noncriminogenic factors (such as emotional distress, self-esteem issues) unless they act as a barrier to changing criminogenic factors.
- *Responsivity principle*: The ability and learning style of the offender should determine the style and mode of intervention. Research has shown the general effectiveness of using both social learning and cognitive-behavioral style interventions.

IN MY EXPERIENCE . . .

As a police officer, I readily identified with other police officers. This happened even if I met someone from another department or state. That same feeling of being in the company of family didn't happen when I met probation or parole officers—not at first, anyway. It was a while before I realized we really did have a lot in common! When criticism of the "job" becomes excessive, people begin to feel as if they are personally responsible for the failings of the profession—and outsiders tend to blame you for every bad thing that someone else in the profession has done. It is not unusual to feel emotionally exhausted and really negative about the work that you do. I know a few people that wouldn't even admit to someone that they worked as probation officers. Having unlisted phone numbers and a small circle of friends is one way to keep the negativity away. But that can also isolate you from the people who could provide the most support. Now, more than ever before, it is acceptable to admit to being burnt out and getting some help!

Question for discussion: What are some of the contributing factors to work-related stress among probation and parole officers?

Community supervision professionals increasingly refer to themselves as *change agents* in contrast to merely being *case managers* (Bourgon, Gutierrez, and Ashton, 2012). This transition is due to increasing demands on supervision officers' knowledge, skills, and abilities in risk assessment, classification and in case-management planning. A primary responsibility for community corrections professionals is determining the level of risk that a repeat offender poses to the community. Risk assessment is an ongoing process that may change as the condition of the person changes, for example, as when an event triggers negative behavioral responses and the offender responds with heightened levels of anxiety or stress. The appropriate type of intervention depends largely on the person's risk of re-offending, matching services that consider the individual's ability to benefit from them. Factors that may be considered to determine the intervention strategy include the age, culture, level of cognitive function, language, maturity, mental illness, and motivation to change.

5. CH12-05: *Stress Among Community Corrections Officers.* Heavy caseloads and workplace violence contribute to the high incidence of stress among probation and parole officers. Stress training programs may be helpful in improving the negative effects of stress and reducing officer burnout. Copyright mangostock/Bigstock.com

Job Stress

Like others who work in the corrections field, probation and parole officers also experience high levels of PTSD and stress. Their overall risk is around 30 percent (Denhof and Spinaris, 2013). The National Institute of Justice reports that levels of stress have increased among community corrections officers in recent years, due in part to more violent offenders being on probation and parole. Offenders involved in community corrections commit more serious crimes than in the past and many have serious drug abuse histories, showing less hesitation in using violence. As many as 55 percent of probation and parole officers have been victimized by work-related violence or threats in some jurisdictions.

A major source of stress for law corrections professionals is the heavy caseloads that they typically carry. One study found that the ratio of probation officers to probationers was one to 124; in other words, 353 officers oversee 44,000 probationers (Glazier and Chapman, 2005). Associated with the high numbers of probationers and parolees is the unwieldy amount of paperwork that goes along with each case. Some officers cite the failure to be recognized for a job well done, few chances for advancement, and low salaries as related stress factors. Because the officers take responsibility for their clients, some feel they are held accountable for offender misconduct. Others feel frustrated at the lack of rehabilitation for offenders and limited options for imposing sanctions.

Recent years have witnessed a greater awareness of the problems associated with stressful work conditions which negatively impacts job effectiveness, health, and home life. Physical fatigue, feelings of helplessness, and the development of negative self-images are among the characteristics that result from continued stress. Historically, officers have used sick time, vacation leave and other forms of approved leave as ways to reduce stress. Stress training programs have been found in recent years to improve the officers' knowledge of the effects of stress and to reduce burnout. Wellness training and the establishment of resource centers are other approaches that improve both the mental and physical health of probation and parole officers.

SUMMARY

Community corrections, the supervision of criminal offenders in the community, is made up of probation and parole. Within corrections, there are more offenders in community corrections then those who are incarcerated in jails and prisons. The clear majority of people in community corrections are on probation versus parole. The mission of corrections sounds relatively simple, to protect society by deterring crime. The question is, how do we deter crime and measure whether offenders have been deterred from committing crime in the future? There are some promising approaches to reduce recidivism that have been developed in recent years which involve intensive services and treatment intervention.

Millions of offenders will serve community sentences under probation supervision, it is the most widely used sanction in the criminal justice system. Parole practices have been radically revised to limit the discretionary aspect of parole during the 1970s and 1980s. Some states and the federal system have abolished discretionary parole altogether. This means that some offenders may be incarcerated for longer periods of time with mandatory releases at the end of their sentence, minus time for good behavior, if the jurisdiction recognizes that option.

Returning to society as law-abiding citizens is difficult for many individuals who have been involved in the criminal justice system by serving time in all aspects of the correctional system. Health care access, employment, and housing are all critical issues that need to be addressed during community corrections to improve recidivism rates and assure reentry success.

The men and women employed in community corrections experience high levels of work-related stress and PTSD. An increase in violent offenders with serious drug abuse histories on both probation and parole has been cited as one of the reasons. Job frustrations include their carrying heavy caseloads of offenders, few chances for advancement, and feeling that they are held accountable for offender misconduct with limited options for imposing sanctions.

CHAPTER QUESTIONS FOR REVIEW

1. How would you describe the mission and goal of community corrections?
2. What is the difference between probation and parole?
3. What is the prevalence of individuals with mental illness in community corrections?
4. What is it about the specialty probation officer programs that make them different from a standard probation approach?
5. What is the potential impact of work on community corrections officers?

REFERENCES

Babchuk, L. C., and Lurigio, A. J. (2012). Responding to probationers with mental illness. *Fed. Probation, 76*, 41.

BJS. (2015). Reentry trends in the U.S.: Releases from state prison. Retrieved November 17, 2015, from http://www.bjs.gov/content/reentry/releases.cfm

Bonczar, T., Kaeble, D., and Maruschak, L. (2015). Probation and Parole in the United States, 2014. Washington, D.C.: Bureau of Justice Statistics.

BOP. (2014). Legal resource guide to the Federal Bureau of Prisons. Washington, D.C.: U.S. Department of Justice, Federal Bureau of Prisons.

Grattet, R., Petersilia, J., and Lin, J. (2008). Parole violations and revocations in California (pp. 134). Washington, D.C.: U.S. Department of Justice.

Hawken, A., and Kleiman, M. (2009). Managing drug involved probationers with swift and certain sanctions: Evaluating Hawaii's HOPE (pp. 67). Washington, D.C.: National Institute of Justice.

Kuziemko, I. (2013). How should inmates be released from prison? An assessment of parole versus fixed-sentence regimes. *Quarterly Journal of Economics, 128*(1), 371.

Louden, J., and Skeem, J. (2013). How do probation officers assess and manage recidivism and violence risk for probationers with mental disorder? An experimental investigation. *Law and Human Behavior, 37*(1), 22–34.

Lurigio, A. J., Epperson, M. W., Canada, K. E., and Babchuk, L. C. (2012). Specialized probation programs for people with mental illnesses: a review of practices and research. *Journal of Crime and Justice, 35*(2), 317–326.

NIC. (2010). Core competencies: A resource for parole board chairs, members and executive staff *Parole essentials: practice guides for parole leaders*. Washington, D.C.: National Institute of Corrections, U.S. Department of Justice.

NSDUH. (2014). Results from the 2013 *National Survey on Drug Use and Health*: Mental health findings *NSDUH Series H-49* (Vol. HHS Publication No. (SMA) 14-4887). Rockville, MD: Substance Abuse and Mental Health Services Administration.

Osher, D'Amora, D., Plotkin, M., Jarrett, N., and Eggleston, A. (2012). Adults with behavioral health needs under correctional supervision: A shared framework for reducing recidivism and promoting recovery. New York, NY: Council of State Governments Justice Center.

Pearsall, B. (2014). Replicating HOPE: Can others do it as well as Hawaii? (NIJ 244148). Retrieved November 28, 2015, from National Institute of Justice http://nij.gov/journals/273/pages/replicating-hope.aspx

Pew Charitable Trusts. (2013). Managing prison health care spending. (NCJ 247358). Retrieved November 10, 2015, from Pew Charitable Trust http://www.pewtrusts.org/~/media/legacy/uploadedfiles/pcs_assets/2014/pct correctionshealthcarebrief050814pdf.pdf

Shannon, L. M., Hulbig, S. K., Birdwhistell, S., Newell, J., and Neal, C. (2015). Implementation of an enhanced probation program: Evaluating process and preliminary outcomes. *Evaluation and Program Planning, 49*, 50–62.

Skeem, J. L., Manchak, S., and Peterson, J. K. (2010). Correctional policy for offenders with mental illness: Creating a new paradigm for recidivism reduction. *Law and Human Behavior* (2), 110.

Williams, B., Sudore, R., Greifinger, R., and Morrison, R. (2011). Balancing punishment and compassion for seriously ill prisoners. *Annals of Internal Medicine, 155*(2), 122–126.

Wolff, N., Epperson, M., Shi, J., Huening, J., Schumann, B. E., and Sullivan, I. R. (2014). Mental health specialized probation caseloads: Are they effective? *International Journal of Law and Psychiatry, 37*(5), 464–472. doi: http://dx.doi.org/10.1016/j.ijlp.2014.02.019

CHAPTER 13

Juvenile Justice

INTRODUCTION

Juvenile justice is a system of law enforcement, courts, and corrections which in many ways resembles the adult system. It looks like the adult criminal justice system at times, as when minors are accused of committing a crime. Over the past thirty years, juvenile offenders have increasingly been afforded more legal protections and constitutional rights. Despite increasing legalization, the basic purpose and function of the juvenile justice system remains the same: to avoid stigmatizing juvenile offenders while holding them accountable for their actions. Juvenile courts recognize the diminished capacity of young people to fully realize the consequences of their actions. Rehabilitation rather than punishment is the primary goal of the juvenile system.

There are numerous procedural differences in juvenile versus adult systems. The procedures in juvenile court are designed to protect and rehabilitate young people. The juvenile courtroom may be closed to outsiders during hearings. Juvenile records of delinquency may be sealed when the person becomes an adult, although it is not automatic nor is it constitutionally required that they be sealed. A young person is charged with being delinquent, not criminal. Only juveniles may be detained as "status offenders" for acts that are not crimes at all, such as truancy and being a runaway. Juvenile courts also hold hearings on matters of child protection and custody. One startling similarity to the adult system is the increasing numbers of individuals that experience mental disorders who are being detained and processed through the juvenile justice system.

Key Terms

AFTERCARE

COST-BENEFIT ANALYSIS

DETENTION

DIVERSION

JUVENILE

PSYCHOSIS

ROOM CONFINEMENT

SPECIALIZED JUVENILE PROBATION

Chapter Objectives

After completing this chapter, you should be able to:

- Explain the mission of the juvenile justice system
- Describe diversion, probation, and court issues of the juvenile justice system
- Explain the mental health disorders that are frequently encountered in juvenile justice
- Discuss the controversies of juvenile detention

THE MISSION AND GOALS OF JUVENILE JUSTICE

The juvenile justice system attempts to empower victims and promote parental responsibility. The juvenile justice system is generally rehabilitative, with procedures designed to minimize juvenile involvement in the adult criminal justice system. Specifically, the professionals in the juvenile justice system seek to protect the constitutional and procedural rights of young offenders. **JUVENILE** is a legal term used to refer to a person at or below the upper age of original jurisdiction who is not old enough to be treated as an adult in the criminal justice system or young enough to be excluded due to infancy, in most states and the federal system this refers to a person under the age of 18. State statutes define the original jurisdiction of a juvenile by the age of the person or by the severity of crime that he is charged to have committed. Some states have determined that the upper age of original juvenile court jurisdiction is fifteen or sixteen. Many States have higher upper ages of juvenile court jurisdiction in status offense, abuse, neglect, or dependency matters, often through age twenty.

Law enforcement officers are the most frequent group who refer minors to the juvenile court system for processing. Less frequently, referrals come from parents, child welfare agencies, and juvenile probation officers. Diversion from prosecution is a frequent resolution in the juvenile justice process; case dismissal or informal case handling are also common ways to divert a young person from further juvenile justice involvement. Slightly more than half of cases referred to the juvenile court continue through the process and are handled formally. If a youthful offender is accused of committing a major crime, there are some circumstances when he may be tried as an adult in criminal court.

Cost-Benefit Analysis

An awareness that a large proportion of minors in the juvenile justice system have at least one diagnosable mental health disorder and commonly have more than one disorder has led to a re-examination of current youth reform practices to assess their value in meeting the needs of this population. The *National Conference of State Legislators* specifically recommends a cost-benefit analysis as defined by the Vera Institute (NCSL, 2011). The **COST-BENEFIT ANALYSIS** is an approach that turns all program outcomes into monetary values which allows for comparisons of juvenile initiatives that have different goals. Program assessments and evaluations made by utilizing this method maximize the allocation of scarce juvenile justice resources. Evaluating programs to address youthful offending in cost-effective ways is a recent trend that is likely to allow juvenile justice programming which meets the needs of juvenile offenders and protects public interests through affordable treatment initiatives.

Despite the challenges of intervention, the benefits to saving a high-risk youth can be substantial. To illustrate the importance of early intervention, Cohen and Piquero (2009) put a monetary value on high-risk youthful offenders. They estimate that 50 percent of juvenile crimes are committed by high risk youth with six or more police contacts. Each juvenile cost society as much as $7 million in today's dollar. On the other hand, preventing one fourteen-year-old high-risk youth from entering a life of crime would save $2.6 to $5.3 million (Cohen and Piquero, 2009). Early youth intervention, to reduce recidivism, is gaining popularity among advocates, researchers, and policy makers. The use of cost-benefit analysis as an evaluation approach is gaining national interest as a legitimate decision making tool to access juvenile justice programs.

JUVENILES AND MENTAL HEALTH

Mental illness is a condition that typically strikes early in life. Because half of all long-term mental illnesses begins by age fourteen and three-quarters emerges by age twenty-four, the *National Alliance on Mental Illness* (NAMI) advocates for early mental health intervention (NAMI, 2014). Among the many challenges of young people who experience mental disorders is the struggle to remain in school, at home, and out of the juvenile justice system. Prompt intervention holds the hope of building resilience and ultimately, self-reliance. Depression, psychosis, and the risk of suicide are some of the pressing juvenile mental health issues that the juvenile justice system may encounter.

Depression

Depression is now recognized as occurring in both children and adults. It is a serious mental health issue and brain disorder that can arise from a combination of genetic vulnerability, early developmental experiences, and exposure to stresses. A diagnosis of depression may only be made if the symptoms occur daily for more than two weeks. In 2013, more than 1.6 million minors received specialty mental health services for feelings of depression, which is the most common reason for seeking specialty mental health services (NSDUH, 2014). The 2013 *National Survey on Drug Use and Health* reports that, there were 2.6 million children and adolescents who experienced a major depressive episode (MDE) during the previous year. Among these, females were three times more likely than males to have past year MDE.

Psychosis

When psychosis occurs, it most commonly happens in men during the late teenage and young adult years, whereas in women, it emerges during the mid-twenties to early thirties. **PSYCHOSIS** is a serious medical symptom in which a person has trouble telling the difference between what is real and what is not real, typically with symptoms such as delusions and/or hallucinations (NAMI, 2011). The psychosis risk syndrome refers to the period of onset before the individual's symptoms pass the threshold of clinically diagnosable psychosis. The majority of people who develop symptoms consistent with the psychosis risk syndrome will not develop psychosis. Early intervention has been identified as a key component in addressing juvenile psychosis.

Untreated psychosis has a devastating effect on the life trajectory of young people, yet many experience these symptoms for years before they are accurately diagnosed and treated. Approximately 100,000 adolescents and young adults in the United States experience First Episode Psychosis (FEP) each year (Heinssen, Goldstein, and Azrin, 2014). Congress has required states to allocate 5 percent of their 2015 federal mental health block grant funds to early intervention with young people who experience FEP. Based on ground breaking international research that identified an array of effective early intervention services, the FEP set-aside initiative has the potential to transform lives. While most states are just beginning to implement FEP programs, Oregon and New York State are examples of states that offer First Episode Psychosis (FEP) intervention programs on a statewide basis (NAMI, 2014).

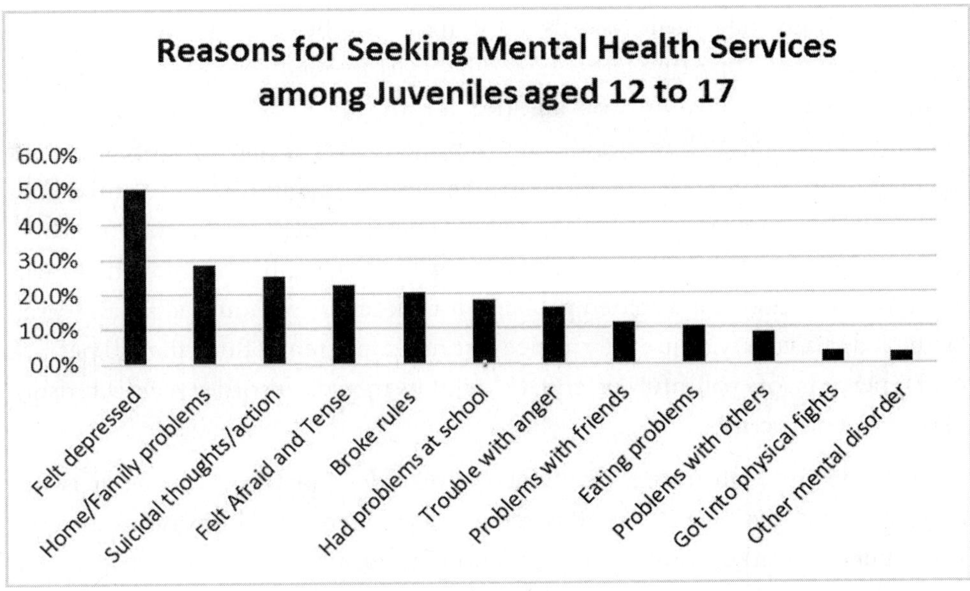

1. CH13-01: *Mental Health Services.* More than 3 million juveniles between the ages of twelve to seventeen received mental health services in 2013. Feeling depressed is the most common reason for seeking help, having suicidal thoughts or actions is the third most common reason for seeking mental health services. Source: *NSDUH,* 2014.

Risk of Suicide

Youth suicide is recognized as a major public health problem. Among juveniles aged ten to twenty-four, suicide is the third leading cause of death and is the second leading cause of death for fifteen to twenty-four-year-olds (CDC, 2015). Risk factors include a history of mental illness and/or substance use, involvement in special education, legal and disciplinary problems, prior disciplinary action, prior offenses, previous suicide attempts or ideation, referral to juvenile court, and being placed on room confinement (National Action Alliance for Suicide Prevention, 2013). Suicide prevention action is particularly necessary in juvenile detention settings given the high-risk population who are in emotionally charged situations. More than half of the adolescents that received inpatient mental health services in 2013 reported that the primary reason for their seeking services was having thought about or attempted suicide (NSDUH, 2014).

PREVALENCE OF MENTAL HEALTH DISORDERS

It is difficult to determine whether the number of juveniles with mental health disorders who become involved with the juvenile justice system has increased. The perception of an increase may be due to better recognition of psychosocial disorders by juvenile professionals or it may also be due to the severity of problems the youthful offenders exhibit. Difficulty in obtaining mental health care is often cited as a reason for an increase of juveniles arrested by police. Deinstitutionalization has negatively impacted the availability of inpatient psychiatric beds for both juveniles and adults. An additional problem is that aggressive and violent youthful offenders may be excluded from the scarce residential programs which accept juveniles. Difficulty in obtaining treatment within the community is a shared problem for juveniles and adults alike. Research conducted in a variety of juvenile justice settings consistently finds that 50 percent to 70 percent of youthful offenders exhibit mental disorder characteristics (Skowyra and Cocozza, 2007).

Despite the high incidence of mental disorders among juveniles, it is not unusual to find that fewer than 20 percent receive mental health services in some communities (Burke, Mulvey, and Schubert, 2015). External barriers that contribute to lower rates of mental health treatment include poverty and poor education in addition to racial and ethnic minority status, as well as having a history of arrest, and having a small social network. While some progress is being made towards getting individuals the help that they need, services currently do not meet the needs of the population. More than 3 million adolescents between the ages of twelve and seventeen did receive mental health care in 2013 (NSDUH, 2014).

The clear majority of detention centers now screen offenders for mental illness and other disorders. Alcohol, drug, and mental health disorders are commonly cited as problems for youthful offenders. Not surprisingly, in 2013, drug and alcohol related crimes made up the largest proportion of juvenile arrests (FBI, 2014). Most juvenile offenders are believed to have unmet mental health treatment needs. Extreme behaviors exhibited by juveniles with psychosocial disorders present challenges to the entire justice system. Research estimates that juveniles in detention experience the following rates of mental disorders (Hayes, 2009):

- ODD and Conduct Disorder, 50 percent–90 percent;

Oppositional defiant disorder (ODD) is characterized by a pattern of developmentally inappropriate, negative, aggressive, and defiant behavior. Juveniles with ODD frequently lose their temper, argue with adults, defy or refuse to comply with rules, deliberately annoy others, blame their behavior on others, are easily annoyed, and are spiteful or vindictive. Children with conduct disorder frequently ignore the basic rights of others and violate social norms and rules to an extent far beyond the usual behavior of his age group.

- ADHD up to 46 percent;

Attention-deficit hyperactivity disorder (ADHD) is characterized by developmentally inappropriate levels of inattention, impulsivity, and excessive activity, resulting in significant impacts on various areas of daily life functioning. It is considered one of the most prevalent psychiatric disorders of childhood.

- Anxiety Disorder, 6 percent–41 percent;

There are a wide variety of anxiety disorders, including post-traumatic stress disorder, obsessive-compulsive disorder, and specific phobias to name a few. Anxiety disorders include a range of conditions characterized by feelings of depression, exaggerated anxiety or fear, and low self-esteem. These commonly occur in children with poor social skills, substance use disorder, sexual risk-taking behaviors, and criminal behavior.

- Substance Use Disorder, 25 percent–50 percent;

Substance use disorder can lead to poor academic performance, health problems, accidents and injuries, overdose, addiction, and unintended pregnancy. Common substance use disorders are those related to alcohol, tobacco, cannabis (marijuana), stimulants, hallucinogens, and opioids.

- Psychotic Disorder, 1 percent–6 percent;

The defining characteristic of psychotic disorders is abnormalities in one or more of five domains: delusions, hallucinations, disorganized thinking, grossly disorganized or abnormal motor behavior, and negative symptoms, which include diminished emotional expression and a decrease in the ability to engage in self-initiated activities. Disorders in this category include schizotypal disorder, schizoaffective disorder, and schizophreniform disorder. The most common diagnosis in this category is schizophrenia. Juveniles may have difficulty with goal-directed behaviors such as basic self-care, relationships, schoolwork, and employment.

- Co-occurring Mental Health and Substance Use Disorders, more than 50 percent.

The coexistence of both a mental health and a substance use disorder is referred to as co-occurring disorders. The conditions may exist separately or they may trigger or aggravate one another.

One recent approach to the issue of unmet treatment needs is restructuring mental health services within the juvenile justice system. In 2013, 59,000 youths received mental health services in a juvenile justice setting (NSDUH, 2014). Numbers were greater for male than for female youths, with 41,000 males and 18,000 females having received mental health services in a juvenile justice setting. Mental health service access for juveniles between the ages of twelve to seventeen is more commonly accomplished through outpatient services and education settings, however.

In a recent study among juveniles in detention who had substance use disorder or any mental health disorder, the detainees most commonly believed that the problem would go away or that they could solve the problem without help (Abram et al., 2015). Some reported that they were not sure where to go for help, and many of the young people denied that they had a mental health problem at all. These common barriers that juvenile detainees report are not dissimilar from those faced by adults with mental health disorders. Services are unlikely to be sought when issues are not acknowledged or not perceived as being a problem.

LAW ENFORCEMENT INTERVENTION

As first responders to crime and disorder, law enforcement officers are the gatekeepers of the juvenile justice system. State statutes define the power of law enforcement officers and the circumstances under which juveniles may be taken into custody by the police. States are making efforts to simplify the process of treating youth for mental health disorders through the juvenile justice system. For example, a recent change in Illinois law specifically allows for police officers to take minors into custody and transport them to a mental health facility, when necessary (NAMI, 2014). The officer must have reasonable grounds to believe that the minor is eligible for admission and is in such a condition that immediate hospitalization is necessary to protect the minor or others from physical harm. Wisconsin has streamlined the process for inpatient mental health treatment of minors by eliminating the need to file a court petition for a minor under the age of fourteen or for older youths who agree to participate in inpatient treatment, according to NAMI.

IN MY EXPERIENCE . . .

Recently, I visited the Mayo Clinic Child and Family Advocacy Center in Rochester, Minnesota. It is one of over 700 children's advocacy centers accredited in the U.S. by the National Children's Alliance. The medical model of response to child abuse includes diagnosis by a physician and staff of mental health specialists. Medical and mental health treatment, if needed, is provided to the child and family members. When law enforcement or child protective services believes a child has been abused, the center provides a safe place to tell his or her story, once. Law enforcement officers and child protection professionals are part of the team that view the videotaped forensic interview and make decisions on whether to prosecute the case.

The Mayo Clinic has decided to meet the challenges of protecting victims from *Munchausen by proxy* who present at the clinic. Doctors, nurses, and mental health staff are trained on the characteristics of this mental disorder and are vigilant when screening parents of very sick children who are brought to the clinic as a last resort. Suspected cases of this rare disorder have been referred to the world-renown clinic which is known for compassion and patient care.

Question for discussion: What do you think would be the benefit of conducting child abuse investigations using this team approach?

Crisis Intervention Team for Youth

It is recognized that children and adolescents express their distress differently than do adults. Cognitive and emotional deficits, fear, paranoia, and anxiety are among the issues that juveniles with psychosocial disorders experience that may affect their interactions with police officers during crisis encounters. Failure to comply with directives from the police can escalate these encounters, increasing the risk that force may be used to control the situation. To meet the specific needs of youth, communities around the country have begun to expand their *Crisis Intervention Team* (CIT) programs. *CIT for Youth* programs train police officers on adolescent brain development, how mental health symptoms affect juveniles, crisis intervention, de-escalation, and communication techniques.

Crisis Intervention Team for Youth training is an advanced course that is typically offered as an eight-hour add-on to the standard CIT training. The youth version of CIT is designed to improve the interactions between law enforcement officers and juveniles who experience mental disorders. The National Alliance of Mental Illness suggests a model for implementing the training that places emphasis on identifying community mental health resources and agency collaborations (NAMI, 2011). In a descriptive study on *CIT for Youth* programs, researchers noted that participating police officers self-selected and that they were highly motivated to receive the training (Douglas and Lurigio, 2014). Identified barriers for the training were finding time needed in addition to the identification of community resources. While the specific topics of the training programs vary somewhat, the common goal is the linkage of schools, service providers, and police departments to provide appropriate treatment options for young people in crisis.

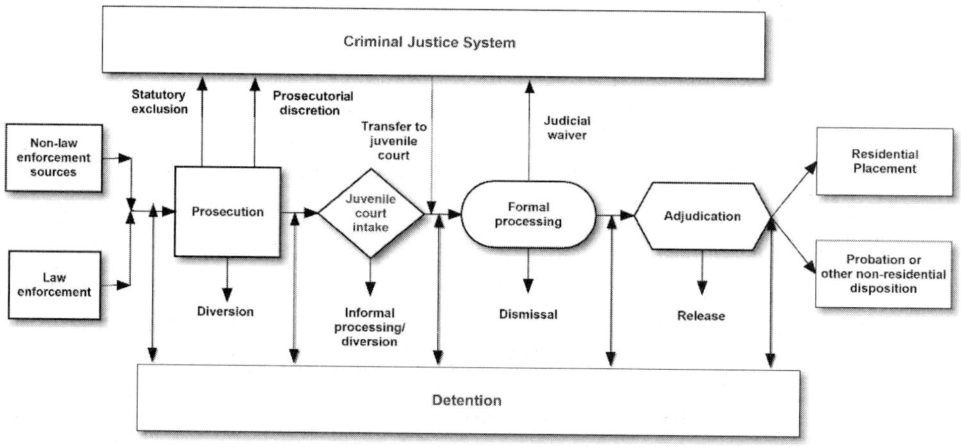

2. CH13-02: *Juvenile Justice System Process.* There are numerous times during the juvenile justice process when delinquents can be diverted for trial within the adult criminal justice system or released for informal processing. Source: *OJJDP,* 2015.

JUVENILE DIVERSION

DIVERSION is designed to allow a juvenile to complete program requirements in lieu of being formally processed for adjudication in the courts. In recent years, there has been an increase in juvenile diversion programs designed to meet the unique needs of youth with psychosocial disorders who have come to the attention of the juvenile justice system. Juvenile diversion comes in many different forms and varies between states. If you look at Minnesota's Criminal Code (Minn. Stat. § 609.092) which went into effect in 2009, for example, you will see an emphasis on the use of restorative justice programming for first-time juvenile petty offenders, which is one approach to diversion. Inclusion of the victim in proceedings, victim restoration, and agreed upon appropriate sanctions for the juvenile offender are characteristics of the approach.

Other diversion programs are designed as specialized case management, individual treatment approaches, youth court, and family treatment approaches. An example of the case management approach to juvenile diversion is when specialized probation teams are officially designed with small individualized caseloads and community services, including therapeutic interventions. The individualized treatment approach to juvenile diversion requires that treatment plans involve mental health professionals for evaluation and treatment. Mental health courts and drug courts are examples of the youth court diversion model. Family treatment approaches are unique in that they treat not only the minor but also involve family members in the belief that the juvenile's problems are largely a function of disordered family relationships. Adopting one model as the primary approach does not exclude the use of others.

Very few studies have considered the outcomes of juvenile diversion, so there is no consensus on what type of program works best. In one of the rare studies comparing multiple diversion programs, different approaches to juvenile diversion were identified by researchers who reported on the effects of each (Schwalbe, Gearing, MacKenzie, Brewer, and Ibrahim, 2012). Included in the study were diversion programs that utilized specialized case management, individual treatment approaches, youth courts, family treatment, and restorative justice. Researchers concluded that the overall effect of diversion programs on recidivism was not significant, with the exception of the family treatment model. This finding does not rule out the possibility that some diversion efforts are poorly run and others are extremely successful. In contrast, a few studies have documented lower recidivism rates among participants involved in juvenile mental health court diversion (Callahan, Cocozza, Steadman, and Tillman, 2012; Ramirez, Andretta, Barnes, and Woodland, 2015). More research is needed to determine what works and what does not work in juvenile diversion programs.

Juvenile Mental Health Courts

The first mental health court for juveniles was implemented in 2001 in Santa Clara County, California to address the needs of minors who were both charged with crimes and suffering from severe mental illness (Pennypacker, 2008). Mental health courts are specialized courts that divert selected offenders away from the regular court processing into judicially supervised, community-based treatment. The *Juvenile Behavioral Diversion Program* (JBDP), which was developed in the District of Columbia in 2011, is an example of a problem-solving specialized court response, an alternative to detaining juveniles with mental illness. Its goal is reducing juvenile recidivism by treating psychiatric symptoms that often accompany delinquent behaviors. There is concern among some experts regarding the potential misuse of the mental health court system, that parents may petition the court or that police may arrest nonviolent offenders to obtain mental health services. This wider net could lead to the inclusion of non-delinquent youth in the juvenile justice system, particularly if jurisdictions rely on the courts to provide treatment to youth with mental health issues. Net-widening is a frequent concern in every aspect of juvenile justice. There is a risk that criminalizing juveniles will stigmatize youths that might not otherwise become involved with the juvenile justice system. Additionally, despite the voluntary nature of the court diversion, juveniles who participate in mental health courts may feel they are being coerced into treatment.

The GAINS Center provides technical assistance and support to help expand community services for those in the criminal justice system and experiencing a mental disorder (GAINS is an acronym for Gather, Assess, Integrate, Network, and Stimulate). The GAINS Center has identified juvenile mental health treatment courts in twenty-one states, with the majority being in California and Ohio (SAMHSA.gov, 2015). Refer to figure CH11-03 to see the states that have established juvenile mental health courts. A major impediment to developing effective juvenile mental health courts, according to the authors, is the high cost of the multi-disciplinary team approach which involves intensive supervision and other services. Juvenile mental health courts are designed to meet the unique needs of youthful offenders. While similar philosophies developed in the adult system are applicable, these are not simply adult courts for young people.

The mental health courts use a problem-solving approach with two primary goals: to reduce recidivism among youthful offenders and to oversee individualized treatment plans of counseling and drug therapies. Generally, these courts operate under a framework of therapeutic jurisprudence to promote a non-adversarial, treatment-oriented approach while still upholding juvenile due process rights. Day-to-day activities and eligibility criteria for mental health courts vary in different jurisdictions (Callahan et al., 2012). Approximately half of courts surveyed only accept individuals with serious mental illness. The rest accept young offenders with any identified mental health issue. Court caseloads can range from less than ten up to seventy-five juvenile cases, dependent upon the availability of psychiatric resources. The average length of court involvement is between ten to eighteen months. The most commonly-reported mental disorders of juvenile mental health court participants are bipolar, depressive, and attention-deficit-hyperactivity disorders.

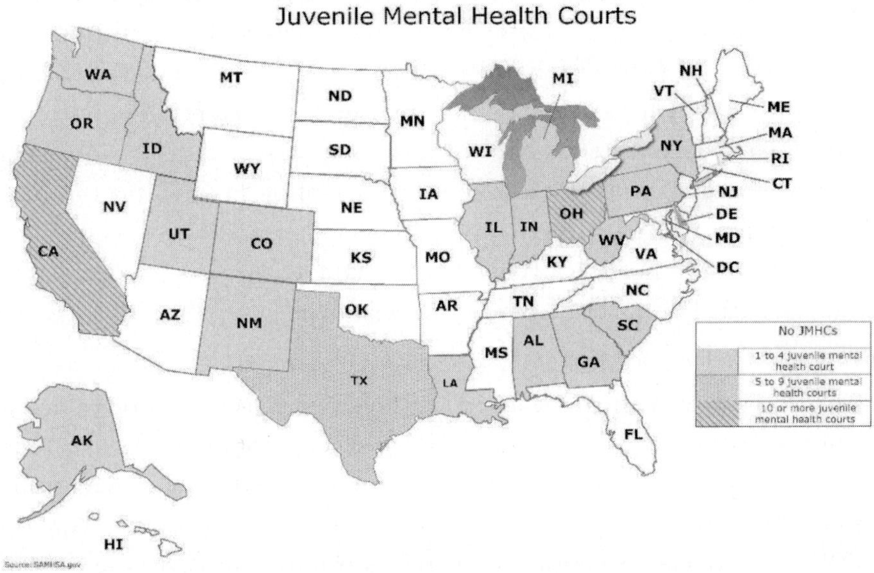

3. CH13-03: Juvenile mental health courts have been established in just twenty-one states. These are similar to the specialized courts in the adult system in that the court personnel are trained to work with this population with a rehabilitative emphasis. Source: SAMHSA.gov, 2015.

JUVENILE DETENTION

DETENTION is the term used to refer to the holding of a juvenile after adjudication and before or during the trial period. Detention during the trial period occurs when juvenile courts hold youthful offenders in secure detention facilities to ensure their appearance at subsequent court hearings, to protect the community from the juveniles, or to secure the juveniles' own safety. The placement of juveniles in an adult facility is discouraged unless no other option exists. Juvenile facilities in some states are separate from adult facilities, and in other states juveniles are held in the same facility and separated from adults by sight and sound. According to the National Conference of State Legislatures, if a juvenile is found delinquent and sentenced to confinement, on average, they are sentenced from four to six months (NCSL, 2011).

A current juvenile justice reform movement to find pretrial detention alternatives has gained momentum in the United States. The *Juvenile Detention Alternatives Initiative*, known as the JDAI model was initiated by the Casey Foundation in the 1990s (Mendel, 2014). Developed to demonstrate that juvenile detention populations could be substantially and safely reduced, among participating jurisdiction, the total average daily detention population was 43 percent lower in 2011 than in the year before joining JDAI. Thirty-four percent of the reporting sites have reduced their average daily detention populations by more than half since entering JDAI. Also, the data show that participating jurisdictions admitted 59,000 fewer youth to detention in 2012 than in the year prior to launching JDAI, a drop of 39 percent. The model has been extremely successful. Per the Office for Juvenile Justice and Delinquency Prevention, youth detention was used in about 20 percent of delinquency cases in 2013, the lowest rate since 1985.

Residential placement in the juvenile justice system is the period of detention which occurs after a juvenile is adjudicated as delinquent. It is reserved for serious or repetitive offenders. A primary source of information on the characteristics of youth in juvenile detention is the *Census of Juveniles in Residential Placement* (CJRP). The CJRP is conducted every two years to gather information on youths living in detention, correctional, and other shelter facilities. Per the CJRP, 54,148 juvenile offenders were held in residential placement facilities in 2013 (OJJDP, 2015). There is a substantial downward trend in the number of residential placement facilities and the number of juvenile offenders confined. Between 2000 and 2012, the number of residential placement facilities fell by 35 percent and there was nearly 50 percent decrease in the number of juvenile offenders held in placement during those years (Hockenberry, Sickmund, and Sladky, 2015).

Youths in juvenile justice are at a higher risk of having mental health disorders, substance use disorders, and educational problems compared to those outside of the juvenile justice system. They are also significantly more likely to have been abused or neglected. Great strides have been made to address these issues in the juvenile justice system through mental health and suicide risk screening. Contrary to beliefs that juveniles in detention have insufficient access to mental health services, one recent study found that almost 75 percent of youth in detention had received services prior to being detained in the justice system (Abram et al., 2015).

Suicide in Juvenile Facilities

The characteristics of juvenile detention itself may increase the risk of suicide, and the population most likely to be detained within the juvenile justice system is predisposed to these high-risk factors. In addition to having mental disorders prior to detention, many confined juveniles have experienced physical, sexual, and emotional abuse which often results in self-injurious behavior (HHS.gov, 2012). Taken together, the risk for suicide among minors in detention is estimated to be high. The first national study to examine the characteristics of juvenile deaths in custody found that more than 70 percent of those who died had histories of suicidal behavior, ideation or self-mutilation (Hayes, 2009). In 2012, there were five suicides in juvenile detention centers nationally (Hockenberry et al., 2015). Increased staff training in suicide prevention and detention screening may have contributed to the declining number of suicides in juvenile facilities.

Room Confinement

Rarely is the term "segregation" used in the juvenile justice system. The practice is instead referred to as **ROOM CONFINEMENT**, which includes the use of isolation, segregation, time-out, or a quiet room imposed on youths as a behavioral sanction. The controversial practice has been banned for use in juvenile facilities in twenty-one states due to its association with juvenile suicide and depression (Kraner, Barrowclough, Weiss, and Fisch, 2015). Half of the victims of juvenile suicide in the Hayes (2009) study were on room confinement status at the time of their death. The reasons for the room confinement in the Hayes study included failure to follow program rules, inappropriate behavior, and threat of or actual physical abuse of staff or peers. Like adult research, studies confirm that placing juveniles in isolation can cause psychological harm that can exacerbate mental health problems. Many other states place time limits for the use of punitive room confinement or require administrative approval for its use. In 2016, the Department of Justice issued its final report on the use of restrictive housing and recommended an end to the practice of placing juveniles in room confinement (DOJ, 2016).

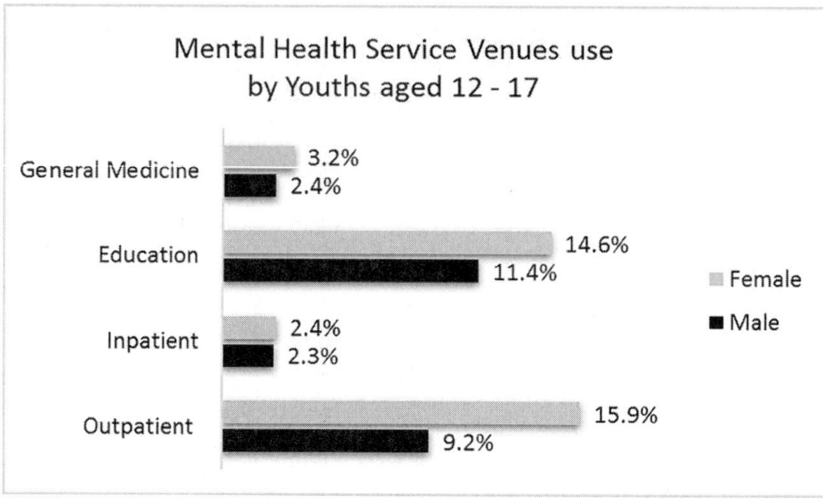

4. CH13-04: The *youth mental health service utilization* measures whether juveniles aged twelve to seventeen received any treatment or counseling for problems with emotions or behaviors in several settings. Most commonly, females received outpatient specialty mental health services and males received treatment in education setting. Source: *NSDUH*, 2014.

JUVENILE PROBATION

All states offer both voluntary and mandatory juvenile probation services. Voluntary probation occurs when a case is disposed of informally with the offender agreeing to abide by certain conditions. Typically, the case is dismissed after the successful probation period. Probation that is mandatory occurs during the period after release from residential placement or when a delinquent is sentenced to supervision; in either situation, the youth has been formally processed though the court. Probation supervision was the outcome for 541,400 juvenile trials, more than 35 percent of all delinquency cases in 2010 (Livsey, 2012).

Research suggests that "aftercare programs" which take place during probation may be effective at reducing recidivism in youthful offenders (James, Stams, Asscher, De Roo, and der Laan, 2013). **AFTERCARE** is the period of probation after a juvenile delinquent has been released from correctional institutions, sometimes referred to as reentry. The National Conference of State Legislatures report that this population is more likely than their peers to have learning disabilities, ADHD, and developmental disabilities (NCSL, 2011). Researchers conclude that aftercare is most effective if it is directed at older and high-risk youth. Increasing the length of community-based supervision following residential placement was found to increase the likelihood that juveniles would attend school, go to work, and avoid further involvement with the juvenile justice system (Sickmund and Puzzanchera, 2014).

Specialized Juvenile Probation

SPECIALIZED JUVENILE PROBATION is an example of a case management approach to diversion. In response to a growing body of research demonstrating that youth in the juvenile justice system frequently experience psychiatric disorders, the Mental Health/Juvenile Justice Action Network has developed and implemented a front-end, pre-adjudication diversion initiative (Espinosa and Skowyra, 2015). This probation strategy relies heavily on specialized juvenile probation officers with a reduced caseload and mental health training. The program is based on similar specialized probation officer programs that have been developed for adults. Pre-adjudication diversion, known as the Front-End Diversion Initiative (FEDI), involves officers that focus less on monitoring, enforcement, and punishment and instead function more like case managers. Probation officers in this model develop enhanced relationships with the offender, obtaining compliance through therapeutic and social controls.

Funded by the John D. and Catherine T. MacArthur Foundation, the first FEDI was implemented and evaluated in Texas. The Specialized Juvenile Probation Officer in FEDI is a certified juvenile probation officer who receives training on family and systems engagement, crisis management, and motivational interviewing, in addition to the Mental Health Training Curriculum for Juvenile Justice. Maintaining a caseload of no more than 15 youths who receive intensive supervision during the period of probation, the officer formulates aftercare plans with multidisciplinary involvement for ongoing support. Initial findings in 2012 conclude that juveniles who participated in FEDI were more likely to access community services and significantly less likely to be adjudicated than those in traditional supervision programs (Espinosa and Skowyra, 2015).

IN MY EXPERIENCE . . .

The Supreme Court has walked a fine line in recent decisions on juvenile sentencing in recognition of the fact that adolescent brain development studies demonstrate a clear difference in juvenile and adult cognitive development. While the vast majority of juvenile offenders are non-violent, those who commit homicide may receive a sentence of life without parole in the worst cases. One such case involved a juvenile who lay in waiting with a baseball bat that he used in the killing a fifteen-year-old girl. The reason for his beating his school mate to death was that she had refused to go out on a date with him. The perpetrator was transferred to adult court and found guilty of the murder. He remains incarcerated to this day.

Question for discussion: Which Supreme Court decisions since 2005 limit the sentencing options in this situation?

JUVENILES IN ADULT COURT

Juveniles may be tried as adults in criminal courts under specific circumstances in all fifty states and the District of Columbia. In Massachusetts, for example, individuals 14 years old or older who are charged with murder are automatically tried as adults rather than juveniles ("Youthful Offender," 1996). Research has shown that juveniles who are processed as criminals in adult court, rather than delinquents in juvenile court, experience similarly high rates of psychosocial disorders (Washburn et al., 2015). The need for psychiatric services for juveniles that have been transferred to the adult system appears to be greater than for detained adults. The Washburn study (2015) concluded that 35 percent of detained adults experience a psychiatric disorder, in contrast to 64 percent of the transferred youth in the adult system.

The last decade has brought about greater reluctance to sentence violent juvenile offenders as harshly as adults. In light of changing attitudes, the U.S. Supreme Court abolished the death penalty as a sentence for those who had committed a capital crime prior to reaching age eighteen (*Roper v. Simmons*, 2005). The Court reasoned that adolescent brain development studies demonstrate clear differences in juvenile and adult cognitive development. Following *Roper*, the Court next held that life without parole could not be used as a sentence for juveniles convicted of non-homicide offenses (*Graham v. Florida*, 2010). Writing for the majority, Justice Kennedy first noted that juvenile non-homicide defendants had diminished culpability. He concluded that it is a violation of the

Eighth Amendment to deny those defendants the chance to later demonstrate that they are fit to rejoin society, based solely on a non-homicide crime committed while they were children in the eyes of the law. Two years later, the U.S. Supreme Court also barred mandatory life without parole for juveniles who were under the age of eighteen at the time of their crime (*Miller v. Alabama*, 2012). The Court, in *Miller,* held that the Eighth Amendment prohibits mandatory life sentences without parole for juveniles as "cruel and unusual punishment," since children are different from adults for the purposes of sentencing. The Court cited differences in culpability and greater prospects for reform as well as a lack of maturity and underdeveloped sense of responsibility. *Miller v. Alabama's* prohibition on mandatory minimum life sentences for juveniles applies retroactively (*Montgomery v. Louisiana*, 2016). However, the use of discretionary life sentences without parole is not a settled issue. The Court refused to consider a total ban on life sentences without parole for juveniles, acknowledging that the penalty is expected to be uncommon and reserved for the worst offenders and in the worst cases.

SCHOOLS

An estimated 55 million students in the United States are enrolled in pre-kindergarten through twelfth grade, according to the *National Center for Education Statistics*. Colleges and universities are attended by another 20 million students. Because children and adolescents spend more time at school than in any other environment outside the home, educators are in an excellent position to identify children with mental health needs. Acknowledging this opportunity, states have enacted laws on school culture, mental health and anti-bullying training for school personnel, and have made moves to reduce the use of restraint and seclusion. Schools, along with law enforcement, mental health services, and community programs, can build valuable collaborative relationships with juvenile justice.

5. CH13-05: School violence is a cause for concern for everyone. Bullying has serious mental health consequences for children and young adults, whether they are victims, perpetrators, or witnesses. Females vs. males are more likely to seek mental health treatment in every venue, including mental health education services. Copyright Creatista/Bigstock.com

School Violence

School shootings provide the misleading impression that American schools are extremely dangerous. Violent deaths associated with schools are very rare, with less than 1 percent of all youth homicides occurring at school each year (National Center for Injury Prevention and Control, 2015). The amount of violent deaths occurring in schools has been relatively stable for the past decade, according to the National Center for Injury Prevention and Control (2015). Regardless of the relative safety of schools, the loss of even one child due to violence is tragic. The heart-wrenching effects of death resulting from school violence are awful and are felt by everyone. Establishing and maintaining safe schools is a top priority for communities, parents, and policy-makers.

Any amount of school violence is cause for concern. Nonfatal injuries and exposure to youth violence at school are statistically minor, but must be addressed. These can lead to unhealthy behaviors such as use of alcohol and drugs and suicide. Bullying, including cyberbullying, has serious mental health consequences for children, whether they are victims, perpetrators, or witnesses. Associated psychological problems may include depression, anxiety, and fear. The clear majority of states have enacted anti-bullying legislation. California, Massachusetts, and Michigan are examples of states that now authorize school officials to refer bullying victims, offenders, and witnesses to school support service staff for counseling and services (NAMI, 2014).

School-Based Services

Mental health privacy standards are acknowledged as an obstruction to necessary coordination between educators, families and mental health providers. Overcoming the obstacles to information sharing is a priority, dictated by the fact that more males receive services through the educational setting than from any other venue; for females, it is the second most frequent source of services. Schools are excellent settings for psychiatric intervention. In 2013, 3.1 million youths received mental health services in an educational setting (NSDUH, 2014).

Some states are responding to the need for juvenile mental health services through legislation that can protect privacy, while still enhancing mental health and educational services to benefit children. Recent legislative initiatives in Massachusetts established a "safe and supportive school" framework by bringing together services to address mental health, reduce bullying and truancy, provide inclusion for students with disabilities and promote positive behavioral approaches. To address suicide among minors, the state of Pennsylvania mandates training on youth suicide awareness and prevention every five years for professional educators of grades six through nine.

SUMMARY

Juvenile justice is a system of justice devoted to hearing cases and settling disputes involving defendants who are, generally, under the age of eighteen. The clear majority of cases involve non-violent crimes and status offenses. Some juvenile courts have embraced the concept of restorative justice in efforts to repair the harm done to victims while still holding juvenile offenders accountable for their behaviors. The system foundations are still paternalistic and rehabilitative, but have increasingly become more legalistic. More than fifty years ago the Supreme Court of the U.S. addressed abusive court procedures by granting juveniles basic due process rights and increased constitutional protections.

Today, professionals are wrestling with the reality that the needs of the delinquent population are substantial. Many juvenile offender's experience mental health disorders, co-occurring disorders, and physical and sexual abuse. These issues challenge the system that is working to decrease recidivism and provide treatment and services. Diversion program efforts hold promise for some youths. Innovative specialty mental health courts and probation services have emerged to provide avenues for collaboration and coordination of needed services. The current trend towards rehabilitation rather than punishment is evident in the modern juvenile justice system.

CHAPTER QUESTIONS FOR REVIEW

1. Explain the mission of the juvenile justice system.
2. What are among the three most pressing juvenile mental health issues encountered by the juvenile justice system?
3. What are the mental disorders that are frequently seen in juveniles who are in detention?
4. What is the current legal status of room confinement for juveniles in detention?
5. What does the term *aftercare* refer to? How does this relate to the adult system?

REFERENCES

Abram, K., Paskar, L., Washburn, J., Teplin, L., Zwecker, N., and Azores-Gococo, N. (2015). Perceived barriers to mental health services among detained youth. Rockville, MD: Office of Juvenile Justice and Delinquency Prevention.

Burke, J., Mulvey, E., and Schubert, C. (2015). Prevalence of mental health problems and service use among first-time juvenile offenders. *Journal of Child and Family Studies, 24*(12), 3774–3781.

Callahan, L., Cocozza, J., Steadman, H., and Tillman, S. (2012). A national survey of U.S. juvenile mental health courts. *Psychiatric Services, 63*(2), 130–134.

CDC. (2015). Deaths: Final Data for 2013 *National Vital Statistics Reports* (vol. 64). Hyattsville, MD: Centers for Disease Control.

Cohen, M., and Piquero, A. (2009). New Evidence on the Monetary Value of Saving a High Risk Youth. *Journal of quantitative criminology, 25*(1), 25–49.

Cuomo, G. (2015). Governor Cumo offers Executive Pardons to New Yorkers convicted of crimes at ages 16 and 17. Retrieved January 30, 2016, from https://www.governor.ny.gov/news/governor-cuomo-offers-executive-pardons-new-yorkers-convicted-crimes-ages–16–and–17

DOJ. (2016). Report and recommendations concerning the use of restrictive housing. Washington, D.C.: U.S. Department of Justice.

Douglas, A., and Lurigio, A. (2014). Juvenile *Crisis Intervention Teams* (CITs): A qualitative description of current programs. *Police Journal: Theory, Practice, and Principles, 87*(2).

Espinosa, E., and Skowyra, K. (2015). Diverting youth at probation intake: The front-end diversion initiative (Vol. 2). Delmar, NY: National Center for Mental Health and Juvenile Justice.

FBI. (2014). Juvenile crime: NIBRS. Retrieved December 17, 2015, from https://www.fbi.gov/about-us/cjis/ucr/nibrs/2013/the-advantage-of-nibrs-data/juvenile-crime

Graham v. Florida, 560 U.S. 48 (2010).

Hayes, L. (2009). Juvenile suicide in confinement: A national survey. Washington, D.C.: OJJDP Report.

Heinssen, R., Goldstein, A., and Azrin, S. (2014). *Evidence based treatment for first episode of psychosis: Components of coordinated specialty care.* Washington, D.C.: National Institute of Mental Health Retrieved from http://www.nimh.nih.gov/health/topics/schizophrenia/raise/nimh-white-paper-csc-for-fep_147096.pdf

HHS.gov. (2012). National strategy for suicide prevention: goals and objectives in action: A report of the U.S. Surgeon General and of the National Action Alliance for suicide prevention. Washington, D.C.: Department of Health and Human Services.

Hockenberry, S., Sickmund, M., and Sladky, A. (2015). Juvenile Residential Facility Census, 2012: Selected findings *Juvenile Offenders and Victims: National Report Series.* Washington, D.C.: OJJDP.

James, C., Stams, G. J. J. M., Asscher, J. J., De Roo, A. K., and der Laan, P. H. v. (2013). Aftercare programs for reducing recidivism among juvenile and young adult offenders: A meta-analytic review. *Clinical Psychology Review, 33*(2), 263–274.

Kraner, N., Barrowclough, N., Weiss, C., and Fisch, J. (2015). Jurisdiction survey of juvenile solitary confinement rules in juvenile justice systems. New York, NY: Lowenstein Center for the Public Interest.

Livsey, S. (2012). Juvenile delinquency probation caseload, 2009. Rockville, MD: Office of Juvenile Justice and Delinquency Prevention.

Mendel, R. (2014). Juvenile detention alternatives initiative progress report: 2014. Baltimore, MD: The Annie E. Casey Foundation.

Miller v. Alabama, No. 567 U.S. ___, 132 S. Ct. 2455, 183 L. Ed. 2d 407, 567 (2012).

Montgomery v. Louisiana, 577 U.S. ___ (2016).

NAMI. (2011). *First episode: Psychosis.* Manual. Arlington, VA: The National Alliance on Mental Illness.

NAMI. (2011). Responding to youth with mental health needs: A CIT for Youth Implementation Manual. Arlington, VA: The National Alliance on Mental Illness.

NAMI. (2014). State Mental Health Legislation 2014: Trends, Themes and Effective Practices. Arlington, VA: National Alliance on Mental Illness.

National Action Alliance for Suicide Prevention: Youth in Contact with the Juvenile Justice System Task Force. (2013). Need to know: A fact sheet series on juvenile suicide—juvenile court judges and staff. Washington, D.C.: Author.

National Center for Injury Prevention and Control. (2015). Understanding school violence. Retrieved December 7, 2015, from http://www.cdc.gov/violence prevention/pdf/school_violence_fact_sheet-a.pdf

NCSL. (2011). *Juvenile justice guidebook for legislators* Retrieved from http://www. ncsl.org/research/civil-and-criminal-Vjustice/juvenile-justice-guidebook-Vfor-legislators.aspx

NSDUH. (2014). Results from the 2013 *National Survey on Drug Use and Health*: Mental health findings *NSDUH Series H-49* (Vol. HHS Publication No. (SMA) 14-4887). Rockville, MD: Substance Abuse and Mental Health Services Administration.

OJJDP. (2015). Custody data. Retrieved December 19, 2015, from http://www. ojjdp.gov/ojstatbb/corrections/faqs.asp

Pennypacker, J. (2008). *Adult and juvenile mental health courts honored by State of California.* Retrieved from http://www.scscourt.org/general_info/news_ media/newspdfs/NRCOMIOawardsVer3.pdf

Ramirez, A. M., Andretta, J. R., Barnes, M. E., and Woodland, M. H. (2015). Recidivism and psychiatric symptom outcomes in a juvenile mental health court. *Juvenile and Family Court Journal, 66*(1), 31–46.

Roper v. Simmons, 543 U.S. 551 (2005).

SAMHSA.gov. (2015). Juvenile mental health treatment court locator. Retrieved December 15, 2015, from http://www.samhsa.gov/gains-center/mental-health-treatment-court-locator/juveniles

Schwalbe, C. S., Gearing, R. E., MacKenzie, M. J., Brewer, K. B., and Ibrahim, R. (2012). A meta-analysis of experimental studies of diversion programs for juvenile offenders. *Clinical Psychology Review, 32*(1), 26–33.

Sickmund, M., and Puzzanchera, C. (2014). Juvenile offenders and victims: 2014 National Report. Pittsburgh, PA: National Center for Juvenile Justice.

Skowyra, K., and Cocozza, J. (2007). Mental health screening within juvenile justice: The next frontier (pp. 34). Delmar, NY: National Center for Mental Health and Juvenile Justice (NCMHJJ).

Washburn, J., Teplin, L., Voss, L., Simon, C., Abram, K., McClelland, G., and Olson, N. (2015). Detained youth processed in juvenile and adult court: Psychiatric disorders and mental health needs. Rockville, MD: Office for Juvenile Justice and Delinquency Prevention.

Youthful Offender, Chapter 119, MA General Law, § 52 Stat. (1996).

PART V

Global Issues

Photo copyright Dmitry Zimin/Bigstock.com

The following chapter is covered in PART V

14. GLOBAL PERSPECTIVES

A crucial question is: How does the international community frame the rights of individuals with mental disorders?

This text has been about the realizations, initiatives, and responses to the needs of people who have mental illness that encounter the criminal justice system. As we stand and look out at our world, wondering how to manage, we should remember that our issues are not unique. We are not alone; the issues are global. Chapter 14 is a brief look at crime and mental disorders at the international level.

CHAPTER 14

Global Perspectives

INTRODUCTION

The world is a very small place and one cannot assume that the challenges faced by the United States criminal justice system are unique to us or insignificant in other nations. A range of documents have outlined disability as a human rights issue since the 1980s and psychosocial disabilities are among the human rights experiences protected under international law. Among developed nations, deinstitutionalization occurred at roughly the same time, though some have yet to stop the practice of warehousing individuals who have disabilities.

Various countries, including the United States, report high rates of involvement between the criminal justice system and populations who have mental disorders. This is the case even though serious mental disorders have been found to be rare in general populations. Research shows that victimization is more likely to occur against persons who experience psychosocial disabilities. Most agree that mental health conditions do not cause crime. So, we are at a loss to fully understand the criminalization of mental illness and are struggling to find humane answers for intervention. At times there is difficulty since definitions of mental illness and treatment don't always translate cross-country or even cross-culturally here in the United States. This chapter will introduce you to the international perspective of criminal justice and mental health disorders along with examples from selected countries around the world. Deinstitutionalization has caused social struggles and common concerns. It is possible that the lack of alternatives to institutionalization is the foundation for the current international crisis.

Key Terms

BLASPHEMY

BURDEN OF DISEASE

DISABILITY

DISABILITY-ADJUSTED LIFE YEARS

PASUNG

SOMATIC SYSTEM DISORDER

Chapter Objectives

After completing this chapter, you should be able to:

- State the position on mental disorder taken by the United Nations
- Name the international organizations involved in mental health fact-gathering initiatives
- Discuss the criminal justice response to mental illness around the world
- Explain the global prevalence of mental health disorders

UNITED NATIONS

Human rights are an international issue, respected and protected at the state level. Chartered to protect human rights since 1948, the United Nations (UN) is an international organization currently made up of 193 countries across the globe. They are referred to as Member States. The International Community, through the UN, has passed international human rights laws which recognize basic human rights and the obligations of governments to promote and protect them. There are UN offices around the world including one of the headquarters is in New York City. The World Health Organization (WHO) is one of the many programs of the United Nations. The UN appointed the first Special Rapporteur with a focus on disability in 1984. The title of Special Rapporteur is given to an expert who works on behalf of the UN on a human rights issue.

Numerous international documents have highlighted the fact that disability, including psychosocial disabilities, is a human rights issue. United Nations resolutions include the Convention on the Rights of the Child (1989), Principles for the Protection of Persons with Mental Illness (1991) and the Standard Rules on the Equalization of Opportunities for People with Disabilities (1994). In 1998, the UN Commission on Human Rights confirmed through resolution thirty-one that disability is a human rights issue. The UN declared that the institutionalization of persons solely due to disability, physical or psychosocial, is a violation of their human rights. **DISABILITY** is defined by the Inter-American Convention for the Elimination of all Forms of Discrimination against Persons with Disabilities (Multilateral Treaties, 1999):

> "a physical, mental, or sensory impairment, whether permanent or temporary, that limits the capacity to perform one or more essential activities in daily life, and which can be caused or aggravated by the economic and social environment" (Article I, para. 1).

1. CH14-01: *United Nations*. The United Nations has framed mental disorder within the context of a psychosocial disability. The institutionalization of individuals solely due to disability, physical, or psychosocial is an international violation of human rights. Photo copyright AlexMax/Bigstock.com

Rights of Children

The number of children from birth to age fourteen that experience moderate or severe disability is estimated to be 93 million worldwide by the World Health Organization, and 13 million children experience severe disabilities. WHO cautions that while this estimate is widely used, it is considered an underestimation. Accurate estimates are difficult to obtain in countries where children with disabilities are often not registered and are therefore unable to obtain birth certificates. The Convention on the Rights of Persons with Disabilities (CRPD) and the Convention on the Rights of the Child (CRC) outline the rights of children with disabilities, including those with psychosocial disabilities, and provide a framework for promoting the right of children with disabilities to live with their families, or in home-like environments within the community. The U.N. Convention of the Rights of the Child, adopted in 1989, has been ratified by 192 nations. The CRC explicitly prohibits the imposition of the sentence of life without parole for crimes committed by juveniles.

It is widely accepted that a strong association exists between parental psychopathy and an elevated risk of mental disorders in their children. Violence toward children and adolescents is prevalent worldwide (Belfer, 2008). Both genetic and environmental conditions can impose this risk. Few large studies have focused on the issue of whether having a parent with a mental disorder increases the risk of a child having the same condition or whether the risk is more generalized to a range of disorders. This question was addressed by WHO researchers using the WMH survey information (McLaughlin et al., 2013). Results of the study involving twenty-two countries indicated that every parent disorder that was examined, except for suicide, was associated with an increased risk for a non-specific type of mental disorder among their offspring. The study suggests that negative parental behaviors, in addition to genetic vulnerability, may explain the intergenerational transmission of mental disorders. Violence against children with disabilities occurs at annual rates at least 1.7 times greater than for their non-disabled peers per the Convention on the Rights of Persons with Disabilities (UN, 2006).

WORLD HEALTH ORGANIZATION

Mental disorders are leading causes of disability around the globe. Nearly one in ten people on the planet are estimated to experience mental disorders (WHO, 2015a). Findings suggest that the prevalence does not differ significantly across cultures for either adult or child populations (Belfer, 2008; WHO, 2015b). It is no easy task to draw these conclusions. Those who have attempted to determine the prevalence of mental disorder around the world have faced daunting challenges. Among the difficulties in measuring the magnitude of the problem are a lack of data-gathering abilities, limits on resources for diagnostic and treatment options, inadequacies in cultural and cross-cultural understanding, and improper assessment (Belfer, 2008). Diagnostic classifications are a western concept that are not necessarily shared by developing countries. Despite these problems, research finds that rates and types of mental disorders globally are consistent with those in the United States (WHO, 2015a).

The World Health Organization (WHO) leads the global initiative on mental health research and treatment. Formed in 1948 by sixty-one Member States, the constitution of WHO was adopted at the International Health Conference. More than 7,000 people now work for the organization to provide leadership, develop standards, and monitor health trends. The World Mental Health (WMH) surveys published by the WHO represent the largest ongoing cross-national series of mental disorder surveys ever attempted. The WMH survey approach is unique because it measures the burden of disease to determine the gap in the health of a population. **BURDEN OF DISEASE** is a complicated measuring technique which combines data from multiple sources to count the total fatal and non-fatal health loss from diseases and injuries in a population. One measure of burden of disease is the **DISABILITY-ADJUSTED LIFE YEARS** (DALY) which combines estimates of years of life lost due to premature death (YLL) and years lived with disability (YLD) to count the total years of healthy life lost from disease and injury. Determining the burden of disease with a survey approach is now the standard technique used in disability studies around the world. The standard has made possible both national and international comparisons.

2. CH14-02: *WHO.* The World Health Organization (WHO) carries out the largest global initiative of determining the burden of mental disorders. By standardizing the burden of disease technique, the prevalence of mental disorders and its impact on society can be calculated and compared across nations and among different cultures. Photo copyright Frith's Photography/Bigstock.com

The WHO compiles the *World Health Atlas* through surveys in countries around the world (WHO, 2015b). As such, the *Atlas* is an important source of information on the global status of mental health. Data is collected on legislative protections, policies, prevalence of psychosocial disabilities, mental health resources and their allocation. Mental disorders make up a large global burden of disease. Mental health and substance abuse disorders, together with neurological and developmental disorders, are responsible for over 10 percent of the global disease burden. Findings from the *Atlas* also reveal that the prevalence of depression among women is substantially higher than among men. At its worst, depression can lead to suicide. An estimated 804,000 suicide deaths occurred worldwide in 2012, amounting to an annual global suicide death rate of 11.4 per a population of 100,000. Bear in mind that for every suicide there are many more suicide attempts.

It has been documented by WHO (2015b) that half of the world's countries have a standalone law on the governance of mental health. Mental disorders, including dementias, are among the leading causes of disease worldwide. A large proportion of mental disorders is caused by depression and anxiety, largely affecting people between the ages of fifteen to fifty-nine. Dementia has become a global health issue, primarily in the high-income countries that reflect the higher proportion of elderly people in the population. Approximately 46 million people are living with dementia, a number that is estimated to grow to 75 million by 2030.

Low and Middle Income Countries

The primary value of collecting data is to provide feedback and recommendations for improvements. Participating countries are selected based on how much they could benefit from an assessment. In the WHO-AIMS report on low and middle income countries (LAMICs), forty-two countries were represented (WHO, 2009). These studies enable countries to develop mental health policy and service delivery plans based on actual data rather than conjecture. The study found that among LAMICs the treatment rate for individuals experiencing mental disorders is only a small fraction of what would be expected. The prevalence of untreated mental health disorders in LAMICs is estimated to be as high as 78 percent. For children and adolescents, one in twenty have a severe mental disorder and the treatment rate is an abysmal 0.16 percent.

One third of the participating countries selected in the WHO-AIMS Report do not have formal mental health collaboration with their criminal justice systems. The clear majority of these countries have provided mental health education to only a few police officers, lawyers, and judges within the previous five years. No country reported providing education for all or almost all (81 percent–100 percent) of criminal justice personnel. Mental health care for prisoners is low to nonexistent in most LAMICs.

Latin American Countries

There are thirty-four countries and territories that make up Latin America and the Caribbean Region within the WHO-AIMS Report. These include South America, the Caribbean countries and territories, Central America, and Mexico. The socioeconomic conditions of the region range from low to high; languages include English, Dutch, Spanish and local languages; some are independent states and others remain territories. Per the WHO-AIMS Report, mental and neurological disorders account for almost 23 percent of the total burden of disease in the region (PAHO, 2013). Gaps in mental health care are up to 71 percent for some disorders. Mental health legislation exists only in a minority of countries. Despite the high psychiatric risk among the prison population, this population is a low priority and the availability of services is quite limited. In countries where forensic beds are available, there is a range of .5 to three beds per 100,000 people; these services are located both in psychiatric hospitals and in prisons.

European Countries

Mental health disorders commonly occur in all surveyed countries around the world. In a study to determine the prevalence of mental disorders in Europe (which included the twenty-seven member states of the EU, plus Switzerland, Iceland, and Norway) researchers found that more than 38 percent of the population experiences mental disorders annually, an estimated 165 million people (Wittchen et al., 2011). In 2005, it had been estimated by the same authors that the population experienced mental disorders at the rate of 27 percent. At first glance it appears as though there is a large increase of mental disorders. However, authors state that the higher estimate is entirely due to the inclusion of fourteen new disorders, including disorders specific to childhood and elderly populations.

The newest WHO (Witchen et al., 2001) study concludes that the four most debilitating disorders of the brain are depression, dementias, alcohol use disorders and stroke. The most frequently occurring disorders are anxiety disorders (14.0 percent), insomnia (7.0 percent), major depression (6.9 percent), somatic symptom disorder (6.3 percent), alcohol and drug dependence (4 percent), ADHD among youth (5 percent), and dementia (1–30 percent, depending on age). **Somatic system disorder**, formally called hysteria, is a mental disorder that describes a constant exaggerated worry about one's health, experiences of pain or other physical symptoms that cannot be medically explained through a diagnosis which disrupts at least one primary area of the person's life (APA, 2014). Except for alcohol and drug dependence, these common mental disorders are not typically associated with criminal activity. However, they may be experienced by individuals within the criminal justice system.

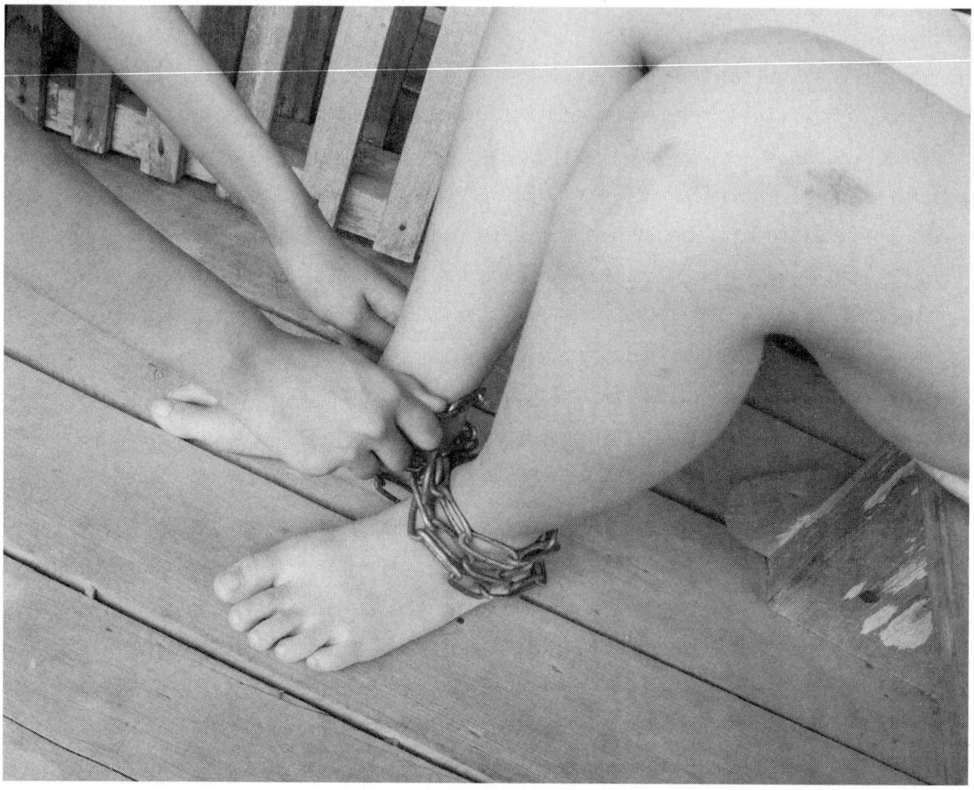

3. CH14-03: *Pasung*. The practice of pasung was banned in 1977 but continues to this day. Stigma, lack of understanding about mental disorders, and an absence of alternative options for intervention are among the contributing factors for the continuing cultural practice of restraining individuals with ropes and chains when mental disorders are suspected in Indonesia. Photo copyright Padchara/Bigstock.com

HUMAN RIGHTS WATCH AND INDONESIA

Established in 1978, Human Rights Watch is a nonprofit, nongovernmental human rights organization with staff located around the world. Human Rights Watch investigates human rights abuses and publishes reports on living conditions in over ninety countries. A recent investigation, for example, reported that over 19 million Indonesians experience psychosocial disabilities, while an estimated 57,000 of them literally live in chains (Sharma, 2014). The Indonesian term **PASUNG** refers to the physical restraint or confinement of criminals and dangerously aggressive people. The practice was banned in 1977 but continues due to cultural beliefs that individuals with mental disorders are possessed by evil spirits. One person in the report described being rubbed with garlic and salt by a family member who was eager to cure the evil within him. Visits to the local healer are common practices in response to mental disorders.

The widespread practice of *pasung* involves physically restraining someone by securing their ankles in wooden stocks, chaining, caging, or lashing them to a building or tree (Puteh, Marthoenis, and Minas, 2011). Destitute and desperate family members with no access to psychiatric treatment services have little option but to physically restrain violent individuals with mental illness, often under the instruction of town officials. Even in provinces where the government pays for mental health treatment, the burden of cost for transportation to the clinics can be insurmountable. In the recent release of fifty-nine patients, 90 percent of whom were diagnosed with schizophrenia, Puteh et al. (2011) documented that the duration of *pasung* varied from a few days to twenty years. An Indonesian mental health care law was passed in 2015 which promises to address the treatment gap of persons with mental disabilities.

IN MY EXPERIENCE . . .

Anto is a young man from Indonesia who has been chained in *pasung* countless times during his life. His experiences are documented in a recent article which he co-authored with Erminia Colucci (SG and Colucci, 2015). His symptoms of depression began prior to high school when Anto began living in a state of overwhelming sadness and fatigue. His self-described unusual behaviors caused adults in his neighborhood to avoid him. Children on the streets yelled at him, calling him crazy. Wanting to escape the taunting and rejection, Anto was unsuccessful in his attempt to commit suicide. He ran away several times. Each time he was returned home and tied with ropes and chains. "Chained like an animal," he said.

Anto's parents believed that he would benefit from being restrained during these periods of darkness, that the chains would somehow tame him. The use of *pasung* as his cure lasted from three days to twenty-eight days each time. His sadness sometimes turned to anger at the torture of the ropes and chains. The traditional healer did not help. Neither did the exorcism or long periods of being tied to a hospital bed. He was given medicine by a primary care physician and a nurse who told him it was a vitamin. That did not help either. He has never seen a psychiatrist or been diagnosed with an illness. Now in his third year of college, Anto dreams of completing a degree in English. He dares to survive and struggle for a better tomorrow. Anto and I exchanged emails and he has graciously given me permission to tell his story.

Question for discussion: What are the mental and physical consequences of *pasung*?

GLOBAL COSTS

Based on 2010 data, the World Economic Forum estimated that mental disorders are the largest medical cost driver at $2.5 trillion in global costs in 2010 and projected costs of $6.0 trillion by 2030 (Bloom et al., 2011). Indirect costs make up two thirds of that figure. The costs for mental disorders are greater than the costs of diabetes, respiratory disorders, and cancer combined. The greatest cost to society, however, is in the personal suffering of the individual, loved ones, and family members. Mental health conditions are the leading cause of Disability-Adjusted Life Years worldwide and account for 37 percent of healthy life years lost from non-communicable diseases (WHO, 2011a). Among these conditions, unipolar depressive disorder, alcohol use disorders and *schizophrenia* constitute the greatest global burden in terms of disability. Appropriate intervention will benefit individuals who have mental disorders as well as society in general.

The difficulties in educating professionals in addition to the costs of providing care for individuals with mental disorders are staggering, according to WHO (2015b). Treatment of dementia alone represented a financial burden of $604 billion in 2010. A shortage of professionals is evidenced internationally. There are fewer than one mental health worker for every 10,000 people to handle the growing needs. Professionals in the field are often untrained in mental health issues, which only compounds the problem. An estimated median of just over 2 percent of physicians and 1.8 percent of nurses and midwives received up to two days of training in mental health in the previous two years. If these numbers from the WHO are accurate, the global burden for mental health needs is high and the world is not yet prepared to meet the challenges.

Crime and Victimization in Brazil

Brazil is an extremely violent country with alarmingly high homicide rates. Between 1980 and 2010 there were 1 million homicides in Brazil, giving it the distinction of having one of the highest murder rates in the world (Murray, Cerqueira, and Kahn, 2013). The authors report that adult prison population has more than tripled for men between 1989 and 2009; an even greater rate of increase was noted for women during the same period. There is an urgent need for data collection on crime and violence according to Murray et al. (2013), as criminal justice data about Brazil is incomplete and unreliable. A recent study has attempted to shine some light on the Brazilian prison population by examining crime categories and psychiatric disorders among prisoners in Salvador. Considering the major categories of mental disorders, the authors concluded that

ADHD, anxiety disorder, bipolar disorder, and depression are not associated with any specific type of crime committed by the inmates (Pondé, Caron, Mendonça, Freire, and Moreau, 2014). A different picture emerged when personality disorders and substance abuse disorders were considered; these were often associated with serious crimes such as robbery, homicide, and sex crimes.

Given that the levels of crime are high in Brazil, researchers wondered about the impact of violence on mental health. A recent study examined the impact of violence exposure to levels of mental disorder in a longitudinal study over a six-year period. Among the population studied, individuals exposed to direct or indirect violence (as documented by an earlier study) were more than six times more likely to experience psychological distress over a six-year period (Lopes et al., 2015). Their conclusion is that exposure to violence will increase/trigger mental health disorders over time.

THE HOMELESS OF BRITISH COLUMBIA AND HUNGARY

It is well documented in the United States that individuals experiencing substance abuse and severe mental disorders are highly represented among homeless populations. They also frequently encounter the criminal justice system. Lifetime arrest rates are very high among the homeless, ranging from 62 percent to 90 percent (Roy, Crocker, Nicholls, Latimer, and Ayllon, 2014). Victimization of the homeless is even more prevalent than criminal offending. Self-reported rates of victimization are between 73.7 percent to 87 percent (Roy et al., 2014). Persons with co-occurring disorders, particularly substance abuse and at least one mental health disorder, seem to the fare the worst. A strong relationship with both crime and victimization among the homeless exists when the co-occurring disorder involves substance abuse. A few international studies have added interesting insight to the global picture of these relationships.

A homeless intervention project (HIP) in British Columbia that was designed to provide housing and support to chronic homeless persons identified 536 participants for inclusion (Patterson, Somers, and Moniruzzaman, 2012). It was believed that an interagency approach would be helpful in meeting the complex needs of the project group so that criminal justice involvement might be reduced when housing and mental health needs were met. Consistent with trends in the U.S., 74 percent of the participants were diagnosed with both a substance use disorder and at least one other mental disorder. The participants had each been convicted of a crime an average of eight times in the two-year period prior to program enrollment. At the end of six months, the program assessment showed a significant decrease in offenses along with an increased use of physician primary care services. Agency collaboration and information sharing by key agencies was credited for the excellent results.

Another recent study examined the prevalence of psychiatric disorders among the homeless in Hungary. Researchers found that 86 percent of the sample suffered from a diagnosable psychiatric disorder (Braun and Gazdag, 2015). Results suggested that personality and alcohol disorders are more frequently associated with males; females more commonly experience personality and anxiety disorders. Less than 40 percent of the sample with a severe mental health diagnosis were receiving psychiatric care at the time of the study. Of interest to the study was the relationship between mental disorders and violence. The authors concluded that criminal behavior was not more frequent among the homeless who experience mental disorders, with one exception. Among the homeless with mental disorders, for individuals who have a drug or prescription dependence there is a significant correlation with both violent and nonviolent offending.

LAW ENFORCEMENT INTERVENTION IN CANADA AND CHINA

Criminal justice systems around the world share common frustrations that came about as consequences of deinstitutionalization. The Canadian police sought to change the situation through improved law enforcement education on mental disorders and a coordinated crisis team response. The police response in Halifax, Nova Scotia now involves a Regional Mental Health Mobile Crisis Team or MHMCT (Cotton and Coleman, 2010). The MHMCT worked with the Dalhousie University Department of Psychiatry to develop an education and training matrix with four levels of education/training for first responders that ranges from three and one half days to ten days of training. A two-hour introduction course, the *Recognition of Emotionally Disturbed Persons*, is available online through the Canadian Police Knowledge Network. Coleman and Cotton (2014) report that the most outstanding feature of the training was the focus on assessment and feedback of an officer's attitudes and behaviors during the training.

The initial contact with an individual experiencing mental health crisis in China is handled differently than in other countries. Researchers Lo and Wang (2010) suggest that the person may be apprehended by family members, a work unit, or neighborhood committee where the person lives. The neighborhood committee is the first level of security in the community; they typically handle what Western countries would consider to be civil or misdemeanor crimes. The incident would then be reported to the police, who would notify a special response unit if necessary. Police officers are not trained on mental health issues in China. Excessive force is common when apprehending individuals with mental disorders (Lo and Wang, 2010). Procedures vary between jurisdictions and there is no standardization for mandatory commitment. Individuals who are found not guilty by reason of a mental disorder are released to surveillance and medical treatment. In reality, over 60 percent of those released due to a mental disorder were discharged to their families, some of whom were chained or otherwise restrained inside the house or left without supervision due to a fear of the person or lack of resources (Lo and Wang, 2010).

DIVERSION IN EUROPE

Several countries have added pretrial diversion to their justice systems, these are based on the American innovation. Of the fifty-one jurisdictions surveyed by WHO, twenty-two persons were diverted to treatment either in lieu of arrest, pending trial, or as an alternative to incarceration following sentencing (NAPSA, 2009). In France, defendants that comply with a court-determined treatment order are not liable to prosecution; in Germany, treatment can be credited against a custodial sentence. In France and Italy, individuals who complete voluntary treatment are given what is called a "pardon." This means that they receive a certificate as evidence of the program completion to protect against subsequent prosecution for offenses committed prior to treatment.

Diversion programs in the UK have been promoted since the early 1990s. Approximately 150 court-based diversion programs now exist across England and Wales in addition to forty police liaison systems which use the police station as the main point of entry (McGilloway and Donnelly, 2004). Police station diversion programs are thought to be the most effective in meeting the needs of mentally ill offenders. A unique approach in some rural areas of the UK has been to employ on-call psychiatric nurses, sometimes at police stations directly, to facilitate collaboration (Moore, 2010). Multi-agency collaborations have also proved important as a mechanism for appropriate diversion to health and social services, as needed.

IMAGINE THAT . . .

Consider, for example, the best practices forwarded by the Mental Health Network (MHN) and the Association of Chief of Police Officers in the United Kingdom, which set forth how to provide care for individuals in mental health crisis (NHS, 2015). The UK estimates that 50 percent of detainees in police custody had mental health problems in 2013 (NHS, 2015). The UK *Mental Health Crisis Care Concordat* launched in 2014 commits agencies to work together to stop the use of police stations as places for holding individuals in mental health crisis, unless exceptional circumstances exist. Best practices include the use of ambulances for transportation and the employment of psychiatric professionals stationed within the police department for twenty-four-hour access to mental health services even during nights and weekends. Establishing sufficient hospital and community care services are a priority. Multi-agency training in mental health issues includes police officers, community and ward nurses, fire fighters, social workers, and troubled families. In short, caring for those in crisis requires a community response, with the help of police officers at the frontline.

Question for discussion: Do you think this approach would work in the US? Why or why not?

4. CH14-04: *Irish Police Service.* Garda Siochana is a term that refers to the Irish Police Service. Although police officers are legally able to divert individuals for assessment when mental disorders are suspected, officers here complain of difficulties in obtaining these medical assessments and long delays when emergency departments or psychiatric hospital were needed as interventions. Photo copyright Editorialz/Bigstock.com

COURTS AND THE IRISH EXPERIENCE

The Garda Siochana (Irish Police Service) have the legal right in Ireland under the Criminal Law (Insanity) Act of 2006, to directly divert, for assessment, those individuals who appear to have mental disorders. However, a survey of the numerous rural stations found officers describing both difficulties in obtaining medical assessments in police stations and long delays when emergency departments or psychiatric hospitals were used (McInerney et al., 2013). Program initiators McInerney et al. (2013) met with other stakeholders and found that District Court judges also were frustrated at the lack of rapid referral to psychiatric services. Prison officials were also dissatisfied that they could only refer patients in need of psychiatric care to high and medium security hospitals where there were long waiting lists. Even the mental health services programs were dissatisfied with the manner in which patients came for treatment.

In response to these concerns in Ireland the *Prison Inreach and Court Liaison Service* (PICLS) was initiated in 2007. This court liaison model consists of a multi-disciplinary mental health team of psychiatrists, nurses, and a team administrator that provides service Monday through Friday at the primary intake center. Each new detainee is screened for mental disorders, suicide risk, and psychiatric history. Several triage options exist for the team. In cases where admission to a local psychiatric hospital is recommended, defendants are accompanied to court by a member of the PICLS to provide evidence to the court for possible transfer to the hospital. In review of a six-year period, a total of 572 prisoners with severe mental illness were diverted from prison to mental health services (McInerney et al., 2013).

CORRECTIONS IN EUROPE

Most studies examining mental illness have been conducted in developed countries and consistently show that a very high proportion of prisoners suffer from poor mental health. In a study which included England, Germany, Italy, the Netherlands, Spain, and Sweden, researchers found that since deinstitutionalization in Europe, the general prison population in each country had increased at rates between 16 percent and 104 percent (Priebe et al., 2005). Prison populations grew and the numbers of available psychiatric beds declined despite an increase in community financed forensic beds in all countries. The authors concluded that a new form of institutionalization has become a reality, with jails and prisons increasingly becoming surrogate mental hospitals. Priebe et al. (2005) concluded that transinstitutionalism of individuals with mental disorders exists as an international phenomenon. Potential explanations for the trend were that there may be a greater frequency or severity of illness, possibly influenced by the increasing use of illegal drugs.

Charges that prisons are the new asylums have surfaced globally (Konrad, 2002). A follow-up study which included Austria, Denmark, Ireland, and Switzerland also found a trend towards transinstitutionalized mental health care throughout Europe (Priebe et al., 2008). An analysis concluded that while Europeans imprison at lower rates than does the United States, all the studied prison populations had increased considerably since deinstitutionalization in Europe. Around the world, serious mental illness is significant within the justice systems. We do not know the extent to which mental disorders influence criminal behavior in cases that do not come to the attention of criminal justice professionals. A study examining the historical trends of mental health services in Norway from 1950 to 2007 concluded that deinstitutionalization resulted in fewer beds but not fewer patients who need continued treatment (Pedersen and Kolstad, 2009). Improvement in the quality of care is the current goal.

Moore (2010) states that a frequently used sanction in England and Wales was created by the *Criminal Justice Act of 2003* and implemented in 2005. Called the Imprisonment for Public Protection (IPP) sentence, it is an "indeterminate" sanction used to incarcerate offenders who are identified by the courts as dangerous, but whose offenses do not carry a life sentence. Highly criticized as the means to imprison persons who were mentally ill, an estimated 90 percent of inmates in England and Wales are believed to have at least one mental health disorder (Moore, 2010). Continued controversy amid claims of prison overcrowding due to the IPP sentence option, the law was revisited and revised in 2008 (Strickland, 2015). Revisions included a new "seriousness threshold" as a requirement to be satisfied before the court could impose an IPP sentence. The lack of mental health services is believed to be responsible for rising numbers of persons who are sentenced under this provision (Moore, 2010). Further efforts to ease prison overcrowding ultimately led to the repeal of the IPP in 2012 (Strickland, 2015).

SPECIFIC DISORDERS AND OFFENDING

Efforts to understand the relationship between mental disorders and crime are emerging in all major countries around the world. One common approach is to examine prevalence rates of specific disorders represented among criminal offenders. Researchers from the United Kingdom reviewed available literature from scholars around the world on persons with autism spectrum disorders and criminal offending (King and Murphy, 2014). The authors describe a great variability in the quality of studies and point out the potentially biased and small sample studies that examine this population alongside criminal behavior. They concluded that individuals with autism spectrum disorders are not disproportionately over-represented in the criminal justice system, although individuals do exhibit problematic behaviors due to rigid rule adherence and social naivety and they do commit crimes. The debate about relationships between specific mental disorders and criminal offending is far from settled, however.

In another study involving more than 33,500 prisoners from twenty-four countries, researchers found a prevalence rate of psychosis of 3.6 percent in male prisoners and 3.9 percent in female prisoners (Fazel and Seewald, 2012). Learning and communication difficulties and addiction problems among these prison populations were also more common than in the general population. In addition, prevalence studies in many countries show that as many as 15 percent of the prison population suffers from severe mental illnesses such as schizophrenia, bipolar disorder, and autism disorders (Durcan and Zwemstra, 2014).

Australia

Australia has deinstitutionalized its mental health system and now relies heavily on community-based health care. Recent studies have found that responding to individuals in psychiatric crisis is a large part of modern policing in Australia. Due to the high prevalence of serious mental disorders among offending populations, along with cases of fatal use of force in police encounters, the effectiveness of the community service model is under scrutiny. In an examination of over 2,500 attempted suicide-by-cop incidents, common characteristics of those involved were identified. The offenders were mostly middle-aged males with a record of substance abuse and a history of contact with police. The majority were known to the public mental health services and had a notable psychiatric history (McLeod, Thomas, and Kesic, 2014). Results of the study suggest that police in Victoria potentially encounter suicidal persons trying to provoke police to shoot them two to three times a week. While most attempts are resolved through nonfatal means, researchers found the only statistically significant difference in resolutions was that those who were killed had a more significant history of violent offending.

In a case study by Kesic, et al. (2012), over 4,260 incidents between 1995 and 2008 were examined to determine the rates of diagnosed mental disorders in incidents of nonfatal force between Victorian police and its citizens. Researchers found that there was a history of mental disorder for more than a third of people on whom the police resorted to using force (Kesic, Thomas, and Ogloff, 2012).

Even after considering age, gender, intoxication and violent behavior, however, they were no more likely to be injured by police than those without a recorded history of mental disorder. Within the group studied, there was a significant overrepresentation of individuals with psychosis and schizophrenia. Programs intended to reduce the risk of injury to police and mental health consumers and to improve collaboration with other agencies in response to mental health crisis events have recently been initiated (Coleman and Cotton, 2014).

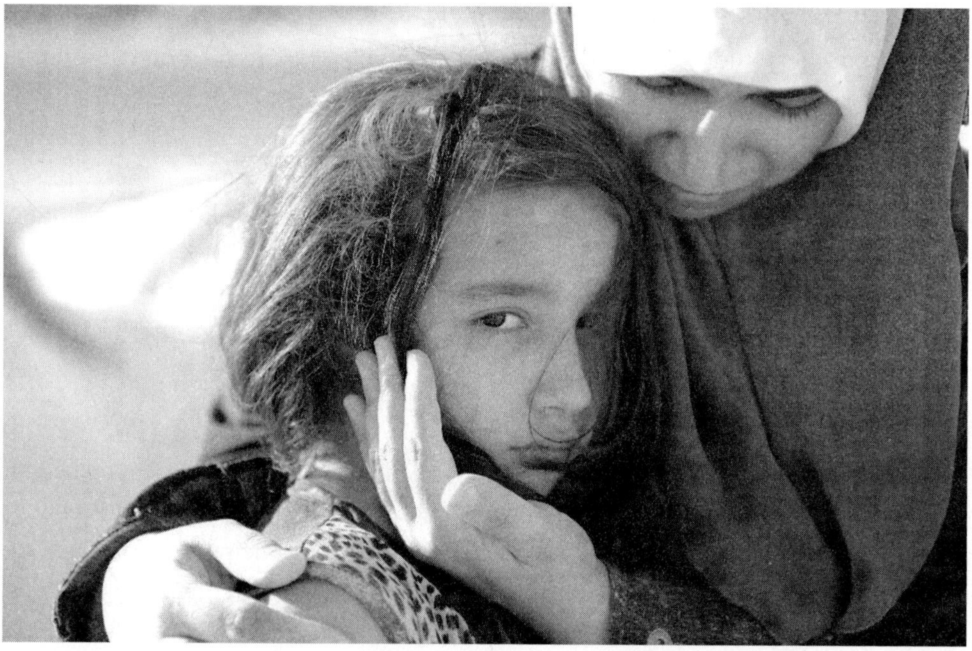

5. CH14-05: *Pakistan.* Evidence suggests that over a thousand of cases alleging blasphemy have been raised in Pakistan. Some of these cases are against individuals with autism and intellectual disability, as well as religious minorities who are incapable of showing the required reverence for the Quran due to mental disorders. Death is a common outcome in these allegations. Photo copyright ZouZou/Shutterstock.com

Pakistan

The Republic of Pakistan, founded in 1947, is located in South Asia. It is the sixth most populous country in the world. Evidence suggests that persons experiencing mental disorders are overrepresented among the defendants prosecuted under the blasphemy laws of Pakistan (Husain, 2014). **BLASPHEMY**, which means speaking evil of sacred matters, was forbidden as far back as ancient Roman and Greek law (Levy, 1993). Incorporated into the English criminal law during the 1600s, these laws were abolished in the UK in 2008, though they experienced a renewed interest in Pakistan during the 1980s. An estimated 1,274 persons have been arrested since 1986 and at least fifty-one blasphemy defendants were murdered by the public following an allegation; officials who oppose the laws have been assassinated (Husain, 2014). Cases of blasphemy have been raised in allegations where perpetrators of sexual abuse fear discovery, and against individuals with autism and intellectual disability as well as religious minorities who, due to mental disorders, are incapable of showing the required reverence for the Quran.

It is estimated that 20 million people in Pakistan suffer from some form of mental disorder, and about 2 million of those cases are severe (Mirza, Tareen, Davidson, and Rahman, 2009). Pakistan also has one of the highest rates of childhood intellectual disabilities (ID) in the world; estimates vary from 19.1/1000 for serious ID to 65/1000 for mild ID (Mirza et al., 2009). Legal protections for individuals who are mentally ill through court diversion and mandatory psychiatric assessment of blasphemy defendants has recently been passed in the province of Sindh (Raza-ur-Rahman, Siddiqi, and Ahmed, 2015). Researchers suggest that implementing mental health services will require significant resources, including funding, training mental health professionals, and mental health care facilities. Protecting the human rights of the mentally ill, one of the most vulnerable population of Pakistan, has begun in earnest.

Regions of Africa

Africa is the second largest continent in the world with fifty-four countries and nine recognized territories. The diversity of governments, ethnicities, cultures, and languages make it impossible to generalize on its criminal justice policies. The United Nations' Human Development Report states that the poorest 25 nations in the world are all in Africa. To reflect international human rights and best practice standards, South Africa adopted a national *Mental Health Care Act,* 2002. The law promotes an integrated approach to mental health and has driven service reform at provincial and district levels. It codifies a number of rights for people with mental health conditions and promotes voluntary treatment. It includes oversight mechanisms such as a Mental Health Review Board which is aimed at protecting against human rights violations. The low priority provided to mental health in this developing country, however, hinders the implementation of mental health policy (Draper et al., 2009). In South Africa, HIV/AIDS has received a fair amount of government and public attention while mental health has not, despite the connection between the two major health issues. Individuals with HIV/AIDS are at an elevated risk of experiencing mental health issues. One study showed that 44 percent of people living with HIV/AIDS have a diagnosable mental health condition while the prevalence of mental health conditions in the general population is only 17 percent (Freeman, Nkomo, Kafaar, and Kelly, 2008). Researchers have also found that children orphaned due to AIDS deaths have significantly higher rates of depression, posttraumatic stress disorder, and suicidal ideation than non-orphaned children.

In the country of Kenya, the life expectancy at birth is fifty-seven years. Until 2014 Kenya was considered a low-income country. Recent discoveries of oil and gas changed its status to a lower-middle income country. This change benefits only a minority and poverty levels remain high. In a study to determine the current prevalence rate of mental disorders among the population of this Sub-Saharan country, it was estimated that over 10 percent of the population suffers from mental disorders (Jenkins et al., 2015). Researchers found that the overall prevalence of mental disorders was unchanged from 2004 despite government intervention and services. Of note was a significant drop in the prevalence of mental illnesses among men and a corresponding increase among women. It was theorized that high rates of domestic violence against women (50 percent), poverty, low levels of education, and the lack of land ownership by women contribute to the higher burden of mental disorders among females vs. that of males (Jenkins et al., 2015). Being over age sixty was also significantly related to mental illness, compared to those under age thirty.

6. CH14-06: *Africa.* Despite mental health reforms aimed at reflecting the international human rights and best practice standards, progress is difficult in the impoverished nations of Africa. Photo copyright francovolpato/Bigstock.com

Sweden

The legal system in Sweden is unique in its handling of individuals who commit crime when experiencing mental disorders. An individual in Sweden is considered an adult for criminal responsibility in the court system at the age of fifteen. Since 1965, the current legal system does not recognize a relationship between mental disorders and criminal offending. Therefore, offenders are presumed capable of forming criminal intent regardless of having severe mental disorders (Svennerlind et al., 2010). However, a prison sentence is not allowed if an offender was determined to have committed a criminal act under the influence of a severe mental disorder. Instead, psychiatric treatment, fines, and other sanctions are imposed.

According to Svennerlind et al. (2010), the concept of accountability has been slowly reintroduced into the legal system since 2008. A defendant who induces their own mental instability through intoxication or some other means may receive a prison sentence. Pending legislative changes remove psychiatric care as a sanction and lift the prohibition against prison, bringing Sweden into line with most legal systems. Offenders diverted to forensic mental health care will be remanded to complete a sentence in jail when the individual can function without psychiatric care.

The nationwide multi-generation register in Sweden has provided records of crimes and individuals having mental disorders that are available for review. One study on violent criminal offending, among a large Swedish population of convicts, found a greater rate of crime among individuals with bipolar disorder who had co-occurring substance disorders (S. Fazel, Lichtenstein, Grann, Goodwin, and Långström, 2010). Interestingly, the study also found an increased rate of violent offending among non-disordered siblings of the group. The authors concluded that substance abuse and genetic or early environmental factors may influence violent crime offending more significantly than does mental disorders.

Another recent study in Sweden attempted to determine the prevalence of abuse against men with a substance use disorder, mental health issues, and a history of abuse. Almost half of the men in the sample reported having experienced some form of abuse; those with mental health problems in addition to substance use disorder were more likely to have a lifetime history of abuse (Lundgren et al., 2013). Men in the study with a history of inpatient psychiatric care were 60 percent more likely to report a history of sexual abuse than their counterparts in the general population, suggesting that self-reporting sexual abuse is strongly associated with mental health symptoms.

SUMMARY

The international community has come together through the United Nations to establish mental disability as a human rights issue. This is important in establishing a right to dignity and health care for all people regardless of their disorder. It is a mechanism to hold nation states accountable for violations of human rights. The World Health Organization is not a punitive arm of the UN. Its function is to set best standards and practices, conduct research, and assist countries in developing legislation and policies for the care of those in need. In addition, WHO provides estimates on world health and projects the burden of illness for the future.

Increased contact between police officers and individuals experiencing mental disorders is reported worldwide. Undesirable outcomes for those experiencing mental illness is a common concern. Problems range from an increase in arrest-related fatalities to the lack of treatment options. Police department resources are stretched beyond their capacity and the best response option is frequently a jail cell. When appropriate mental health services do exist, they are few and far between—meaning that police officers, by default, provide mental health care. Diversion initiatives at the point of police involvement and from the criminal courts are commonly used.

Prisons around the world report increased numbers of incarcerated individuals who have a variety of mental disorders. The handling of inmates with severe mental disorders varies greatly by country and their prioritization of mental health issues. It appears that underdeveloped countries lack appropriate psychiatric responses at every level of criminal justice contact. Initiatives to inform the public about mental disorders are as imperative as the care itself.

There is an emerging trend to include conditions such as substance use disorders, dementias, and stroke in the category of mental disorders. Recent data has shown that mental disorders have increased dramatically in recent years, though this is partly due to more conditions meeting the categorical criteria, so caution should be used in interpreting data by only looking at the numbers. The approach is helpful, however, in determining the true burden on societies. The rise in individuals with dementia signals an impending crisis around the world. As people are living longer there is a marked increase of the disability which requires significant resources from the community.

CHAPTER QUESTIONS FOR REVIEW

1. What position has the United Nations taken on mental disabilities?
2. What contributions has the World Health Organization made towards a global understanding of mental disorders?
3. Explain the relevance of the theory on intergenerational transmission of mental disorder.
4. How did Ireland address its mental health court frustrations through collaborations?
5. What legislative changes have occurred in Sweden that will likely change the way it copes with the burden of individuals who are mentally disordered and are involved in the criminal justice system?

REFERENCES

APA. (2014). *Understanding mental disorders: Your guide to DSM-5*. Washington, D.C: APA.

Belfer, M. L. (2008). Child and adolescent mental disorders: the magnitude of the problem across the globe. *Journal of Child Psychology and Psychiatry, 49*(3), 226–236.

Bloom, D., Cafiero, E., Jané-Llopis, E., Abrahams-Gessel, S., Bloom, L., Fathima, S., . . . Weinstein, C. (2011). The Global Economic Burden of Noncommunicable Diseases. Retrieved July 1, 2015, from http://www3.weforum.org/docs/WEF_Harvard_HE_GlobalEconomicBurdenNonCommunicableDiseases_2011.pdf

Braun, E., and Gazdag, G. (2015). Prevalence of psychiatric disorders in homeless population. *Psychiatr Hung, 30*(1), 60–67.

Coleman, T., and Cotton, D. (2014). TEMPO: A contemporary model for police education and training about mental illness. *International Journal of Law and Psychiatry, 37*(4), 325–333.

Cotton, D., and Coleman, T. G. (2010). Canadian police agencies and their interactions with persons with a mental illness: a systems approach. *Police Practice and Research, 11*(4), 301–314.

Draper, C. E., Lund, C., Kleintjes, S., Funk, M., Omar, M., Flisher, A. J., and Consortium, t. M. R. P. (2009). Mental health policy in South Africa: development process and content. *Health Policy and Planning, 24*(5), 342–356.

Durcan, G., and Zwemstra, J. C. (2014). Mental health in prison *Prisons and health* (pp. 87–95). Copenhagen, Denmark: WHO/Europe.

Fazel, S., Lichtenstein, P., Grann, M., Goodwin, G. M., and Langström, N. (2010). Bipolar disorder and violent crime: New evidence from population-based longitudinal studies and systematic review. *Arch Gen Psychiatry, 67*(9), 931–938.

Fazel, S., and Seewald, K. (2012). Severe mental illness in 33,588 prisoners worldwide: systematic review and meta-regression analysis. *British Journal of Psychiatry, 200*(5), 364–373.

Freeman, M., Nkomo, N., Kafaar, Z., and Kelly, K. (2008). Mental disorder in people living with HIV/AIDS in South Africa. *South African Journal of Psychology, 38*(3), 489–500.

Husain, M. (2014). Blasphemy laws and mental illness in Pakistan. *Psychiatric Bulletin, 38*, 40–44.

Jenkins, R., Othieno, C., Ongeri, L., Sifuna, P., Ongecha, M., Kingora, J., . . . Ogutu, B. (2015). Common mental disorder in Nyanza province, Kenya in 2013 and its associated risk factors—an assessment of change since 2004, using a repeat household survey in a demographic surveillance site. *BMC Psychiatry, 15*(1), 1–12.

Kesic, D., Thomas, S., and Ogloff, J. (2012). Estimated rates of mental disorders in, and situational characteristics of, incidents of nonfatal use of force by police. *Social Psychiatry and Psychiatric Epidemiology, 48*(2), 225–232.

King, C., and Murphy, G. H. (2014). A systematic review of people with autism spectrum disorder and the criminal justice system. *Journal of Autism and Developmental Disorders, 44*(11), 2717–2733.

Konrad, N. (2002). Prisons as new asylums. *Current Opinion in Psychiatry, 15*(6), 583–587.

Levy, L. (1993). *Blasphemy: Verbal offense against the sacred, from Moses to Salman Rushdie.* Chapel Hill, NC: The University of North Carolina Press.

Lo, T. W., and Wang, X. (2010). Policing and the mentally ill in China: challenges and prospects. *Police Practice and Research, 11*(4), 342–354.

Lopes, C. S., Moraes, C. L., Junger, W. L., Werneck, G. L., Ponce de Leon, A. C., and Faerstein, E. (2015). Direct and indirect exposure to violence and psychological distress among civil servants in Rio de Janeiro, Brazil: a prospective cohort study. *BMC Psychiatry, 15*(1), 1–9.

Lundgren, L. M., Brännström, J., Chassler, D., Wilkey, C., Sullivan, L., and Nordström, A. (2013). Mental health, substance use, and criminal justice characteristics of males with a history of abuse in a Swedish national sample. *Journal of Dual Diagnosis, 9*(1), 47–60.

McGilloway, S., and Donnelly, M. (2004). Mental illness in the UK criminal justice system: A police liaison scheme for mentally disordered offenders in Belfast. *Journal of Mental Health Counseling, 13*(3), 263–275.

McInerney, C., Davoren, M., Flynn, G., Mullins, D., Fitzpatrick, M., Caddow, M., . . . O'Neill, C. (2013). Implementing a court diversion and liaison scheme in a remand prison by systematic screening of new receptions: a six-year participatory action research study of 20,084 consecutive male remands. *International Journal of Mental Health Systems, 7*(1), 1–11.

McLaughlin, K., Gadermann, A., Hwang, I., Sampson, N., Andrade, L., Almeida, J. C. d., . . . Kessler, R. (2013). Parent psychopathology and offspring mental disorders. In J. Alonso, S. Chatterji, and Y. He (Eds.), *The burdens of mental disorders: Global perspectives from the WHO Mental Health Surveys* (pp. 39–55). Cambridge, NY: Cambridge University Press.

McLeod, L. C., Thomas, S. D. M., and Kesic, D. (2014). The frequency and nature of resolution of potential police provoked shooting encounters. *International Journal of Law and Psychiatry, 37*(4), 383–389. http://dx.doi.org/10.1016/j.ijlp.2014.02.009

Mirza, I., Tareen, A., Davidson, L. L., and Rahman, A. (2009). Community management of intellectual disabilities in Pakistan: a mixed methods study. *Journal of Intellectual Disability Research: JIDR, 53*(6), 559–570.

Moore, R. (2010). Current trends in policing and the mentally ill in Europe: a review of the literature. *Police Practice and Research, 11*(4), 330–341.

Multilateral Treaties. (1999). Inter-American Convention for the Elimination of all Forms of Discrimination against Persons with Disabilities. Retrieved December 28, 2015, from Organization of American States. http://www.oas.org/juridico/english/treaties/a–65.html

Murray, J., Cerqueira, D. R. d. C., and Kahn, T. (2013). Crime and violence in Brazil: Systematic review of time trends, prevalence rates and risk factors. *Aggression and Violent Behavior, 18*(5), 471–483.

NAPSA. (2009). Promising practices in pretrial diversion. Washington, D.C.: National Association of Pretrial Services Agencies.

NHS. (2015). Mental health and policing: Improving crisis care *Briefing* (Vol. 279). London, England: Mental Health Network and the Association of Chief Police Officers.

PAHO. (2013). WHO—AIMS regional report on mental health systems in Latin America and the Caribbean. Washington, D.C.: Pan American Health Organization.

Patteron, M., Somers, J., and Moniruzzaman, A. (2012). Sealing the cracks: preliminary findings from an inter-ministry initiative to address chronic homelessness in British Columbia. *Journal Of Interprofessional Care, 26*(5), 426–428.

Pedersen, P. B., and Kolstad, A. (2009). De-institutionalization and trans-institutionalization—changing trends of inpatient care in Norwegian mental health institutions 1950–2007. *International Journal of Mental Health Systems, 3*(1), 1–20.

Pondé, M. P., Caron, J., Mendonça, M. S. S., Freire, A. C. C., and Moreau, N. (2014). The Relationship Between Mental Disorders and Types of Crime in Inmates in a Brazilian Prison. *Journal of Forensic Sciences (Wiley-Blackwell), 59*(5), 1307–1314.

Priebe, S., Badesconyi, A., Fioritti, A., Hansson, L., Kilian, R., Torres-Gonzales, F., . . . Wiersma, D. (2005). Reinstitutionalization in mental health care: comparison of data on service provision from six European countries. *BMJ, 330*(7483), 123–126.

Priebe, S., Frottier, P., Gaddini, A., Kilian, R., Lauber, C., Martínez-Leal, R., . . . Wright, D. (2008). Mental Health Care Institutions in Nine European Countries, 2002 to 2006. *Psychiatric Services, 59*(5), 570–573.

Puteh, I., Marthoenis, M., and Minas, H. (2011). Aceh Free Pasung: Releasing the mentally ill from physical restraint. *International Journal of Mental Health Systems, 5*(1), 1–5.

Raza-u-Rahman, Siddiqi, M. N., and Ahmed, S. H. (2015). Implementation of the Mental Health Act; are we ready? *J Pak Med Assoc. 65*(12), 1339–1343.

Roy, L., Crocker, A. G., Nicholls, T. L., Latimer, E. A., and Ayllon, A. R. (2014). Criminal behavior and victimization among homeless individuals with severe mental illness: A systematic review. *Psychiatric Services, 65*(6), 739–750.

SG, A., and Colucci, E. (2015). Free from *pasung:* A story of chaining and freedom in Indonesia told through painting, poetry and narration. *World Cultural Psychiatry Research Review, September/December*, 149–167.

Sharma, K. (2014). Break the shackles of stigma on mental health care in Indonesia. Retrieved December 30, 2015, from Human Rights Watch https://www.hrw.org/news/2014/09/16/break-shackles-stigma-mental-health-care-indonesia

Strickland, P. (2015). Sentences of imprisonment for public protection. (Report #06086). Retrieved May 23 2016, from Parliament of the United Kingdom www.parliament.uk/briefing-papers/Sn06086.pdf

Svennerlind, C., Nilsson, T., Kerekes, N., Andiné, P., Lagerkvist, M., Forsman, A., . . . Malmgren, H. (2010). Mentally disordered criminal offenders in the Swedish criminal system. *International Journal of Law and Psychiatry, 33*(4), 220–226.

WHO. (2009). Mental health systems in selected low- and middle-income countries: A WHO-AIMS crossnational analysis. Geneva, Switzerland: WHO.

WHO. (2011). Global status report on non-communicable diseases 2010. Geneva: World Health Organization.

WHO. (2015a). Clinical Management of Mental, Neurological and Substance Use Conditions in Humanitarian Emergencies: Mental health Gap Action Programme Humanitarian Intervention Guide. Geneva, Switzerland: World Health Organization.

WHO. (2015b). Mental Health Atlas 2014. Geneva, Switzerland: World Health Organization.

Wittchen, H. U., Jacobi, F., Rehm, J., Gustavsson, A., Svensson, M., Jönsson, B., . . . Steinhausen, H. C. (2011). The size and burden of mental disorders and other disorders of the brain in Europe 2010. *European Neuropsychopharmacology, 21*(9), 655–679.

Index